Blackstone's
POLICE MANUAL

CRIME

Blackstone's
POLICE MANUAL

CRIME

2002 edition

Fraser Sampson, LLB, LLM, MBA

Blackstone Press

Published by
Blackstone Press Limited
Aldine Place
London
W12 8AA
United Kingdom

Sales enquiries and orders
Telephone +44-(0)-20-8740-2277
Facsimile +44-(0)-20-8743-2292
e-mail: sales@blackstone.demon.co.uk
website: www.blackstonepress.com

ISBN 1-84174-241-4
© Fraser Sampson, 1998
First published 1998
Reprinted with amendments, November 1998
Second edition, 1999
Third edition, 2000
Fourth edition, 2001

British Library Cataloguing in Publication Data
A catalogue record for this book is available from the British Library

Typeset in 11/13 Plantin by Style Photosetting Ltd, Mayfield, East Sussex
Printed and bound in Great Britain by Ashford Colour Press Ltd, Gosport, Hampshire

CONTENTS

CONTENTS

CONTENTS

CONTENTS

PREFACE

The Police Service has been under increasing pressure — both from outside and within its ranks — to develop and apply occupational standards. Now they have arrived, the Police Skills and Standards Organisation will hasten the implementation of those standards together with concepts of continuing professional development, which must include knowledge, understanding and application of the law. The imminent arrival too of the National Competency Framework will also focus clearly on the skills and knowledge required of all police officers in all ranks and roles. Police staff of all ranks and positions are expected by those they serve and by the courts to know the law. As the additions to this Manual show, that law is being made at a phenomenal rate. More and more, the responsibility for keeping abreast of legal developments is being placed upon individuals with the emphasis now being clearly on 'life-long learning' and continuing professional development.

Although they began life as a text for promotion candidates, *Blackstone's Police Manuals* have become the leading reference source on police law. With plans underway to make the Manuals available in electronic format on-line, they will become more accessible and comprehensive than ever, providing an invaluable resource for the changing times ahead.

The Manuals are fully indexed and cross-referenced and will be published each year to keep them up to date, thus doing away with the need for inserts or supplements. More importantly for OSPRE candidates, if the law isn't in the latest edition of the Manual, it won't be in the exam.

You will find many different types of crime in this book: recordable crimes, indictable crimes, crimes of specific intent and ulterior intent, incomplete crimes. Whatever their legal classification, all crimes have one thing in common — an ultimate victim. I do not believe that there is such a thing as a 'victimless' crime, whether that victim is an individual, an organisation or the community as a whole. Crime often leaves a lasting impression on its students; it frequently has the same effect on its victims. What follows focuses primarily on defendants, but it may help to bear in mind the consequences that their behaviour can have on those caught up in their offending. The government has recognised the impact of crime upon victims as a significant issue and has introduced a national scheme whereby victims will be able to give their views and feelings about that impact, as well as introducing a victim's charter.

While every care has been taken to ensure the accuracy of the contents of this Manual, neither the author nor the publishers can accept any responsibility for any actions taken, or not taken, on the basis of the information contained in this Manual.

The law is stated as at 27 July 2001.

ACKNOWLEDGEMENTS

One of the aims in introducing the Manuals to the police service was to produce well-thought out, well-used and well-respected books on police law. Entering their fourth year, the Manuals' feedback from individual officers, police training centres and research departments, along with the specific audiences of promotion examination candidates and probationers, testifies to their success in achieving that objective.

Having become established as a 'household name' in the context of police law, *Blackstone's Police Manuals* are the product, not just of the authors and the editorial team, but also the wide and varied input of many people — police officers serving and retired, junior and senior, uniformed, detectives and specialists; human resources and support staff; supporters and detractors; lawyers and lecturers, friend and foe.

Thanks to all — in whatever category you see yourselves.

Thanks in particular to David Anson, Paul Murphy, George Cooper and Stuart Fairclough past whom no legal or typographical nuance can slip. Thanks to Chris Jay at the Royal Military Police Training School and DS Pat Whelan at West Yorkshire Police Detective Training. Thanks also to Chief Inspector Howard Veigas at Derbyshire for his observations on the Regulation of Investigatory Powers Act 2000 material. Further thanks to the Crown Prosecution Service for their permission to include the CPS National Casework Guidelines.

As ever, thanks to the 'manual workers' at Blackstone Press, especially Alistair, Heather, Ruth and Mandy and, naturally, to CC, TA and AC for more things than we've room for here.

TABLE OF CASES

TABLE OF CASES

TABLE OF CASES

TABLE OF STATUTES

TABLE OF STATUTES

TABLE OF STATUTES

International legislation

Rules and Regulations

CHAPTER ONE

STATE OF MIND

1.1   Introduction

There is a cardinal rule in the criminal law of England and Wales that acts alone cannot amount to a crime unless they are accompanied by a 'guilty mind' or '*mens rea*'. There is another rule of our legal system that even cardinal rules must have exceptions and this one is no different!

The idea of 'guilty knowledge' suggested by the original Latin terminology is misleading and there are many different mental states which will fulfil the requirements of many different offences which have nothing to do with 'guilty knowledge' or, sometimes, any other kind of 'knowledge'.

The key to proving *mens rea* in any criminal charge is to show that a defendant had *the required state of mind at the required time*. The coincidence of the state of mind with the criminal act (the *actus reus*) is critical and is dealt with in the next chapter.

1.2   Strict Liability

Turning to the exceptions first, some criminal offences are said to be offences of 'strict liability'. This expression generally means that there is little to prove beyond the act itself and that the state of mind of the defendant is immaterial. However, in most cases it is more accurate to say that there is no need to prove *mens rea* in relation to one particular aspect of the criminal activity or behaviour.

Most of the authoritative case law in this area is fairly old; however, that does not affect its validity, even today.

Take for example the fairly ancient case of *Cundy v Le Cocq* (1884) 13 QBD 207 where the defendant was convicted of selling intoxicating liquor to someone who was drunk (**see General Police Duties, chapter 10**). In spite of the fact that the accused showed that he had no idea that the person was drunk, the court held that such knowledge (*mens rea*) was not necessary; if the person supplied with the drink was in fact drunk, that

1

would suffice in proving the offence. In the equally ancient and equally harsh case of *Parker* v *Alder* [1899] 1 QB 20 the defendant was charged with selling adulterated milk. The milk had only become adulterated while it was being transported to the buyer. The seller could not have known of this fact but was nevertheless found guilty as there was no need to prove any *mens rea* in relation to the adulterated state of the milk, merely that he sold it and it was in an adulterated state.

In some other, albeit rare, cases absolute liability is imposed, reducing even further the burden on the prosecution (see, e.g. *Smedleys Ltd* v *Breed* [1974] 2 All ER 21). (See also *R* v *Larsonneur* (1933) 24 Cr App R 74 where a person who was the subject of a deportation was arrested and detained for an offence. She was then convicted of 'remaining in the country' while under arrest!)

The situations where strict or absolute liability is imposed are usually to enforce statutory regulation (e.g. road traffic offences), particularly where there is some social danger or concern presented by the proscribed behaviour. So, where a defendant was charged with possessing a 'prohibited' weapon (**see General Police Duties, chapter 6**) the court held that it did not matter whether he *knew* he had the weapon — a CS gas canister — in order to prove 'possession' (*R* v *Bradish* [1990] 1 QB 981: contrast this with other decisions on 'possession' generally, **see para. 6.5**). See also *Gammon (Hong Kong) Ltd* v *Attorney-General of Hong Kong* [1985] AC 1.

Some other offences such as public nuisance at common law require only strict liability in relation to some elements of the criminal conduct (**see General Police Duties, chapter 3**).

1.3 States of Mind

Criminal offences generally can be classified in terms of the level of *mens rea* required. In descending order they are:

1.3.1 Offences Requiring a Particular *Mens Rea*

These are crimes of *specific* intent or *ulterior* intent, a distinction which is important when considering defences (**see chapter 4**). Crimes of specific intent are only committed where the defendant is shown to have had a particular intention to bring about a specific consequence at the time of the criminal act. Murder is such a crime, requiring proof of an intention to kill or seriously injure (**see chapter 5**). Other examples would be offences such as:

- wounding or inflicting grievous bodily harm *with intent* (Offences Against the Person Act 1861, s. 18 (**see chapter 8**));

- assault *with intent* to commit buggery (Sexual Offences Act 1956, s. 16 (**see chapter 10**));

- blackmail (Theft Act 1968, s. 21 (**see chapter 12**));

- contamination of goods (Public Order Act 1986, s. 38(1) (**see chapter 14**)).

Ulterior intent means an intention beyond the basic intent of carrying out the criminal act. Where a defendant is charged with burglary (**see chapter 12**) under the Theft Act

1968, s. 9(1)(a), you must show the intention, not just to enter a building as a trespasser, but also to *rape, inflict grievous bodily harm, cause damage, steal* etc. The italicised intention makes this a crime of ulterior intent.

1.3.2 Offences of Basic Intent

Many criminal offences require no further proof of anything other than a basic intention to bring about the given circumstances, e.g. theft (**see chapter 12**), offences involving simple possession of prohibited articles (**see General Police Duties, chapter 6**), or drink/driving offences (**see Road Traffic, chapter, 5**).

Whereas an offence of burglary under s. 9(1)(a) of the Theft Act 1968 requires proof of the ulterior intent described above, burglary under *s. 9(1)(b)* simply requires proof that the person entered the building/part of a building as a trespasser and that he/she went on to commit one of the prohibited acts (theft/attempted theft; inflicting/ attempting to inflict grievous bodily harm; **see chapter 12**). As well as easing the burden of proof on the prosecution in cases of basic intent, the distinction can also be significant when dealing with possible defences (**see chapter 4**).

A further important difference in offences of specific or ulterior intent and those requiring only basic intent is that, in the case of the latter type of offence, *recklessness* will often be enough to satisfy the mental element. Recklessness is a particularly important concept in the area of *mens rea* and is dealt with at **para. 1.4.2**.

1.3.3 Negligence

A few, relatively rare, offences can be committed by 'negligence'. Although many commentators argue that, by definition, negligence should not appear alongside discussions of *mens rea* as it is not a 'state of mind', it is useful to include it here. Negligence is generally concerned with the defendant's compliance with the standards of reasonableness of ordinary people. Like strict liability, the concept of negligence focuses on the consequences of the defendant's conduct rather than demanding proof of a particular state of mind at the time. Unlike strict liability, negligence still ascribes some notion of 'fault' or 'blame' to the defendant who must be shown to have acted in a way that runs contrary to the expectations of the reasonable person.

The most important criminal offence that can be committed by negligence is manslaughter (**see chapter 5**), which is also one of the only offences to include specific reference — at common law — to the word 'negligence'. The requirement to show that an *individual person* was negligent has been one of the main problems in the development of 'corporate manslaughter'. Other offences that can be committed by negligence do not usually contain the word itself but attract that test in relation to the mental element. Good examples are offences involving the standard of driving (**see Road Traffic**).

1.4 Statutory Expressions

Statutory offences use a number of different terms to describe the respective states of mind which must be proved. The more common expressions are:

* intent
* recklessness
* wilfully.

These have been developed through our common law system and now have the following meanings.

1.4.1   **Intent**

If a defendant intends something to happen, he/she wishes to bring about certain consequences. In some offences, say burglary under s. 9(1)(a) of the Theft Act 1968, the defendant's *intention* may be very clear; he/she may enter a house as a trespasser *intending* to steal property inside. As a crime *of ulterior* intent (**see para. 1.3.1**), it would need to be proved that the defendant not only entered the house or part of it in such a way, but that at the time he/she also *intended* to steal. Provided there is enough admissible evidence (e.g. the possession of articles for use in the theft, a 'shopping list', an admission by the defendant and an arrangement for the disposal of the property once stolen), this element of the defendant's intention is relatively straightforward.

However, there will often be consequences following from a defendant's actions that he/she did not *intend* to happen. An example might be where, in the above burglary, it was late at night and the householder came across the burglar and suffered a heart attack as a result of the shock. In such an event it would be reasonable to suggest that it was the defendant's behaviour or actions that had brought about the victim's heart attack (**see chapter 2**). The defendant, however, may well argue that, although he/she intended to break in and steal, there had never been any *intention* of harming or frightening the occupant. At this point you might well say that the defendant should have thought about that before breaking into someone else's house in the middle of the night. This then brings in the concept of *foresight*, a concept that has caused the courts considerable difficulty over the years — for a number of reasons.

First, there is the Criminal Justice Act 1967 which says (under s. 8) that a court/jury, in determining whether a person has committed an offence:

> *(a)   shall not be bound in law to infer that he intended or foresaw a result of his actions by reason only of its being a natural and probable consequence of those actions; but*
> *(b)   shall decide whether he did intend or foresee that result by reference to all the evidence, drawing such inferences from the evidence as appear proper in the circumstances.*

Secondly, there is the body of case law which has developed around the area of 'probability', culminating in two cases in the House of Lords (*R* v *Moloney* [1985] AC 905 and *R* v *Hancock* [1986] AC 455). Following those cases it is now settled that foresight of the probability of a consequence *does not amount to an intention to bring that consequence about, but may be evidence of it.*

In other words, you cannot claim that a defendant *intended* a consequence of his/her behaviour simply because it was virtually certain to occur. What you can do is to put evidence of the defendant's foresight of that probability before a court who may infer an intention from it. In proving such a point the argument would go like this:

•   at the time of the criminal act there was a *probability* of a consequence

•   the greater the probability, the more likely it is that the defendant *foresaw* that consequence

•   if the defendant foresaw that consequence, the more likely it is that the defendant *intended* it to happen.

Whether or not a defendant intended a particular consequence will be a question of fact left to the jury (or magistrate(s) where appropriate). Most of the problematic cases in this area have arisen in relation to murder (**see chapter 5**). In such circumstances, where death or serious bodily harm was a *virtual certainty* from the defendant's actions and he/she had appreciated that to be the case, the jury *may* infer that the defendant intended to bring about such consequences (*R* v *Nedrick* [1986] 3 All ER 1). Therefore, where the defendant threw a three-month-old baby down onto a hard surface in a fit of rage, the jury *might* have inferred both that death/serious bodily harm was a virtual certainty from the defendant's actions and that he must have appreciated that to be the case; they should therefore have been directed by the trial judge accordingly (*R* v *Woollin* [1998] 4 All ER 103).

1.4.2   Recklessness

Much time — and even more money — has been spent on arguing over the meaning of 'recklessness' in our criminal courts. The concept itself goes beyond a statutory expression and has probably become more important in proving criminal offences than the concept of 'intent' above as proof of recklessness is often enough to fulfil the requirement of *mens rea* (although not in offences requiring 'dishonesty' — **see chapter 12**).

An advantage of recklessness over intention is that the former is easier to prove by the attendant circumstances; a disadvantage is the different elements attributed to the word 'reckless' by different courts considering different offences — there are different sorts of recklessness.

Example

Consider a schoolgirl who throws a stone into a neighbour's garden, breaking the glass of a greenhouse window. She tells you that she was only 'having a laugh' and did not stop to think of what damage might be caused by the stone. Does the fact that she gave no thought to the consequences of her actions make her 'reckless' or blameless? Had she stopped to think about the possible consequences, would she have seen the risk? Does that matter?

If some reasonable person walking past at the time had seen her about to throw the stone, would that person have realised the possible risk? What if the person walking past had been another schoolgirl of the same age and understanding as the one who threw the stone? Are these questions relevant in determining recklessness?

Taking the last question first, yes — all of the above deliberations can be relevant, both to the type of recklessness involved and the liability of the defendant.

In addition, there are not only different types of recklessness, but they are *applied* in different ways to different offences.

Take the example of assault occasioning actual bodily harm (**see chapter 8**). In such an offence recklessness can suffice in proving the mental element (*R* v *Venna* [1976] QB 421). But recklessness as to what? The defendant may have been reckless as to the assault itself and/or to the *harm* that was actually caused *by* the assault. The courts have held that assault occasioning actual bodily harm only requires proof of recklessness *as to the assault* and there is no need to show that the defendant was reckless as to the extent of the harm caused by his/her assault (see *R* v *Savage* [1992] 1 AC 699).

In an offence of criminal damage (**see chapter 14**) however, it is necessary to show that the defendant was reckless, not only in relation to the causing of the damage, but also in relation to the property belonging to another. Therefore where a defendant intended to damage his own property and could not be shown to have been reckless as to the possibility of someone else's property being damaged, he was found not guilty (*R v Smith* [1974] QB 354).

The House of Lords has concluded (*R v Reid* [1992] 1 WLR 793) that the word reckless may not necessarily be expected to have the same meaning in all statutory provisions. To the practitioner this view causes many problems; to the student of criminal law it is perhaps hardly more helpful than Lewis Carroll's Humpty Dumpty whose words meant whatever he wanted them to mean.

Recklessness can be classified as follows:

Objective Recklessness

Objective recklessness, also known as *Caldwell* recklessness (from the House of Lords decision in *Metropolitan Police Commissioner* v *Caldwell* [1982] AC 341), involves the defendant's failure to consider an *obvious* risk. In such cases a defendant cannot claim to have had no *mens rea* simply because he/she had not thought the matter through. If the prosecution show that the relevant risk (in our schoolgirl example above, the risk to property) would have been apparent to a reasonable person, it is not necessary to show that the defendant realised that risk. If the defendant *did* in fact see the risk then clearly this strengthens the prosecution's case but it is not an essential element in proving offences which require objective recklessness.

Some difficulty has arisen where the defendant, because of his/her mental condition or personal attributes, would not have been able to appreciate the risk *even if they had stopped to consider the consequences*. Although it has resulted in some 'harsh' decisions (*Elliot v C* [1983] 1 WLR 939; *R v Stephen (Malcolm R)* (1984) 79 Cr App R 334) the courts have applied the ruling in *Caldwell* strictly, deciding that it is immaterial whether or not the defendant could have *actually* seen the risk; the test is that of a reasonable person who does not have to share the physical or mental characteristics of the defendant. The abolition of the *doli incapax* rule (**see chapter 4**) means that, where objective recklessness is the appropriate test — e.g. manslaughter and criminal damage — children who were incapable of appreciating the risks arising from their actions may still be found guilty. Similarly, adults whose mental characteristics prevent them from appreciating the risks created by their behaviour are not able to raise those characteristics as a defence to charges requiring objective recklessness.

This type of recklessness will generally apply to all statutory offences requiring 'recklessness' as to consequences (e.g. criminal damage). Note that in the offence of rape, however, (**see chapter 10**) the 'recklessness' required is recklessness as to the victim's consent, not to the act of sexual intercourse, placing it almost in a category of its own (see *R v S (Satnam)* (1983) 78 Cr App R 149). The notion of objective recklessness has no application in relation to assaults and woundings (**see chapter 8**).

Subjective Recklessness

Although objective recklessness will be enough to satisfy the required state of mind in the majority of offences, there are some where the test will be *subjective*. The requirement of subjective recklessness can be found in the case of *R* v *Cunningham* [1957] 2 QB 396 and are satisfied in situations where the defendant foresees the consequences of his/her actions as being probable or even possible. The main difference from objective recklessness is that, in cases requiring subjective or *Cunningham* recklessness, the fact that the consequences *ought to have been foreseen* by the defendant will not be enough. The most important group of offences where this will be the case is those requiring 'malice' under the Offences Against the Person Act 1861 (**see chapter 8**). In such cases the term 'malice' is misleading. What the prosecution will need to show is that the defendant either intended to do harm to the victim or that he/she *foresaw that harm* (though not the extent of that harm) *may be caused but nevertheless went on to take that risk* (*R* v *Savage* [1992] 1 AC 699). This is a more difficult element to prove than objective recklessness but, it is suggested by some commentators, one which is fairer to the defendant.

1.4.3 Wilfully

This term implies that a defendant must be shown to have desired the consequences of his/her actions or at least to have foreseen them (subjective recklessness). The term 'wilfully' however is *not* restricted to such occasions and has been taken to include *objective* (*Caldwell*) recklessness (*R* v *Sheppard* [1981] AC 394; *R* v *Newington* (1990) 91 Cr App R 247).

'Wilful' can also mean simply that an action was voluntary, that is, it describes the criminal conduct (*actus reus*) rather than the state of mind (*mens rea*) as in the offence of child destruction (**see chapter 7** and *Blackstone's Criminal Practice*, 2001, section B1.59).

1.5 Transferred Malice

The state of mind required for one offence can, on occasions, be 'transferred' from the original target or victim to another. Known generally as the doctrine of 'transferred malice' because it originates from a case involving malicious wounding (**see chapter 8**), the doctrine only operates if the crime remains the same. For example, in the original case (*R* v *Latimer* (1886) 17 QBD 359) the defendant lashed out with his belt at one person but missed, striking a third party instead. As it was proved that the defendant had the required *mens rea* when he swung the belt, the court held that the same *mens rea* could support a charge of wounding against any other victim injured by the same act. If the *nature of the offence* changes, then the doctrine will not operate. Therefore if a defendant is shown to have thrown a rock at a crowd of people intending to injure one of them, the *mens rea* required for that offence cannot be 'transferred' to an offence of criminal damage if the rock misses them and breaks a window instead. The House of Lords has acknowledged that this doctrine is somewhat arbitrary and is an exception to the general principles of law (*Attorney-General's Reference (No. 3 of 1994)* [1998] AC 245).

The issue of transferred *mens rea* (which is really what this doctrine amounts to) can be important in relation to the liability of accessories (as to which, **see chapter 2**). If the principal's intentions are to be extended to an accessory, it must be shown that those intentions were either contemplated and accepted by that person at the time of the offence, or that they were 'transferred' by this doctrine.

Example

A person (X) incites another (Y) to assault Z. Y decides to attack a different person instead. X will not be liable for that assault because it was not contemplated or agreed by X. If, however, in trying to assault Z, Y happens to injure a third person inadvertently, the doctrine of 'transferred malice' may result in X being liable for those injuries even though X had no wish for that person to be so injured.

CHAPTER TWO

CRIMINAL CONDUCT

2.1   Introduction

For a person to be found guilty of a criminal offence you must show that they:

- acted in a particular way;
- failed to act in a particular way; or
- brought about a state of affairs.

Known as the *actus reus*, this essential characteristic of any offence is the behavioural element. It is important to remember that the element of *actus reus* can also be proved by showing an *omission* to act in certain circumstances.

2.2   *Actus Reus*

Mens rea is what a defendant must have had; *actus reus* is what a defendant must have done — or failed to do.

When proving the required *actus reus* you must show:

- that the defendant's conduct was voluntary; and
- that it occurred while the defendant still had the requisite *mens rea*.

2.2.1   Voluntary Act

Other than in the few specific instances where an 'omission' will suffice (**see para. 2.3**), you must generally show that a defendant acted 'voluntarily', that is, by the operation of his/her own free will.

If a person is shoved into a shop window, he/she cannot be said to have damaged it for the purposes of criminal liability, even though he/she was the immediate physical cause of the damage. Similarly, if a person was standing in front of a window waiting to break it and someone came up and pushed that person into the window, the presence of the requisite *mens rea* (**see chapter 1**) would still not be enough to attract criminal liability for the resultant damage. In each case, the person being pushed could not be said to be acting of his/her own volition in breaking the window and therefore could not perform the required *actus reus*.

This aspect of voluntariness becomes important, not just when considering offences committed under physical compulsion, but also where the defendant has lost control of his/her own physical actions. Reflexive actions are generally not classed as being willed or voluntary, hence the (limited) availability of the 'defence' of automatism (**see chapter 4**).

Likewise, the *unexpected* onset of a sudden physical impairment (such as severe cramp when driving; actions when sleepwalking) can also render any linked actions 'involuntary'. If the onset of the impairment could reasonably have been foreseen or anticipated (e.g. where someone is prone to blackouts) the defendant's actions may be said to have been willed in the respect that he/she could have prevented the loss of control or at least avoided the situation (e.g. driving) which allowed the consequences to come about.

2.2.2   Coincidence with *Mens Rea*

Generally it must be shown that the defendant had the requisite *mens rea* at the time of carrying out the *actus reus*. However, there is no need for that 'state of mind' to remain unchanged throughout the entire commission of the offence. If a person (X) poisons another (Y) intending to kill Y at the time, it will not alter X's criminal liability if X changes his mind immediately after giving the poison or even if X does everything he can to halt its effects (see *R* v *Jakeman* (1983) 76 Cr App R 223). Similarly, if a person 'appropriates' another's property while having the required *mens rea*, giving it back later will not prevent them from committing theft (*R* v *McHugh* (1993) 97 Cr App R 335 (**see chapter 12**)).

Conversely, if the *actus reus* is a continuing act, as 'appropriation' is (**see chapter 12**), it may begin without any particular *mens rea* at the start but the required 'state of mind' may come later while the *actus reus* is still continuing. If this happens, whereby the *mens rea* 'catches up' with the *actus reus*, the offence is complete.

This principle can be seen in the offence of rape. The sexual intercourse may be consensual at the time it starts but, if that consent is later withdrawn, any continued intercourse will amount to an offence (*Kaitamaki* v *The Queen* [1985] AC 147).

A further illustration can be found in a case where a motorist was being directed to pull his car over to the kerb by a police officer. In doing so, the motorist inadvertently drove onto the officer's foot. Having no *mens rea* at the time of driving onto the officer's foot, the defendant was not at that point guilty of assault. However, once the situation was pointed out to him, the fact that he left the car where it was (the *actus reus*) was then joined by the appropriate *mens rea* and he was convicted of assault (*Fagan* v *Metropolitan Police Commissioner* [1969] 1 QB 439).

2.3   Omissions

Criminal conduct is most often associated with *actions*: damaging or stealing property, injuring or deceiving others. In some cases more than one action is required to give rise to criminal liability (e.g. harassment: **see General Police Duties, chapter 3**). But occasionally liability is brought about by a failure to act (e.g. constructive manslaughter, **see chapter 5**).

Most of the occasions where failure or omission will attract liability are where a *duty to act* has been created. Such a duty can arise from a number of circumstances the main ones being:

D The creation of a **D**angerous situation by the defendant. See, for example, *R* v *Miller* [1983] 2 AC 161 where the defendant, having accidentally started a fire in a house, moved to another room taking no action to counteract the danger he had created.

U **U**nder statute, contract or a person's public 'office'. Examples would be where a police officer failed to intervene to prevent an assault (*R* v *Dytham* [1979] QB 722) or where a crossing keeper omitted to close the gates at a level crossing and a person was subsequently killed by a train (*R* v *Pittwood* (1902) 19 TLR 37).

T Where the defendant has **T**aken it upon himself/herself to carry out a duty and then fails to do so. Such a duty was taken up by the defendant in *R* v *Stone* [1977] QB 354 when she accepted a duty to care for her partner's mentally-ill sister who subsequently died.

Y In circumstances where the defendant is in a parental relationship with a child or a **Y**oung person.

In each situation there may be a *duty* to act. Having established such a duty, you must also show that the defendant has *voluntarily* omitted to act as required or that he/she has not done enough to discharge that duty. If a defendant is unable to act (e.g. because someone else has stopped them) or is incapable of doing more because of their own personal limitations, the *actus reus* will *not* have been made out (see *R* v *Reid* [1992] 1 WLR 793).

Some statutory offences are specifically worded to remove any doubt as to whether they can be committed by omission as well as by a positive act (e.g. torture under the Criminal Justice Act 1988, s. 134, **see chapter 9**). Other offences have been held by the courts to be capable of commission by both positive acts and by omission (e.g. false accounting under the Theft Act 1968, s. 17, **see chapter 13**). Occasionally, some statutory offences arise where the only *actus reus* involves failing to take action under certain circumstances, such as the offence of retaining a wrongful credit under the Theft Act 1968, s. 24A (**see chapter 12**).

The distinction between acts and omissions was considered by the High Court in a recent case concerning withholding medical treatment from chronically ill patients (*NHS Trust A* v *M* [2001] 1 All ER 801). For a discussion of this case, **see General Police Duties, chapter 2**.

2.4   Causal Link

Once the *actus reus* has been proved, you must then show a *causal link* between it and the relevant consequences. That is, you must prove that the consequences would not have happened 'but for' the defendant's act or omission.

In a case of simple criminal damage (**see chapter 14**) it may be relatively straightforward to prove this causal link: a defendant throws a brick at a window; the window would not have broken 'but for' the defendant's conduct. Where the link becomes more difficult to prove is when the defendant's behaviour triggers other events or aggravates existing circumstances. For example, in *R* v *McKechnie* [1992] Crim LR 194 the defendant attacked the victim, who was already suffering from a serious ulcer, causing him brain damage. The brain damage prevented doctors from operating on the ulcer which eventually ruptured, killing the victim. The Court of Appeal, upholding the conviction for manslaughter, held that the defendant's criminal conduct had made a significant contribution to the victim's death even though the untreated ulcer was the actual cause of death.

In a case which had similar facts to our 'simple damage' example above, the defendant entered the house after throwing the brick through the window. Although the defendant did not attack the occupant, an 87-year-old who died of a heart attack some hours later, the Court of Appeal accepted that there could have been a causal link between the defendant's behaviour and the death of the victim. If so, a charge of manslaughter would be appropriate (*R* v *Watson* [1989] 1 WLR 684).

2.5   Intervening Act

The causal link can be broken by a new intervening act provided that the 'new' act is 'free, deliberate and informed' (*R* v *Latif* [1996] 1 WLR 104).

If a drug dealer supplies drugs to another person who then kills himself/herself by overdose, the dealer cannot, without more, be said to have *caused* the death. Death would have been brought about by the deliberate exercise of free will by the user (see *R* v *Armstrong* [1989] Crim LR 149). However, the Court of Appeal has recently accepted that, under certain circumstances, where a person buys a controlled drug from another and immediately injects it, resulting in his/her death, the supplier *can* attract liability for bringing about the person's death (*R* v *Kennedy*, unreported, 31 July 1998). In that case, the court held that the issue of whether or not the supplier's act did in fact cause the death of the drug user should have been left to the jury.

If the medical treatment which a victim is given results in their ultimate death, the treatment itself will not normally be regarded as a 'new' intervening act (*R* v *Smith* [1959] 2 QB 35). However, for an exception, see *R* v *Jordan* (1956) 40 Cr App R 152.

There is also a rule which says defendants must 'take their victims as they find them'. This means that if the victim has a particular characteristic — such as a very thin skull or a very nervous disposition — which makes the consequences of an act against them much more acute, that is the defendant's bad luck. Such characteristics (e.g., where an assault victim died after refusing a blood transfusion on religious grounds (*R* v *Blaue* [1975] 1 WLR 1411)) will not break the causal link.

Actions by the victim will sometimes be significant in the chain of causation such as where a victim of a sexual assault was injured when jumping from her assailant's car (*R* v *Roberts* (1976) 56 Cr App R 95). Where such actions take place, the victim's behaviour will not necessarily be regarded as introducing a new intervening acts. If the victim's actions are those which might reasonably be anticipated from any victim in such a situation, there will be no new and intervening act and the defendant will be responsible for the consequences flowing from them. If, however, the victim's actions are done entirely of his/her own volition (as in *Armstrong* above) or where those actions are, in the words of Stuart-Smith LJ 'daft' (see *R* v *Williams* [1992] 1 WLR 380), they *will* amount to a new intervening act and the defendant cannot be held responsible for them.

2.6   Principals and Accessories

Once you have established the criminal conduct and the required state of mind, you must identify what degree of involvement the defendant had.

CRIMINAL CONDUCT

There are two ways of attracting criminal liability for an offence: either as a *principal* or an *accessory*.

A principal offender is one whose conduct has met all the requirements of the particular offence. An accessory is someone who helped in or procured the commission of the offence. If an accessory 'aids, abets, counsels or procures' the commission of an offence, he/she will be treated by a court in the same way as a principal offender for an indictable offence (Accessories and Abettors Act 1861, s. 8) or for a summary offence (Magistrates' Courts Act 1980, s. 44). The expression 'aid, abet, counsel and procure' is generally used in its entirety when charging a defendant, without separating out the particular element that applies. However, if you are trying to show that a defendant *procured* an offence you must show a causal link between his/her conduct and the offence (*Attorney-General's Reference (No. 1 of 1975)* [1975] QB 773). 'Counselling' an offence requires no causal link (*R v Calhaem* [1985] QB 808). As long as the principal offender is aware of the 'counsellor's' advice or encouragement, the latter will be guilty as an accessory, even if the principal would have committed the offence anyway (*Attorney-General v Able* [1984] QB 795).

2.6.1 State of Mind for Accessories

Although the concept of 'state of mind' was addressed in the previous chapter, it is necessary to consider the particular requirements in relation to accessories here.

Generally, the state of mind (*mens rea*) which is needed to convict an accessory is: 'proof of intention to aid as well as of knowledge of the circumstances' (*National Coal Board v Gamble* [1959] 1 QB 11 at p. 20). The *minimum* state of mind required of an accessory to an offence is set out in *Johnson v Youden* [1950] 1 KB 544. In that case the court held that, before anyone can be convicted of aiding and abetting an offence, he/she must at least know the essential matters that constitute that offence. Therefore the accessory to an offence of drink/driving (**see Road Traffic, chapter 5**) must at least have been aware that the 'principal' (the driver) had been drinking (see *Smith v Mellors* (1987) 84 Cr App R 279).

There must also be a further mental element, namely an intention to aid the principal. Whether there was such an intention to aid the principal is a question of fact to be decided in the particular circumstances of each case. An example of such a case can be seen in *Gillick v West Norfolk & Wisbech Area Health Authority* [1986] AC 112. There a doctor who prescribed a contraceptive pill for a girl under the age of 16 was charged with being an accessory to an offence by the girl's partner of having unlawful sexual intercourse (as to which, **see chapter 10**).

You can see from this requirement that the wider notions of recklessness and negligence (**see chapter 1**) are not enough to convict an accessory.

Occasionally statutes will make specific provision for the state of mind and/or the conduct of accessories and principals. An example can be found in s. 7 of the Protection from Harassment Act 1997 (**see General Police Duties, chapter 3**).

2.6.2 Joint Enterprise

If an accessory is present at the scene of a crime when it is committed, his/her presence may amount to *encouragement* which would support a charge of aiding, abetting, counselling or procuring. For instance, someone who has paid to watch a dog fight or other illegal event may be convicted as an accessory to the principal offence (see *R v*

13

Jefferson [1994] 1 All ER 270). This is also a substantive offence in itself, **see General Police Duties, chapter 8**.

Particular problems have been encountered where one person involved in a joint venture goes beyond that which was agreed or contemplated by the other(s).

Example

A person (the 'accessory'), accompanies a friend (the 'principal'), to a public house where the principal intends to attack a third party. When the two arrive at the public house, the principal produces a knife and stabs the third person. Is the accessory liable for the wounding of the victim? The answer will depend on the nature and extent of the offence that was agreed and contemplated by the accessory and the principal when they set out on their joint enterprise. If the accessory knew that the principal intended to attack the victim, but knew nothing about a knife or any intention to stab the victim, the accessory will generally be liable for the resultant injuries caused by the principal. This is because the joint venture envisaged a physical attack on the third person and the stabbing was simply an 'unusual consequence' arising from the execution of that enterprise (see *R* v *Anderson* [1966] 2 QB 110). If, however, in the example above, the joint enterprise had involved, not an attack on the victim but the theft of his car, then the accessory would not be liable if the principal unexpectedly stabbed a witness or the owner of the car who happened to get in the way. This is because the principal would be going 'beyond what has been tacitly agreed as part of the common enterprise' (*Anderson* above) and therefore the accessory could not be held liable for the consequences of such an 'unauthorised' act.

What would be the liability of the accessory if, in the above example, the victim had subsequently died from his injuries? This situation has caused further problems for the courts and there are many authorities setting out the liability of accessories in such cases. The overall conclusion appears to be that, if at the time they set out on their joint enterprise, the accessory realised:

- that the principal *might* kill someone and
- that, when killing, the principal might have the *intention* to kill or
- an intention to cause *grievous bodily harm*

then the accessory will be liable for murder (*R* v *Powell* [1997] 3 WLR 959). For the *mens rea* of murder, **see chapter 5**.

If the principal cannot be traced or identified, the accessory may still be liable (see *Hui Chi-ming* v *The Queen* [1992] 1 AC 34). Similarly, an accessory may be convicted of procuring an offence even though the principal is acquitted or has a valid defence for his/her actions. The reasoning for this would seem to be that the principal often supplies the *actus reus* for the accessory's offence. If the accessory also has the required *mens rea*, the offence will be complete and should not be affected by the fact that there is some circumstance or characteristic preventing the principal from being prosecuted.

Additionally, if the accessory had some responsibility and the actual ability to control the actions of the principal, his/her failure to do so may attract liability (e.g. a driving instructor who fails to prevent a learner driver from driving without due care and attention (*Rubie* v *Faulkner* [1940] 1 KB 571)).

For the rules regulating the evidence of accessories and co-accused, **see Evidence and Procedure**.

A person whom the law is intended to protect from certain types of offence cannot be an accessory to such offences committed against them. For example, a girl under 16 years of age is protected (by the Sexual Offences Act 1956 (**see chapter 10**)) from people having sexual intercourse with her. If a 15-year-old girl allows someone to have sexual intercourse with her she cannot be charged as an accessory to the offence (*R v Tyrrell* [1894] 1 QB 710).

The European Council has adopted a joint action that will make participation in a 'criminal organisation' an offence (98/733/JHA, OJ L 351, 29 December 1998). The action will require member States to draw up measures for implementing such an offence (or offences) within one year.

2.7 Corporate Liability

Companies which are 'legally incorporated' have a legal personality of their own, that is they can own property, employ people and bring law suits: they can therefore commit offences. There are many difficulties associated with proving and punishing criminal conduct by companies. However, companies have been prosecuted for offences of strict liability (**see para. 1.2** and *Alphacell Ltd v Woodward* [1972] AC 824); offences requiring *mens rea* (*Tesco Supermarkets Ltd v Nattrass* [1972] AC 153); and offences of being an 'accessory' (*R v Robert Millar (Contractors) Ltd* [1970] 2 QB 54 aiding and abetting the causing of death by reckless (now dangerous) driving). There are occasions where the courts will accept that the knowledge of certain employees will be extended to the company (see e.g. *Tesco Stores Ltd v Brent London Borough Council* [1993] 1 WLR 1037).

Clearly there are some offences that would be conceptually impossible for a legal corporation to commit (e.g. some sexual offences) but, given that companies can be guilty as accessories (see *Robert Millar* above), they may well be capable of aiding and abetting such offences even though they could not commit the offence as a principal.

A company (OLL Ltd) has also been convicted, along with its Managing Director, of manslaughter (following the school canoeing tragedy at Lyme Bay in 1994) (*R v Kite and OLL Ltd, The Independent*, 9 December 1994). For manslaughter generally, **see chapter 5**.

2.8 Vicarious Liability

The general principle in criminal law is that liability is *personal*. There are, however, rare occasions where liability can be transmitted *vicariously* to another.

The most frequent occasions are cases where a statutory duty is breached by an employee in the course of his/her employment (see e.g. *National Rivers Authority v Alfred McAlpine Homes (East) Ltd* [1994] 4 All ER 286), or where a duty is placed upon a particular individual such as a licensee who delegates some of his/her functions to another (**see General Police Duties, chapter 10**). The purpose behind this concept is generally to prevent individuals or organisations from evading liability by getting others to carry out unlawful activities on their behalf. A common law exception to the rule that liability at criminal law is personal can be found in the offence of public nuisance (as to which, **see General Police Duties, chapter 3**).

CHAPTER THREE

INCOMPLETE OFFENCES

3.1 Introduction

There are circumstances where defendants are interrupted or frustrated in their efforts to commit an offence. Such circumstances might come about as a result of police intervention (e.g. where intelligence suggests that a serious offence is to take place on a given date) or as a result of things not going as the defendants had hoped (e.g. the property which they intended to steal not being where they thought it was). In these and other cases several general offences, often called inchoate or incomplete offences, may be used to ensure that the defendant's conduct does not go unpunished.

Note that some incomplete offences (i.e. incitements, conspiracies and attempts) will be drug trafficking offences for the purposes of the Drug Trafficking Act 1994 (**see chapter 6**).

3.2 Incitement

Offence — Incitement — Common Law
Triable as per offence incited. Unlimited maximum penalty on indictment;
penalty per offence incited on summary conviction
(Criminal Law Act 1977, ss. 28(1) and 30(4)).
(*Arrestable offence if indictable*)

It is an offence unlawfully to incite another to commit an offence.

Keynote

Incitement involves encouraging or pressurising someone to commit an offence. The other person need not actually commit the substantive offence or even form the intention to do so — though if they do go on to commit the offence, the inciter will become a secondary party (**see chapter 2**).

There are also some specific statutory incitements such as inciting someone to commit an offence under the Misuse of Drugs Act 1971 (**see chapter 6**).

Encouraging motorists to break the speed limit by advertising a radar detector has been held to be 'incitement' (*Invicta Plastics Ltd* v *Clare* [1976] RTR 251).

Incitement to murder is punishable under the Offences Against the Person Act 1861, s. 4.

As with accessories (**see chapter 2**), a defendant cannot incite another to commit an offence which exists for the defendant's own protection (e.g. a girl under 16 inciting a man to have unlawful sexual intercourse with her (*R* v *Tyrrell* [1894] 1 QB 710)).

A defendant cannot incite another to commit conspiracy (Criminal Law Act 1977, s. 5(7)).

A defendant cannot incite another to aid, abet, counsel or procure an offence which is not ultimately committed (*R* v *Bodin* [1979] Crim LR 176).

3.3 Conspiracy

Conspiracies can be divided into statutory and common law conspiracies.

3.3.1 Statutory Conspiracy

Offence — Statutory Conspiracy — Criminal Law Act 1977, s. 1
Triable on indictment. Where conspiracy is to commit murder, an offence punishable by life imprisonment or any indictable offence punishable with imprisonment where no maximum term is specified — life imprisonment. In other cases, sentence is the same as for completed offence.
(*Arrestable offence where substantive offence is arrestable*)

The Criminal Law Act 1977, s. 1 states:

(1)   Subject to the following provisions of this Part of this Act, if a person agrees with any other person or persons that a course of conduct will be pursued which, if the agreement is carried out in accordance with their intentions, either —
   (a)   will necessarily amount to or involve the commission of any offence or offences by one or more of the parties to the agreement; or
   (b)   would do so but for the existence of facts which render the commission of the offence or any of the offences impossible,
he is guilty of conspiracy to commit the offence or offences in question.

Keynote

A charge of conspiracy can be brought in respect of an agreement to commit indictable or summary offences. Conspiracy is triable only on indictment even if it relates to a summary offence (in which case the consent of the Director of Public Prosecutions will be required).

Agreeing with Another

For there to be a conspiracy there must be an agreement. Therefore there must be at least two people involved. Each conspirator must be aware of the overall common purpose to which they all attach themselves. If one conspirator enters into *separate* agreements with different people, each agreement is a separate conspiracy (*R* v *Griffiths* [1966] 1 QB 589).

A person can be convicted of conspiracy even if the other conspirators are unknown (as to the affect of the acquittal of one party to a conspiracy on the other parties, see the Criminal Law Act 1977, s. 5(8)).

A defendant cannot be convicted of a statutory conspiracy if the only other party to the agreement is:

- his/her spouse
- a child/children under 10 years of age
- the intended victim

(Criminal Law Act 1977, s. 2(2)).

A husband and wife can both be convicted of a statutory conspiracy if they conspire with a third party (not falling into the above categories) (*R* v *Chrastny* [1991] 1 WLR 1381). The 'end product' of the agreement must be the commission of an offence by *one or more of the parties to the agreement*. Once agreed upon, any failure to bring about the end result or an abandoning of the agreement altogether will not prevent the statutory conspiracy being committed. If, however, one of only two conspirators is an undercover officer who has no intention of going through with the agreement, there can be no true conspiracy (*Yip Chieu-Chung* v *The Queen* [1995] 1 AC 111).

Note that if an agreement to commit a *summary offence which is not punishable by imprisonment* is done in contemplation or furtherance of a trade dispute, it must be disregarded (Trade Union and Labour Relations (Consolidation) Act 1992, s. 242).

Conspiracy, Incitement and Attempts to Commit Offences Abroad

The law regulating the territorial jurisdiction over offences abroad is complex and has been changed by a number of recent pieces of legislation. The following is only a brief outline of some of that legislation and the advice of the Crown Prosecution Service should be sought in any such cases.

The Criminal Law Act 1977

A conspiracy under the provisions of the Criminal Law Act 1977 must involve an agreement by the respective parties to commit an offence triable under the law of England and Wales. Although this condition (under s. 1(4)) generally restricts statutory conspiracy to an agreement to commit an offence that is to be committed in England and Wales (or to offences planned to be committed on British vessels or aircraft), there are several offences that can be tried by our courts even though they are committed abroad. An example would be manslaughter committed by a British citizen. Therefore a conspiracy in England or Wales to commit such an offence abroad would be triable here.

The Criminal Justice (Terrorism and Conspiracy) Act 1998

In addition, the Criminal Justice (Terrorism and Conspiracy) Act 1998, makes provision to deal with conspiracies in England and Wales to carry out acts outside the United Kingdom. Despite its name, the 1998 Act is not limited to terrorist offences. If the object of the conspiracy would amount to an offence under the jurisdiction of the relevant country *and* of England and Wales, the conspiracy may be tried under the Criminal Law Act 1977, s. 1A. There are, however, procedural restrictions on the prosecution of these conspiracies and the consent of the Attorney-General (or Solicitor-General) must be given before a prosecution can take place.

The Criminal Justice Act 1993

The Criminal Justice Act 1993 (which was only brought into force — in part — in June 1999) implements some of the recommendations of the Law Commission Report 'Jurisdiction over Offences of Fraud and Dishonesty with a Foreign Element' (Law Com. No. 180; 27 April 1989). Section 1(2) sets out a group of substantive offences ('Group A' offences) that can be tried in England and Wales if any relevant act or omission on the part of the defendant took place in England and Wales. Among the offences in Group A are:

- theft
- obtaining property and services by deception
- blackmail
- handling stolen goods
- obtaining a money transfer by deception and retaining a wrongful credit.

This list also contains other offences involving deception and fraud.

Section 1(3) sets out another group of offences ('Group B') and this group covers conspiracies, attempts and incitement to commit a Group A offence, together with conspiracies to defraud.

Both lists, Group A and B, may be amended by the Secretary of State (s. 1(4)).

Section 3 sets out the rules to determine the relevance or otherwise of a defendant's nationality or whereabouts at the time of the commission of a Group A or B offence. This then allows the court to establish whether or not it has jurisdiction over the relevant offence.

Section 5 inserts another section (s. 1A) into the Criminal Attempts Act 1981 (see below) and makes further provision in relation to acts that are 'more than merely preparatory' towards the commission of an offence outside England and Wales.

Conspiracy Abroad to Commit Offences in England and Wales

If people conspire abroad to commit offences in England and Wales they may, under certain circumstances, be indicted under English and Welsh law even, it seems, if none of the conspirators enters the jurisdiction to do so (see *R* v *Manning* [1998] 2 Cr App R 461).

3.3.2 **Common Law Conspiracies**

Offence — Conspiracy to Defraud — Common Law
Triable on indictment. Ten years' imprisonment and/or a fine.
(*Arrestable offence*)

Conspiracy to defraud involves:

. . . an agreement by two or more [persons] by dishonesty to deprive a person of something which is his or to which he is or would or might be entitled [or] an agreement by two or more by dishonesty to injure some proprietary right [of the victim] . . .

(*Scott* v *Metropolitan Police Commissioner* [1975] AC 819).

(See also *Blackstone's Criminal Practice*, 2001, section A6.25.)

Keynote

The common law offence of conspiracy to defraud can be divided into two main types. The first is contained in the *dictum* of Viscount Dilhorne in *Scott* above, the second involves a dishonest agreement to *deceive* another into acting in a way that is contrary to his/her duty (see *Wai Yu-Tsang* v *The Queen* [1992] 1 AC 269).

Although the requirement for an agreement between at least two people is the same, this offence is broader than statutory conspiracy. There is no requirement to prove that the end result would amount to the commission of *an offence*, simply that it would result in depriving a person of something under the specified conditions or in injuring his/her proprietary right.

You must show *intent* (**see chapter 1**) to defraud a victim (*R* v *Hollinshead* [1985] AC 975).

You must also show that a defendant was *dishonest* as set out in *R* v *Ghosh* [1982] QB 1053 (**see chapter 12**).

Clearly there will be circumstances where the defendant's behaviour will amount to both a statutory conspiracy and a conspiracy to defraud. The Criminal Justice Act 1987, s. 12 makes provision for such circumstances and allows the prosecution to choose which charge to prefer.

Examples of common law conspiracies to defraud include:

- Buffet car staff selling their own home-made sandwiches on British Rail trains thereby depriving the company of the opportunity to sell their own products (*R* v *Cooke* [1986] AC 909).

- Directors agreeing to conceal details of a bank's trading losses from its shareholders *Wai Yu-Tsang* above).

- Making unauthorised copies of commercial films for sale (*Scott* above).

3.4 Attempts

The Criminal Attempts Act 1981, s. 1 states:

> *(1)   If, with intent to commit an offence to which this section applies, a person does an act which is more that merely preparatory to the commission of the offence, he is guilty of attempting to commit the offence.*
> . . .
> *(2)   A person may be guilty of attempting to commit an offence to which this section applies even though the facts are such that the commission of the offence is impossible.*

(3)   In any case where—

(a)   apart from this subsection a person's intention would not be regarded as having amounted to an intent to commit an offence; but

(b)   if the facts of the case had been as he believed them to be, his intention would be so regarded, then, for the purposes of subsection (1) above, he shall be regarded as having had an intent to commit that offence.

(4)   This section applies to any offence which, if it were completed, would be triable in England and Wales as an indictable offence, other than—

(a)   conspiracy (at common law or under section 1 of the Criminal Law Act 1977);

(b)   aiding, abetting, counselling, procuring or suborning the commission of an offence;

(c)   offences under section 4(1) (assisting offenders) or 5(1) (accepting or agreeing to accept consideration for not disclosing information about an arrestable offence) of the Criminal Law Act 1967.

Keynote

Most attempts at committing criminal offences will be governed by s. 1. Although some statutory exceptions apply, the sentence generally for such attempts will be:

- for murder — life imprisonment
- for indictable offences — the same maximum penalty as the substantive offence
- for either way offences — the same maximum penalty as the substantive offence *when tried summarily.*

If the attempted offence is triable summarily only, it cannot be an offence under s. 1. However, if the only reason the substantive offence is triable summarily is because of a statutory limit imposed in some cases (e.g. criminal damage to property of a low value) the offence can be attempted (**see chapter 14**). Some summary offences include an element of attempt (e.g. drink drive offences — **see Road Traffic, chapter 5**).

If the offence attempted is triable only on indictment, the attempt will be triable only on indictment. Similarly, if the offence attempted is an 'either way' offence, so to will the attempt be triable either way (s. 4(1)).

Many other statutory offences contain references to 'attempts', including:

- Theft Act 1968, s. 9 (burglary)
- Firearms Act 1968, s. 17 (using firearm to resist arrest)
- Official Secrets Act 1920, s. 7 (encouraging others to commit offences).

Section 3 of the Criminal Attempts Act 1981 deals with such statutory provisions and they will generally be governed by the same principals as those set out here.

Offences having Similar Effects

Other situations where a person tries to bring about a particular result or consequence are addressed by statutory offences which, although not falling within the category of 'criminal attempts' nevertheless have a similar effect.

For example, offences under s. 1 of the Computer Misuse Act 1990 (**see General Police Duties, chapter 11**) can be committed by causing a computer to perform a function under certain circumstances. Under the 1990 Act a defendant could, for example, commit the substantive offence by trying to log-on under someone else's user code or password. Such *actus reus* (criminal conduct) is more often associated with 'incomplete' offences like criminal attempts than substantive offences. Other examples can be found in offences requiring a particular intention such as offences under the

Offences Against the Person Act 1861, s. 58 which is almost an 'attempt' to procure an abortion (**see chapter 7**), and an offence of 'attempting' to cause an explosion under the Explosive Substances Act 1883, s. 3 (**see General Police Duties, chapter 4**).

In some cases acts which *are* merely preparatory towards a given end can still amount to an offence under the relevant statute, the best example of which is probably arranging to 'receive' stolen goods under the Theft Act 1968, s. 22 (**see chapter 12**).

Section 1(4) precludes the 'attempting' of some other incomplete offences. It does not preclude statutory offences involving 'procurement' (e.g. under the Sexual Offences Act 1956) or attempting to aid and abet the suicide of another (**see chapter 5**). Note that a defendant can be convicted of attempting to incite.

More than merely preparatory

A defendant's actions must be shown to have gone beyond mere preparation towards the commission of the substantive offence. Whether the defendant did or not go beyond that point will be a question of fact for the jury/magistrate(s). There is no specific formula used by the courts in interpreting this requirement. Courts have accepted an approach of questioning whether the defendant had 'embarked on the crime proper' (*R* v *Gullefer* [1990] 1 WLR 1063) but there is no requirement for him/her to have passed a point of no return leading to the commission of the substantive offence. However, to prove an 'attempt' you must show an *intention* (**see chapter 1**) on the part of the defendant to commit the substantive offence.

A defendant's intention may be *conditional*, that is, he/she may only intend to steal from a house if something worth stealing is later found inside. The conditional nature of this intention will not prevent the charge of attempt being brought. The defendant's intentions will, in accordance with s. 1(3) above, be judged *on the facts as he/she believed them to be*.

Although 'intent to commit' the offence is required under s. 1(1), there are occasions where a state of mind that falls short of such a precise intention may suffice. For instance, in cases of attempted rape (**see chapter 10**) the courts have accepted that recklessness as to whether the victim is consenting is sufficient *mens rea* for attempted rape because it is sufficient for the substantive offence (*R* v *Khan* [1990] 1 WLR 813).

In proving an 'attempt' it is enough to show that a defendant was in one of the states of mind required for the substantive offence and that he/she did his/her best, so far as he/she was able, to do what was necessary for the commission of the full offence (*Attorney-General's Reference (No. 3 of 1992)* [1994] 1 WLR 409).

For acts that are more than merely preparatory towards the commission of an offence outside England and Wales, **see para. 3.3.1**.

3.4.1   **Interfering with Vehicles**

Offence — Interfering with Motor Vehicles — Criminal Attempts Act 1981, s. 9
Triable summarily. Three months' imprisonment and/or a fine.
(No specific power of arrest)

The Criminal Attempts Act 1981, s. 9 states:

23

(1)   A person is guilty of the offence of vehicle interference if he interferes with a motor vehicle or trailer or with anything carried in or on a motor vehicle or trailer with the intention that an offence specified in subsection (2) below shall be committed by himself or some other person.

(2)   The offences mentioned in subsection (1) above are—

(a)   theft of the motor vehicle or trailer or part of it;

(b)   theft of anything carried in or on the motor vehicle or trailer; and

(c)   an offence under section 12(1) of the Theft Act 1968 (taking and driving away without consent);

and, if it is shown that a person accused of an·offence under this section intended that one of those offences should be committed, it is immaterial that it cannot be shown which it was.

(3)–(4)   . . .

(5)   In this section 'motor vehicle' and 'trailer' have the meanings assigned to them by [section 185(1) of the Road Traffic Act 1988].

Keynote

'Interference' is not defined and there are no conclusive cases on the subject at the time of writing. This offence is one of specific intent (**see chapter 1**) and you must prove that the defendant interfered with the vehicle etc. with one of the intentions listed — (note, however, that it is not necessary to show which *particular* intention).

For the definitions of motor vehicle and trailer, **see Road Traffic, chapter 1**.

See also the offence of tampering, **see Road Traffic, chapter 8**.

3.5   Impossibility

Practical difficulties have arisen where, despite the best (or worst) efforts of the defendant, his/her ultimate intention has been impossible (such as trying to extract cocaine from a powder which is, unknown to the defendant, only talc). Impossibility is now far clearer following the Criminal Attempts Act 1981 and its interpretation through the courts. It differs however in some incomplete offences.

Example

Taking an example of someone who tries to handle goods which are not in fact stolen, the following rules would apply:

- A defendant could *not* be guilty of inciting another, nor of common law conspiracy to defraud in these circumstances. The *physical* impossibility of what they sought to do would preclude such a charge.

- A defendant *could* be guilty of a statutory conspiracy with another to handle 'stolen' goods and also of attempting to handle 'stolen' goods under these circumstances. The physical impossibility would not prelude such charges as a result of the Criminal Attempts Act 1981 and the House of Lords' decision in *R v Shivpuri* [1987] AC 1. The only form of impossibility which would preclude liability under the Criminal Attempts Act 1981 or for a statutory conspiracy would be the *legal* impossibility — for instance if the defendants attempted to commit an offence of 'handling vegetables on a Sunday', an offence which is a clear *legal* impossibility (at least to the author's knowledge).

3.6 Inter-relationship and Police Operations

The subject of incomplete offences can be complicated enough when looking at single offences; they get really silly once you try to mix and match them. A good rule of thumb is that *most* incomplete offences cannot be mixed, and that most cannot be attempted. For instance, you *cannot* conspire to aid and abet, neither can you attempt to conspire. There are, as ever, limited exceptions to this rule. So, for instance, you *can* attempt to incite another to commit an offence. In practical terms, however, the legal niceties are simply a distraction. If in doubt about the appropriateness of a charge you should seek advice from the Crown Prosecution Service.

Where the issues of involvement in an incomplete offence *are* of practical relevance to police officers is in the area of covert operations. Is it a conspiracy if one of the conspirators is an undercover police officer? Can a person commit an offence of incitement if the person they try to incite is a police informer? Such operations by the police and other investigative agencies are recognised as being critical to the management and reduction of crime but what safeguards are in place to protect an individual's rights to privacy under the European Convention on Human Rights from unjustified intrusion? These questions, along with the new regulatory framework governing the whole area of covert police operations, are discussed below.

3.6.1 Police Operations

The involvement of undercover or plain-clothed police officers in some operations has raised a number of questions in this area of criminal law — as the following brief summary shows:

- As a general rule, if one of only two conspirators is an undercover police officer who has no intention of carrying out an agreement, there can be no 'true' conspiracy (see *Yip Chieu-Chung* v *The Queen* [1995] 1 AC 111).

- If a defendant having the relevant *mens rea* asks an undercover police officer to commit a criminal offence (e.g. to supply child pornography), that defendant can still be convicted of incitement, even though the officer had no intention of carrying out the act 'incited' (see *DPP* v *Armstrong* [2000] Crim LR 379).

- Making an offer which amounts to a criminal offence (e.g. an offer to supply a controlled drug) to an undercover officer may still amount to the offence and a defendant cannot claim that the offer was not 'real' because of the identity of the recipient (see *R* v *Kray*, unreported, 10 November 1998).

Although these case decisions stand on their own merits, this area of law has received a great deal of attention recently, primarily as a result of 'sting' operations carried out by public authorities and, more recently, by investigative journalists. So far as the police are concerned, one of the greatest dangers in cases such as these is the possibility that the evidence obtained may be excluded because the officers concerned are deemed to have acted as *agents provocateur* and to have violated the defendant's rights under the European Convention on Human Rights (see *Teixeira de Castro* v *Portugal* (1998) 28 EHRR 101). Generally, the involvement of the officers will be judged in the light of the seriousness of the case (see, for example, *Nottingham City Council* v *Mohammed Amin* [2000] 1 WLR 1071, where it was held that police officers posing as members of the public to flag down unlicensed mini-cab drivers was not unfair to the defendants). However, this entire area of the law has now been revised by the Regulation of Investigatory Powers Act 2000.

3.6.2 The Regulation of Investigatory Powers Act 2000

The title of the 2000 Act is a bit misleading as there are many areas of investigation that it leaves untouched. Similarly, the Act extends beyond activities amounting purely to the investigation of crime. Primarily, the 2000 Act addresses the interception of communications and the covert acquisition of information about people. The Act's main purpose is to make sure that these activities, when carried out by public authorities (as opposed to the journalists referred to above), are subjected to a robust statutory framework which allows for proper independent control and monitoring. One of the main purposes behind the legislation is the need for such practices to conform to the European Convention on Human Rights, particularly since the former regulatory provisions were held to be inadequate in this regard (see *Khan* v *United Kingdom* [2000] Crim LR 684).

Repealing the Interception of Communications Act 1985, the 2000 Act appears in five parts:

- Part I — the interception of communications and the acquisition/disclosure of data;

- Part II — surveillance and use of covert human intelligence sources (informers, agents and undercover officers);

- Part III — the investigation of electronic data (e.g. encrypted files);

- Part IV — the supervision of investigatory powers and Codes of Practice;

- Part V — miscellaneous provisions.

On a practical note, most, if not all, police services have an identified bureau or department that deal centrally with the new procedures under the 2000 Act and any queries as to the practical implementation of what follows in this section should be directed to them. Under s. 71 of the Act, the Secretary of State must draw up Codes of Practice and these must be taken into account by anyone exercising powers or authority given by the Act (s. 72). Breach of the Codes of Practice is not of itself an offence but the Codes will be admissible in evidence. At the time of writing, a draft Code has been issued and further consultation on its content is taking place. Although the rest of this chapter sets out some of the key *legal* features, the Codes of Practice make significant additions (particularly in the requirements for authorisation levels) to the practical implementation of the Act and should be referred to in any practical context.

3.6.3 Independence and Safeguards

Taking the regulatory framework first, Part IV of the 2000 Act provides for a number of independent public appointments, giving the relevant postholders clear duties and powers. The Chief Surveillance Commissioner and the Interception Commissioner are among the key postholders tasked with ensuring the proper supervision of the Act and currently these posts are held by very senior judges. Other appointments include ordinary and assistant Surveillance Commissioners and these posts will generally be held by circuit judges or their equivalent. Part IV also sets up a Tribunal with a very wide remit to consider, among other things, complaints arising from the application of the Act.

3.6.4 Surveillance and Human Intelligence Sources

Part II of the 2000 Act sets up a system for the authorisation and monitoring of various methods of surveillance and the use of 'covert human intelligence sources'. These activities, which are a significant feature of modern crime management, were formerly governed by agreed codes of conduct and guidelines. Now, in the wake of the Human Rights Act 1998, they have been placed on a firm statutory footing. Failure to follow the statutory requirements will render the relevant public authority liable to an action for breaching the 1998 Act and will also risk any evidence that has been obtained as a result being excluded by the courts.

Part II deals with three main types of activity by the police (and other investigators), namely,

- covert human intelligence sources
- directed surveillance and
- intrusive surveillance

(s. 26(1)).

Although only the first of these expressly uses the word, 'covert' for the nature of the activity, it is relevant to *all three* of these areas. Part II is concerned with *covert* activity and so, as a general rule, if it is not covert, it is not covered.

For a discussion of the issues relating to disclosure of evidence obtained through covert operations, **see Evidence and Procedure, chapters 10 and 14**.

3.6.5 Covert Human Intelligence Sources

The 2000 Act introduces the concept of a 'covert human intelligence source' (CHIS). As with the legislation regulating surveillance (see below), it is the *covert* nature of this type of activity that the Act is concerned with. This is because of the effect of such activity on an individual's rights under the European Convention *when carried out by public authorities* (e.g. the police). As the decided cases above show (**see para. 3.6.1**), the use of human intelligence sources has been a significant feature of crime detection and management for many years. However, the various types of activity involving informers, test purchasers and undercover operatives have not been subjected to open statutory regulation. The lack of clear legal regulation of such activity raises the risk of incompatibility with the European Convention and, with the arrival of the Human Rights Act 1998, a robust statutory framework was needed if the activities of the police and other agencies in this area were to avoid fundamental challenge.

What is a CHIS?

Broadly, a covert human intelligence source is someone who establishes or maintains a relationship with another person for the *covert* purpose of:

- obtaining information
- providing access to information

or who *covertly* discloses information obtained by the use of such a relationship.

The full definition is set out in s. 26(8) of the 2000 Act. Clearly this definition would cover the types of police operation involved in the decided cases discussed above (**see para 3.6.1**). A purpose is 'covert' here only if the relationship (and the subsequent disclosure of information) is conducted in a manner that is calculated to ensure that one of the parties is unaware of that purpose (see s. 26(9)). Therefore the definition would not usually apply to members of the public generally supplying information to the police.

Practically there are two broad areas to be considered when considering covert human intelligence sources: 'use' of a CHIS and acting as a CHIS. Both areas are strictly controlled by the legislation and require the relevant authorisation if they are to be lawful. 'Using' a CHIS includes inducing, asking or assisting someone to act as such and obtaining information by means of such a source (s. 26(7)(b)).

Generally, covertly recording conversations and other personal information about a particular person will amount to some form of 'surveillance' (and therefore will be governed by the strict rules regulating such operations: see below). However, such use of a CHIS will not amount to 'surveillance' (s. 48(3)).

Who Can Authorise a CHIS?

Section 27 of the 2000 Act provides that activity involving a CHIS will be lawful for all purposes if it is carried out in accordance with a properly granted authorisation. Such authorisation can cover activity in the United Kingdom or elsewhere.

The people who can grant authorisations for a CHIS are prescribed by s. 30 and the relevant order(s) made by the Secretary of State. The power to authorise the use of a CHIS extends to public authorities far beyond the police (see sch. 1 to the Act). The Regulation of Investigatory Powers Act (Prescription of Offices, Ranks and Positions) Order 2000 (SI 2000 No. 2417) sets out the relevant people who can authorise the activities of a CHIS. The schedule to the Order identifies the relevant roles and ranks of people in a whole series of public authorities from the National Crime Squad to the Egg Marketing Inspectorate! In the case of police services in England and Wales, the relevant rank is superintendent and above. However, where

- it is not reasonably practicable
- to have the application considered
- by someone of that rank in the same organisation
- having regard to the urgency of the case

then an inspector may give the relevant authorisation (see r. 3 of the Order). Given that this issue will most commonly arise where the police are trying to adduce evidence obtained by a CHIS, it will normally fall to the officer seeking the authorisation to prove that all the above ingredients were in fact present.

How Long Will an Authorisation Last?

Unless it is renewed, the authorisation given by a superintendent will ordinarily cease to have effect after 12 months beginning on the day that it was granted (s. 43(3)(b)). If that authorisation was given orally by the superintendent in an urgent case, it will only last for 72 hours unless renewed (s. 43(3)(a)(i)).

Where the case was urgent and the authority was given by an inspector, it will cease to have effect 72 hours later unless renewed (s. 43(3)(a)).

Special provisions exist where the CHIS is under 18 (see below).

When and How Can a CHIS be Used?

A designated person must not authorise any activity by a CHIS unless he or she believes it is necessary:

- for the purpose of preventing or detecting crime or of preventing disorder;
- in the interests of national security, public safety and the economic well-being of the United Kingdom;
- for the purposes of protecting health or collecting or assessing any tax, duty, etc.,
- for any other purpose specified by an order made by the Secretary of State

and that to do so is proportionate to what is sought to be achieved (s. 29).

It will not be enough for a designated person to show that he or she thought the use of a CHIS would be very useful or productive in achieving one of the above purposes; he or she must *believe* that is both *necessary* and *proportionate* to the legitimate objective of the operation. Both the requirements for necessity and proportionality are key features of the European Convention.

Generally, the authorisation must be given in writing but, in urgent cases involving superintendents' authority, it may be given orally (s. 43(1)).

In addition to the requirements surrounding authorisation, the 2000 Act makes provisions for the independent management and supervision of a CHIS. A Code of Practice (in draft form at the time of writing), together with a number of statutory instruments set out clear guidelines for the control and monitoring of CHIS activities and the keeping of records (see, for example, the Regulation of Investigatory Powers Act (Source Records) Regulations 2000 (SI 2000 No. 2725)). These provisions set out detailed requirements which replace any former rules governing the recruitment and handling of informants. This regulatory framework will set out specific conditions in relation to the deployment of different types of CHIS, from undercover operatives who change their entire identity in order to infiltrate criminal organisations, to 'decoys' who have no direct communication with suspects.

Very strict controls have been put in place where the CHIS is under 18 years of age (see the Regulation of Investigatory Powers Act (Juveniles) Order 2000 (SI 2000 No. 2793)). One such control is the time for which a written authorisation will last; in the case of a juvenile it is reduced from 12 months to one month. Further restrictions will be imposed under the Code of Practice.

This discussion is merely a summary of the key aspects of this legislation. To find the full extent of the powers and duties under Part II, the statutory text should be used, along with the relevant Code of Practice in force at the time.

3.6.6   Covert Surveillance

Along with the deployment of CHIS, covert surveillance has become a vital method of obtaining evidence and intelligence in the reduction of crime and the investigation of offences. Surveillance will only be covert for the purposes of Part II of the 2000 Act if it is carried out in a manner that is calculated to ensure that people subject to it are unaware that it is (or might be) taking place (see s. 26(9)). Surveillance includes monitoring, observing, listening to and recording people and their conversations, activities and communications (see s. 48(2)). So, if the police are monitoring a person's movements and are trying to do it without that person knowing, the activities will usually amount to 'covert' surveillance. General monitoring of a particular area such as a shopping precinct by CCTV will not usually be covert and therefore will not be caught by the provisions of Part II. There are, however, exceptions (see below). The proper use of covert TV detector equipment is neither directed nor intrusive surveillance (s. 26(6)).

For the practical considerations when gathering evidence from observation points, **see Evidence and Procedure, chapter 14**.

Directed Surveillance

It can be seen from the list above that there are two particular types of surveillance for the purposes of Part II — 'directed' and 'intrusive'. It is clear from the wording of s. 26 that surveillance must be one or the other; it cannot be both. Why does it matter? Because the controls surrounding *intrusive* surveillance are far tighter than those imposed on *directed* surveillance. If surveillance is:

- covert (but not 'intrusive' — see below)
- for the purposes of a specific investigation or specific operation
- likely to result in the obtaining of private information about a person (including information about their family life)
- whether or not that person has been specifically identified for the purposes of the investigation/operation, and
- not carried out in immediate response to events/circumstances where it would not be reasonably practicable to seek prior authorisation

it will generally be 'directed' surveillance (s. 26(2)).

Therefore, if in the example cited above, the police *specifically* use the CCTV camera in connection with a planned operation or they are covertly filming an area in a way that is likely to result in the obtaining of private information about someone, these may amount to directed surveillance. On the other hand, if a police officer in immediate pursuit of a suspect conceals himself or herself behind an obstacle in order to watch that person briefly, this would not amount to directed surveillance — because the activity was carried out in immediate response to events/circumstances where it would not have been reasonably practicable to seek prior authorisation.

The interception of a communication in the course of its transmission by a postal or telecommunication system will be 'directed' surveillance if the communication is sent or intended to be received by someone who has consented to its interception and there is no interception warrant (as to which, see below) (s. 48(4)). However, the use of a CHIS (see above) to record or obtain information will not usually amount to 'surveillance' (s. 48(3)).

Authorising Directed Surveillance

Directed surveillance must be authorised by a designated person (see below) and the authorisation can cover activity in the United Kingdom or elsewhere. The person must not grant the authorisation unless he or she believes that it is *proportionate* to what is sought to be achieved and *necessary* on the specified grounds (s. 28). These specified grounds are the same as those for 'communications data' (see above) with the exception that there is no provision for emergency actions.

The people who can grant authorisations for directed surveillance are prescribed by s. 30 and the relevant order(s) made by the Secretary of State. The power to authorise directed surveillance extends to other public authorities (see sch. 1 to the 2000 Act). The Regulation of Investigatory Powers Act (Prescription of Offices, Ranks and Positions) Order 2000 (SI 2000 No. 2417) sets out the relevant roles and ranks of the people in those public authorities who can authorise directed surveillance. In the case of police services, the relevant rank will generally be superintendent and above. However, where it is not reasonably practicable:

- to have the application considered
- by someone of that rank in the same organisation
- having regard to the urgency of the case

then an inspector may give the relevant authorisation (see r. 3 of the Order).

Authorisations must generally be made in writing but, in urgent cases, a superintendent may give an oral authorisation (s. 43(1)(a)).

Additional procedural safeguards may be made under the Codes of Practice.

How Long Will an Authorisation Last?

Unless it is renewed, the authorisation given by a superintendent will ordinarily cease to have effect after three months beginning on the day that it was granted (s. 43(3)(c)). If that authorisation was given orally by the superintendent in an urgent case, it will only last for 72 hours unless renewed (s. 43(3)(a)(i)).

Where the case was urgent and the authority was given by an inspector, it will cease to have effect 72 hours later unless renewed (s. 43(3)(a)).

Intrusive Surveillance

Intrusive surveillance is broadly what it says — surveillance activity that immediately intrudes on someone's private life (as protected by Article 8 of the European Convention, **see General Police Duties, chapter 2**). The statutory regulation of this activity is concerned as much with the intrusive *effects* of such surveillance as the means by which they are carried out and is designed to keep such intrusions by public authorities to an absolute minimum. If surveillance is:

- covert
- carried out in relation to anything taking place on any *residential premises* or in any *private vehicle*, and
- involves the presence of an individual on the premises or in the vehicle, or is carried out by means of a surveillance device

it will generally be 'intrusive' surveillance (s. 26(3)).

The definition of residential premises extends much wider than a conventional home. Covert rural surveillance operations and the use of specialist devices in houses or hotel rooms will generally fall into the category of intrusive surveillance. In addition to the activities authorised under Part II of the 2000 Act, the Police Act 1997 makes further provision governing the interference with property for the purposes of evidence/intelligence. These highly specialised areas of property interference are beyond the scope of this book.

The elements of intrusive surveillance listed above require the presence of people or devices on the relevant premises/vehicle. However, if the surveillance:

- involves a surveillance device, and
- relates to activities taking place on residential premises or in private vehicles
- but without the device being present on the premises or in, on or under the vehicle

it will still be 'intrusive' if that device *consistently* provides information of the same quality and detail as might be expected from a device that was actually present on the premises or in the vehicle (s. 26(5)). This is in keeping with the aims of Part II of the Act in this area, namely to minimise the intrusive effects of such surveillance on people's legitimate right to conduct their private and family life without interference from the State.

Surveillance carried out by means of a device for the purpose of providing information about the location of a vehicle (e.g. a tracking device) is not 'intrusive' (s. 26(4)(a)).

Authorising Intrusive Surveillance

Given the type of activity that is covered by this category, the restrictions on its authorisation are very tight. In addition, many types of activity under this heading will involve applications for 'multiple' authorisations and specialist advice must be sought.

Generally, the person who will authorise intrusive surveillance by the intelligence services, the armed forces and other specified bodies is the Secretary of State. In relation to the police (including the armed services police) the authority will be sought from senior authorising officers. Broadly these will be Chief Officers, the Commissioners/ Assistant Commissioners of the Metropolitan and City of London Police and the Directors General of the National Criminal Intelligence Service and the National Crime Squad (s. 32). Provision is also made for authorisations by designated deputies in some cases. In keeping with the tenor of the Act, these officers must not grant the relevant authorisation unless they believe that it is necessary and proportionate to do so:

- in the interests of national security;

- for the purpose of preventing or detecting 'serious crime', for example, offences for which a person aged 18 or over could reasonably expect to be sentenced to at least three years' imprisonment on his or her first offence, or offences resulting in substantial financial gain, involving the use of violence or a large number of people pursuing a common purpose (s. 81(3));

- for the purpose of safeguarding the economic well-being of the United Kingdom.

These are very similar to the grounds on which an interception warrant may be authorised (see below). The 2000 Act makes detailed provision for the recording and notification of authorisations. Anyone granting a police or customs authorisation for intrusive surveillance must notify a Surveillance Commissioner (as to which, see above) in writing as soon as reasonably practicable (s. 35). This is because, except in urgent cases, the authorisation will not take effect until the Surveillance Commissioner has approved it and given written notification to that effect to the authorising officer (s. 36). The purpose behind this process is to make the system open to independent scrutiny and monitoring, largely in satisfaction of the requirements of the Human Rights Act 1998. Surveillance Commissioners can quash or revoke authorisations and order the destruction of certain records and materials obtained by intrusive surveillance. Senior authorising officers may appeal against decisions of Surveillance Commissioners to the Chief Surveillance Commissioner.

3.6.7   Interception of Communications

The interception of communications is relevant to police operations for two reasons — first, because there are several substantive offences caught by this area (including listening in to police communications) but, more importantly, because the interception and monitoring of some communications have become important tools for the police and other investigatory bodies, particularly in proving a defendant's involvement in some of the incomplete offences covered by this chapter.

As with the other aspects of police operations in this area, the Regulation of Investigatory Powers Act 2000 puts the whole matter of intercepting communications and related data on a firm statutory footing for the first time. The 2000 Act sets out the relevant offences and also the procedures that will permit the interception of communications. The Act also makes certain provisions to address the 'international' nature of modern communications. The part of the Act dealing with the interception of communications is Chapter I.

On a practical point, all police services will have an identified Single Point of Contact (SPOC) who is registered with the telecommunications industry and queries as to the practical implementation of this following section should be directed to them.

Offence — Unlawful Interception of Public Communications — Regulation of Investigatory Powers Act 2000, s. 1(1)
Triable either way. Two years' imprisonment and/or a fine on indictment; a fine summarily.
(No specific power of arrest)

The Regulation of Investigatory Powers Act 2000, s. 1(1) states:

> *(1)   It shall be an offence for a person intentionally and without lawful authority to intercept, at any place in the United Kingdom, any communication in the course of its transmission by means of—*
> *(a)   a public postal service; or*
> *(b)   a public telecommunication system.*

Keynote

This offence is similar to the former offence under the Interception of Communications Act 1985 (which it repeals). It cannot be prosecuted without the prior authority of the Director of Public Prosecutions.

The offence relates to public postal services and public telecommunication systems. Broadly, these are:

- Public postal service — any postal service which is offered or provided to the public in any part of the United Kingdom.

- Public telecommunication system — the parts of a public telecommunications service that are located within the United Kingdom.

The full definition is set out at s. 2(1). Under the former offence under the 1985 Act, interception of a communication between a cordless handset and the base set of a domestic telephone was held to fall outside the concept of a 'public' system, even though the line ultimately connected with a public system (*R* v *Effik* [1995] 1 AC 309). Under such circumstances there would now probably be an offence under s. 1(2) (see below).

To prove this offence you must show that the defendant acted intentionally and without lawful authority. For a full discussion of the concept of intent, **see chapter 1**.

For the statutory provisions governing 'lawful authority' here, see below.

As in other Parts of the Act, special provision is made for international mutual assistance.

What Amounts to Interception?

What amounts to 'interception' is set out in s. 2(2) of the 2000 Act. This generally provides that a person only intercepts a communication in the course of its transmission by a telecommunication system if he or she:

- modifies or interferes with the system or its operation
- monitors transmissions made by means of the system or by wireless telegraphy to or from apparatus comprised in the system

so as to make some or all of the contents of the communication available to a person other than the sender or intended recipient *while the communication is being transmitted*.

A communication is 'being transmitted' for the purposes of this offence when it is stored on the system for the intended recipient to collect or access (s. 2(7)). This means that e-mail messages awaiting collection/access by the intended recipient are still 'being transmitted', as are unreceived or uncollected pager messages.

Again, the full definition can be found in s. 2 of the 2000 Act.

There is no equivalent definition for the interception of postal communications and this will presumably be a question of fact to be addressed on the merits of each case. Having set out what the offence covers, the Act goes on to specify particular activities that will *not* be caught by this section. These include:

- the interception of any communication broadcast for general reception — this covers broadcasts such as television and radio; it does not extend to pagers and mobile phone communications and these *are* covered by the Act;

- the interception of certain types of 'traffic data' — this means certain types of information that are needed to deliver or route the communication.

INCOMPLETE OFFENCES

Offence — Unlawful Interception of Private Communications — Regulation of Investigatory Powers Act 2000, s. 1(2)

Triable either way. Two years' imprisonment and/or a fine on indictment; a fine summarily.
(No specific power of arrest)

The Regulation of Investigatory Powers Act 2000, s. 1(2) states:

> (2) It shall be an offence for a person—
>
> (a) intentionally and without lawful authority, and
>
> (b) otherwise than in circumstances in which his conduct is excluded by subsection (6) from criminal liability under this subsection,
>
> to intercept, at any place in the United Kingdom, any communication in the course of its transmission by means of a private telecommunication system.

Keynote

This offence is new and had no equivalent under the Interception of Communications Act 1985. Like the offence under s. 1(1), this offence also requires the authority of the Director of Public Prosecutions before being prosecuted.

Although sharing many of the other features of the offence under s. 1(1), this offence applies only to the interception of a communication that is being transmitted by a private telecommunication system.

A 'private telecommunication system' is defined at s. 2(1). Generally, it must satisfy the following criteria. It must be:

- attached (directly or indirectly) to a public telecommunication system (see above); and

- have apparatus comprised in it which is located in the United Kingdom and used for attaching it to that public telecommunication system.

Therefore a privately-owned office telephone system in England and Wales which is locally attached to a public telecommunication system would now come under s. 1. So too would the type of police station payphone which was routed via the internal telephone system in *R* v *Ahmed* [1995] Crim LR 246 (under the former provisions, these types of telephone system fell outside the statutory controls preventing interception of calls). Interestingly, one of the earliest cases in this area of alleged human rights infringement within the UK arose out of the tapping of a senior police officer's telephone calls by her employer (*Halford* v *United Kingdom* (1997) 24 EHRR 523).

As with the s. 1(1) offence, the above offence requires proof of intention and also the absence of lawful authority (as to which, see below). However, it contains a further stipulation that the interception is not excluded by s. 1(6). Subsection (6) exempts some interception of communications where the interceptor has a right to control the operation or use of the system or has the consent of such a person to intercept the communication. The sort of interception envisaged here is where organisations intercept and monitor communications made on their telecommunication systems. Monitoring and recording communications in this way is permitted by the Telecommunications (Lawful Business Practice) (Interception of Communications) Regulations 2000 (SI 2000 No. 2699). In addition the Data Protection Commissioner has issued a code of conduct for employers, setting out conditions that should be observed when monitoring employee's communications at work.

Returning to the above offence. Bottom line? You must show that the person intercepted the communication intentionally, without lawful authority and under circumstances that are not exempted by s. 1(6).

Lawful authority is discussed below.

Lawful Authority

Under s. 1(5) lawful authority for the purposes of the s. 1 offences above is broken down into three areas:

- conduct in accordance with any statutory power (apart from this section) for the purpose of obtaining information or of taking possession of any document or other property in relation to any *stored communication*;

- conduct authorised under s. 3 or 4; or

- conduct in accordance with a warrant under s. 5.

Each of these is considered below.

Stored Communication

The first exception referred to above relates to occasions where the person is exercising a statutory power other than s. 1 of the 2000 Act for the purpose of obtaining information or taking possession of any document or other property *in relation to any stored communication*. The example given by the Home Office of such a situation is where police officers have recovered a pager from a person in custody and they apply to a circuit judge for an order under sch. 1 to the Police and Criminal Evidence Act 1984 to access its messages.

Conduct Authorised under Section 3 or 4

Section 3 of the 2000 Act authorises certain *types of interception* without the need for a warrant. In general, it covers interception where:

- both the sender and intended recipient have consented or the person intercepting has reasonable grounds to believe they have both consented;

- either the sender or intended recipient have consented and surveillance by means of that interception has been authorised under Part II (as to which, see below) — this might cover the situation where the police are monitoring threatening telephone calls made to a victim or calls made in connection with blackmail demands;

- the interception is by/on behalf of the provider of the postal or telecommunications service for purposes connected with it (examples of this conduct would include postal workers who need to open mail in order to return it to the sender);

- the person is authorised under the Wireless Telegraphy Act 1949, s. 5 (as to which, see below).

INCOMPLETE OFFENCES

Section 4 of the 2000 Act generally sets out occasions where *other authorities* might permit the interception of certain communications without the need for a warrant such as communications to/from prisons and high security psychiatric hospitals. Section 4 also makes provision for interception of communications involving people who are (or are believed to be) outside the United Kingdom.

Interception Warrants

Section 5 of the 2000 Act allows the Secretary of State to issue interception warrants under certain, very stringent, conditions. Section 5(2) says that the Secretary of State must not issue an interception warrant unless he or she *believes* that the warrant is *necessary*:

- in the interests national security;

- for the purpose of preventing or detecting 'serious crime', for example, offences for which a person aged 18 or over could reasonably expect to be sentenced to at least three years' imprisonment on his or her first offence, or offences resulting in substantial financial gain, involving the use of violence or a large number of people pursuing a common purpose (s. 81(3));

- for the purpose of safeguarding the economic well-being of the United Kingdom (where the relevant acts or intentions relate to people outside the United Kingdom (s. 54));

- for the purpose of 'international mutual assistance'.

Note that, emphasised in italics above, it is not enough that the Secretary of State 'suspects' that these threats or needs exist, nor that he or she considers that an interception warrant might be useful, valuable or effective. The Secretary of State must believe that the warrant is necessary for one of the purposes set out. The wording used in s. 5 is in accordance with Article 8 of the European Convention (as to which, **see General Police Duties, chapter** 2). Furthermore, the Secretary of State must consider whether the information that is sought under the application for a warrant could be obtained by other means (s. 5(4)). In urgent cases an interception may be signed by a senior official who has been expressly authorised to do so by the Secretary of State (s. 7).

As a general rule, most interception warrants are valid for three months unless cancelled (s. 9). Interception warrants issued in urgent cases by a senior official last for five working days only (s. 9(1) and (6)(a)).

You can apply for an interception warrant only if you are doing so on behalf of one of the people set out in s. 6(2). These people include the Commissioner of the Metropolitan Police, the Director General of the National Criminal Intelligence Service and various chief officers of the intelligence and Customs & Excise services.

The 2000 Act makes several provisions relating to the providers of communications services (telecommunications companies, etc.) and imposes duties on them to help implement the execution of interception warrants. It also goes on to provide a system of general safeguards against abuse or misuse of the powers in relation to interception of communications.

Finally — and somewhat ominously — Chapter I creates the following offence:

INCOMPLETE OFFENCES

Offence — Unauthorised Disclosures — Regulation of Investigatory Powers Act 2000, s. 19

Triable either way. Five years' imprisonment and/or a fine on indictment; six months' imprisonment and/or a fine summarily.

(*Arrestable offence*)

The Regulation of Investigatory Powers Act 2000, s. 19 states:

(1)   Where an interception warrant has been issued or renewed, it shall be the duty of every person falling within subsection (2) to keep secret all the matters mentioned in subsection (3).

(2)   The persons falling within this subsection are—

(a)   the persons specified in section 6(2);

(b)   every person holding office under the Crown;

(c)   every member of the National Criminal Intelligence Service;

(d)   every member of the National Crime Squad;

(e)   every person employed by or for the purposes of a police force;

(f)   persons providing postal services or employed for the purposes of any business of providing such a service;

(g)   persons providing public telecommunications services or employed for the purposes of any business of providing such a service;

(h)   persons having control of the whole or any part of a telecommunication system located wholly or partly in the United Kingdom.

(3)   Those matters are—

(a)   the existence and contents of the warrant and of any section 8(4) certificate in relation to the warrant;

(b)   the details of the issue of the warrant and of any renewal or modification of the warrant or of any such certificate;

(c)   the existence and contents of any requirement to provide assistance with giving effect to the warrant;

(d)   the steps taken in pursuance of the warrant or of any such requirement; and

(e)   everything in the intercepted material, together with any related communications data.

(4)   A person who makes a disclosure to another of anything that he is required to keep secret under this section shall be guilty of an offence . . .

Keynote

This offence carries a far greater sentence than the offences of unlawful interception of communications. It is clearly intended to apply to police officers and others involved in an investigation, and it extends to support staff as well.

It will be a defence for a person charged with this offence to show that he or she could not reasonably have been expected, after first becoming aware of the matter disclosed, to take steps to prevent the disclosure (s. 19(5)). Nevertheless, this offence imposes a very clear duty on the people set out above. The offence makes no specific requirement as to state of mind.

Further defences exist for some communications with professional legal advisors and other proper communications with the Interception of Communications Commissioner.

Wireless Telegraphy

The unauthorised interception of radio communications has been a summary offence for many years under the Wireless Telegraphy Act 1949, s. 5 and has been used where defendants have deliberately tuned in to police radio messages (*DPP* v *Waite* [1997]

Crim LR 123). Although the Regulation of Investigatory Powers Act 2000 leaves this offence on the statute book (moving it to s. 5(1) of the 1949 Act), it makes certain changes to the wording of the offence to make the 1949 Act 'human rights' proof. The 2000 Act now greatly restricts the ability of a designated person to authorise interception of wireless telegraphy. This type of interception is outside the scope of this book.

Communications Data

Chapter II of the 2000 Act (which was still not in force at the time of writing) deals with the concept of 'communications data'. This is broadly information that relates to the use of the particular communications service but not the *content* of the communication itself. The full definition can be found in s. 21(4).

Examples of communications data would include:

- itemised telephone bills;
- telephone subscriber details;
- addresses or other marks on the outside of postal packages and letters.

Access to this type of data is clearly useful to the investigation of crime and the gathering of criminal intelligence. However, in line with the European Convention, this activity must be regulated by clear and accessible legal rules.

Chapter II deals with the obtaining and disclosure of this communications data; it does not apply to any *interception* of such data while the communication is being transmitted (as to which, see above).

Section 22 sets out the circumstances when, and the purposes for which such communications data may be obtained. In order to obtain communications data the designated person (see below) must *believe* it is *necessary* to obtain the data:

- for the purpose of preventing or detecting crime or preventing disorder
- in the interests of national security, public safety and the economic well-being of the United Kingdom
- for the purposes of protecting health or collecting or assessing any tax, duty, etc.;
- in an emergency, for the purpose of preventing (or mitigating) death, injury or damage to a person's physical or mental health
- for any other purpose specified by an order made by the Secretary of State

and that to do so is *proportionate* to what is sought to be achieved

Both the requirements for necessity and proportionality are key features of the European Convention.

Note that, although the requirements for *necessity* are the same here as for interception warrants, the grounds contain significant differences. In particular, a much wider class of people can authorise the obtaining of communications data under Chapter II and there is no stipulation that 'serious crime' is involved.

The 'designated person' who can authorise communications data to be obtained is the person holding a specified rank or office in one of the relevant public authorities. Those public authorities here include police forces, the National Criminal Intelligence Service, the National Crime Squad, Customs & Excise and any other public authority specified by the Secretary of State in appropriate regulations. The data can be obtained by an authorised person collecting it themselves or by serving a notice on the holder of the data requiring him or her to comply with the terms of the notice.

The format for recording authorisations and notices is set out in s. 23. Generally any such authorisations or notices will last for one month unless cancelled or renewed.

This discussion is merely a summary of the key aspects of this legislation. To find the full extent of the powers and duties under the Act, the statutory text should be used along with the relevant Code of Practice in force at the time.

CHAPTER FOUR

DEFENCES

4.1 Introduction

The idea of a person having a 'defence' to a criminal charge suggests a carefully crafted argument being put before a court which excuses the alleged behaviour or which presents a different version of events from that outlined by the prosecution.

Although there are times when such a picture would be accurate, the so-called 'general defences' in criminal law are more concerned with cases where the prosecution are unable to prove all elements beyond reasonable doubt because of some specific characteristics of the defendant or circumstances of a particular offence. This failure may come about at trial but will often be apparent at the evidence gathering stage of a proposed prosecution. In addition, any interview plan drawn up in advance of a suspect interview would be expected to address any possible defences. It is therefore an area of practical relevance to police officers and investigators.

Some offences have particular defences attached to them (e.g. criminal damage), others exist only in relation to murder. These defences are discussed in the relevant chapters. This chapter is concerned with 'general defences', that is, those circumstances which may negate a conviction or even the bringing of a charge for a number of different offences.

When considering defences, either statutory or at common law, it will now be necessary to examine the impact of the Human Rights Act 1998 and any relevant provisions made under the European Convention on Human Rights. In particular the right to life (Article 2), the rights to liberty and security of person (Article 5) and the right to the peaceful enjoyment of property and possessions (Protocol 1, Article 1) may be relevant in assessing the lawfulness or otherwise of a person's conduct. For a full discussion of the Convention and its impact following the Human Rights Act 1998, **see General Police Duties**.

In addition, it has been argued that some statutory defences infringe the presumption of innocence (imposed at both common law and under Article 6). This argument was considered by the House of Lords in the context of the statutory defences under the

Misuse of Drugs Act 1971 (**see chapter 6**) in *R v Lambert* (2001) LTL 5 July. In *Lambert* it was argued that the statutory defence effectively shifted the legal burden of proof from the prosecution to the defendant, making it incompatible with the Convention. Among other things, their Lordships decided that the statutory defence did not shift the *legal* burden of proof at all, but could be read in a way that moved the *evidential* burden onto the defendant. Such an approach was compatible with the Convention and the Human Rights Act 1998. In *Lambert* their Lordships also considered the effects of some other statutory defences and held that there was no general incompatibility between them and the presumption of innocence. For a further discussion of these issues **see Evidence and Procedure, chapter 11**.

4.2 Automatism

Strictly speaking, automatism is not a 'defence'; it is an absence of a fundamental requirement for any criminal offence, namely the 'criminal conduct' (*actus reus*). In **chapter 1** we considered the need for criminal conduct to be *voluntary* and *willed*. It therefore follows that, if a defendant has total loss of control over his/ her actions, he/she cannot be held liable for those actions and provided the loss of control is *total*, there may be grounds to claim a defence of automatism. The most well known example of this defence is the case of *Hill v Baxter* [1958] 1 QB 277 where a swarm of bees flew into a car. The reflex action by the driver resulted in an accident but the driver's actions were involuntary and therefore not sufficient to support a criminal charge. Other examples might include a person inadvertently dropping and damaging property when suddenly seized by cramp or discharging a firearm as a result of an irresistible bout of sneezing.

If the loss of control is brought about by voluntary intoxication or by insanity, the defence becomes narrower and more complicated (see below).

4.3 Intoxication: Voluntary or Involuntary

There is no general defence of intoxication. If there were, a high proportion of criminal behaviour would clearly go unpunished. There are several summary offences which involve drunkenness, **see General Police Duties, chapters 4 and 10**: there are also some statutory offences where specific provision is made for drunkenness (e.g. the Public Order Act 1986, **see General Police Duties, chapter 4**). Additionally, if a defendant is *involuntarily* intoxicated (say, through having his/her drink 'spiked'), he/she may lack the relevant *mens rea* or state of mind for an offence.

If a defendant simply misjudges the amount or strength of intoxicants which he/she takes, this will not be regarded as involuntary and the restrictions discussed below will apply (*R v Allen* [1988] Crim LR 698). Similarly, if the defendant can be shown to have formed the required *mens rea* (**see chapter 1**) the limited defence of intoxication — whether involuntary or otherwise — will not be available (*R v Kingston* [1995] 2 AC 335).

The source of the intoxication can be drink or drugs. In the latter case, however, the courts will consider the known effects of the drug in deciding whether or not the defendant had formed the required degree of *mens rea*; the characteristics of the drugs will also be relevant in determining whether the defendant behaved recklessly in taking them.

DEFENCES

4.3.1 Specific and Basic Intent

The division of crimes into specific and basic intent (**see chapter 1**) is relevant when considering a defendant's intoxication.

If a defendant was intoxicated voluntarily at the time of the alleged offence, he/she can only rely on that fact *if the offence is one of specific intent*. The courts have accepted that, when so intoxicated, a defendant may be incapable of forming the specific intent required (such as an intention to steal or to wound in the case of burglary, **see chapter 12**).

Conversely, the courts have also accepted that a defendant is still capable of forming basic intent even when completely inebriated (see *DPP v Majewski* [1977] AC 443). Therefore, when gathering evidence to support a criminal prosecution, it is important to establish whether:

- the defendant was intoxicated at the time
- the intoxication was voluntary or involuntary
- the alleged offence is one of basic or specific intent.

The defence of voluntary intoxication applies to offences where a specific intent is required (e.g. murder or s. 18 wounding or criminal attempts); it is also suggested (see *Blackstone's Criminal Practice*, 2001, section A3.10) that the defence would logically extend to other offences requiring particular states of mind such as 'dishonesty'.

Where the defendant forms a 'mistaken belief' based on the fact that he/she is intoxicated and not thinking straight, that belief may sometimes be raised as a defence. In cases of criminal damage where a defendant has mistakenly believed that the property being damaged is his/her her own property, and that mistaken belief has arisen from the defendant's intoxicated state, the courts have accepted the defence under s. 5 of the Criminal Damage Act 1971 (**see chapter 14**). However, this appears to be confined to the wording of that particular statute and the courts have refused to accept similar defences of mistaken, drunken belief (see *R v O'Grady* [1987] QB 995 where the defendant mistakenly believed he was being attacked and so 'defended' himself).

One further qualification is that if a defendant becomes intoxicated in order to gain false courage to go and commit a crime, he/she will not be able to claim a defence of intoxication *even if the crime is one of specific intent*. This is because he/she has already formed the intent required and the intoxication is merely a means of plucking up courage to carry it out (*Attorney-General for Northern Ireland v Gallagher* [1963] AC 349).

4.4 Insanity

There is a presumption in law that all people are sane. That presumption is clearly rebuttable (**see Evidence and Procedure, chapter 11**) and evidence of a defendant's insanity may be put before a court.

If a defendant claims to have been 'insane' at the time of the offence (to attract an acquittal in a summary trial or an order of the court when tried on indictment), that claim will be judged against the M'Naghten rules. The rules (*M'Naghten's Case* (1843) 10 Cl & F 200) state:

. . . to establish a defence on the ground of insanity, it must be clearly proved that, at the time of the committing of the act, the party accused was labouring under such a defect of reason, from disease of the mind, as not to know the nature and quality of the act he was doing; or, if he did know it, that he did not know he was doing what was wrong.

The question of whether the defendant's attributes or condition amount to a 'disease of the mind' is a question of law and not a question of medical opinion (*R* v *Sullivan* [1984] AC 156). (Contrast the 'special defence' to murder in **chapter 5**.)

An epileptic fit has been deemed to be similar to insanity in respect of a defence to a criminal charge and therefore the M'Naghten rules above should be applied — *Sullivan*.

A special verdict of 'not guilty by reason of insanity' is provided by the very politically incorrect Trial of Lunatics Act 1883. This area, together with the recent amendments provided by the Criminal Cases Review (Insanity) Act 1999 are fairly involved and beyond the scope of this book. For further guidance see *Blackstone's Criminal Practice*, 2001, section A3.12.

4.5   Inadvertance and Mistake

In addition to mistaken belief brought about by intoxication (**see para. 4.3.1**), there are also occasions where a defendant makes a mistake about some circumstance or consequence. Claims that a defendant 'made a mistake' or did something 'inadvertantly' will only be an effective defence if they negate the *mens rea* for that offence. Therefore, if someone picks up another person's shopping at a supermarket till or wanders out of a shop with something they have yet to pay for, their mistake or inadvertence, in each case, might negative any *mens rea* (of 'dishonesty', **see chapter 12**). As the requirement for the *mens rea* in such a case is *subjective* then the defendant's mistake or inadvertence will be judged subjectively. The same will generally be true for offences requiring subjective recklessness. It does not matter whether the mistake was 'reasonable' (*DPP* v *Morgan* [1976] AC 182). If the alleged offence is one which will be judged *objectively* (**see chapter 1**) then inadvertence will not be a defence (it would almost be an admission!) and any 'mistake' will have to involve the defendant ruling out any risk of the prohibited consequence. (See *Chief Constable of Avon and Somerset* v *Shimmen* (1986) 84 Cr App R 7 where a martial arts 'expert' mistakenly believed he could aim a kick at a window without breaking it. As he had not 'ruled out any risk' of the window breaking — which it did — his mistake was not accepted as a defence.) There are occasions where a genuine mistake on the part of the defendant will amount to a defence (see rape and indecent assault (**chapter 10**) and the Indecency with Children Act 1960 s. 1 (**see chapter 11**).

In *R* v *Lee* [2000] Crim LR 991, a case arising from an assault on two arresting police officers, the Court of Appeal reviewed the law in this area, reaffirming the following points:

- A genuine or honest mistake could provide a defence to many criminal offences requiring a particular state of mind, including assault with intent to resist arrest (*R* v *Brightling* [1991] Crim LR 364).

- A defence of mistake had to involve a mistake of fact, not a mistake of law (see below).

- People under arrest are not entitled to form their own view as to the lawfulness of that arrest. They have a duty to comply with the police and hear the details of the charge against them (*R* v *Bentley* (1850) 4 Cox CC 406).

- Belief in one's own innocence, however genuine or honestly held, cannot afford a defence to a charge of assault with intent to resist arrest under s. 38 of the Offences Against the Person Act 1861 (as to which, **see chapter 8**).

In relation to offences involving negligence, inadvertance would clearly not amount to a defence and any 'mistake' would generally need to be shown to be a reasonable one.

Generally, it is no defence to claim a mistake as to the law because all people are presumed to know the law once it is made (if only . . .). With statutory instruments a defendant can show that the instrument in question was not in force at the time of the offence or that the behaviour that it sought to control was beyond the powers (*ultra vires*) of that instrument (see *Boddington* v *British Transport Police* [1998] 2 WLR 639 where the defendant sought to challenge the bye-laws preventing smoking on trains formerly owned by British Rail but now operated by private companies).

There is one particular example, however, where a mistaken belief in the legal position is specifically provided for in a criminal offence. This is where a person appropriates property in the belief that he/she has a legal right to deprive another person of it under s. 2 of the Theft Act 1968 (**see chapter 12**).

4.6   Duress

Where a person is threatened with death or serious physical injury unless they carry out a criminal act, they may have a defence of *duress* (see *R* v *Graham* [1982] 1 WLR 294). The threat of serious physical injury does not appear to include serious *psychological* injury (see *R* v *Baker* [1997] Crim LR 497), which seems slightly at odds with the situation regarding injury generally (see *R* v *Ireland* [1998] AC 147 and **chapter 8**).

It would seem that the threat need not be made solely to the person who goes on to commit the relevant offence and there are authorities to suggest that threats of death/serious harm to loved ones may allow a defence of duress (see *Blackstone's Criminal Practice*, 2001, section A3.21).

The defence is not available in respect of an offence of murder (*R* v *Howe* [1987] AC 417) or attempted murder (*R* v *Gotts* [1992] 2 AC 412), as a principal or secondary offender. It is, however, available in other offences even in offences of strict liability (*Eden DC* v *Braid* [1998] COD 259 — taxi driver threatened and forced to carry excessive number of people in breach of his licensing conditions).

There are several key elements to this defence:

- the threat must have driven the defendant to commit the offence;

- the defendant must have acted as a sober and reasonable person sharing his/her characteristics would have done;

- the threatened injury must be anticipated at or near the time of the offence (i.e., not sometime in the distant future);

- the defendant must not voluntarily put himself/herself in a position where such compulsion is likely if the defendant can avoid the effect of duress by escaping without risk to himself/herself or family, he/she must do so (*R v Baker* [1999] 2 Cr App R 335).

If a defendant knowingly exposes himself/herself to a risk of such a threat of death or serious physical injury, he/she cannot then claim duress as a defence. For instance, if a person joins a violent gang or an active terrorist organisation, he/she cannot then claim duress as a defence to any crimes he/she may go on to commit under threat of death or serious injury from another member or rival of that organisation (see *R v Sharp* [1987] QB 853). However, if the purpose of the organisation or gang is not predominantly violent or dangerous (e.g. a gang of shoplifters) then the defence of duress *may* be available in relation to offences committed while under threat of death or serious physical injury from other gang members (*R v Shepherd* (1987) 86 Cr App R 47).

4.6.1 Marital Coercion

Closely linked to the defence of duress is the somewhat anachronistic defence of 'marital coercion' whereby a *wife* charged with any offence other than treason or murder, may raise the defence that she committed the offence in the presence and under the coercion of her husband (see the Criminal Justice Act 1925, s. 47). The Law Commission has recommended that this defence be abolished.

4.7 Duress of Circumstances

As well as cases where a person receives a direct threat in order to make them commit an offence, there may be times when circumstances leave the defendant no real alternative. If a doctor is suddenly called upon to use his/her car to get someone to hospital for emergency treatment then those circumstances may provide a defence for driving while disqualified (see e.g. *R v Martin* [1989] 1 All ER 652). Similarly, threats of immediate violence may allow a defence of duress of circumstances for someone who drives dangerously in order to escape the threat (*R v Willer* (1986) 83 Cr App R 225). In such cases the court will consider the reasonableness of the defendant's behaviour in light of the prevailing circumstances. If the defendant commits a very serious offence in order to avoid very minor or trivial consequences then this defence is unlikely to be available.

Although it is said that there is no defence of 'necessity' in the law of England and Wales (*see Blackstone's Criminal Practice*, 2001, section A3.27), the expansion of the defence of duress of circumstances appears to have created the same result by a different name (see *R v Pommell* [1995] 2 Cr App R 607).

This type of duress should be distinguished from that at **para. 4.6**. There the duress comes from a threat made to the defendant compelling him/her to commit an offence: a gun to the head type of situation where one person says to another '*Do this or else...*' With duress of circumstances, there is no such threat being made. Rather there is a threatening situation or set of circumstances from which the defendant wishes to escape and, in so doing, feels impelled to commit an offence as the lesser of two present evils. Here the threat is 'situational' and the defendant feels '*If I don't do this, then I will suffer death or serious physical injury . . .*'. A good example is in *R v Willer* (1986) 83 Cr App R 225 where the defendant, while in his car, feared he would be attacked by a gang of youths and drove across a shopping precinct in order to avoid the assault. In answer to a charge of what was then 'reckless' (now 'dangerous', **see Road Traffic, chapter** 2) driving, the defendant raised the defence of duress of circumstances.

This growing defence was examined very recently by the Court of Appeal in a case where someone jumped onto the bonnet of the car that the appellant was driving. The appellant drove for some distance with the man on the bonnet of the car, braking after a short time to go over a speed ramp. The man fell from the bonnet and the appellant drove on, running the man over and causing him grievous bodily harm (as to which, **see chapter 8**). In determining whether or not the defence of 'duress of circumstances' was available, the court held that the jury must ask two questions in relation to the appellant:

• Was he (or might he have been) impelled to act as he did because, as a result of what he reasonably believed, he had good cause to fear he would suffer death or serious injury if he did not do so?

• If so, would a sober person of reasonable firmness and sharing the same character-istics, have responded to the situation in the way that he did?

If each question were answered with a 'yes', the defence would be made out (*R v Cairns* [1999] 2 Cr App R 137).

The important aspect to this defence then is that it will only avail the defendant as long as he/she is acting under compulsion of the prevailing circumstances when committing the offence. It appears that the defendant need only hold an *honest* belief that those circumstances exist without necessarily having *reasonable grounds* for that belief (see *DPP v Rogers* [1998] Crim LR 202) and there is no need for the threat to be 'real'. However, the defendant's actions in order to avoid that perceived threatening situation must be reasonable and in proportion to the threat presented. Therefore defendant(s) in situation(s) like *Willer* and *Cairns* would not be able to claim duress of circumstances if they drove at their victims repeatedly until all had been injured to a point whereby they no longer posed a threat.

It seems that, apart from the offence of murder or attempted murder (or treason), the defence is available against any other charge (including hijacking, *R v Abdul-Hussain* [1999] Crim LR 570). The Court of Appeal has said that there is an urgent need for legislation in this area (*Abdul-Hussain* above).

For the development of this defence in the area of dangerous and careless driving, **see Road Traffic, chapter 2.**

4.8   Defence of Self, Others or Property

There are circumstances where the use of force against person or property will be permissible. This aspect of criminal law has attracted a great deal of interest as a result of several widely-reported court cases recently. As a result, there have been calls for a change in the legislation in order to provide greater perceived protection for those who cause injury in defending their lives or property. Whatever future changes this may bring, it is almost certain that the effect of Human Rights Act 1998 will be to impose even stricter conditions on those occasions whereby a person might lawfully injure — or kill — a person in the defence of another (see below). There are also those cases where a person is specifically empowered to use force, such as when executing a warrant (**see General Police Duties, chapter 2**). But there are times when the use of force generally will be justified by the circumstances, i.e.:

* preventing crime
* defending yourself or another
* protecting property.

4.8.1   Preventing Crime

The Criminal Law Act 1967, s. 3(1) states:

> *A person may use such force as is reasonable in the circumstances in the prevention of crime, or in effecting or assisting in the lawful arrest of offenders or suspected offenders or of persons unlawfully at large.*

There used to be a distinction between the wording of the Criminal Law Act 1967 (above) which applies in cases of the prevention of crime, and the other occasions (defence of self, another and property) which were governed by common law. Now, since the Privy Council decision in *Beckford* v *The Queen* [1988] AC 130 and the case of *R* v *Clegg* [1995] 1 AC 482, the requirements appear to be the same — that is *such force as is reasonable in the circumstances.*

Where such a defence is raised in relation to the taking of someone's life, the provisions of Article 2 of the European Convention on Human Rights will now be applicable. The requirements of Article 2 are more stringent than the test under s. 3. Under Article 2 the test will be whether the force used was no more than *absolutely necessary* and lethal force will be 'absolutely necessary' only if it is strictly proportionate to the legitimate purpose being pursued. In order to meet those criteria, regard will be had to:

* the nature of the aim being pursued
* the inherent dangers to life and limb from the situation
* the degree of risk to life presented by the amount of force employed.

The only circumstances under which lethal force might be permissible here are where the defendant was acting *to defend another person from unlawful violence* (Article 2(2)), not in the general prevention of crime. The other circumstances where such force may be used are in effecting the lawful arrest, or preventing the escape of another and in lawfully acting to quell a riot or insurrection.

For a full discussion on the Convention and the impact of the Human Rights Act 1998, **see General Police Duties**.

4.8.2   Defence of Self or Another

It is uncertain whether 'self-defence' is limited to the defence of oneself and 'friends and family', or whether it extends to acts done in defence of any other person. The distinction is of little importance given the general defence in relation to the prevention of crime under the Criminal Law Act 1967.

A defendant must believe that the degree of force used is reasonable in the circumstances *as he/she honestly believes them to be* (*Beckford*). Therefore if a defendant believes he/she is being attacked or is facing a lethal threat, he/she may use a degree of force which would be reasonable if that were actually the case.

Note that there is no requirement to let the believed attacker 'strike the first blow' (*Beckford*) or for the person defending themselves to retreat (see *R* v *Bird* [1985] 1 WLR 816). A 'pre-emptive' strike may be justified by the circumstances.

Whether or not a defendant did act in self-defence is a question of fact which should be left to a jury — even if the defendant has not raised the issue (*DPP (Jamaica)* v *Bailey* [1995] 1 Cr App R 257).

In deciding whether or not the force used by a defendant was reasonable in the circumstances, the court will have regard to the 'anguish' of the moment and the defendant will not be expected to have *'weighed to a nicety the exact measure of his [/her] necessary defensive actions'* (per Lord Morris in *Palmer* v *The Queen* [1971] AC 814).

If the degree of force used by the defendant is found to have been excessive in a trial for murder, there is no room for an argument of self-defence to *reduce* the defendant's liability to manslaughter; the defence is either accepted completely (in which case the defendant is 'not guilty') or it is not (in which case he/she is convicted) (*R* v *Clegg* [1995] 1 AC 482).

If the defendant mistakenly believes that he/she is being attacked, that belief does not have to be 'reasonable' (*R* v *Williams* [1987] 3 All ER 411). In such cases the defendant's actions will be judged against the circumstances as he/she believed them to be at the time. Therefore, where a defendant mistakenly believed he was being attacked by strangers and 'defended' himself against them, his actions were to be judged as though that were actually the case — even though the strangers were in fact police officers and court officials and the defendant's mistake was not an entirely reasonable one (*Blackburn* v *Bowering* [1994] 1 WLR 1324).

If any lethal force is used, the test under Article 2 of the European Convention on Human Rights will apply (see above).

For the defence of mistake generally, **see para. 4.5**.

4.8.3 Defence of Property

Again it is unclear how far a person may act in defence of his/her own or another's property. For the statutory defences to destroying or damaging another's property in defence of one's own, **see chapter 14**. Given the general requirements of reasonableness set out above, it would be difficult — though not impossible — to argue that deliberately killing another was a reasonable and necessary response to a threat to one's property alone. However, Article 2(2) of the European Convention on Human Rights does not permit the taking of life in order to protect property.

4.9 Infancy

Before the Crime and Disorder Act 1998, children under 14 years of age were presumed at common law to be 'incapable of evil' or *doli incapax*. In relation to children under 10 years of age that presumption was, and still is irrebuttable (**see Evidence and**

Procedure, chapter 11). Consequently, no evidence to the contrary will be entertained by a court and children under 10 cannot be convicted of a criminal offence. Their actions, however, may give rise to a 'parenting order' under the Crime and Disorder Act 1998 (**see Evidence and Procedure, chapter 8**).

The presumption of *doli incapax* in relation to children who were aged 10 or over but who had not yet reached 14 years of age was *rebuttable*. This meant that the prosecution could adduce evidence to show that the child defendant knew that what he/she had done was seriously wrong. If the evidence was accepted, the courts would regard that presumption as having been rebutted and the child defendant could be tried in much the same way as an adult. Some concern as to how appropriate such a presumption was in modern society led the House of Lords in *C (A Minor)* v *DPP* [1996] AC 1 to declare the rule to be outdated but adding that it was up to Parliament to change it. Section 34 of the Crime and Disorder Act 1998 does exactly that and abolishes this second, rebuttable form of the presumption of *doli incapax*, effectively lowering the age of criminal responsibility to 10 years of age. According to many commentators, this change now gives England and Wales one of the lowest ages of criminal responsibility in the world.

Despite the many criticisms and concerns raised over this change in the criminal law, its practical effects are likely to be mitigated by a number of factors, in particular:

- the general requirement for subjective awareness in many criminal offences, **see chapter 1**;

- the provisions for dealing with youth crime, **see Evidence and Procedure, chapter 8**;

- the role of the CPS in decisions to prosecute and the consideration of the public interest, **see Evidence and Procedure, appendix 1**.

CHAPTER FIVE

HOMICIDE

5.1 Introduction

Homicide covers not only the offences of murder and manslaughter, but also other occasions where a person causes, or is involved in, the death of another. The common law which has grown up around the subject of homicide is important, not only because of the gravity of the offences themselves, but also because the cases have defined a number of key issues in criminal law which are applicable to many other offences.

In approaching the offences discussed in this chapter, it is worth noting the statutory duty imposed on chief officers of police and the local probation board for the area, acting jointly as the 'responsible authority' in relation to certain types of offender. Although primarily concerned with sex offenders (as to which, **see chapter 10**), that duty (under s. 67 of the Criminal Justice and Court Services Act 2000) also relates to violent offenders and the responsible authority has a duty to establish appropriate 'arrangements' for the purpose of assessing and managing the risks posed in their area by relevant violent offenders.

In considering any offences set out in this chapter, the right to life enshrined in Article 2 of the European Convention on Human Rights may be significant. In particular, the positive obligation imposed on a State to protect the lives of its citizens may be relevant where a person has been killed or an unlawful attempt has been made on his/her life. Article 2 creates both a duty on the State not to take life and also a positive duty to protect the lives of individuals (see *X* v *United Kingdom* (1978) 14 DR 31). The duty of the State to protect people from the criminal actions of others was examined in the case of *Osman* v *United Kingdom* (2000) 29 EHRR 245. There the European Court of Human Rights held that it is possible for an individual to show that the State had violated Article 2 if the police had failed to protect his/her right to life under certain circumstances. For further discussion of this issue and the importance of it in policing generally, **see General Police Duties, chapter 2**. Recently, in a case concerning withholding medical treatment, the High Court considered the positive and negative duties under Article 2. The court held that the negative obligation was to refrain from taking a life intentionally. It held that this obligation was not breached by a decision made in the patient's best interests to withdraw life support facilities and that the intentional deprivation of life had to involve a deliberate act as opposed to an omission (**see chapter 2**). In relation to the positive obligation, the court held that this required the relevant public authority to take adequate and appropriate steps to safeguard life. Again, the taking of a responsible clinical decision to withhold treatment that was not in the patient's best interests met the state's positive obligation under Article 2 (*NHS Trust A* v *M* [2001] 1 All ER 801).

For offences arising out of pregnancy and childbirth, **see chapter 7**.

5.2 Murder

Offence — Murder — Common Law
Life imprisonment (mandatory).
(***Serious arrestable offence***)

Murder is committed when a person unlawfully kills another human being under the Queen's Peace, with malice aforethought (see *Blackstone's Criminal Practice*, 2001, section B1).

Keynote

A conviction for murder carries a mandatory sentence of life imprisonment (in the case of a defendant who is under 18, 'detention at Her Majesty's pleasure': Powers of Criminal Courts (Sentencing) Act 2000, s. 90).

'Unlawful killing' means actively causing the death of another without justification and includes occasions where someone fails to act after creating a situation of danger (**see chapter 2**).

'Another human being' includes a baby who has been born alive and has an existence independent of its mother. If a person injures a baby while it is in its mother's womb and it subsequently dies from those injuries *after being born*, it may be appropriate to bring a charge of murder (for the situation where the baby is not born alive, see **chapter 7**).

If the defendant intended only to cause serious injury to the mother, that intention cannot support a charge of *murder* in respect of the baby if it goes on to die after being born alive. It may, however, support a charge of *manslaughter*. This departure for the earlier law is clear from the House of Lords' ruling in *Attorney-General's Reference (No. 3 of 1994)* [1998] AC 245, a ruling that overturned the Court of Appeal's previous decision in the same case. The House of Lords ruled that the doctrine of 'transferred malice' (**see chapter 1**) does not fully apply in cases of unborn children (*in utero*). Any liability of the defendant for the subsequent death of a child that he/she injured before it was born alive will depend on the defendant's intentions at the time of causing the injury. Clearly an intention to kill the mother could be sufficient in bringing a charge of murder following the subsequent and connected death of the child.

'Under the Queen's Peace' appears to exclude deaths caused during the legitimate prosecution of warfare (see the War Crimes Act 1991). Under the provisions of the Offences Against the Person Act 1861 any British citizen who commits a murder anywhere in the world may be tried in England or Wales.

It should be noted that the only state of mind or *mens rea* (**see chapter 1**) that will support a charge of attempted murder is an *intention to kill*. Nothing less will suffice (hence the note in the CPS Charging Standards, **see appendix 2**).

Sections 1 and 2 of the Criminal Evidence (Amendment) Act 1997 extending the power to take non-intimate samples without consent apply to this offence and also to conspiracies, attempts or incitements in the circumstances set out in that Act (**see Evidence and Procedure, chapter 16**).

5.2.1 Malice Aforethought

This archaic expression both sounds — and was — very complex and daunting until recently. Now, after the cases of *R v Moloney* [1985] AC 905 and *R v Hancock* [1986] AC 455, the *mens rea* required for murder is an intention:

* to kill, or
* to cause grievous bodily harm.

Murder is therefore a crime of 'specific intent' (**see chapter 1**).

The term 'malice aforethought' is therefore completely misleading and the only place where 'premeditation' is insisted upon is in murder mystery novels.

5.2.2 Year and a Day

Another ancient and awkward rule which no longer applies is the 'year and a day' requirement. Since the Law Reform (Year and a Day Rule) Act 1996 there is no longer a need to show that a victim died within a year and a day of the defendant's actions (s. 1).

If a victim of an alleged murder dies *more than three years after receiving their injury* then the consent of the Attorney-General (or Solicitor-General) is needed before bringing a prosecution (s. 2(b)). That consent is also needed if the defendant has already been convicted of an offence committed under the circumstances connected with the death (s. 2(a)).

5.3 Special Defences

As a conviction for murder leaves a judge no discretion in sentencing a defendant, a number of 'special defences' have developed around the offence. These 'defences' are now provided by the Homicide Act 1957 and, rather than securing an acquittal, allow for a conviction of manslaughter instead of murder. They are dealt with here as they fall outside the more common defences that are generally available in respect of criminal offences (as to which, **see chapter 4**).

These 'special defences' are:

* diminished responsibility
* provocation
* suicide pact.

5.3.1   Diminished Responsibility

The Homicide Act 1957, s. 2 states:

(1) Where a person kills or is party to the killing of another, he shall not be convicted of murder if he was suffering from such abnormality of mind (whether arising from a condition of arrested or retarded development of mind or any inherent causes or induced by disease or injury) as substantially impaired his mental responsibility for his acts or omissions in doing or being a party to the killing.

(2) On a charge of murder, it shall be for the defence to prove that the person charged is by virtue of this section not liable to be convicted of murder.

(3) A person who but for this section would be liable, whether as principal or as accessory, to be convicted of murder shall be liable instead to be convicted of manslaughter.

(4) The fact that one party to a killing is by virtue of this section not liable to be convicted of murder shall not affect the question whether the killing amounted to murder in the case of any other party to it.

Keynote

'Abnormality of mind' has been held to be 'a state of mind so different from that of ordinary human beings that the reasonable man would term it abornmal' (*R* v *Byrne* [1960] 2 QB 396). This includes the mental ability to exert control over one's behaviour and to form rational judgement.

'Impairment of mental responsibility' — this impairment must be 'substantial'. Whether or not that is the case will be a question of fact for the jury to decide. Minor lapses of lucidity will not be enough. There may be any number of causes of the 'abnormality' of the mind. Examples accepted by the courts to date have included pre-menstrual symptoms (*R* v *Reynolds* [1998] Crim LR 679) and 'battered wives' syndrome' (*R* v *Hobson* [1998] 1 Cr App R 31).

The burden of proving these features lies with the defence and the standard required is one of a balance of probabilities (**see Evidence and Procedure, chapter 11**). In *R* v *Lambert, The Times*, 5 September 2000, the Court of Appeal held that this burden of proof did not breach an individual's right to a presumption of innocence or the right to a fair trial under the European Convention on Human Rights.

5.3.2   Provocation

The Homicide Act 1957, s. 3 states:

Where on a charge of murder there is evidence on which a jury can find that the person charged was provoked (whether by things done or by things said or by both together) to lose his self-control, the question whether the provocation was enough to make a reasonable man do as he did shall be left to be determined by the jury; and in determining that question the jury shall take into account everything both done and said according to the effect which, in their opinion, it would have on a reasonable man.

Keynote

The questions to be considered here are:

- Was the defendant actually provoked?

- Might a reasonable person have acted as the defendant did under the same circumstances?

Was the defendant provoked? It is clear that words (*DPP* v *Camplin* [1978] AC 705) or even sounds (*R* v *Doughty* (1987) 83 Cr App R 319 (baby crying)) can amount to 'provocation'. It is also clear that the words or acts need not be directed towards the defendant, nor need they originate from the ultimate victim. Therefore a defendant may be sufficiently provoked by things which X says to Y that he/she kills Z and the 'defence' of provocation could be available. In addition to the 'battered wives' syndrome' mentioned above, where the provocation has been endured by the defendant over a prolonged period (such as the abused wife in *R* v *Ahluwalia* [1992] 4 All ER 889), he/she may be able to show an eventual and sudden lack of self-control brought about by that prolonged behaviour or by a particular event which proved to be 'the last straw' (*R* v *Humphreys* [1995] 4 All ER 1008).

If a defendant simply panics or acts out of fear, as opposed to losing control, the defence will not be made out.

Unlike the general defence of 'duress' (**see chapter 4**), there is no defence of 'provocation by circumstances'; the provocation must come from something done by or to a third person (*R* v *Acott* [1997] 1 WLR 306).

If there is no loss of control by the defendant, then the provocation defence will not be available. See, for example, *R* v *Cocker* [1989] Crim LR 740 where the defendant had endured pleas from his chronically-ill wife to kill her. He had not lost control at the time of the killing — quite the reverse — and the judge had no alternative but to pass a life sentence.

The 'Reasonable Person' Test

In assessing the second point, a jury must consider how a reasonable person *sharing the defendant's characteristics* would have reacted to the provocation. Such characteristics could include disability (*R* v *Roberts* [1990] Crim LR 122 where the defendant was taunted about his deafness), impotence or even an addiction (*R* v *Morhall* [1996] AC 90 where the defendant was taunted about his addiction to glue). Not surprisingly, one characteristic which is not admissible is a defendant's general lack of self-control or tendency to have violent losses of temper.

5.3.3 Suicide Pact

The Homicide Act 1957, s. 4 states:

> *(1) It shall be manslaughter, and shall not be murder, for a person acting in pursuance of a suicide pact between him and another to kill the other or be a party to the other being killed by a third person.*

Keynote

The *defendant* must show that:

- a suicide pact had been made, and
- he/she had the intention of dying at the time the killing took place.

'Suicide pact' is defined by the Homicide Act 1957, s. 4(3) as:

> *a common agreement between two or more persons having for its object the death of all of them, whether or not each is to take his own life, but nothing done by a person who enters into a suicide pact shall be treated as done by him in pursuance of the pact unless it is done while he has the settled intention of dying in pursuance of the pact.*

(See also **para. 5.5** for the offence of assisting a suicide.)

5.4 Manslaughter

Traditionally this subject is divided in two classifications — voluntary and involuntary manslaughter. This is not particularly helpful and, at the time of writing, the government has published a consultation paper on the subject. The real division between the two types of manslaughter centres around the *mens rea* — the state of mind of the defendant.

The three sets of circumstances where 'special defences' may reduce a murder charge to one of manslaughter make up one type or classification of the offence (so-called *voluntary* manslaughter). They have been covered in **paras 5.3.1 to 5.3.3 above**. In that sense, voluntary manslaughter is more a finding by a court than an offence with which someone can be charged. The second classification (*involuntary* manslaughter) occurs where the defendant causes the death of another but is not shown to have had the required *mens rea* for murder.

Offence — Manslaughter — Common Law
Triable on indictment. Life imprisonment.
(Serious arrestable offence)

Keynote

Manslaughter, like murder is the unlawful killing of another human being. What it does not require is the intention to kill or to cause grievous bodily harm.

Sections 1 and 2 of the Criminal Evidence (Amendment) Act 1997 extending the power to take non-intimate samples without consent apply to this offence and also to conspiracies, attempts or incitements in the circumstances set out in that Act (**see Evidence and Procedure, chapter 16**).

The second classification of manslaughter, that is, those cases which do not involve the 'special defences' under the Homicide Act 1957 (**see para. 5.3**) can be separated into occasions where a defendant:

- kills another by an *unlawful act* which was *likely to cause bodily harm*, or
- kills another by *gross negligence*.

5.4.1 Manslaughter by Unlawful Act

In order to prove manslaughter by an unlawful act (constructive manslaughter), you must prove:

- An unlawful act by the defendant, that is, an act which is *unlawful in itself*, irrespective of the fact that it ultimately results in someone's death. The act must be inherently unlawful. An act that only becomes unlawful by virtue of the way in which it is carried out will not be enough. A good example is 'driving'. Driving is clearly not an inherently unlawful act but becomes so if done inconsiderately on a road or public place (**see Road Traffic, chapter 2**). Therefore if someone drives inconsiderately and thereby causes the death of another, the act of driving — albeit carried out in a way that attracts criminal liability — is *not* an 'unlawful act' for the purposes of constructive manslaughter (see *Andrews* v *DPP* [1937] AC 576). This is one reason why there are statutory offences addressing most instances of death that are caused by poor standards of driving. The act need not be directed or aimed at anyone and can include acts committed against or towards property (*R v Goodfellow* (1986) 83 Cr App R 23).

Generally, if the actions of the victim break the chain of causation between the defendant's unlawful act and the cause of death, the defendant will not be responsible for the death of that victim (**see chapter 2**). This has been held to mean that drug dealers cannot generally be held liable for the ultimate deaths of their 'victims' (see *R v Dalby* [1982] 1 All ER 916 and *R v Armstrong* [1989] Crim LR 149).

However, the Court of Appeal has recently accepted that, under certain circumstances, the supply of a controlled drug that was immediately taken (in this case, by injection) by a purchaser who then died as a result, can amount to assistance and encouragement of the taking of the drug. Therefore, the issue of whether the dealer caused the death of the user by the unlawful act of supplying the drug should have left to the jury (*R v Kennedy*, unreported, 31 July 1998).

An *omission* to do something will not suffice (**see chapter 2**). Any unlawful killing caused by an omission would either come under the circumstances outlined in **chapter 2** or under those required to prove gross negligence (**see para. 5.4.2**).

- That the act involved a risk of somebody being harmed. That risk will be judged *objectively*, that is; would the risk be apparent to a reasonable and sober person watching the act? (See *R v Church* [1966] 1 QB 59.) Such acts might include dropping a paving stone off a bridge into the path of a train (*R v Newbury* [1977] AC 500), setting fire to your house (*Goodfellow* above) or firing a gun at police officers and then holding someone else in front of you when the officers return fire (*R v Pagett* (1983) 76 Cr App R 279). 'Harm' must be physical; the risk of emotional or psychological harm does not appear to be enough (see *R v Dawson* (1985) 81 Cr App R 150).

- That the defendant had the required *mens rea* for the relevant 'unlawful act' (e.g. for an assault or criminal damage) which led to the death of a victim. If he/she did not have that *mens rea* then the offence of manslaughter will not be made out. See, for example, *R v Lamb* [1967] 2 QB 981 where the defendant pretended to fire a revolver at his friend. Although the defendant believed that the weapon would not fire, the chamber containing a bullet moved round to the firing pin and the defendant's friend was killed. As Lamb did not have the *mens rea* required for an assault (**see chapter 8**) his conviction for manslaughter was quashed.

There is no logical reason why, if a defendant uses a motor vehicle as a means to commit an 'unlawful act' (e.g. an assault) that he/she cannot be charged with manslaughter as long as the 'act' goes beyond poor driving. There are, however, reasons of policy (see *R v Lawrence* [1982] AC 510) why, in all but the most deliberate of cases, the offence under the Road Traffic Act 1988, as amended, should be used (**see Road Traffic, chapter 2**).

5.4.2 Manslaughter by Gross Negligence

Manslaughter is the only criminal offence at common law capable of being committed by negligence. The degree of that negligence has been the source of considerable debate over the years and particular problems have arisen in trying to distinguish the level of negligence required for manslaughter and that required to prove 'recklessness' (as to which, **see chapter 1**).

A charge of manslaughter may be brought where a person, by an instance of *gross negligence,* has brought about the death of another. Thankfully the most difficult task in defining the degree of negligence that will qualify as 'gross' falls to the trial judge when he/she addresses the jury. Whether a defendant's conduct will amount to gross negligence is a question of fact for the jury to decide in the light of all the evidence (*R v Bateman* (1925) 19 Cr App R 8). What is clear from the decided cases is that civil liability, although a starting point for establishing the breach of a duty of care, is not enough to amount to 'gross negligence', neither is 'recklessness' as defined in *Caldwell* (**see chapter 1**) (*R v Adomako* [1995] 1 AC 171).

For the practical difficulties and the inconsistencies in the case law on this area generally, see *Blackstone's Criminal Practice*, 2001, section B1.39.

5.4.3   Corporate Manslaughter

One area that has caused a great deal of speculation — and not a little confusion — is that of corporate manslaughter. The requirement that there be at least some evidence of the state of mind of defendant even in cases involving gross negligence has always presented problems where the defendant is a limited company. As an entirely separate legal 'person', a limited company can clearly be capable of committing criminal offences and it is not unusual for companies to be prosecuted for criminal offences, particularly those involving strict liability (as to which, **see chapter 1**). Where the offence in question requires proof of a state of mind by the defendant, however, corporate liability becomes a little more problematic. Companies can still commit such offences, which include manslaughter, a fact made very clear by the prosecution of P&O ferries after the sinking of the *Herald of Free Enterprise* in 1987. However, the problem of identifying a 'directing mind' of an officer of the company has prevented the successful prosecution of corporate liability cases on a number of occasions (including in the P&O case). A recent case that has attracted a great deal of attention in this area followed the Southall rail crash. In *Attorney-General's Reference (No. 2 of 1999)* [2000] 3 WLR 195, the Court of Appeal confirmed that a defendant might be convicted of gross negligence manslaughter without the need to prove his/her particular state of mind at the time provided it is shown:

- that the defendant owed the deceased a duty of care

- that the defendant breached that duty of care, and

- that the breach was so grossly negligent that the defendant could be deemed to have had such a disregard for the life of the deceased as to deserve criminal punishment

(per *R v Adomako* [1995] 1 AC 171).

However, the state of mind of the defendant might still be relevant as the jury need to take *all* the circumstances into account when considering the breach of duty of care above. As a result, a 'corporate defendant' could only be convicted of manslaughter by gross negligence through the mind and will of its directors and senior managers.

At the time of writing, the Law Commission is considering this area of criminal law very carefully and the government has proposed the creation of a new offence of 'corporate killing'.

5.5 Aiding Suicide

Offence — Aiding Another to Commit Suicide — Suicide Act 1961, s. 2
Triable on indictment. 14 years' imprisonment.
(*Arrestable offence*)

The Suicide Act 1961, s. 2 states:

> *(1) A person who aids, abets, counsels or procures the suicide of another, or an attempt by another to commit suicide, shall be liable . . .*

Keynote

This offence is an alternative verdict on a charge of murder/manslaughter (Suicide Act 1961, s. 2(2)). Perhaps the most topical aspect of this offence involves so-called mercy killings. It was formerly an offence to *commit* suicide (!) but that was repealed by s. 1 of the 1961 Act. For guidance on the scope of aiding, abetting, counselling and procuring, **see chapter 3**. This offence has the unusual feature of creating criminal liability for aiding and abetting *an attempt*.

Given that this offence is linked to the expected death of another, it might be argued that it will always be a 'serious' arrestable offence even though it is not included under s. 116(2) of the Police and Criminal Evidence Act 1984 (**see General Police Duties, chapter 2**).

5.6 Solicitation of Murder

Offence — Encouraging Another to Murder — Offences Against the Person Act 1861, s. 4
Triable on indictment. Life imprisonment.
(*Arrestable offence*)

The Offences Against the Person Act 1861, s. 4 states:

> *Whosoever shall solicit, encourage, persuade or endeavour to persuade, or shall propose to any person, to murder any other person, whether he be a subject of Her Majesty or not . . . shall be guilty of [an offence] . . .*

Keynote

The proposed victim may be outside the United Kingdom.

It does not matter whether or not the person is in fact encouraged to commit murder. This offence may be appropriate in cases where a person is trying to arrange a 'contract killing' (see *R v Adamthwaite* (1994) 15 Cr App R (S) 241 where the person 'encouraged' was an undercover police officer). For this reason this offence may be preferred in cases where the defendant has 'conspired' with *one* other person and that person is an undercover police officer (**see chapter 2**).

The comments in relation to serious arrestable offences above also apply to this offence.

For the offence of making threats to kill, **see General Police Duties, chapter 3**.

CHAPTER SIX

MISUSE OF DRUGS

6.1   Introduction

The misuse of controlled drugs has become such a pervasive feature of Western society that it now affects almost every aspect of community life. Its impact on crime and community safety has become so significant that it is one of the most frequently encountered areas of criminal law for police officers.

The majority of the law in this area is statutory and is supported by a considerable body of case law.

At the time of writing, drug treatment and testing orders were being piloted under new legislation in certain areas of England and Wales (**see Evidence and Procedure**).

6.2   Drug Trafficking

The Drug Trafficking Act 1994 addresses (amongst other things) the production, movement and storage of controlled drugs, together with the proceeds of drug trafficking. Although the contents of that and related statutes are beyond the scope of this work, references to it have been included as and where it seems appropriate to do so.

6.3   Controlled Drugs

The list of controlled drugs has developed almost as fast as the substances themselves. Schedule 2 to the Misuse of Drugs Act 1971 (**see appendix 1** which defines what those drugs are), is a slightly daunting and bewildering table of chemicals. Practically, defendants are unlikely to know that they are selling or buying 1-diphenylpropanecar-boxylic acid — neither are police officers. Both, however, are likely to know the 'street' name for the more commonly available controlled drugs, but the important classification for the purposes of investigation and prosecution, is that of Class A, B or C drugs.

6.4 Classification

Drugs which are subject to the provisions of the Misuse of Drugs Act 1971 are listed in Parts I to II to Schedule 2.

The divisions are made largely on the basis of each substance's potential effects on both the person taking it and society in general.

Classification is important in determining the sentencing powers of the courts.

- **Class A** — This class includes the most notorious and dangerous drugs such as heroin and morphine, opiates, cocaine, some amphetamines and LSD.

- **Class B** — This class includes cannabis, cannabis resin, codeine and some amphetamines.

- **Class C** — This class includes some commonly-abused prescription drugs, for examples of these drugs, **see appendix 1**.

If the charge alleges possession of one particular drug then that drug must be identified.

It is not necessary, when prosecuting an offence, to distinguish between the various chemical forms in which a drug exists (i.e. as a salt, ester or other form) (*R* v *Greensmith* [1983] 1 WLR 1124).

A defendant's admission may, in some cases, be relied upon to prove his/her knowledge as to what a particular substance is (see *R* v *Chatwood* [1980] 1 WLR 874).

6.4.1 Cannabis

The Misuse of Drugs Act 1971, s. 37 states:

> *'cannabis' (except in the expression 'cannabis resin') means any plant of the genus Cannabis or any part of any such plant (by whatever name designated) except that it does not include cannabis resin or any of the following products after separation from the rest of the plant, namely—*
> *(a)   mature stalk of any such plant,*
> *(b)   fibre produced from mature stalk of any such plant, and*
> *(c)   seed of any such plant,*
> *'cannabis resin' means the separated resin, whether crude or purified, obtained from any plant of the genus Cannabis.*

Keynote

As cannabis and cannabis resin are both Class B drugs there would be no duplicity if a person were charged with possessing either one or the other in the same charge (*R* v *Best* (1979) 70 Cr App R 21).

6.4.2 Drug Testing

When brought fully into force, the Criminal Justice and Court Services Act 2000 will introduce new powers to enable the police to require urine or non-intimate samples to be taken from adults in police detention under certain circumstances. The purpose of such tests is to ascertain whether the person has any specified Class A drug in their body. The power to require such a sample will be activated in one of two ways:

- the person concerned has been charged with a 'trigger' offence (these offences are identified throughout this and other relevant chapters in this Manual); or

- the person concerned has been charged with any offence and a police officer of the rank of inspector or above has reasonable grounds for suspecting that the misuse by that person of any specified Class A drug caused or contributed to the offence.

The Powers of Criminal Courts (Sentencing) Act 2000 makes further provision for the courts to impose drug treatment and testing orders. For a full discussion of these powers, **see Evidence and Procedure, chapter 9**.

6.5   Possession

Possession appears to be a straightforward concept. However, as with many other such 'straightforward' concepts, the courts have wrangled over its meaning for so long that it is not so straightforward after all.

'Possession' in itself is a neutral concept, not implying any kind of blame or fault. This is the key feature to understand first before going on to consider specific offences under *any* legislation. In order to be in possession of *anything,* the common law requires physical control of the object plus knowledge of its presence. This requirement is particularly problematic where containers of some sort (whether they be boxes, handbags, cigarette packets or whatever) are involved or where the person claims not to have realised what it was that he/she 'possessed'. In such cases, the common law makes the same requirements; you need to show that the person had physical control of the container together with a knowledge that it contained *something.* Once you have established possession, you then need to show that the substance/object/material possessed was in fact proscribed by the relevant statute.

In relation to controlled drugs, the issue becomes complicated further by the specific defences provided by the 1971 Act. The very reason those defences (**see para. 6.**7) have been drafted in this way is to reflect the common law concept of possession and to provide some protection from its effects where drugs are concerned (see *R v Bett* [1999] 1 All ER 600).

So, if a person has a container with him/her and that container is found to have controlled drugs in it, he/she is in possession of those drugs *provided he/she knew that there was something in the container.* That does not mean that, at this point, the person necessarily commits an offence (and he/she may still have a statutory defence); it means that he/she was in 'possession' of the drugs. This merely satisfies one element of a number of possible offences; just as if you were trying to prove that a person was 'driving' a vehicle. (Driving is also a neutral concept and only satisfies one element within a number of possible offences.)

The Misuse of Drugs Act 1971 creates offences under certain circumstances where a person has been shown to have been in 'possession' of a controlled drug. However, the Act also provides a defence which unfortunately includes a mental element on the part

MISUSE OF DRUGS

of the defendant. It is true that this situation in relation to possession is impracticable — like many others in our system — and it is not even consistently applied (e.g. in cases of strict liability such as some firearms offences involving 'possession' (see *R* v *Bradish* [1990] 1 QB 981 and **General Police Duties, chapter 5**). Nevertheless, until the concept of 'possession' at common law is changed to include an element of blame or fault, these rules will continue to apply and presumably statutes will continue to contain defences which, like s. 28 of the 1971 Act, are aimed at correcting any unjust results.

Nevertheless it is clear from the House of Lords' decisions in *Warner* v *Metropolitan Police Commissioner* [1969] 2 AC 256 and *R* v *Boyesen* [1982] AC 768, and also the Court of Appeal judgment in *R* v *McNamara* (1988) 87 Cr App R 246 that the basic elements required are that a person 'knows' that he/she is in possession of something which is, in fact, a prohibited or controlled object or substance.

To prove possession of a controlled drug then, you must show that a defendant both:

- *had* a controlled drug in his/her possession; and

- *knew* that he/she had something in his/her possession which was in fact a controlled drug.

The first part of this requirement, the *physical* possession, is fairly obvious. It is the second part, the *mental* element required at common law, which complicates the concept.

Example

Consider the following circumstances: After a stop and search, a defendant is found with a knife in his pocket. The knife has traces of brown powder on the blade. Later examination shows the powder to be heroin.

In order to prove 'possession' of the heroin you must show:

- that the defendant actually had the knife
- that the knife had a substance which was a controlled drug on it and that
- the defendant knew *of the existence of the substance* (i.e., the powder).

6.5.1 Quality

You would not have to show that he/she knew what the powder was. That is, you do not need to show that the defendant knew the *quality* of what he/she possessed.

If the defendant admits to knowing that the powder was there but thought it was sand, he/she is in possession of it (see *R* v *Marriott* [1971] 1 All ER 595).

Therefore if a defendant had a packet of cigarettes with him/her and admitted to knowing that he/she had them, he/she would be in possession of a controlled drug if one cigarette was shown to have contained cannabis. The fact that the defendant thought they contained tobacco would be irrelevant (*Searle* v *Randolph* [1972] Crim LR 779) (although clearly they may be able to raise the defence under s. 28: see below).

64

6.5.2   Quantity

The *quantity* of a controlled drug, however, may be so small that the defendant could not possibly have known about it; therefore it could not be 'possessed'.

Each case will have to be decided on its merits but the House of Lords have suggested that if something is 'visible, tangible and measurable', that may be sufficient (*Boyesen*). If the amount recovered is too small to support a charge of possession, it might be used to prove earlier possession of the drug (see *R* v *Graham* [1970] 1 WLR 113 and *Hambleton* v *Callinan* [1968] 2 QB 427 (traces of a controlled drug in a urine sample held to be possible evidence of earlier possession of that drug)).

6.6   Misuse of Drugs Regulations 1985

The Misuse of Drugs Regulations 1985 (SI 1985 No. 2066) exempt certain drugs and certain people from the main offences of possession, supply and importation.

The key regulations are:

- Regulation 4 which exempts certain types of drugs from offences involving importation when those drugs are contained in a medicinal product.

- Regulation 5 which allows certain people holding a licence issued by the Secretary of State to possess, supply or produce controlled drugs in accordance with the conditions of that licence.

- Regulation 6 which allows certain people — including police officers in the course of their duty — to possess and supply controlled drugs to others under very strict conditions.

Examples of others covered by reg. 6 are veterinary surgeons, postal workers, HM Customs and Excise staff and pharmacists.

The remaining regulations concern further exemptions for medical and research staff.

6.7   Defences

Before considering the various offences under the Misuse of Drugs Act 1971 it is useful to address the specific statutory defences provided by ss. 5 and 28 of the Act.

Section 5(4) provides a defence to an offence of unlawful *possession*:

(4)   In any proceedings for an offence under subsection (2) above in which it is proved that the accused had a controlled drug in his possession, it shall be a defence for him to prove—
(a)   that, knowing or suspecting it to be a controlled drug, he took possession of it for the purpose of preventing another from committing or continuing to commit an offence in connection with that drug and that as soon as possible after taking possession of it he took all such steps as were reasonably open to him to destroy the drug or to deliver it into the custody of a person lawfully entitled to take custody of it; or
(b)   that, knowing or suspecting it to be a controlled drug, he took possession of it for the purpose of delivering it into the custody of a person lawfully entitled to take custody of it and that as soon as possible after taking possession of it he took all such steps as were reasonably open to him to deliver it into the custody of such a person.

Keynote

This defence envisages two distinct situations. The purpose in taking possession of the controlled drug under s. 5(4)(a) must be to:

- prevent *another*
- from committing (in the future) or
- continuing to commit

an offence in connection with *that* drug.

The first situation might arise where a parent, guardian or carer finds a child in possession of something which appears to be a controlled drug. Provided that that person takes all reasonable steps to destroy the drug or to take it to someone lawfully entitled to possess it (like a general practitioner or police officer), *as soon as possible after taking possession of it*, he/she commits no offence *of unlawful possession*.

The second situation (under s. 5(4)(b)) may arise where a person finds what he/she believes to be a controlled drug and he/she takes possession of it *solely for the purpose of delivering it to a person lawfully entitled to take custody of it*. The defendant must prove that this was his/her intention at the time of taking possession (*R v Dempsey* (1985) 82 Cr App R 291).

In either case above, s. 5(4) will not provide a defence to any other offence connected with the controlled drug (e.g. supplying or offering to supply).

General Defence

However, there is a more general defence provided by s. 28 of the Act. Section 28 applies to offences of:

- unlawful production (s. 4(2))
- unlawful supply (s. 4(3))
- unlawful possession (s. 5(2))
- possession with intent to supply (s. 5(3))
- unlawful cultivation of cannabis (s. 6(2))
- offences connected with opium (s. 9).

The defences under s. 28 are *not* available in cases of conspiracy as they are not offences under the 1971 Act (*R v McGowan* [1990] Crim LR 399). In *R v Lambert* (2001) LTL 5 July the House of Lords considered the requirements of the defences under ss. 5(4) and 28 in relation to their effect on the presumption of innocence (imposed at both common law and under Article 6). It was argued that the statutory defence shifted the legal burden of proof from the prosecution onto the defendant and, therefore, was incompatible with the Convention. Their Lordships held that the defences could legitimately be read by the courts in a way that moved the *evidential* burden onto the defendant. Such an approach, they held, was compatible with the Convention and the Human Rights Act 1998. For a further discussion of these issues **see Evidence & Procedure, chapter 11**.

Section 28 states:

> *(2)   Subject to subsection (3) below, in any proceedings for an offence to which this section applies it shall be a defence for the accused to prove that he neither knew of nor suspected nor had reason to*

suspect the existence of some fact alleged by the prosecution which it is necessary for the prosecution to prove if he is to be convicted of the offence charged.

(3) Where in any proceedings for an offence to which this section applies it is necessary, if the accused is to be convicted of the offence charged, for the prosecution to prove that some substance or product involved in the alleged offence was the controlled drug which the prosecution alleges it to have been, and it is proved that the substance or product in question was that controlled drug, the accused—

(a) shall not be acquitted of the offence charged by reason only of proving that he neither knew nor suspected nor had reason to suspect that the substance or product in question was the particular controlled drug alleged; but

(b) shall be acquitted thereof—

(i) if he proves that he neither believed nor suspected nor had reason to suspect that the substance or product in question was a controlled drug; or

(ii) if he proves that he believed the substance or product in question to be a controlled drug, or a controlled drug of a description, such that, if it had in fact been that controlled drug, or a controlled drug of that description, he would not at the material time have been committing any offence to which this section applies.

Keynote

This defence envisages three distinct situations:

- a lack of knowledge by the defendant of some fact which is alleged by the prosecution;

- a general lack of knowledge by the defendant about the drug in question;

- a conditional belief held by the defendant about the drug in question.

These situations are discussed below.

6.7.1 Lack of Knowledge of Some Alleged Fact

Section 28(2) allows a defence where the defendant did not *know*, *suspect* or *have reason to suspect* the existence of some fact which is essential to proving the case.

Example

Consider the following example. A youth is stopped in the street by a stranger who asks him to drop off an envelope at a nearby address in exchange for £1. As the youth approaches the address he is arrested for possessing a controlled drug (which had been inside the envelope), with intent to supply.

Section 28(2) would allow the youth to prove that he neither knew, nor suspected that the envelope contained a controlled drug, and that he neither knew nor suspected that he was supplying it to another. Both of these elements would be facts which the prosecution would have to allege in order to prove the offence.

The youth must also show that he had no reason to suspect these facts. If he knew the person to be a local drug dealer, or the reward for his errand was disproportionately large — say £100 — then he may not be able to satisfy this last requirement.

It has been held that the test for 'reason to suspect' is an *objective* one (*R v Young* [1984] 2 All ER 164). Consequently, where a 'reason to suspect' was not apparent to a defendant because he/she was too intoxicated to see it, the defence will not apply.

6.7.2 General Lack of Knowledge about Drug in Question

The wording of s. 28(3)(a) prevents defendants from claiming a 'defence' when what they thought was one type of controlled drug was in fact another, different controlled drug.

Section 28(3)(b) however, has two strands, one concerned with the defendant's general lack of knowledge about the drug in question and the other (see below) concerning the defendant's conditional belief.

Section 28(3)(b)(i) will allow a defendant to prove that he/she did not believe or suspect the substance in question to be a controlled drug and that he/she had no reason so to suspect.

This clearly overlaps with s. 28(2) and the youth in the above example would also be able to claim this lack of knowledge. If he believed the envelope to contain amphetamine when it turned out to contain heroin, however, this lack of knowledge would not be permitted as a defence under s. 28(3).

6.7.3 Conditional Belief about Drug in Question

In contrast to s. 28(3)(a), the second strand of s. 28(3)(b) allows a defendant to show that he/she *did* believe the drug in question to be a particular controlled drug. It is then open to them to prove that, had the drug in question actually been the drug which he/she believed it to be, then he/she would not have committed any of the offences in **para. 6.7** above.

Example

A registered heroin addict may have been prescribed methadone. If she collects her prescription from a chemist but is mistakenly given pethidine instead, she may be able to prove that she *believed* the drug in question to be methadone *and* that, if it had been, she would not have committed an offence by possessing it.

6.8 Offences Involving the Misuse of Controlled Drugs

Clearly there are occasions when the production, supply and possession of controlled drugs will be lawful and most of these occasions are addressed in either the Misuse of Drugs Regulations 1985 or in s. 28 of the Misuse of Drugs Act 1971 (**see para. 6.7**).

In the offences which follow, the aspects which generally make the behaviour 'unlawful' are either the lack of authority under the relevant regulations, or the absence of the circumstances outlined in the defences under s. 28.

6.8.1 Production

Offence — Producing Controlled Drug — Misuse of Drugs Act 1971, s. 4(2)
Triable either way. Class A (life imprisonment and/or fine on indictment;
six months' imprisonment and/or prescribed sum summarily); Class B (14 years'
imprisonment and/or fine on indictment; six months' imprisonment and/or prescribed
sum summarily); Class C (five years' imprisonment and/or fine on indictment;
three months' imprisonment and/or fine summarily).
(Serious arrestable offence)

The Misuse of Drugs Act 1971, s. 4 states:

(2) Subject to section 28 of this Act, it is an offence for a person—
    (a) to produce a controlled drug in contravention of subsection (1) . . .; or
    (b) to be concerned in the production of such a drug in contravention of that subsection by another.

Keynote

'Produce' means producing by manufacture, cultivation or any other method and 'production' has a corresponding meaning (Misuse of Drugs Act 1971, s. 37).

Converting one form of a Class A drug into another has been held to be 'producing' (*R* v *Russell* (1991) 94 Cr App R 351) as has harvesting, cutting and stripping a cannabis plant (*R* v *Harris* [1996] 1 Cr App R 69).

Section 4(2) is a drug trafficking offence for the purposes of the Drug Trafficking Act 1994 (**see para. 6.2**). It is also a serious arrestable offence under s. 116(2) of the Police and Criminal Evidence Act 1984 (**see General Police Duties, chapter 2**).

If committed in relation to specified Class A drugs (heroin, cocaine and 'crack' cocaine), this will be a 'trigger' offence under s. 63B of the Police and Criminal Evidence Act 1984 which can activate police powers to require a sample from a person in police detention in some force areas (**see Evidence and Procedure, chapter 15**).

6.8.2 Supply

Offence — Supplying Controlled Drug — Misuse of Drugs Act 1971, s. 4(3)
Triable either way. Class A (life imprisonment and/or fine on indictment;
six months' imprisonment and/or prescribed sum summarily); Class B (14 years'
imprisonment and/or fine on indictment; six months' imprisonment and/or prescribed
sum summarily); Class C (five years' imprisonment and/or fine on indictment;
three months' imprisonment and/or fine summarily).
(*Serious arrestable offence*)

The Misuse of Drugs Act 1971, s. 4 states:

(3) Subject to section 28 of this Act, it is an offence for a person—
    (a) to supply or offer to supply a controlled drug to another in contravention of subsection (1); or
    (b) to be concerned in the supplying of such a drug to another in contravention of that subsection; or
    (c) to be concerned in the making to another in contravention of that subsection of an offer to supply such a drug.

Keynote

The word supply 'connotes more than the mere transfer of physical control of [something] from one person to another' (per Lord Keith in *Holmes* v *Chief Constable of Merseyside* [1976] Crim LR 125). The offence of supplying requires a further element, namely that the person receiving the item (the controlled drug) is thereby enabled to apply it to his/her own purposes. Whether or not a person has 'supplied' a controlled drug to another is a question of fact.

'Supplying' includes distributing (s. 37(1)).

This offence most frequently occurs where one person hands over a controlled drug to another, in which case there is little argument about the meaning of supply.

Where a person leaves a controlled drug with another for safekeeping however, the situation is more problematic. It has been held that, where a person holds on to a controlled drug belonging to another for a short while and then hands it back, there is no 'supply' (although there may be unlawful possession) (*R* v *Dempsey* (1985) 82 Cr App R 291, see below). If the person looking after the drugs for another is in some way benefiting from that activity, then the return of those drugs to the depositor *will* amount to 'supplying', and the offences of supplying or possession with intent to supply will be applicable (*R* v *Maginnis* [1987] AC 303, see below). *Dempsey* involved a registered drug addict who was in lawful possession of a controlled drug and who asked his partner to hold on to some of that drug while he went to administer the remainder of it to himself in a gents' toilet. Both the addict and his partner were arrested, the addict being subsequently charged with 'supplying' his partner with the drug. The Court of Appeal held that, if the partner had simply been given the drug for safekeeping until the addict's return, there would be no 'supplying'. If however, she had been given the drug for her own use, then there clearly *would* be a 'supplying' of that drug and the offence under s. 4(3)(a) would be complete.

Other situations where the *initial* possession of the controlled drug is itself unlawful have also raised difficult questions. If a drug trafficker leaves drugs with a third person temporarily, what criminal liability is incurred by the third person when he/she returns the drugs to the trafficker? Will returning the drug to its owner under these circumstances, which are different from those in *Dempsey* (above) amount to 'supplying'? This situation was faced by the House of Lords in *R* v *Maginnis* [1987] AC 303. In that case their Lordships decided that Maginnis would have been 'supplying' the controlled drug had he returned it to the drug trafficker who had left a package of cannabis resin in Maginnis' car. Therefore he was in possession with intent to supply and so committed an offence under s. 5(3) (**see para. 6.8.4**). Once again however, the court expressed the view that if the person left with temporary possession of the controlled drug was not benefiting from so possessing it, there would be no 'supplying'. That being the case, it is at least arguable that the third person is *aiding and abetting* the trafficker to possess with intent to supply (as to which, **see chapter 2**).

This issue has been further complicated by a decision involving a person who claimed that he had been coerced into holding controlled drugs for unnamed dealers. When found in possession of the drugs, the defendant claimed the defence of duress (as to which, **see chapter 4**) and said that he had only been an 'involuntary custodian' of them, intending to return them at a later date. The Court of Appeal decided that it was irrelevant whether a person was a voluntary or involuntary custodian of the drugs and that an intention to return them to their depositor amounted to an 'intention to supply' (*R* v *Panton* [2001] All ER (D) 134).

If a police informer provides a controlled drug to another in order that the other be arrested, there will still be a 'supplying' of the drug (*R* v *X* [1994] Crim LR 827).

Injecting another with his/her own controlled drug has been held not to amount to 'supplying' in a case where the defendant assisted pushing down the plunger of a syringe that the other person was already using. Parker CJ's comments in that case suggest that simply injecting another person with their own drug would not amount to 'supplying' (*R* v *Harris* [1968] 1 WLR 769). It may, however, amount to an offence of 'poisoning' under s. 23 of the Offences Against the Person Act 1861 (**see chapter 9**). If a person supplies another with a drug and the other person then takes it and dies as a result, the supplier will not *generally* be responsible for causing that death (**see para. 5.4.1**). However, if the circumstances are such that, in supplying the drug, the defendant was assisting or encouraging the person to take it, he/she may be liable for a number of offences including manslaughter and poisoning (*R* v *Kennedy*, unreported, 31 July 1998). Section 4(3) is a drug trafficking offence for the purposes of the Drug Trafficking Act 1994 (**see para. 6.2**). It is also a serious arrestable offence under s. 116(2) of the Police and Criminal Evidence Act 1984 (**see General Police Duties, chapter 2**).

Dividing up controlled drugs which have been jointly purchased will amount to 'supplying' (*R* v *Buckley* (1979) 69 Cr App R 371).

The offence of offering to supply a controlled drug is complete when the offer is made. It is irrelevant whether or not the defendant actually has the means to meet the offer or even intends to carry it out (see *R* v *Goodard* [1992] Crim LR 588). If the offer is made by conduct alone (i.e. without any words), it may be difficult to prove this offence. If words are used, the defence under s. 28 (**see para. 6.7**) does not appear to apply (see *R* v *Mitchell* [1992] Crim LR 723). If the offer is made to an undercover police officer, the offence is still committed and the defendant cannot claim that such an offer was not a 'real' offer (*R* v *Kray*, unreported, 10 November 1998).

In each case it will be a question of fact for the magistrate(s)/jury to decide whether or not the conduct amounted to a supply or offer to supply.

In order to prove the offence of being concerned in the supply/offer to supply a controlled drug, you must show:

- the actual supply of, or making of an offer to supply, a controlled drug

- the participation of the defendant in that enterprise, and

- knowledge by the defendant that the enterprise involved the supply of, or making of an offer to supply, a controlled drug

(per the Court of Appeal in *R* v *Hughes* (1985) 81 Cr App R 344).

If the object of a conspiracy (**see chapter 3**) is to supply a controlled drug to a co-conspirator, any subsequent charge must make that clear; stating that the defendants conspired to supply the drug to 'another' implies that the supply was to be made to someone *other than any of the conspirators* (*R* v *Jackson*, *The Times*, 13 May 1999).

If committed in relation to specified Class A drugs (heroin, cocaine and 'crack' cocaine), this will be a 'trigger' offence under s. 63B of the Police and Criminal Evidence Act 1984 which can activate police powers to require a sample from a person in police detention in some force areas (**see Evidence and Procedure, chapter 15**).

6.8.3   Possession

Offence — Possession of Controlled Drug — Misuse of Drugs Act 1971, s. 5(2)
*Triable either way. Class A (seven years' imprisonment and/or fine on indictment; six months'
imprisonment and/or prescribed sum summarily); Class B (five years' imprisonment
and/or fine on indictment; three months' imprisonment and/or fine summarily).*
(Arrestable offence)
*Class C (two years' imprisonment and/or fine on indictment; three months' imprisonment
and/or fine summarily).*
(No specific power of arrest)

The Misuse of Drugs Act 1971, s. 5 states:

> (2)   Subject to section 28 of this Act and to subsection (4) below, it is an offence for a person to
> have a controlled drug in his possession in contravention of subsection (1) . . .

Keynote

See **para. 6.5** above for meaning of 'possession'.

If committed in relation to specified Class A drugs (heroin, cocaine and 'crack'
cocaine), this will be a 'trigger' offence under s. 63B of the Police and Criminal
Evidence Act 1984 which can activate police powers to require a sample from a person
in police detention in some force areas (**see Evidence and Procedure, chapter 15**).

6.8.4   Possession with Intent to Supply

Offence — Possession with Intent to Supply — Misuse of Drugs Act 1971, s. 5(3)
*Triable either way. Class A (life imprisonment and/or fine on indictment;
six months' imprisonment and/or prescribed sum summarily); Class B (14 years'
imprisonment and/or fine on indictment; six months' imprisonment and/or prescribed
sum summarily); Class C (five years' imprisonment and/or fine on indictment;
three months' imprisonment and/or fine summarily).*
(Serious arrestable offence)

The Misuse of Drugs Act 1971, s. 5 states:

> (3)   Subject to section 28 of this Act, it is an offence for a person to have a controlled drug in his
> possession, whether lawfully or not, with intent to supply it to another in contravention of section 4(1)
> of this Act.

Keynote

This is a crime of *specific* intent (**see chapter 1**).

It is important to note that the lawfulness or otherwise of the *possession* is irrelevant;
what matters here is the lawfulness of the intended supply. If a vet or a police officer
or some other person is in lawful possession of a controlled drug but they intend to
supply it unlawfully to another, this offence will be made out.

You must show that the intention was that the *possessor* supply the controlled drug, not
some third party in the future (*R v Greenfield* (1983) 78 Cr App R 179).

If more than one person has possession of the relevant controlled drug, you must show an individual intention to supply it by each person charged; it is not enough to show a joint venture whereby one or more parties simply knew of another's intent (*R* v *Downes* [1984] Crim LR 552). Given the decision of the Court of Appeal in *Kray* (**see para. 6.8.2**), possession with intent to supply a controlled drug to a person who is in fact an undercover police officer would appear to amount to an offence under this section.

All that is necessary in proving the offence under s. 5(3) is to show that the defendant had a controlled drug in his/her possession and intended to supply that substance to another. If the substance in the defendant's possession is a Class A drug and he/she intended to supply it to another person, the fact that he/she thought the drug was some other type of drug does not matter (*R* v *Leeson*, *The Times*, 2 November 1999).

In proving an intention to supply you may be able to adduce evidence of the defendant's unexplained wealth (*R* v *Smith* [1995] Crim LR 940) or the presence of large sums of money with the drugs seized (see *R* v *Wright* [1994] Crim LR 55).

For the meaning of 'supply', **see para. 6.8.2**.

Section 5(3) is a drug trafficking offence for the purposes of the Drug Trafficking Act 1994 (**see para. 6.2**). It is also a serious arrestable offence under s. 116(2) of the Police and Criminal and Evidence Act 1984 (**see General Police Duties, chapter 2**).

If committed in relation to specified Class A drugs (heroin, cocaine and 'crack' cocaine), this will be a 'trigger' offence under s. 63B of the Police and Criminal Evidence Act 1984 which can activate police powers to require a sample from a person in police detention in some force areas (**see Evidence and Procedure, chapter 15**).

6.8.5   **Cultivation of Cannabis**

Offence — Cultivation of Cannabis — Misuse of Drugs Act 1971, s. 6
Triable either way. Fourteen years' imprisonment and/or a fine on indictment;
six months' imprisonment and/or prescribed sum summarily.
(*Arrestable offence*)

The Misuse of Drugs Act 1971, s. 6 states:

(1)   *Subject to any regulations under section 7 of this Act for the time being in force, it shall not be lawful for a person to cultivate any plant of the genus Cannabis.*
(2)   *Subject to section 28 of this Act, it is an offence to cultivate any such plant in contravention of subsection (1) above.*

Keynote

'Cultivate' is not defined but it appears that you would have to show some element of attention (such as watering or feeding) to the plant by the defendant in order to prove this offence. This offence does not permit police officers to tend plants which have been seized as evidence in order to preserve them as exhibits for court!

In proving the offence, you need only show that the plant is of the genus *Cannabis* and that the defendant cultivated it; you need not show that the defendant knew it to be a cannabis plant (*R* v *Champ* (1982) 73 Cr App R 367).

6.8.6   **Supply of Articles**

Offence — Supplying Articles for Administering or Preparing Controlled Drugs — Misuse of Drugs Act 1971, s. 9A
Triable summarily. Six months' imprisonment and/or fine.
(No specific power of arrest)

The Misuse of Drugs Act 1971, s. 9A states:

> *(1)   A person who supplies or offers to supply any article which may be used or adapted to be used (whether by itself or in combination with another article or other articles) in the administration by any person of a controlled drug to himself or another, believing that the article (or the article as adapted) is to be so used in circumstances where the administration is unlawful, is guilty of an offence.*
> *(2)   . . .*
> *(3)   A person who supplies or offers to supply any article which may be used to prepare a controlled drug for administration by any person to himself or another believing that the article is to be so used in circumstances where the administration is unlawful is guilty of an offence.*

Keynote

This offence is designed to address the provision of drug 'kits'.

'Supply' for these purposes is likely to be interpreted in the same way as for the earlier sections in the 1971 Act.

Hypodermic syringes, or parts of them, are not covered by this offence (s. 9A(2)).

The administration for which the articles are intended must be 'unlawful'. Section 9A states:

> *(4)   For the purposes of this section, any administration of a controlled drug is unlawful except—*
> *(a)   the administration by any person of a controlled drug to another in circumstances where the administration of the drug is not unlawful under section 4(1) of this Act, or*
> *(b)   the administration by any person of a controlled drug to himself in circumstances where having the controlled drug in his possession is not unlawful under section 5(1) of this Act.*
> *(5)   In this section, references to administration by any person of a controlled drug to himself include a reference to his administering it to himself with the assistance of another.*

6.8.7   **Opium**

Offence — Opium Misuse — Misuse of Drugs Act 1971, s. 9
Triable either way. Fourteen years' imprisonment and/or a fine on indictment; six months' imprisonment and/or fine summarily.
(Arrestable offence)

The Misuse of Drugs Act 1971, s. 9 states:

> *Subject to section 28 of this Act, it is an offence for a person—*
> *(a)   to smoke or otherwise use prepared opium; or*
> *(b)   to frequent a place used for the purpose of opium smoking; or*
> *(c)   to have in his possession*
> *(i)   any pipes or other utensils made or adapted for use in connection with the smoking of opium, being pipes or utensils which have been used by him or with his knowledge and permission in that connection or which he intends to use or permit others to use in that connection; or*
> *(ii)   any utensils which have been used by him or with his knowledge and permission in connection with the preparation of opium for smoking.*

Keynote

These offences are relatively rare. Prepared opium includes dross and other residues (s. 37(1)).

The defence under s. 28 applies to these offences.

6.8.8 Occupiers etc.

Offence — Occupier or Manager of Premises Permitting Drug Misuse — Misuse of Drugs Act 1971, s. 8
Triable either way. Class A or B (14 years, imprisonment and/or fine on indictment; six months' imprisonment' and/or prescribed sum summarily); Class C (five years' imprisonment and/or a fine on indictment; three months' imprisonment and/or fine summarily)
(Arrestable offence)

The Misuse of Drugs Act 1971, s. 8 states:

> *A person commits an offence if, being the occupier or concerned in the management of any premises, he knowingly permits or suffers any of the following activities to take place on those premises, that is to say—*
>
> *(a)   producing or attempting to produce a controlled drug in contravention of section 4(1) of this Act;*
> *(b)   supplying or attempting to supply a controlled drug to another in contravention of section 4(1) of this Act, or offering to supply a controlled drug to another in contravention of section 4(1);*
> *(c)   preparing opium for smoking;*
> *(d)   smoking cannabis, cannabis resin or prepared opium.*

Keynote

The courts have adopted a 'common sense' approach to the interpretation of whether someone is an 'occupier' or not (see *R* v *Tao* [1977] QB 141). You will not need to prove that a defendant falls within some narrow legal meaning of an occupier. What is important in proving this offence is showing that the defendant had enough control over the premises to prevent the sort of activity listed above (see *R* v *Coid* [1998] Crim LR 199).

If a person cannot be shown to be an occupier in this sense, it may be that he/she can be shown to be involved in the planning, organising and actual use of the premises by taking part in more than just menial tasks. If so, this level of involvement may amount to 'management' of the premises (see *R* v *Josephs* (1977) 65 Cr App R 253).

'Premises' is not defined and has not been clarified at common law but the meaning has been given a wide definition elsewhere (such as in the Police and Criminal Evidence Act 1984; **see General Police Duties, chapter 2**).

The permitting or suffering of these activities requires a degree of *mens rea* (**see chapter 1**) — *Sweet* v *Parsley* [1970] AC 132 — even if that degree is little more than wilful blindness (see *R* v *Thomas* (1976) 63 Cr App R 65). For the purposes of s. 8(b) — and therefore presumably s. 8(a) — it is not necessary to show that the defendant knew exactly which drugs were being produced, supplied etc.; only that they were 'controlled drugs' (*R* v *Bett* [1999] 1 All ER 600).

The Criminal Justice and Police Act 2001 makes provision to extend this offence. At the time of writing, that Part of the 2001 Act had not been brought into force.

An occupier who permits the growing of cannabis plants also commits this offence (*Taylor* v *Chief Constable of Kent* [1981] 1 WLR 606).

6.8.9 Importation of Controlled Drugs

It is an offence under the Misuse of Drugs Act 1971, s. 3 to import or export a controlled drug unless authorised by the regulations made under the Act. The relevant offences and their respective penalties are contained in the Customs and Excise Management Act 1979. Schedule 1 to the 1979 Act provides for the following penalties for the improper importation or exportation of controlled drugs:

- **Class A** — life imprisonment
- **Class B** — 14 years' imprisonment
- **Class C** — five years' imprisonment.

All are **serious arrestable offences** (**see General Police Duties, chapter 2**).

6.8.10 Assisting or Inducing Offence Outside United Kingdom

**Offence — Assisting or Inducing Misuse of Drugs Offence Outside UK —
Misuse of Drugs Act 1971, s. 20**
*Triable either way. Fourteen years' imprisonment and/or a fine on indictment;
six months' imprisonment and/or fine summarily.*
(Arrestable offence)

The Misuse of Drugs Act 1971, s. 20 states:

A person commits an offence if in the United Kingdom he assists in or induces the commission in any place outside the United Kingdom of an offence punishable under the provisions of a corresponding law in force in that place.

Keynote

In order to prove this offence, you must show that the offence outside the United Kingdom actually took place. The circumstances where this offence is likely to be committed will clearly overlap with the offences of importation/exportation (**see para. 6.8.9**).

'Assisting' has been held to include taking containers to another country in the knowledge that they would later be filled with a controlled drug and sent on to a third country (*R* v *Evans* (1977) 64 Cr App R 237).

For an offence to amount to one under 'corresponding law' for these purposes, a certificate relating to the domestic law concerned with the misuse of drugs must be obtained from the government of the relevant country (s. 36).

Section 20 is a drug trafficking offence for the purposes of the Drug Trafficking Act 1994 (**see para. 6.2**).

6.8.11   Incitement

Offence — Incitement — Misuse of Drugs Act 1971, s. 19
Triable and punishable as for substantive offence incited.
(*Arrestable offence if offence incited is arrestable*)

The Misuse of Drugs Act 1971, s. 19 states:

It is an offence for a person to incite . . . another to commit [an offence under this Act].

Keynote

Although the offence of incitement exists for most other offences generally (**see chapter 3**), the Act makes a specific offence of inciting another to commit an offence under its provisions. On the arguments in *DPP* v *Armstrong* [2000] Crim LR 379 (**see chapter 3**), it would seem that a person inciting an undercover police officer may commit an offence under s. 19 even though there was no possibility of the officer actually being induced to commit the offence.

Section 19 is a drug trafficking offence for the purposes of the Drug Trafficking Act 1994 (**see para. 6.2**).

6.9   Enforcement

6.9.1   Powers of Entry, Search and Seizure

The Misuse of Drugs Act 1971, s. 23 states:

(1)   A constable or other person authorised in that behalf by a general or special order of the Secretary of State (or in Northern Ireland either of the Secretary of State or the Ministry of Home Affairs for Northern Ireland) shall, for the purposes of the execution of this Act, have power to enter the premises of a person carrrying on business as a producer or supplier of any controlled drugs and to demand the production of, and to inspect, any books or documents relating to dealings in any such drugs and to inspect any stocks of any such drugs.

(2)   If a constable has reasonable grounds to suspect that any person is in possession of a controlled drug in contravention of this Act or of any regulations made thereunder, the constable may—

(a)   search that person, and detain him for the purpose of searching him;

(b)   search any vehicle or vessel in which the constable suspects that the drug may be found, and for that purpose require the person in control of the vehicle or vessel to stop it;

(c)   seize and detain, for the purposes of proceedings under this Act, anything found in the course of the search which appears to the constable to be evidence of an offence under this Act.

In this subsection 'vessel' includes a hovercraft within the meaning of the Hovercraft Act 1968; and nothing in this subsection shall prejudice any power of search or any power to seize or detain property which exercisable by a constable apart from this subsection.

(3)   If a justice of the peace (or in Scotland a justice of the peace, a magistrate or a sheriff) is satisfied by information on oath that there is reasonable ground for suspecting—

(a)   that any controlled drugs are, in contravention of this Act or of any regulations made thereunder, in the possession of a person on any premises; or

(b)   that a document directly or indirectly relating to, or connected with, a transaction or dealing which was, or an intended transaction or dealing which would if carried out be, an offence under this Act, or in the case of a transaction or dealing carried out or intended to be carried out in a place outside the United Kingdom, an offence against the provisions of a corresponding law in force in that place, is in the possession of a person on any premises,

he may grant a warrant authorising any constable acting for the police area in which the premises are situated at any time or times within one month from the date of the warrant, to enter, if need be by force, the premises named in the warrant, and to search the premises and any persons found therein and, if there is reasonable ground for suspecting that an offence under this Act has been committed in relation to any controlled drugs found on the premises or in the possession of any such persons, or that a document so found is such a document as is mentioned in paragraph (b) above, to seize and detain those drugs or that document, as the case may be.

Keynote

For the procedure involved in applying for, and executing warrants, **see General Police Duties, chapter 2**.

6.9.2 Obstruction

Offence — Obstruction — Misuse of Drugs Act 1971, s. 23(4)
Triable either way. Two years' imprisonment and/or a fine on indictment; six months' imprisonment and/or fine summarily.
(**No specific power of arrest**)

The Misuse of Drugs Act 1971, s. 23 states:

> *(4)   A person commits an offence if he—*
> *(a)   intentionally obstructs a person in the exercise of his powers under this section; or*
> *(b)   conceals from a person acting in the exercise of his powers under subsection (1) above any such books, documents, stocks or drugs as are mentioned in that subsection; or*
> *(c)   without reasonable excuse (proof of which shall lie on him) fails to produce any such books or documents as are so mentioned where their production is demanded by a person in the exercise of his powers under that subsection.*

Keynote

The offence of obstructing a person in the exercise of his/her powers is only committed if the obstruction was intentional (*R* v *Forde* (1985) 81 Cr App R 19). For the offence of obstructing a police officer generally, **see chapter 8**.

6.10 Intoxicating Substances

Offence — Supply of Intoxicating Substance —
Intoxicating Substances (Supply) Act 1985, s. 1
Triable summarily. Six months' imprisonment and/or a fine.
(**No specific power of arrest**)

The Intoxicating Substances (Supply) Act 1985, s. 1 states:

> *(1)   It is an offence for a person to supply or offer to supply a substance other than a controlled drug—*
> *(a)   to a person under the age of 18 whom he knows, or has reasonable cause to believe, to be under that age; or*
> *(b)   to a person—*
> *(i)   who is acting on behalf of a person under that age; and*
> *(ii)   whom he knows, or has reasonable cause to believe, to be so acting, if he knows or has reasonable cause to believe that the substance is, or its fumes are, likely to be inhaled by the person under the age of 18 for the purpose of causing intoxication.*

Keynote

This offence is aimed at curbing 'glue sniffing'. Retailers who sell solvents to people apparently under 18, or to people apparently acting on the behalf of someone under 18, would commit this offence.

The requirement as to the personal knowledge of the age and intentions of the person supplied makes this a difficult offence to prove.

It is a defence for a person charged with this offence to show that at the time he/she made the supply or offer he/she was both:

- under the age of eighteen; and
- acting otherwise than in the course or furtherance of a business

(s. 1(2)).

For the law relating to the supply of alcohol to people under 18, **see General Police Duties, chapter 10**.

Offence — Supply of Butane Lighter Refill to Person under 18 — Cigarette Lighter Refill (Safety) Regulations 1999 (SI 1999 No. 1844), reg. 2
Triable summarily. Six months' imprisonment and/or a fine.
(No *specific power of arrest*)

The Cigarette Lighter Refill (Safety) Regulations 1999, reg. 2 states:

No person shall supply any cigarette lighter refill canister containing butane or a substance with butane as a constituent part to any person under the age of eighteen years old.

Keynote

For this offence there is no requirement that the person believed or even suspected the person to be under 18. The 1999 Regulations are made under the Consumer Protection Act 1987, s. 12.

For the meaning of 'supply', **see para. 6.8.2**.

CHAPTER SEVEN

OFFENCES ARISING OUT OF PREGNANCY AND CHILDBIRTH

7.1 Introduction

This chapter addresses the law relating to pregnancy and childbirth, an extremely emotive subject crossing all manner of religious, professional and ethical boundaries. Indeed, there are few more contentious areas of criminal law than those relating to abortion. What is produced here is a statement of the existing law; the ethics of its application — or misapplication — are another matter.

The provisions of Article 2 of the European Convention on Human Rights may be of relevance in cases falling under the law in this chapter. In one reported case the Commission was petitioned by a husband trying to use Article 2 to prevent his estranged wife from having an abortion (*Paton* v *United Kingdom* (1980) 19 DR 244). Although the Commission decided that the Article only extended the right to life to people once they had actually been born, this decision is one that may need to be reconsidered, both in light of the changing standards of society and also against the rapid advances that have been made in medicine and genetics. For a full discussion of the Convention and its impact following the Human Rights Act 1998, **see General Police Duties**.

7.2 Infanticide

Offence — Infanticide — Infanticide Act 1938, s. 1
Triable on indictment. Life imprisonment.
(*Arrestable offence*)

The Infanticide Act 1938, s. 1 states:

> *(1) Where a woman by any wilful act or omission causes the death of her child being a child under the age of 12 months, but at the time of the act or omission the balance of her mind was disturbed by reason of her not having fully recovered from the effect of giving birth to the child or by reason of the effect of lactation consequent upon the birth of the child, then, notwithstanding that the circumstances were such that but for this Act the offence would have amounted to murder, she shall be guilty of [an offence], to wit of infanticide, and may for such offence be dealt with and punished as if she had been guilty of the offence of manslaughter of the child.*

Keynote

This offence is designed for very unusual and extreme circumstances. It can only be committed by a mother. It is similar to 'diminished responsibility' (**see chapter 5**) and it can be found proven as an alternative verdict to a charge of murder (s. 1(2)).

The meaning of 'wilful' is explained in **chapter 1**.

7.3 Concealing Birth

Offence — Concealing Birth — Offences Against the Person Act 1861, s. 60
Triable either way. Two years' imprisonment.
(**No specific power of arrest**)

The Offences Against the Person Act 1861, s. 60 states:

If any woman shall be delivered of a child, every person who shall, by any secret disposition of the dead body of the said child, whether such child died before, at, or after its birth, endeavour to conceal the birth thereof, shall be guilty of [an offence], and being convicted thereof shall be liable . . . to be imprisoned . . .

Keynote

There is no specific stage of gestation or 'age' of a foetus at which point it will become a 'child' for the purpose of this offence. It has been held that the 'child' must have reached that stage of maturity which would mean '*that it might have been a living child*' (*R v Berriman* (1854) 6 Cox CC 388).

The *actus reus* is the secret disposition, that is hiding the body of the child and the intention is that the birth itself be concealed. There are also common law offences of disposing of a body to prevent an inquest and preventing the burial of a body (see *Blackstone's Criminal Practice*, 2001, section B1.79).

7.4 Abortion

Offence — Abortion — Offences Against the Person Act 1861, s. 58
Triable on indictment. Life imprisonment.
(**Arrestable offence**)

Every woman, being with child, who, with intent to procure her own miscarriage, shall unlawfully administer to herself any poison or other noxious thing, or shall unlawfully use any instrument or other means whatsoever with the like intent, and whosoever, with intent to procure the miscarriage of any woman, whether she be or be not with child, shall unlawfully administer to her or cause to be taken by her any poison or noxious thing or shall unlawfully use any instrument or other means whatsoever with the like intent, shall be guilty of [an offence] . . .

Keynote

This offence can be committed by the woman herself or a third party. The wording makes a distinction between occasions where the woman herself can commit the offence — when she is actually pregnant — and when third parties may commit the offence — whether she is 'with child' or not.

However, if a woman who only believed herself to be pregnant tried to bring about her own miscarriage, she might be guilty of a criminal attempt (**see chapter 3**) and, if acting with another, she might be guilty of aiding and abetting that other (**see chapter 2** and *R* v *Sockett* (1908) 1 Cr App R 101).

7.4.1   'Legal' Abortion

The Abortion Act 1967, ss. 1 and 5 states:

1.—(1)   Subject to the provisions of this section, a person shall not be guilty of an offence under the law relating to abortion when a pregnancy is terminated by a registered medical practitioner if two registered medical practitioners are of the opinion, formed in good faith—

(a)   that the pregnancy has not exceeded its twenty-fourth week and that the continuance of the pregnancy would involve risk, greater than if the pregnancy were terminated, of injury to the physical or mental health of the pregnant woman or any existing children of her family; or

(b)   that the termination is necessary to prevent grave permanent injury to the physical or mental health of the pregnant woman; or

(c)   that the continuance of the pregnancy would involve risk to the life of the pregnant woman, greater than if the pregnancy were terminated; or

(d)   that there is a substantial risk that if the child were born it would suffer from such physical or mental abnormalities as to be seriously handicapped.

(2)   In determining whether the continuance of a pregnancy would involve such risk of injury to health as is mentioned in paragraph (a) or (b) of subsection (1) of this section, account may be taken of the pregnant woman's actual or reasonably foreseeable environment.

(3)   Except as provided by subsection (4) of this section, any treatment for the termination of pregnancy must be carried out in a hospital vested in the Minister of Health or the Secretary of State under the National Health Service Acts, or in a place for the time being approved for the purposes of this section by the said Minister or the Secretary of State.

(3A)   The power under subsection (3) of this section to approve a place includes power, in relation to treatment consisting primarily in the use of such medicines as may be specified in the approval and carried out in such manner as may be so specified, to approve a class of places.

(4)   Subsection (3) of this section, and so much of subsection (1) as relates to the opinion of two registered medical practitioners, shall not apply to the termination of a pregnancy by a registered medical practitioner in a case where he is of the opinion, formed in good faith, that the termination is immediately necessary to save the life or to prevent grave permanent injury to the physical or mental health of the pregnant woman.

5.—(1)   . . .

(2)   For the purposes of the law relating to abortion, anything done with intent to procure a woman's miscarriage . . . is unlawfully done unless authorised by section 1 of this Act and, in the case of a woman carrying more than one foetus, anything done with intent to procure her miscarriage of any foetus is authorised by that section if—

(a)   the ground for termination of a pregnancy specified in subsection (1) (d) of that section applies in relation to any foetus and the thing is done for the purpose of procuring the miscarriage of the foetus, or

(b)   any of the other grounds for termination of the pregnancy specified in that section applies.

Keynote

Section 1 applies to unsuccessful attempts to terminate a pregnancy (*Royal College of Nursing* v *DHSS* [1981] AC 800). The key element in this section is that two registered medical practitioners are of the relevant opinion(s) and that the opinion is formed in good faith. This effectively means the decision to approve an abortion is one of medical ethics. Note also that, where a medical practitioner is of the opinion, similarly held in good faith, that an abortion is immediately necessary to save the life of the woman or to prevent grave permanent injury to her physical or mental health, the need for two medical practitioners is removed (s. 1(4)).

A pregnant woman may refuse medical treatment for herself even if that refusal jeopardises the life of her child (*St George's NHS Trust* v *S*, *The Times*, 8 May 1998).

7.4.2 **Supplying or Procuring Means for Abortion**

Offence — Supplying or Procuring Means for Abortion —
Offences Against the Person Act 1861, s. 59
Triable on indictment. Five years' imprisonment.
(***Arrestable offence***)

The Offences Against the Person Act 1861, s. 59 states:

Whoever shall unlawfully supply or procure any poison or other noxious thing, or any instrument or thing whatsoever, knowing that the same is intended to be unlawfully used or employed with intent to procure the miscarriage of any woman, whether she be or be not with child, shall be guilty of [an offence] . . .

Keynote

This offence requires the actual supplying or procuring, of instruments, poisons, drugs etc. Simple possession would not be enough. The defence under the Abortion Act 1967, s. 1 (**see para. 7.4.1**) applies to this offence. Again, it is not necessary that the woman is actually pregnant, simply that the articles are intended to be used in the proscribed way. On a literal interpretation, the use of a 'morning after' pill could amount to this offence if 'implantation' of a fertilised egg had occurred (see *Association of Lawyers for the Defence of the Unborn Newsletter*, Spring 1998).

7.5 Child Destruction

Offence — Child Destruction — Infant Life (Preservation) Act 1929, s. 1
Triable on indictment. Life imprisonment.
(***Arrestable offence***)

The Infant Life (Preservation) Act 1929, s. 1 states:

(1)   Subject as hereinafter in this subsection provided, any person who, with intent to destroy the life of a child capable of being born alive, by any wilful act causes a child to die before it has an existence independent of its mother, shall be guilty of [an offence] . . .
Provided that no person shall be found guilty of an offence under this section unless it is proved that the act which caused the death of the child was not done in good faith for the purpose only of preserving the life of the mother.
(2)   For the purposes of this Act, evidence that a woman had at any material time been pregnant for a period of 28 weeks or more shall be prima facie proof that she was at that time pregnant of a child capable of being born alive.

Keynote

This offence supplements the offence of abortion (**see para. 7.4**) which is an alternative verdict on a charge of child destruction. Child destruction would cover an occasion where a child is killed *during birth* (i.e. where there has been no attempt to bring about a miscarriage). As well as the statutory presumption at s. 1(2), it can be shown that a child was *in fact* 'capable of being born alive' (see *Rance v Mid-Downs Health Authority* [1991] 1 QB 587). This offence cannot be committed by an omission and requires a 'wilful' (that is, a *voluntary*) act. The slightly awkward wording of the proviso in s. 1(1) means that the prosecution must show that the relevant act was *not* done in good faith to preserve the life of the mother; the absence of binding case law on this point illustrates the practical difficulties of doing so.

A further defence is provided for medical practitioners by the Abortion Act 1967, s. 5(1) which states:

(1)   No offence under the Infant Life (Preservation) Act 1929 shall be committed by a registered medical practitioner who terminates a pregnancy in accordance with the provisions of this Act.

CHAPTER EIGHT

OFFENCES AGAINST THE PERSON

8.1 Introduction

Non-fatal offences against others cover a wide range of behaviour from a raised fist to a calculated wounding. The importance of this subject lies not only in the number of occasions when officers will need to refer to it, but also because it deals with violence and the fear of violent crime — areas in which victims are particularly traumatised. As courts are being urged to focus on the effects of a defendant's conduct upon their victim, the scope for bringing a charge of assault is widening. In addition, there are now clear guidelines for the charging of offences against the person, **see appendix 2**.

As with the offences discussed in **chapter 5**, the statutory duty imposed on chief officers of police (and the local probation board) to establish appropriate 'arrangements' for assessing and managing the risks posed by certain violent offenders may be relevant when considering some of the offences in this chapter and **chapter 9**.

8.2 Key Issues

8.2.1 Assault and Battery

Assault and battery are, strictly speaking, two separate things. What people generally think of as being an 'assault' (e.g. a punch on the nose) is a 'battery', that is, the infliction of unlawful force on someone else. While it would cover a punch on the nose, an 'assault' in its proper legal sense has a much wider meaning and includes any act whereby the defendant 'intentionally — or possibly recklessly — causes another person to apprehend immediate and unlawful personal violence' (*Fagan* v *Metropolitan Police Commissioner* [1969] 1 QB 439).

8.2.2 Assault or Battery?

Although these terms — assault and battery — have distinct legal meanings they are often referred to as simply 'assaults' or 'common assault'. It is, however, important to separate the two expressions when charging or laying an information against a defendant as to include both may be bad for duplicity (*DPP* v *Taylor* [1992] QB 645).

The term battery, or the application of 'force', creates a misleading impression as a very small degree of physical contact will be enough. That force can be applied directly or indirectly. For example, where a defendant punched a woman causing her to drop and injure a child she was holding, he was convicted of assaulting that child (*Haystead v Chief Constable of Derbyshire* [2000] 3 All ER 890. The *actus reus* needed to prove an assault is an act which caused the victim to apprehend the immediate infliction of unlawful force. The force or violence apprehended by the victim does not have to be a 'certainty'. Causing a fear of some possible violence can be enough (see *R v Ireland* [1998] AC 147) provided that the violence feared is about to happen in the immediate future (see *R v Constanza* [1997] 2 Cr App R 492).

Both battery and assault are offences under the Criminal Justice Act 1988 (**see para. 8.3**).

While some offences can be committed by an act or an *omission* (e.g. manslaughter (**see chapter 5**)) for a charge of assault to succeed there must be an *act* (*Fagan*).

It also is important to remember that the state of mind of the *victim* in an assault is relevant to the *actus reus*. The victim must apprehend the immediate use of unlawful force. For these reasons, if a defendant threatened someone with an imitation pistol, he/she could still be charged with assault provided the victim *believed* that the pistol was real — the defendant had caused an apprehension of possible immediate force being used (*Logdon v Director of Public Prosecutions* [1976] Crim LR 121). There would also be an offence under the Firearms Act 1968, **see General Police Duties, chapter 5**.

Words can amount to an assault provided they are accompanied by the required *mens rea*. This was made clear by the decision in *R v Ireland* [1998] AC 147 where it was held that telephone calls to a victim, followed by silences, could amount to an assault. In *Ireland*, the House of Lords accepted that '*a thing said is also a thing done*' and rejected the view that words can never amount to an assault. *Ireland* involved the making of threatening telephone calls which led the victims to fear that unlawful force would be used against them. The House of Lords accepted that, in such cases, even *silence* could fulfil the requirements for the *actus reus* of assault if it brought about the desired consequences (e.g. fear of the immediate use of unlawful force).

Where the words threatening immediate unlawful force come in the form of letters, the Court of Appeal has held that an assault may have been committed (see *Constanza* above).

As well as constituting an assault, words can also *negate* an assault if they make a conditional threat, e.g., where you attend an incident and one person says to another '*If these officers weren't here I'd chin you!*'.

Although the force threatened must be immediate, that immediacy is — like most legal interpretation — somewhat elastic. Courts have accepted that, where a person makes a threat from outside a victim's house to the victim who is inside, an assault is still committed even though there will be some time lapse before the defendant can carry out the threat.

In *Ireland* the House of Lords suggested that a threat to cause violence 'in a minute or two' might be enough to qualify as an assault. The victim must be shown to have feared the use of *force*; it will not be enough to show that a person threatened by words — or silence — feared more calls or letters. The fear of force is the key to assault.

8.2.3 Intentionally or Recklessly

The *mens rea* needed to prove common assault is either:

- an intention to cause apprehension of immediate unlawful violence, or
- subjective recklessness as to that consequence (**see chapter 1**).

When considering the *mens rea of* any assault, it is important to separate the assault or battery (**see para. 8.2.2**) from *any further consequences caused by* that assault or battery. The *mens rea* needed for the assault/battery is set out above. If a defendant's behaviour causes another to fear immediate and unlawful personal violence, he/she commits an 'assault' provided it can be shown that, at the time, the defendant *intended* to cause that fear or was *subjectively reckless* as to whether such a fear would result from his/her actions.

So what happens where the defendant's actions cause more than just fear; they cause more serious injury? Unfortunately that appears to depend on the extent of the injury and the wording of the offence charged. Among the more serious offences under the Offences Against the Person Act 1861 (**see para. 8.4**) are causing 'actual bodily harm' (s. 47) and 'wounding' or inflicting/causing 'grievous bodily harm' (ss. 18 and 20). The *mens rea* required for an offence under s. 47, causing actual bodily harm, is the same as that required for the basic offence of assault (*R* v *Savage* [1992] 1 AC 699). This is because s. 47 makes no specific requirement for any greater degree of *mens rea* by the defendant and, in effect, the offence of causing actual bodily harm becomes simply an assault or battery with a more serious outcome. From the defendant's point of view this is really pot luck because there is no requirement for him/her to have intended or even foreseen the actual bodily harm. In the case of woundings and grievous bodily harm, the situation is different because ss. 18 and 20 use the word 'maliciously' (**see para. 8.4.2**). This element introduces the element of intention or subjective recklessness *in relation to the injuries suffered by the victim* (*Savage* above), thereby adding a further requirement to the *mens rea*.

Example

Take the example of two people in a pub. They are arguing. One person, the defendant, threatens to throw a pint of beer over the other, the victim. At this point the defendant has caused the victim to fear that immediate unlawful personal violence will be used against him — an 'assault'. In order to prove an offence of assault under the Criminal Justice Act 1988, you must show that, at the time of the threat, the defendant either intended to cause the fear of violence or was subjectively reckless in that regard. If such an intention or recklessness cannot be shown, there is no offence of assault.

After the threat, a third person pushes past the defendant, accidentally knocking him into the victim and spilling the beer over him. At this point there has been no 'assault' by the defendant because there has been no *actus reus* by him, irrespective of his intentions.

The defendant continues to argue and then raises his glass and throws the contents over the victim. Clearly there has now been a voluntary application of unlawful force — a 'battery' — which the defendant intended to apply and he commits an offence under the Criminal Justice Act 1988. In the act of throwing the beer, however, the defendant's hand slips and he in fact hits the victim in the face with his beer glass causing a broken tooth. At this point the defendant's actions have gone beyond those intended by him and his victim has suffered injuries which the defendant had neither intended nor considered. Nevertheless, at the time of the assault (and battery) the defendant had the required *mens rea* for the assault/battery and therefore is liable for any actual bodily harm suffered by the victim as a result. Therefore the defendant commits the offence of assault occasioning actual bodily harm under s. 47 of the Offences Against the Person Act 1861, even though he neither intended nor considered the injuries to his victim.

Having a small amount of beer left in the glass, the defendant flicks the 'dregs' from the glass at the victim. The defendant loses his grip on the glass and it flies from his hand, hitting the victim in the eye and breaking on impact. The victim suffers a deep wound to the eye. Although the defendant is still liable for any actual bodily harm, he can only be liable for the more serious offences of wounding and causing/inflicting *grievous* bodily harm if it can be shown that he acted 'maliciously'. Malice for these purposes means that he must have intended to cause the harm or realised that there was a risk of at least some harm being suffered by the victim. If he did realise that the victim was at risk of being harmed by his actions, the defendant may be liable for an offence under s. 20 of the Offences Against the Person Act 1861 (**see para. 8.4.2**). If it can be shown that he intended to bring about *serious* harm, the defendant may be liable for the offence under s. 18 of the 1861 Act (**see para. 8.4.3**).

Given the requirements for *mens rea*, together with the respective penalties, it is not surprising that charges of 'actual bodily harm' might be preferred over charges of malicious wounding or inflicting grievous bodily harm.

8.2.4 Consent

A key element in proving an assault is the *unlawfulness* of the force used or threatened. Therefore, you might argue, if a person consents to the use of force, it cannot be unlawful and no assault or battery is committed. If only life were so simple! Although the courts have accepted consent as a feature which negatives any offence, they have been reluctant to accept this feature in a number of notable cases. These cases have developed as a question of public policy and were summarised in the House of Lords in the so-called 'spanner trial' (*R* v *Brown* [1994] 1 AC 212).

That case involved members of a sado-masochist group who inflicted varying degrees of injuries on one another for their own gratification. Charged with many offences against the person, the group claimed that they had consented to the injuries and therefore no assault or battery had taken place. Their Lordships followed an earlier policy that *all assaults which result in more than transient harm will be unlawful unless there is good reason for allowing the plea of 'consent'*. Good reason will be determined in the light of a number of considerations:

* the practical consequences of the behaviour
* the dangerousness of the behaviour
* the vulnerability of the 'consenting' person.

Further difficulties in clarifying what will amount to 'true' or effective consent were added by the decision of the Court of Appeal in *R* v *Wilson* [1996] 2 Cr App R 241. In that case the court accepted that a husband might lawfully brand his initials on his wife's buttocks with a hot knife provided she consented (as she appeared to have done). The reasoning behind the judgment seems to be based on the fact that the branding was similar to a form of tattooing (see below), but also on the policy grounds that consensual activity between husband and wife is not a matter for criminal investigation. This causes several problems, not least of which is the fact that sado-masochistic 'branding' was denounced by the House of Lords in *Brown* above. Therefore, if a situation arose where a husband and wife took part in mutual branding in the privacy of their home, their criminal liability would arguably depend on whether they caused the harm for purposes of sado-masochistic pleasure or out of some affectionate wish to be permanently adorned with the mark of their loved one. It is also unclear how far the policy aspect of the decision in *Wilson* would extend and whether or not it would encompass unmarried or homosexual couples.

Sado-masochistic injury may justifiably be made the subject of criminal law on grounds of the 'protection of health'. It was for this reason that the European Court of Human Rights held that there had been no violation of the defendants' right to private life (under Article 8) in the *Brown* case above. Although the defendants asserted that the interference by the criminal law in their consensual sexual practices amounted to an unnecessary restriction of their individual rights under Article 8, the Court held that this was a justifiable intrusion on the grounds set out above (*Laskey* v *United Kingdom* (1997) 24 EHRR 39).

Clearly there are times when a person may consent to even serious harm such as during properly-conducted sporting events (see *Attorney-General's Reference (No. 6 of 1980)* [1981] QB 715), tattooing and medical operations. Where the activity falls outside those parameters, such as an off-the-ball incident in a football match (*R* v *Lloyd* (1989) 11 Cr App R (S) 36) or an unauthorised prize fight, the plea of consent will not apply.

Other more straightforward policy considerations would include the implied consent by people getting on to crowded tube trains or moving around at a packed concert venue. In these cases it will be a matter of fact to decide whether the behaviour complained of went beyond what was acceptable in those particular circumstances.

Where a dentist who had been suspended by the General Dental Council continued to operate on patients, her failure to inform those patients of her suspension did not affect their true 'consent' and the dentist's actions were not an 'assault' (*R* v *Richardson* [1998] 2 Cr App R 200). The situation would be very different if the dentist had no formal qualifications at all, or if her actions went beyond the proper professional activities of a dentist (e.g. an indecent touching of patients).

8.2.5　Lawful Chastisement

There is an increasingly narrow head under which force might lawfully be applied to children. Those acting in *loco parentis* of a child appear to be able to use reasonable force in controlling the behaviour of that child (see *Blackstone's Criminal Practice*, 2001, section B2.10). What is 'reasonable' is likely to vary widely and would be difficult to define given the breadth and depth of social attitudes and conventions within England and Wales.

In a case involving an allegation of assault by a stepfather on his stepson, the European Court of Human Rights held that the United Kingdom was in breach of its obligation to protect individuals from inhuman or degrading punishment (under Article 3 of the European Convention on Human Rights) because the law in this area was not clear enough (*A* v *United Kingdom* (1999) 27 EHRR 611). The issues of reasonable chastisement and its compatibility with the Convention was examined recently by the Court of Appeal in *R* v *H*, *The Times*, 25 April 2001. Among other things, the Court held that the defence should be considered in the light of the nature and context of the defendant's behaviour, its duration, its physical and mental effects on the child, the age and personal characteristics of the child, and the reasons for the punishment. Additionally, Protocol 1, Article 2 (the right to education) of the Convention requires a State to have regard to the religious and philosophical convictions of parents in its schools. This requirement was at the centre of a successful challenge against corporal punishment in a State school (*Campbell* v *United Kingdom* (1982) 4 EHRR 293). The School Standards and Framework Act 1998 now outlaws corporal punishment in all British schools, although staff may use reasonable force in restraining violent or disruptive pupils (Education Act 1996, s. 550A). For further guidance on the Convention, **see General Police Duties**.

8.3 Offences

8.3.1 Common Assault and Battery

Offence — Common Assault/Battery — Criminal Justice Act 1988, s. 39
Triable summarily. Six months' imprisonment.
Offence — Racially Aggravated — Crime and Disorder Act 1998, s. 29(1)(c)
Triable either way. Two years' imprisonment and/or a fine on indictment;
six months' imprisonment and/or a fine summarily.
(***No specific power of arrest***)

See paras 8.2.1 and 8.2.2 above.

Keynote

Under certain circumstances the magistrates must issue a certificate of dismissal following the bringing of a charge of common assault (Offences Against the Person Act 1861, ss. 44 and 45). In order for a certificate of dismissal to be issued it must be shown that the party aggrieved (the victim) brought the charge or it was so preferred on the victim's behalf *and* the magistrates find:

• the offence not to have been proved or
• the assault to have been justified or
• the assault to be so trifling that it did not merit any punishment.

The certificate releases the defendant from all further proceedings, civil or criminal, *arising from the same cause*. Therefore, although such a certificate would absolve the defendant from further criminal or civil action in respect of the *actus reus* that amounted to the assault/battery), it would not protect him/her from further proceedings arising from some distinct but related matter (e.g. acts committed immediately before or after the assault/battery).

If the prosecution is not brought by or on behalf of the aggrieved party, the certificate will not be applicable.

Common assault was deemed by the legislators to be one of those offences where it was necessary to increase the maximum penalty available to the courts if it was committed under racially aggravated circumstances (see the Crime and Disorder Act 1998, s. 29(1)(c)). A further effect of the racially aggravated offence is that it can be tried on indictment without having to be included alongside another indictable offence as is the case with common assaults generally (see the Criminal Justice Act 1988, s. 40).

In a recent decision, the Divisional Court held that the words 'white man's arse licker' and 'brown Englishman' when used to accompany an assault on an Asian victim did not necessarily make the assault 'racially aggravated' and that the prosecution had not done enough to show that the assailants' behaviour fell under the definition set out in s. 28 of the 1998 Act (*DPP* v *Pal* [2000] Crim LR 756).

For a full explanation of the meaning of 'racially aggravated', **see General Police Duties, chapter 3**.

Under the racially aggravated public order offences the courts have held that police officers are entitled to the same protection under the legislation as anyone else (see *R* v *Jacobs, The Times*, 28 December 2000) and the same principle ought to apply to physical assault.

If an assault upon a police officer is 'racially aggravated' per the requirements of s. 28 of the Crime and Disorder Act 1998, it may be preferable to consider this offence rather than one of the offences under the Police Act 1996 (as to which, **see para. 8.3.3**).

It should be noted that there are potential problems with the availability of alternative verdicts in cases of racially aggravated assault and, in cases of doubt, the advice of the Crown Prosecution Service should be sought.

8.3.2   Assault with Intent to Resist Arrest

Offence — Assault with Intent to Resist Arrest — Offences Against the Person Act 1861, s. 38
Triable either way. Two years' imprisonment.
(No *specific power of arrest*)

The Offences Against the Person Act 1861, s. 38 states:

> *Whosoever . . . shall assault any person with intent to resist or prevent the lawful apprehension or detainer of himself or of any other person for any offence, shall be guilty of an offence . . .*

Keynote

This is a crime of *specific intent* (**see chapter 1**). It must be shown that the defendant intended to resist or prevent a lawful arrest. It must also be shown that the defendant knew the arrest was lawful. Provided they were acting within their powers, this offence can apply to arrests made, not only by police officers, but also by store detectives, Benefits Agency staff and custody assistants. There are other specific offences created for the protection of court security officers and prisoner custody officers (not police officers) under the Criminal Justice Act 1991, ss. 78 and 90. If the person assaulted was assisting a police officer in the execution of his/her duty, the offence below may also apply.

Once the lawfulness of the arrest is established, the state of mind necessary for the above offence is an intention to resist/prevent that arrest, accompanied by knowledge that the person assaulted was trying to make or help in the arrest. It is irrelevant whether or not the person being arrested had actually committed an offence. These principles were set out recently by the Court of Appeal in a case where the defendant mistakenly believed that the arresting officers had no lawful power to do so. The Court held that such a mistaken belief does not provide a defendant with the defence of 'mistake' (**see chapter** 4). Similarly, a belief in one's own innocence, however genuine or honestly held, cannot afford a defence to a charge under s. 38 (*R v Lee* [2000] Crim LR 991).

8.3.3   Assaults on Police

There is an offence which deals specifically with assaults on police officers.

Offence — Assault Police — Police Act 1996, s. 89
Triable summarily. Six months' imprisonment and/or a fine.
(No specific power of arrest)

The Police Act 1996, s. 89 states:

(1)   *Any person who assaults a constable in the execution of his duty, or a person assisting a constable in the execution of his duty, shall be guilty of an offence . . .*

Keynote

It is critical to this offence that the officer was acting in the execution of his/her duty when assaulted. Given the almost infinite variety of situations that police officers may find themselves in, it is difficult to define the precise boundaries of the execution of their duty. There have been many instances of officers being assaulted after entering premises as technical 'trespassers' or not following statutory or common law requirements when stopping and questioning people. If it is not proved that the constable was in the execution of his/her duty then part of the *actus reus* will be missing. However, a court may infer from all the circumstances that an officer was in fact acting in the execution of his/her duty (*Plowden v DPP* [1991] Crim LR 850).

Where the assault is made in reaction to some form of physical act by the officer, it must be shown that the officer's act was not in itself unlawful. Other than the powers of arrest and detention (**see General Police Duties, chapter** 2), police officers have no general power to take hold of people in order to question them or keep them at a particular place while background enquiries are made about them. Therefore, if an officer does hold someone by the arm in order to question them without arresting them, there may well be a 'battery' by that officer (*Collins v Wilcock* [1984] 1 WLR 1172). The courts have accepted, however, that there may be occasions where a police officer is justified in taking hold of a person to attract their attention or to calm them down (*Mepstead v DPP* (1996) 160 JP 475).

However, where a prisoner is arrested and brought before a custody officer, that officer is entitled to assume that the arrest has been lawful. Therefore, if the prisoner goes on to assault the custody officer, that assault will nevertheless be an offence under s. 89(1) about *even if the original arrest turns out to have been unlawful* (*DPP v L* [1999] Crim LR 752).

There is no need to show that the defendant knew — or suspected — that the person was in fact a police officer or that he/she was acting in the lawful execution of his/her duty (*Blackburn v Bowering* [1994] 1 WLR 1324). However, if the defendant claims to have been acting in self-defence under the mistaken and honestly held belief that he/she was being attacked, there may not be sufficient *mens rea* for a charge of assault (for defences of mistake generally, **see chapter** 4).

94

These offences are simply a form of common assault upon someone carrying out a lawful power of arrest. There is a further offence which deals with behaviour not amounting to an actual assault.

Offence — Obstruct Police — Police Act 1996, s. 89
Triable summarily. One month's imprisonment and/or a fine.
(No specific power of arrest)

The Police Act 1996, s. 89 states:

> (2) *Any person who resists or wilfully obstructs a constable in the execution of his duty, or a person assisting a constable in the execution of his duty, shall be guilty of an offence* . . .

Keynote

Resistance suggests some form of physical opposition; obstruction does not and may take many forms. For instance, warning other drivers of a speed check operation (*Betts* v *Stevens* [1910] 1 KB 1, providing misleading information (*Ledger* v *DPP* [1991] Crim LR 439), or deliberately drinking alcohol before providing breath specimen (*Ingleton* v *Dibble* [1972] 1 All ER 275). Obstruction has been interpreted as making it more difficult for a constable to carry out his/her duty (*Hinchcliffe* v *Sheldon* [1955] 1 WLR 1207). Refusing to answer an officer's questions is not obstruction (*Rice* v *Connolly* [1966] 2 QB 414) — unless perhaps the defendant was under some duty to provide information. Any obstruction must be *wilful*, that is the defendant must intend to do it (**see chapter 1**). The obstruction will not be 'wilful' if the defendant was simply trying to help the police, even if that help turned out to be more of a hindrance (*Wilmot* v *Atack* [1977] QB 498).

Obstruction can be caused by omission but only where the defendant was already under some duty towards the police or the officer. There is also a common law offence of refusing to go to the aid of a constable when asked to do so in order to prevent or diminish a breach of the peace (*R* v *Waugh*, *The Times*, 1 October 1986).

Tipping off people who were about to commit crime has been held to amount to obstruction (*Green* v *Moore* [1982] QB 1044), and some extreme forms of obstruction may amount to more serious offences such as perverting the course of justice or concealing offences (**see chapter 15**). There are also specific statutory offences of 'tipping off' in relation to money laundering and drug trafficking offences under s. 93D of the Criminal Justice Act 1988 and s. 53 of the Drug Trafficking Act 1994 respectively.

Note that there is no power of arrest unless the obstruction involves a breach of the peace (as to which, **see General Police Duties, chapter 4**).

8.4 Offences Involving Significant or Lasting Injury

If an assailant causes any significant or lasting injury then one of the following offences may apply.

8.4.1   Assault Occasioning Actual Bodily Harm

**Offence — Assault Occasioning Actual Bodily Harm —
Offences Against the Person Act 1861, s. 47**
*Triable either way. Five years' imprisonment on indictment; six months' imprisonment
and/or a fine summarily.*
(***Arrestable offence***)
Offence — Racially Aggravated — Crime and Disorder Act 1998, s. 29(1)(b)
*Triable either way. Seven years' imprisonment and/or a fine on indictment;
six months' imprisonment and/or a fine summarily.*
(***Arrestable offence***)

The Offences Against the Person Act 1861, s. 47 states:

> *Whosoever shall be convicted . . . of any assault occasioning actual bodily harm shall be liable . . .
> to [imprisonment] . . .*

Keynote

It must be shown that 'actual bodily harm' was a consequence, directly or indirectly, of
the defendant's actions. Such harm can include shock (*R v Miller* [1954] 2 QB 282)
and mental 'injury' (*R v Chan-Fook* [1994] 1 WLR 689).

For a discussion of the relevant *mens rea* for this offence, **see para. 8.2.3**. The state of
mind required is the same as that for an assault or battery.

Examples of what will amount to 'actual bodily harm' can be found in the CPS
Charging Standards (**see appendix 2**) and include:

- loss or breaking of teeth
- temporary loss of sensory functions
- extensive or multiple bruising
- minor fractures and cuts requiring stitches
- psychiatric injury going beyond fear, distress or panic.

As with common assault, this offence was deemed by the legislators to be one where it
was necessary to increase the maximum penalty available to the courts if it was
committed under racially aggravated circumstances (see Crime and Disorder Act 1998,
s. 29(1)(b)).

Again it should be noted that there are potential problems with the availability of
alternative verdicts in cases of racially aggravated assault and, in cases of doubt, the
advice of the Crown Prosecution Service should be sought.

For a full explanation of the meaning of 'racially aggravated', **see General Police
Duties, chapter 3**.

Sections 1 and 2 of the Criminal Evidence (Amendment) Act 1997 extending the power
to take non-intimate samples without consent apply to this offence and also to
conspiracies, attempts or incitements in the circumstances set out in that Act (**see
Evidence and Procedure, chapter 16**).

8.4.2   Wounding or Inflicting Grievous Bodily Harm

**Offence — Wounding or Inflicting Grievous Bodily Harm —
Offences Against the Person Act 1861 s. 20**
*Triable either way. Five years' imprisonment on indictment; six months' imprisonment
and/or a fine summarily.*
(**Arrestable offence**)
Offence — Racially Aggravated — Crime and Disorder Act 1998, s. 29(1)(a)
*Triable either way. Seven years' imprisonment and/or a fine on indictment;
six months' imprisonment and/or a fine summarily.*
(**Arrestable offence**)

The Offences Against the Person Act 1861, s. 20 states:

> *Whosoever shall unlawfully and maliciously wound or inflict any grievous bodily harm upon any other person, either with or without any weapon or instrument, shall be guilty of [an offence] . . .*

Keynote

Wounding is a breaking of the 'whole' skin or the continuity of the skin. A cut which goes right through all the layers of a person's skin, whether caused externally (e.g. a knife wound) or internally (a punch causing a tooth to puncture the cheek), will amount to a wound.

The word 'inflict' has caused problems in the past. However, the House of Lords in *R v Ireland* [1998] AC 147 has made it clear that no 'assault' (**see para. 8.2.2**) is needed for this offence and that harm could be 'inflicted' indirectly (in this case by menacing telephone calls inflicting psychiatric harm). Therefore there is now little if any difference between inflicting harm and 'causing' harm (**see para. 8.4.3**). It should be enough to show that the defendant's behaviour brought about the resulting harm to the victim.

There have also been many judicial attempts at defining grievous bodily harm. In *R v Saunders* [1985] Crim LR 230 it was held that the expression meant 'serious or really serious harm'. This harm will now include psychiatric harm (*Ireland*). Examples of what will amount to 'grievous bodily harm' can be found in the CPS Charging Standards (**see appendix 2**) and include:

- injury resulting in some permanent disability or visible disfigurement
- broken or displaced limbs or bones
- injuries requiring blood transfusion or lengthy treatment.

For a discussion of the relevant *mens rea* for this offence, **see para. 8.2.3**.

'Maliciously' — although the word maliciously suggests some form of evil premeditation, 'malice' here amounts to subjective recklessness (**see chapter 1**). It means that the defendant must realise that there is a risk of some harm being caused to the victim. The defendant does not need to foresee the degree of harm which is eventually caused, only that his/her behaviour may bring about some harm to the victim.

Section 1 and 2 of the Criminal Evidence (Amendment) Act 1997 extending the power to take non-intimate samples without consent apply to this offence and also to conspiracies attempts or incitements in the circumstances set out in that Act (**see Evidence and Procedure, chapter 16**).

As with common assault and assault occasioning actual bodily harm, this offence was deemed by the legislators to be one where it was necessary to increase the maximum penalty available to the courts if it was committed under racially aggravated circumstances (see Crime and Disorder Act 1998, s. 29(1)(a)).

Again, it should be noted that there are potential problems with the availability of alternative verdicts in cases of aggravated assaults and the advice of the Crown Prosecution Service should be sought.

For a full explanation of the meaning of 'racially aggravated', **see General Police Duties, chapter 3**.

8.4.3 Wounding or Causing Grievous Bodily Harm with Intent

Offence — Wounding or Causing Grievous Bodily Harm with Intent — Offences Against the Person Act 1861, s. 18
Triable on indictment only. Life imprisonment.
(*Arrestable offence*)

The Offences Against the Person Act 1861, s. 18 states:

> *Whosoever shall unlawfully and maliciously by any means whatsoever wound or cause any grievous bodily harm to any person with intent to do some grievous bodily harm to any person, or with intent to resist or prevent the lawful apprehension or detainer of any person, shall be guilty of [an offence] . . .*

Keynote

This is a crime of *specific intent* (**see chapter 1**). The word 'cause', together with the expression 'by any means whatsoever', seems to give this offence a wider meaning than s. 20. However, the increasingly broad interpretation of the s. 20 offence means that there is little difference in the *actus reus* needed for either offence.

The state of mind for this offence is the same as that for s. 20 with the added intention of bringing about serious harm or to resist/prevent arrest.

Where the intent was to cause grievous bodily harm, the issue of 'malice' will not arise. However, where the intent was to resist or prevent the lawful arrest of someone, the element of maliciousness as set out above (**see para. 8.4.2**) will need to be proved.

Sections 1 and 2 of the Criminal Evidence (Amendment) Act 1997 also apply to this offence (and to conspiracies, attempts or incitements in the circumstances set out in that Act) (**see Evidence and Procedure, chapter 16**).

The provisions of ss. 28 and 29 of the Crime and Disorder Act 1998 in relation to racially aggravated assaults do not apply to this offence as it was felt by the legislators that there was nothing to be gained by creating a special offence, given that the maximum sentence available is already life imprisonment. However, the courts must still take notice of any element of racial aggravation when determining sentence (s. 153 of the Powers of Criminal Courts (Sentencing) Act 2000).

Perhaps in these cases more than any other, there are potential problems with the availability of alternative verdicts in cases of racially aggravated assaults and the advice of the Crown Prosecution Service should be sought.

CHAPTER NINE

MISCELLANEOUS OFFENCES AGAINST THE PERSON

9.1 Introduction

In addition to the more common offences against the person there are some, relatively rare but important offences which are set out below.

9.2 Torture

Offence — Torture — Criminal Justice Act 1988, s. 134
Triable on indictment. Life imprisonment.
(*Serious arrestable offence*)

The Criminal Justice Act 1988, s. 134 states:

(1)   A public official or person acting in an official capacity, whatever his nationality, commits the offence of torture if in the United Kingdom or elsewhere he intentionally inflicts severe pain or suffering on another in the performance or purported performance of his official duties.

(2)   A person not falling within subsection (1) above commits the offence of torture, whatever his nationality, if—

(a)   in the United Kingdom or elsewhere he intentionally inflicts severe pain or suffering on another at the instigation or with the consent or acquiescence—

(i)   of a public official; or

(ii)   of a person acting in an official capacity; and

(b)   the official or other person is performing or purporting to perform his official duties when he instigates the commission of the offence or consents to or acquiesces in it.

(3)   It is immaterial whether the pain or suffering is physical or mental or whether is caused by an act or an omission.

Keynote

The consent of the Attorney-General (or Solicitor-General) is needed before bringing a prosecution under s. 134. This offence, although it sounds quite extreme, could be committed by a police officer in the course of his/her duties, and may have significant implications for Custody Officers.

Although the offence has a statutory defence of 'lawful authority, justification or excuse' (see below), Article 3 of the European Convention on Human Rights contains an absolute prohibition on torture. Irrespective of the prevailing circumstances, there can be no derogation from an individual's absolute right under Article 3 to freedom from torture, inhuman or degrading treatment or punishment.

These three features have been identified as having the following broad characteristics:

• Torture — deliberate treatment leading to serious or cruel suffering.

• Inhuman treatment — treatment resulting in intense suffering, both physical and mental.

• Degrading treatment — treatment giving rise to fear and anguish in the victim, causing feelings of inferiority and humiliation.

(See *Ireland* v *United Kingdom* (1978) 2 EHRR 25.)

It has been held by the European Commission of Human Rights that causing mental anguish without any physical assault could be a violation of Article 3 (see *Denmark* v *Greece* (1969) 12 YB Eur Conv HR special Vol.).

Article 3 does not only prohibit the deliberate application of pain and suffering, but also a range of other behaviour. Oppressive interrogation techniques such as sleep deprivation, exposure to continuous loud noise and forcing suspects to adopt uncomfortable postures for prolonged lengths of time have been held to fall within the second and third categories of inhuman and degrading treatment (*Ireland* v *United Kingdom*).

In each case, it must be shown that the prohibited behaviour went beyond the 'minimum level of severity'. In determining whether the behaviour did go beyond that level, and under which particular category that behaviour falls, the courts will take into account factors such as the age, sex, state of health and general life experience of the victim. 'Severe pain or suffering' can be mental as well as physical and can be caused by omission.

For a full discussion of this and the implications of the Convention in light of the Human Rights Act 1998, **see General Police Duties**.

9.2.1 Defence

The Criminal Justice Act 1988, s. 134 states:

(4) It shall be a defence for a person charged with an offence under this section in respect of any conduct of his to prove that he had lawful authority, justification or excuse for that conduct.

9.3 Poisoning

Offence — Poisoning — Offences Against the Person Act 1861, s. 23
Triable on indictment. Ten years' imprisonment.
(Arrestable offence)

The Offences Against the Person Act 1861, s. 23 states:

Whosoever shall unlawfully and maliciously administer to or cause to be administered to or taken by any other person any poison or other destructive or noxious thing, so as thereby to endanger the life of such person, or so as thereby to inflict upon such person any grievous bodily harm, shall be guilty of [an offence] . . .

Keynote

For the meaning of 'malicious', **see chapter 8**. Other than the requirement for 'malice', this offence is mainly concerned with the consequences caused to the victim and not the defendant's intentions.

'Causing to be administered' would cover indirect poisoning or even inducing someone to poison themselves. 'Administering' is a very broad term which has been held to include the spraying of gas into another's face (*R v Gillard* (1988) 87 Cr App R 189). As such this would appear to include the use of CS spray by police officers but the 'administering' would also have to be shown to be both unlawful and malicious. A decision of the Court of Appeal has suggested that the supply of a controlled drug to someone who then immediately takes that drug can amount to an offence under this section in certain circumstances (*R v Kennedy*, unreported, 31 July 1998, **see para. 6.8.2**).

Whether a substance is poisonous, destructive or noxious will depend on both its quality and quantity. Some substances may become poisonous or noxious only in large amounts whereas others may be so *per se*.

This offence would certainly cover the administering of a controlled drug to another or inducing another to take a controlled drug.

There is a requirement to prove a consequence with this offence, namely the endangering of a person's life or the infliction of grievous bodily harm.

Offence — Poisoning with Intent — Offences Against the Person Act 1861, s. 24
Triable on indictment. Five years' imprisonment.
(*Arrestable offence*)

The Offences Against the Person Act 1861, s. 24 states:

Whosoever shall unlawfully and maliciously administer to or cause to be administered to or taken by any other person any poison or other destructive or noxious thing, with intent to injure, aggrieve, or annoy any such person, shall be guilty of [an offence] . . .

Keynote

Unlike the previous offence under s. 23, there is no requirement as to the actual consequences of a defendant's actions under s. 24 and this offence is concerned with the defendant's intentions.

This is an offence of *specific intent* which means that recklessness will not suffice and that self-induced intoxication may provide a defence (**see chapters 1 and 4**).

This offence may be considered in relation to the administering of so-called 'date rape' drugs, particularly where there is insufficient evidence of sexual activity. The offence was recently considered by the Court of Appeal in a case where the defendant had slipped Zolpidem (a prescription-only drug designed to alleviate insomnia) into the wine of a female friend. In that case, although the defendant had written some suggestive comment on the victim's abdomen, there had been no evidence of sexual assault. Nevertheless, the court held that administering a drug to another without their knowledge or consent was a 'most serious offence' (*R* v *Callaghan* (2001) LTL 6 February).

9.4 False Imprisonment

Offence — False Imprisonment — Common Law
Triable on indictment. Unlimited maximum penalty.
(*Arrestable offence*)

It is an offence at common law falsely to imprison another person.

Keynote

This offence is the first in an ascending order of aggravated offences against the person and is more usually dealt with under civil law or as kidnapping/abduction (see below).

The elements required for this offence are the unlawful and intentional/reckless restraint of a person's freedom of movement (*R* v *Rahman* (1985) 81 Cr App R 349). Locking someone in a vehicle or keeping them in a particular place for however short a time may amount to false imprisonment if done unlawfully. An unlawful arrest may amount to such an offence (**see General Police Duties, chapter 2**) and it is not uncommon for such an allegation to be levelled at police officers against whom a public complaint has been made.

The state of mind required to prove this offence is 'subjective' recklessness (*R* v *James*, *The Times*, 2 October 1997). (For a discussion of this concept, **see chapter 1**.)

Sections 1 and 2 of the Criminal Evidence (Amendment) Act 1997 apply to this offence and also to conspiracies, attempts or incitements in the circumstances set out in that Act (**see Evidence and Procedure, chapter 16**).

9.5 Kidnapping

Offence — Kidnapping — Common Law
Triable on indictment. Unlimited maximum penalty.
(*Serious arrestable offence*)

It is an offence at common law to take or carry away another person without the consent of that person and without lawful excuse.

Keynote

Kidnapping is the second of the aggravated offences described above. The required elements of this offence are the unlawful taking or carrying away of one person by another by force or fraud (*R* v *D* [1984] AC 778). These requirements go beyond those of mere restraint needed for false imprisonment. Parents may be acting without lawful excuse, for instance, if they are acting in breach of a court order in respect of their children (**see chapter 11**).

The taking or carrying away of the victim must be without the consent of the victim. If the victim consents to an initial taking but later withdraws that consent, the offence would be complete. If the victim is a child, the consent will probably be that of the parents but the more appropriate charge in such a case may be one under the Child Abduction Act 1984 (**see chapter 11**).

The state of mind required for this offence appears to be the same as that for false imprisonment, indeed the only thing separating the two offences seems to be *actus reus* (*R v Hutchins* [1988] Crim LR 379). For *actus reus* generally, **see chapter 2**).

Sections 1 and 2 of the Criminal Evidence (Amendment) Act 1997 above also apply to this offence (and to conspiracies, attempts or incitements in the circumstances set out in that Act) (**see Evidence and Procedure, chapter 16**).

9.6 Hostage Taking

Offence — Hostage Taking — Taking of Hostages Act 1982, s. 1
Triable on indictment. Life imprisonment.
(***Serious arrestable offence***)

The Taking of Hostages Act 1982, s. 1 states:

> *(1) A person, whatever his nationality, who, in the United Kingdom or elsewhere—*
> *(a) detains any other person ('the hostage'), and*
> *(b) in order to compel a State, international governmental organisation, or person to do or abstain from doing any act, threatens to kill, injure or continue to detain the hostage, commits an offence.*

Keynote

The consent of the Attorney-General (or Solicitor-General) is needed before bringing a prosecution for this, the third aggravated offence. To be guilty, a defendant must detain a person *and* threaten to kill, injure or continue to detain them with the intentions outlined under s. 1(1)(b). It is therefore an offence of 'ulterior' or 'specific' intent (**see chapter 1**).

9.7 False Imprisonment, Kidnapping and Hostage Taking Compared

To summarise:

- Detaining someone without any lawful authority can amount to false imprisonment. The detention or restraint may be committed recklessly.

- Taking or carrying someone away without any lawful authority or without the person's consent can amount to kidnapping. Again this may be done 'recklessly'.

- Detaining a person (with or without authority) in order to compel a state, governmental organisation or person to do/not to do something will be hostage taking if it is accompanied by the relevant threats. This offence cannot be committed by recklessness and requires proof of the requisite intent.

In any of these cases the overall motive of the defendant or the wider consequences of the offence may bring it within the category of 'terrorism' (as to which **see General Police Duties, chapter 4**).

CHAPTER TEN

SEXUAL OFFENCES

10.1 Introduction

Sexual offences represent a particularly important area of criminal law for two main reasons: the sensitivity required in their investigation and prosecution and their potential effect on the victim.

Many legal textbooks include sexual offences under 'non-fatal offences against the person'. However, such offences can cause significant emotional harm to the victim, harm which may take far longer to 'heal' than many physical injuries. For that reason, together with the growth in the range of legal provisions that have been created to tackle the behaviour of sex offenders, sexual offences have been addressed in this separate chapter. Most of this area of criminal law is contained in statute and there are many, sometimes overlapping, offences.

A further factor affecting this area of criminal law is the relevance of the European Convention on Human Rights. It is clear that sexual activities are aspects of a person's 'private life' as protected by Article 8 of the Convention (see *Dudgeon* v *United Kingdom* (1981) 4 EHRR 149 and *ADT* v *United Kingdom* [2000] Crim LR 1009). It is also clear that this applies to homosexual relationships as well as heterosexual ones (*X* v *United Kingdom* (1997) 24 EHRR 143).

As such, any attempt by the criminal law to place restrictions on the consensual sexual activities of individuals will have to be considered very carefully in light of the Human Rights Act 1998 (as to which, **see General Police Duties, chapter 2**). Indeed some changes to primary legislation in this area have already been made in response to the 1998 Act.

10.1.1 Anonymity

Under the Sexual Offences (Amendment) Acts 1976 and 1992, victims of most sexual offences (including rape, incest, buggery and indecency with children) are entitled to anonymity throughout their lifetime. This means that there are restrictions on the way in which trials and cases may be reported and the courts have powers to enforce these provisions. This area has been the subject of many campaigns for legal reform over the last 20 years. Further protection preventing victims from cross-examination by their alleged attackers is provided by the Youth Justice and Criminal Evidence Act 1999. The 1999 Act also imposes restrictions on the introduction of evidence in most of the sexual offences covered in this chapter. For the restrictions on the use of victims' statements in sexual offences, **see para. 10.2.3**.

10.2   Control of Sex Offenders

10.2.1   The Sex Offenders Act 1997

Statutory Regulation

Statutory regulation of the behaviour of sex offenders has increased significantly over recent years. The Sex Offenders Act 1997 was introduced for two main purposes: to create a system whereby the movement and whereabouts of certain sex offenders (in particular paedophiles) could be monitored (Part I) and to impose further controls on sexual offences committed against children outside the United Kingdom by UK residents (Part II).

The Criminal Justice and Court Services Act 2000 has since extended some of the provisions in relation to sex offenders in several ways. First, it has imposed a requirement upon chief officers of police to assess and manage the risks posed by sex offenders. Under s. 67 of the 2000 Act, chief officers of police and the local probation board for the area, acting jointly as the 'responsible authority', have a statutory duty to establish 'arrangements' for the purpose of assessing and managing the risks posed in that area by relevant sexual and violent offenders. This duty also extends to the assessment and management of risks posed by any other people who, by reason of offences they have committed *anywhere* (including abroad) are considered by the responsible authority to be people 'who may cause serious harm to the public'. Sexual and violent offenders are generally those who:

- are subject to the notification requirements of Part I of the Sex Offenders Act 1997 (see below);

- are convicted of a sexual or violent offence under the Powers of Criminal Courts (Sentencing) Act 2000 and have been sentenced to 12 months' imprisonment or more (these offences cover most sexually motivated offences and offences intended/ likely to lead to death or physical injury including arson);

- have been tried for a sexual/violent offence as above but found not guilty by reason of insanity and have been admitted to a hospital under the Mental Health Act 1983; or

- have been convicted of an 'offence against a child' (**see chapter 11 and appendix 3**).

The responsible authority must also prepare and publish an annual report in relation to the arrangements they have made under s. 67. In addition, local probation boards have a further duty to consult victims of violent/sex offenders as to any conditions or requirements that might be imposed on those offenders when they are released (s. 69).

In addition to the provisions of the Sex Offenders Act 1997, the Crime and Disorder Act 1998 introduced the concept of sex offender orders whereby magistrates' courts could impose conditions on the activities of certain sex offenders (**see para. 10.3**).

SEXUAL OFFENCES

Paedophiles

Perhaps the best description of the reason for enacting some of this legislation is the explanation provided by Baroness Blatch, Minister of State for the Home Office. During the 1997 Act's passage through Parliament, Baroness Blatch said:

Paedophiles are markedly different from other criminals. . . . Their offending behaviour often intensifies with the passage of time. One of the problems of dealing with hardened paedophiles is that they do not consider their behaviour to be wrong — rather the opposite, they do not always understand or accept efforts to stop their activities. This makes them especially dangerous.

(*Hansard*, 579 HL (5th series) col. 545, 14 March 1997.)

Who? — Offenders Covered by Part I

Part I of the Sex Offenders Act 1997 — which imposes requirements for notifying local police forces — applies, not just to paedophiles, but to people who:

* have been convicted of an offence under sch. 1;
* have been found 'not guilty' by reason of insanity of such an offence;
* have committed such an offence while under a disability;
* have been cautioned by the police after admitting such an offence (s. 1(1) and (2)).

Offenders who are currently serving sentences, or who are subject to detention or guardianship orders for offences under sch. 1 are also covered by the notification requirements (s. 1(3)), as are offenders serving sentences imposed by military courts (see s. 4).

Under the law as it currently stands, however, offenders who are given a conditional or absolute discharge are not required to register as sex offenders. This gap in the law has attracted considerable criticism and is under review.

Young sex offenders are also covered by the provisions of Part I, as are those who have parental responsibility for them under certain circumstances (see below). Under the former process of cautioning juvenile offenders, parents of juveniles who had been cautioned for relevant sexual offences were required to ensure that the juveniles' names and addresses were included on the sex offenders' register (*R v Greater Manchester Police, ex parte R* (2000) ILR 23 October).

Although the system of cautioning has been replaced by the system of reprimands and final warnings (as to which, **see Evidence and Procedure, chapter** 7), the requirement for parents to register their children's details in such cases would still appear to apply.

There are reductions in the period for which the requirements will apply in relation to some young offenders (see below).

Schedule 1 Offences

The following offences under the Sexual Offences Act 1956 appear in sch. 1 of the Sex Offenders Act 1997:

- rape (s. 1)
- intercourse with girl under 13 (s. 5)
- intercourse with girl between 13 and 16 (s. 6 only if *offender* was aged 20+)
- causing prostitution of, intercourse with or indecent assault on girl under 16 (s. 28).

The following offences under the Sexual Offences Act 1956 are covered by sch. 1 *provided the victim or other party is under 18:*

- incest by man (s. 10)

- buggery (s. 12) (only if *offender* was aged 20+)

- indecency between men (s. 13) (only if *offender* was aged 20+)

- assault with intent to commit buggery (s. 16)

- an offence under s. 3 of the Sexual Offences (Amendment) Act 2000 (abuse of position of trust) (only if offender was aged 20+).

The following offence under the Sexual Offences Act 1956 is covered by sch. 1 *provided the victim or other party is under 18,* **or** *the offender was sentenced to at least 30 months' imprisonment or admitted to a hospital under a restriction order:*

- indecent assault (ss. 14 and 15).

Other offences covered by sch. 1 are:

- indecent conduct towards a child (Indecency with Children Act 1960, s. 1)

- inciting girl under 16 to have incest (Criminal Law Act 1977)

- indecent photographs of children (Protection of Children Act 1978)

- possessing indecent photographs of children (Criminal Justice Act 1988, s. 160)

- importing indecent photographs of children under 16 (Customs and Excise Management Act 1979).

These offences are addressed in this chapter and **chapter 11**.

Schedule 1 also includes the counterparts of these offences under Scottish law, military law and the law in respect of Northern Ireland.

It also includes attempting, conspiracy, incitement and aiding and abetting the offences set out.

What? — Notification Requirements

Although the Sex Offenders Act 1997 Act does not create a special 'register' of sex offenders, it requires offenders who fall within its ambit to notify the police of their name and address and every other name which they use (s. 2(1)).

Under s. 2(2), sex offenders must also notify the police of:

- any use they make of a name which has not previously been notified;

- any change of home address (which includes their sole or main residence in the UK or, if there is no such residence, premises which they regularly visit);

- their having resided or stayed for a 'qualifying period' at any premises in the UK which has not been notified.

Under s. 2(7) the 'qualifying period' is:

- 14 days, or
- two or more times within any 12 month period which amount to 14 days.

In determining any periods under s. 2(1) and (2) no account will be taken of time spent under remand or sentence by a court, detention in a hospital or time spent outside the UK (s. 2(4)). (Note that the UK does not include the Isle of Man nor the Channel Islands but that s. 9 makes provision for regulations to extend the 1997 Act thereto.)

Section 2(6D) allows the Secretary of State to make regulations requiring sex offenders who are subject to the notification requirements to provide travel and residence details on leaving and returning to the UK, along with any other related information set out in the regulations.

Under s. 2(3), any notification to the police under s. 2(1) or (2) above must always state the offender's:

- date of birth;
- name on the relevant date and any other name used; and
- home address.

When? — Time Limits

Sex offenders must comply with the notification requirements above within three days of the relevant date or the commencement of the Sex Offenders Act 1997 Act.

How? — Method of Notification

Under s. 2(5) of the Sex Offenders Act 1997, sex offenders may give notification:

- by attending the police station in the area where their home is situated or a police station prescribed by statutory instrument and giving oral notification to any police officer or authorised person; or

- by sending written notification to such a police station.

A person giving notification must also, if requested by the police officer or other authorised person, allow that officer/person to take his/her fingerprints and/or photograph for the purpose of verifying his/her identity (s. 2(6A)).

SEXUAL OFFENCES

For How Long? — Applicable Period for Notification Requirement

The Sex Offenders Act 1997 Act imposes an incremental scale on the period of time for which sex offenders will be required to give the notification set out in Part I. Offenders sentenced to life, to 30 months' imprisonment or more, or those admitted to hospital under a restriction order will be subject to the notification requirements indefinitely.

The relevant times are set out in the Table under s. 1(4):

TABLE

Description of person	Applicable period
A person who, in respect of the offence, is or has been sentenced to imprisonment for life or for a term of 30 months or more	An indefinite period
A person who, in respect of the offence or finding, is or has been admitted to a hospital subject to a restriction order	An indefinite period
A person who, in respect of the offence, is or has been sentenced to imprisonment for a term of more than 6 months but less than 30 months	A period of 10 years beginning with the relevant date
A person who, in respect of the offence, is or has been sentenced to imprisonment for a term of 6 months or less	A period of 7 years beginning with that date
A person who, in respect of the offence or finding, is or has been admitted to a hospital without being subject to a restriction order	A period of 7 years beginning with that date
A person of any other description	A period of 5 years beginning with that date

Keynote

In the case of an offender who is under 18, the applicable notification periods of 10, 7 and 5 years are halved (s. 4(2)).

Section 4(3) makes provision for those having parental responsibility for some young sex offenders to comply with the provisions for notification *and* to become liable in the event of any failure to comply.

Section 4(6) sets out the formula for calculating consecutive or concurrent sentences.

One of the effects of a court passing a sex offender order (see below) is that the person must register as a sex offender.

In addition to the requirements imposed on offenders by the 1997 Act, the police have a duty to disclose the identity of a convicted sex offender to members of the public where there is a pressing need to do so (R v *Chief Constable of North Wales*, ex parte *Thorpe, The Times*, 5 May 1998).

The provisions of the Criminal Evidence (Amendment) Act 1997 extending the power to take non-intimate samples without consent apply to all offences under the Sexual Offences Act 1956 except ss. 30, 31, 33 or 36 (**see Evidence and Procedure, chapter 16**).

Offence — Failing to Comply with Notification Requirements — Sex Offenders Act 1997, s. 3(1)

Triable either way. Five years' imprisonment on indictment; six months' imprisonment.
(*Arrestable offence*)

Section 3 states:

> *(1)   If a person—*
> *(a)   fails, without reasonable excuse, to comply with section 2(1) or (2) above; or*
> *(b)   notifies to the police, in purported compliance with section 2(1) or (2) above, any information which he knows to be false,*
> *he is guilty of an offence.*
> *(1A)   . . .*
> *(1B)   If without reasonable excuse—*
> *(a)   a person fails to comply with section 2(6A) above, or*
> *(b)   a person fails to comply with any requirement imposed by virtue of section 2(6D)above to give a notice, or gives a notice which does not disclose the required information or which discloses information which he knows to be false,*
> *he is guilty of an offence . . .*

Keynote

The sanctions for non-compliance with the notification requirements were strengthened considerably by the Criminal Justice and Court Services Act 2000, which also added the offence under s. 3(1B). The requirements referred to in the new s. 3(1B) offence are the requirement to allow the taking of fingerprints and the requirement to give notice when leaving or returning to the UK, both of which are discussed above.

Reasonable excuse will be a question of fact to be determined by the court. In order to prove the offence under s. 3(1)(b) you will have to show knowledge on the part of the defendant (**see chapter 1**).

Under s. 3(1)(a) and 3(1B) a person continues to commit the offence throughout any period of non-compliance but he/she can only be prosecuted once in respect of the same failure (s. 3(2)). Therefore, if a person began to use a different name on 10 September 2000 but did not notify the police until 5 January 2001, he/she would commit one continuing offence over that period. Presumably, if he/she changed address or stayed for the qualifying period (see above) during that time without notifying the police, he/she would commit a further offence.

Proceedings for the offence under s. 3(1) can be brought in any place where the offender resides or where he/she is found (s. 3(3)).

10.2.2   Restraining Orders

In addition to the other amendments to the Sex Offenders Act 1997, the Criminal Justice and Court Services Act 2000 also introduced the concept of restraining orders.

Restraining orders can be made by the Crown Court or the Court of Appeal when they impose a sentence of imprisonment for a relevant sexual offence under the 1997 Act. Restraining orders are *discretionary*, a feature that distinguishes them from disqualification orders that are available in relation to offences involving children (as to which, **see chapter 11**). Restraining orders are available when the relevant courts are satisfied that it is necessary to protect the public in general, or any people in particular, from serious harm from the offender (s. 5A(1)). Such orders can prohibit the offender from doing anything described in the order (in much the same way as a 'sex offender order'; **see para. 10.3**). Restraining orders will have effect for as long as the order specifies or until a further order is made and any notification requirements imposed on the sex offender are unaffected by it. Offenders have a right of appeal against a restraining order and either the offender or the chief officer of police (or local probation board) may apply for an order to be varied or discharged.

Offence — Breaching a Restraining Order — Sex Offenders Act 1997, s. 5A(8)

Triable either way. Five years imprisonment on indictment; six months' imprisonment and/or fine summarily.

(Arrestable offence)

The Sex Offenders Act 1997, s. 5A states:

> *(8) If without reasonable excuse the offender does anything which he is prohibited from doing by an order under this section, he is guilty of an offence.*

Keynote

Given that restraining orders are passed at the same time as a criminal sentence, it would seem that they are *criminal* orders. This again distinguishes them from sex offender orders (**see para. 10.3**) and anti-social behaviour orders (as to which, **see General Police Duties, chapter 3**) and will be relevant when the courts are assessing their compatibility with the Human Rights Act 1998.

10.2.3 Statements in Sexual Offence Cases

For some time convicted sex offenders and prisoners remanded for sexual offences have used their entitlement to have a copy of all complainant statements as a form of 'currency' in prisons, swapping and trading their statements for sexual gratification.

The Sexual Offences (Protected Material) Act 1997 was passed to address this problem which is particularly distressing for victims of sexual offences.

The 1997 Act regulates access by the defendant and others to victim statements and other material in sexual offences (s. 3). The material includes photographs of victims and medical reports on their physical condition (s. 1).

The 1997 Act requires the defendant's legal adviser to give an undertaking in relation to the copying and retention of the protected material by the defendant (s. 4).

The Youth Justice and Criminal Evidence Act 1999 places restrictions on the cross-examination of victims of most sexually-motivated offences and the introduction at trial of certain details of the victim's history (**see Evidence and Procedure, chapter 6**).

10.3 Sex Offender Orders

In common with the anti-social behaviour order available under s. 1 of the Crime and Disorder Act 1998 (**see General Police Duties, chapter 3**), the sex offender order

114

under s. 2 creates a new means whereby the activities of individuals can be restrained through the courts and enforced with criminal sanctions.

There have been other pieces of recent legislation aimed at curbing the activities of sex offenders (**see chapter 11**; see also the Children (Protection from Offenders) (Miscellaneous Amendments) Regulations 1997 (SI 1997 No. 2308) which place requirements on people who run children's homes to obtain information about prospective employees). Additionally, s. 85 of the Powers of Criminal Courts (Sentencing) Act 2000 provides for extended sentences in respect of certain sexual offences. However, the sex offender order gives the courts much broader powers to impose restrictions on the day to day activities of sex offenders.

10.3.1 Sex Offenders

For the purposes of a sex offender order under the Crime and Disorder Act 1998, a person is a 'sex offender' if he/she:

> (a) has been convicted of a sexual offence to which Part I of the Sex Offenders Act 1997 applies;
> (b) has been found not guilty of such an offence by reason of insanity, or found to be under a disability and to have done the act charged against him in respect of such an offence;
> (c) has been cautioned by a constable, in England and Wales or Northern Ireland, in respect of such an offence which, at the time when the caution was given, he had admitted; or
> (d) has been punished under the law in force in a country or territory outside the United Kingdom for an act which—
> > (i)   constituted an offence under that law; and
> > (ii) would have constituted a sexual offence to which that Part applies if it had been done in any part of the United Kingdom.

(s. 3(1)).

Keynote

For the sexual offences to which Part I of the Sex Offenders Act 1997 applies, **see para. 10.2.1**.

The provisions of s. 3(1) and (2) (see below) will extend to reprimands or warnings under s. 65 of the 1998 Act (as to which, **see Evidence and Procedure, chapter 7**).

A person will also be a 'sex offender' if he/she has been punished under the law of another jurisdiction for an act which was both an offence in that jurisdiction *and* which would have amounted to an offence under Part I of the Sex Offenders Act 1997 had it been committed in the UK.

Section 3 goes on to state:

> (2) In subsection (1) of section 2 . . . 'the relevant date', in relation to a sex offender, means—
> (a) the date or, as the case may be, the latest date on which he has been convicted, found, cautioned or punished as mentioned in subsection (1) above; or
> (b) if later, the date of the commencement of that section.
> (3) Subsections (2) and (3) of section 6 of the Sex Offenders Act 1997 apply for the construction of references in subsections (1) and (2) above as they apply for the construction of references in Part I of that Act.
> (4) In subsections (1) and (2) above, any reference to a person having been cautioned shall be construed as including a reference to his having been reprimanded or warned (under section 65 below) as a child or young person.

(5)   An act punishable under the law in force in any country or territory outside the United Kingdom constitutes an offence under that law for the purposes of subsection (1) above, however it is described in that law.

(6)   Subject to subsection (7) below, the condition in subsection (1)(d)(i) above shall be taken to be satisfied unless, not later than rules of court may provide, the defendant serves on the applicant a notice—

(a)   stating that, on the facts as alleged with respect to the act in question, the condition is not in his opinion satisfied;

(b)   showing his grounds for that opinion; and

(c)   requiring the applicant to show that it is satisfied.

(7)   The court, if it thinks fit, may permit the defendant to require the applicant to show that the condition is satisfied without the prior service of a notice under subsection (6) above.

Keynote

Section 3(6) is a rebuttable presumption of law (see **Evidence and Procedure, chapter 11**) designed to prevent a lengthy examination of foreign law. That presumption is subject to the power given to the court under s. 3(7) to require an applicant to prove that an offence punished abroad meets the requirements set out at s. 3(1)(d)(i).

10.3.2   Applying for a Sex Offender Order

Section 2 of the Crime and Disorder Act 1998 states:

(1)   If it appears to a chief officer of police that the following conditions are fulfilled with respect to any person in his police area, namely—

(a)   that the person is a sex offender; and

(b)   that the person has acted, since the relevant date, in such a way as to give reasonable cause to believe that an order under this section is necessary to protect the public from serious harm from him, the chief officer may apply for an order under this section to be made in respect of the person.

(2)   Such an application shall be made by complaint to the magistrates' court whose commission area includes any place where it is alleged that the defendant acted in such a way as is mentioned in subsection (1)(b) above.

(3)   If, on such an application, it is proved that the conditions mentioned in subsection (1) above are fulfilled, the magistrates' court may make an order under this section (a 'sex offender order') which prohibits the defendant from doing anything described in the order.

(4)   The prohibitions that may be imposed by a sex offender order are those necessary for the purpose of protecting the public from serious harm from the defendant.

Keynote

Unlike the procedure relating to an anti-social behaviour order (see **General Police Duties, chapter 3**), where an application can be made by the local authority or the police, both of whom must have consulted with each other first, the applicant for a sex offender order will be the relevant chief officer of police.

In order to apply for a sex offender order, it must:

- *appear* to the chief officer that

- the person is a sex offender as defined above, *and*

- that the person has acted in a way *which gives reasonable cause to believe* that an order is necessary

- to protect *the public* from *serious harm* from that person.

The acts must have occurred since the commencement date of the section (1 December 1998) and since the person's conviction or punishment which qualifies him/her as a sex offender.

The requirement here to show *reasonable cause to believe* that an order is necessary to protect the public from serious harm is different from the lesser requirement found in s. 1 in relation to anti-social behaviour orders (**see General Police Duties, chapter 3**). For a discussion of the expression 'reasonable cause to believe', **see General Police Duties, chapter 2**.

In contrast to the anti-social behaviour order, here the defendant's acts need not be criminal or even a source of annoyance and could include behaviour such as using public lavatories, waiting in the proximity of a school or even using a public transport system. As this procedure is a *civil* one, the standard of proof required in proving the elements above would seem to be on a balance of probabilities (**see Evidence and Procedure, chapter 11**).

10.3.3 The Order

Section 2 of the 1998 Act goes on to state:

> (5) *A sex offender order shall have effect for a period (not less than five years) specified in the order or until further order; and while such an order has effect, Part I of the Sex Offenders Act 1997 shall have effect as if—*
> (a) *the defendant were subject to the notification requirements of that Part; and*
> (b) *in relation to the defendant, the relevant date (within the meaning of that Part) were the date of service of the order.*
> (6) *Subject to subsection (7) below, the applicant or the defendant may apply by complaint to the court which made a sex offender order for it to be varied or discharged by a further order.*
> (7) *Except with the consent of both parties, no sex offender order shall be discharged before the end of the period of five years beginning with the date of service of the order.*

Keynote

A sex offender order runs for a minimum of five years, unless it is varied or discharged following an application by either the defendant or the police (s. 2(6)). The ability to vary an order could be used to add further restrictions or to extend its lifespan.

Under s. 2(7), no sex offender order can be discharged before the end of five years *except with the consent of both parties*.

The effect of s. 2(5) is that the person who is subject to a sex offender order will become subject to the registration requirements that apply to sex offenders under the Sex Offenders Act 1997 (**see para. 10.2.1**).

The further effect is that the person must refrain from doing any act set out in the order (s. 2(3) above). Given the very wide ambit of the court's power under this section, a person might be prevented from doing almost anything that the court deems to be necessary in order to protect the public.

If a person does not fall within the definition of a 'sex offender', the anti-social behaviour order may be considered (**see General Police Duties, chapter 3**).

The procedure for application for sex offender orders and anti-social behaviour orders is governed by the Magistrates' Courts (Sex Offenders and Anti-social Behaviour Orders) Rules 1998 (SI 1998 No. 2682).

10.3.4   The Offence

**Offence — Breach of a Sex Offender Order — Crime and Disorder Act 1998,
s. 2(8)**
*Triable either way. Five years' imprisonment and/or fine on indictment;
six months' imprisonment and/or a fine summarily.*
(*Arrestable offence*)

The Crime and Disorder Act 1998, s. 2 states:

> *(8)   If without reasonable excuse a person does anything which he is prohibited from doing by a
> sex offender order, he shall be liable . . .*

Keynote

As the punishment provided by a conditional discharge (under s. 12 of the Powers of
Criminal Courts (Sentencing) Act 2000) has the same general effect as a sex offender
order, a court cannot impose a conditional discharge on a defendant found guilty of
committing an offence under s. 2(8) above (s. 2(9)).

Given the breadth of a sex offender order, which may restrain a defendant from doing
the most ordinary, every day activities, the behaviour required to commit this offence
could be relatively minor. Many commentators and practitioners believe that this
breadth of application, coupled with severe criminal sanctions, means that the sex
offender order system represents an unjustifiable violation of an individual's right to
private life under Article 8 of the European Convention on Human Rights and it is
anticipated that the above legislation will be challenged on these grounds. However, the
use of statutory administration provisions to keep sex offenders away from past or future
victims was expressly approved by the European Court of Human Rights in *K* v *United
Kingdom*, unreported, 9 January 2001. For a full discussion of the implications of the
Convention and the 1998 Act, **see General Police Duties**. The advice of the Crown
Prosecution Service may need to be sought in cases involving what appear to be
innocuous but technical breaches of such an order.

It appears from the wording of the 1998 Act that a person might have a sex offender
order made against him/her in his/her absence. Although a magistrates' court has the
power to issue a summons and then a warrant (under the Magistrates' Courts Act 1980)
in order to compel the person to come to court when an application for a sex offender
order is being heard, it does seem that the court can go on to make an order *ex parte*
(i.e. in the person's absence). Again, if this is the case, there are serious human rights
implications that may allow the procedure to be challenged.

10.3.5   Appeal

Section 4 of the Crime and Disorder Act 1998 states:

> *(1)   An appeal shall lie to the Crown Court against the making by a magistrates' court of [a] . . .
> sex offender order.*
> *(2)   On such an appeal the Crown Court—*
>   *(a)   may make such orders as may be necessary to give effect to its determination of the appeal; and*
>   *(b)   may also make such incidental or consequential orders as appear to it to be just.*
> *(3)   Any order of the Crown Court made on an appeal under this section (other than one directing
> that an application be re-heard by a magistrates' court) shall, for the purposes of section 1(8) or 2(6)*

118

above, be treated as if it were an order of the magistrates' court from which the appeal was brought and not an order of the Crown Court.

Keynote

There is no right of appeal open to the chief officer against a decision of a court to make an order. That would not preclude the applicant from requiring the court to 'state a case' for consideration by the Divisional Court in appropriate circumstances (**see Evidence and Procedure, chapter 2**).

10.4   Rape

Offence — Rape — Sexual Offences Act 1956, s. 1
Triable on indictment. Life imprisonment.
(*Serious arrestable offence*)

The Sexual Offences Act 1956, s. 1 states:

(1)   It is an offence for a man to rape a woman or another man.
(2)   A man commits rape if—
    (a)   he has sexual intercourse with a person (whether vaginal or anal) who at the time of the intercourse does not consent to it; and
    (b)   at the time he knows that the person does not consent to the intercourse or is reckless as to whether that person consents to it.
(3)   A man also commits rape if he induces a married woman to have sexual intercourse with him by impersonating her husband.

Keynote

Until 1994 the offence of rape could only be committed by a man against a woman. Section 142 of the Criminal Justice and Public Order Act 1994 amended the s. 1 offence to include male victims. A further amendment to the law relating to sexual offences was brought about by the Sexual Offences Act 1993, s. 1 which abolished the presumption that a male under the age of 14 was incapable of sexual intercourse.

10.4.1   Criminal Conduct

To prove rape you must show that the defendant had 'sexual intercourse' with the victim. Sexual intercourse will include any degree of penetration either of the anus or the vagina. It is not necessary to prove the completion of the intercourse 'by emission of seed' (ejaculation) (Sexual Offences Act 1956, s. 44). However, the presence of semen is clearly important in proving the elements of a sexual offence, as is other scientific evidence recovered from the victim, the offender and the scene etc.

Oral sex will not amount to 'sexual intercourse' (*R* v *Gaston* (1981) 73 Cr App R 164) but it can amount to indecent assault (**see para. 10.10**). Wives are now protected by the offence of rape since the case of *R* v *R* [1992] 1 AC 599, where the House of Lords made it clear that a husband can be convicted of raping his wife even if he is still living with her and has not begun separation or divorce proceedings. In *SW* v *United Kingdom* (1995) 21 EHRR 363, a defendant tried to argue that this change in the common law, which had previously not extended the offence of rape to wives, amounted to a violation of Article 7 of the European Convention on Human Rights. Article 7 prohibits the imposition of punishment without a clear criminal offence being in existence at the time of the defendant's act. In the *SW* case, the Court held that the extension of the law in this area had been sufficiently foreseeable to meet the requirements of Article 7 (as to which, **see General Police Duties**).

A husband can also be guilty of assisting others to rape his wife (*R* v *Cogan* [1976] QB 217), a decision that is only really of historical relevance given the extension of the law by *R* v *R*.

The government has abandoned the idea of creating a specific offence of 'date rape'.

10.4.2 Consent

The issue of consent is a question of fact and is critical to proving the offence of rape. It is also potentially the most difficult aspect of the offence to prove. Whereas the act of intercourse or physical intimacy may be proved or corroborated by forensic evidence, the true wishes of the victim at the time of the offence are much more difficult to prove beyond a reasonable doubt. Any consent given must be 'true' consent, not simply a *submission* induced by fear or fraud. Some people however are not capable of giving the required consent. Someone who has a mental disability may be incapable of providing true consent as might someone who is too drunk to exercise rational judgment (*R* v *Lang* (1975) 62 Cr App R 50) or someone who is asleep (*R* v *Mayers* (1872) 12 Cox CC 311).

There is no requirement that the complainant demonstrate or communicate a lack of consent to the defendant and earlier cases to the contrary need not be followed (*R* v *Malone (Thomas Patrick)* [1998] 2 Cr App R 447). What is required is evidence that the victim did not consent at the time and such evidence might include (as in Malone's case) the fact that the victim was too drunk or insensible to give consent or to understand what was going on.

Even if consent is freely given, it may still be withdrawn at any time. Once the 'passive' party to sexual penetration withdraws consent, any continued penetration can amount to rape (*R* v *Cooper* [1994] Crim LR 531). 'Consent' obtained by impersonating the victim's partner or by procuration will not be true consent (see Sexual Offences Act 1956, s. 1(3) and ss. 2 and 3 (see below)). Neither will consent to sexual penetration be valid when the act itself is misrepresented (see *R* v *Williams* [1923] 1 KB 340 where a teacher told the victim that sexual intercourse was a technique to improve her singing voice). If, however, it is not the act that is misrepresented but the *intentions* or *attributes* of the person seeking consent (such as a hollow promise to marry the victim afterwards or a pretence that the victim will be paid (*Papadimitropoulos* v *The Queen* (1957) 98 CLR 249)) the consent so obtained will be valid as it amounts to a sexual consensus. Inducing another into an act of prostitution with no intent of paying will not invalidate 'consent' as to the act of sexual intercourse and therefore will not amount to rape (*R* v *Linekar* [1995] QB 250).

In *Linekar*, the Court of Appeal also considered the situation of impersonating another person in order to have sexual intercourse. In addition to the statutory provision at s. 1(3) above (impersonating the husband), Morland J held that the common law extended the offence of rape to occasions where the defendant impersonated *any* man to whom the victim was ostensibly giving consent. In the Court's view, if the victim's consent extended only to a particular individual and the person with whom she had sexual intercourse was in fact an entirely different person, the element of true consent was missing and the offence of rape would be complete. On this basis, the impersonation of any partner or lover which fools the victim into having sexual intercourse will amount to rape. In these cases it is the *identity of the person to whom consent is granted* that is disguised. This is very different from those cases where the *act of intercourse* is disguised or the later intentions of the defendant (e.g. to pay the victim).

10.4.3 State of Mind

The *mens rea* required for this offence is:

- knowledge that the other person does not consent at the time, or
- recklessness as to whether he/she consents or not.

If a defendant knows that the other person might not be consenting at the time but goes on to have intercourse anyway, that behaviour may amount to 'recklessness' (*R v S (Satnam)* (1983) 78 Cr App R 149). In a rape trial the prosecution does not have to choose whether they are proceeding on the basis of the 'knowing' or 'reckless' elements of the required *mens rea* (*R v Flitter* [2001] Crim LR 328).

The Sexual Offences (Amendment) Act 1976, s. 1 states:

> *(2)   It is hereby declared that if at a trial for a rape offence the jury has to consider whether a man believed that a woman or man was consenting to sexual intercourse, the presence or absence of reasonable grounds for such a belief is a matter to which the jury is to have regard, in conjunction with any other relevant matters, in considering whether he so believed.*

Whether a defendant *believed* that the victim was consenting is therefore a matter for a jury to decide and the presence or absence of *reasonable grounds* for such a belief will be just one relevant matter to consider in making that decision. An honestly held mistake as to the other person's consent, even if unreasonable, will prevent a conviction for rape.

If it can be shown that the defendant did not in fact believe that the other person was consenting, that absence of belief will amount to recklessness (*R v Gardiner* [1994] Crim LR 455).

Where a defendant is inebriated and, as a result, mistakenly believes that the other person is consenting to sexual intercourse, he cannot rely on that mistake as a defence (*R v Fotheringham* (1988) 88 Cr App R 206).

10.5   Procuration

Offence — Procuration — Sexual Offences Act 1956, ss. 2 and 3
Triable on indictment. Two years' imprisonment.
(*No specific power of arrest*)

The Sexual Offences Act 1956, ss. 2 and 3 state:

> *2.—(1)   It is an offence for a person to procure a woman, by threats or intimidation, to have sexual intercourse in any part of the world.*
> *3.—(1)   It is an offence for a person to procure a woman, by false pretences or false representations, to have sexual intercourse in any part of the world.*

Keynote

These offences would cover the occasions above where the victim has been conned or induced — by one of the listed conditions — into having sexual intercourse. The victim must actually have sexual intercourse — which may take place any where in the world — *as a result of* the threats, intimidation, false pretences or false representations. An example of this offence can be found in *R* v *Harold* (1984) 6 Cr App R (S) 30 where the defendant discovered that a woman who had once been a prostitute was working as an employee of a firm. The defendant threatened to tell the woman's employer of her former lifestyle unless she had sexual intercourse with him. He was convicted of an offence under s. 2(1) above.

'Procuring' means persuading the woman by whatever means to have sexual intercourse. The act of procurement is not complete until the desired outcome is achieved (*R* v *Johnson* [1964] 2 QB 404).

10.6 Prostitution

There are many offences connected with the 'profession' of prostitution. Some of these offences still involve the ancient distinction between a 'common prostitute' and others who occasionally take part in acts of lewdness for payment or reward. A 'common prostitute' is a woman who offers her body *commonly* in return for payment. In order to be a common prostitute a woman need not be merely submissive, that is she may take an active part in the relevant 'acts' which may or may not include sexual intercourse. The important feature is her apparent readiness to engage in such acts with 'all and sundry'. See *R* v *De Munck* [1918] 1 KB 635. The term does not appear to include men although there are offences which involve men selling sexual favours and premises to which men resort for homosexual activity can be 'brothels' (see below).

10.6.1 Procuring Prostitution

Offence — Procuring Prostitution — Sexual Offences Act 1956, ss. 22 and 23
Triable on indictment. Two years' imprisonment.
(*Arrestable offence*)

The Sexual Offences Act 1956, ss. 22 and 23 state:

22.—(1)   *It is an offence for a person—*
(a)   *to procure a woman to become, in any part of the world a common prostitute; or*
(b)   *to procure a woman to leave the United Kingdom, intending her to become an inmate of or frequent a brothel elsewhere; or*
(c)   *to procure a woman to leave her usual place of abode in the United Kingdom, intending her to become an inmate of or frequent a brothel in any part of the world for the purposes of prostitution.*

23.—(1)   *It is an offence for a person to procure a girl under the age of 21 to have unlawful sexual intercourse in any part of the world with a third person.*

Keynote

'Procure' has the same meaning as at **para. 10.5** above.

Given the above discussion about prostitution, any procuration under s. 22(1)(b) and (c) above need only be for indecent or lewd acts; it is not necessary for the procuration to be for full sexual intercourse. If a defendant believes that the woman concerned is already a common prostitute, he/she does not commit this offence. The expression 'unlawful' sexual intercourse means outside marriage (see *R* v *Chapman* [1959] 1 QB 100) — an expression now restricted to a small number of offences.

The above offences are made 'arrestable' by virtue of the Police and Criminal Evidence Act 1984, s. 24 (**see General Police Duties, chapter 2**).

10.6.2 Taking/Detaining a Woman

Offence — Taking/Detaining a Woman for Marriage or Unlawful Sexual Intercourse — Sexual Offences Act 1956, s. 17
Triable on indictment. Two years' imprisonment.
(**No specific power of arrest**)

The Sexual Offences Act 1956, s. 17 states:

(1) It is [an offence] for a person to take away or detain a woman against her will with the intention that she shall marry or have unlawful sexual intercourse with that or any other person, if she is so taken away or detained either by force or for the sake of her property or expectations of property.

(2) In the foregoing subsection, the reference to a woman's expectations of property relates only to property of a person to whom she is next of kin or one of the next of kin, and 'property' includes any interest in property.

Offence — Detaining a Woman Against Her Will for Unlawful Sexual Intercourse — Sexual Offences Act 1956, s. 24
Triable on indictment. Two years' imprisonment.
(**No specific power of arrest**)

The Sexual Offences Act 1956, s. 24 states:

(1) It is an offence for a person to detain a woman against her will on any premises with the intention that she shall have unlawful sexual intercourse with men or with a particular man, or to detain a woman against her will in a brothel.

(2) Where a woman is on any premises for the purpose of having unlawful sexual intercourse or is in a brothel, a person shall be deemed for the purpose of the foregoing subsection to detain her there if, with the intention of compelling or inducing her to remain there, he either withholds from her her clothes or any other property belonging to her or threatens her with legal proceedings in the event of her taking away clothes provided for her by him or on his directions.

(3) A woman shall not be liable to any legal proceedings, whether civil or criminal, for taking away or being found in possession of any clothes she needed to enable her to leave premises on which she was for the purpose of having unlawful sexual intercourse or to leave a brothel.

Keynote

The offence under s. 17 extends to taking the woman away or detaining her, while s. 24 envisages the act of detaining only. Though requiring a female victim, either offence can be committed by a man or a woman.

On many occasions, the act of taking or detaining the woman against her will may also amount to the more serious common law offences of false imprisonment and kidnapping (**see chapter 9**).

SEXUAL OFFENCES

For the meaning of 'unlawful sexual intercourse', **see para. 10.6.1**.

For similar offences where the victim is under 18 or suffering from a mental impairment, **see chapter 11**.

The provisions of the Criminal Evidence (Amendment) Act 1997 do not apply to these offences (**see Evidence and Procedure, chapter 16**).

10.6.3   Immoral Earnings

Offence — Living on Immoral Earnings — Sexual Offences Act 1956, s. 30
Triable either way. Seven years' imprisonment on indictment; six months' imprisonment and/or a fine summarily.
(*Arrestable offence*)

The Sexual Offences Act 1956, s. 30 states:

(1)   It is an offence for a man knowingly to live wholly or in part on the earnings of prostitution.
(2)   For the purposes of this section a man who lives with or is habitually in the company of a prostitute, or who exercises control, direction or influence over a prostitute's movements in a way which shows he is aiding, abetting or compelling her prostitution with others, shall be presumed to be knowingly living on the earnings of prostitution, unless he proves the contrary.

Offence — Living on Immoral Earnings — Sexual Offences Act 1967, s. 5
Triable either way. Seven years' imprisonment on indictment; six months' imprisonment and/or a fine summarily.
(*Arrestable offence*)

The Sexual Offences Act 1967, s. 5 states:

(1)   A man or woman who knowingly lives wholly or in part on the earnings of prostitution of another man shall be liable [for an offence].

Keynote

For the purposes of these offences there is no need to prove the presence of a 'common prostitute'. A single act of lewdness — such as masturbating a client in a massage parlour — would amount to 'prostitution' for this purpose. The first offence above is committed by a man living on a woman's earnings; the second offence can be committed by a man or a woman living on another man's earnings. The question of whether a defendant was living wholly or in part on such earnings can be difficult to prove. You must show a direct link between *any* money received by a defendant and the 'profession' of prostitution. There is no need to prove any joint venture (see *R v Stewart* (1986) 83 Cr App R 327) but you do need to show some form of participation by the defendant in the prostitute's business, i.e. supplying the prostitute's advertising cards and stickers (*R v Howard* (1990) 92 Cr App R 223).

The presumption in s. 30(2) of the 1956 Act will help in this regard, however it is a rebuttable one (**see Evidence and Procedure, chapter 11**).

The offences above are not committed simply by letting premises to a prostitute (*Shaw v DPP* [1962] AC 220) (however, **see para. 10.6.5**). If it can be shown that the landlord and the prostitute(s) are engaged in some form of joint venture however, the offence of living off immoral earnings by the landlord may be made out. Features such as:

- the adaptation of the premises to facilitate prostitution
- a personal relationship between the prostitute and the landlord
- the amount of rent and method of payment

may all provide evidence that establishes such a venture or enterprise.

When evidence raising the presumption at s. 30(2) has been given, the onus moves to the defendant to prove that he was not living (wholly or partly) on the earnings of prostitution.

'Exercising control, direction or influence' is a wide expression that has been held to encompass taxi drivers regularly ferrying prostitutes to clients (see *Calvert* v *Mayes* [1954] 1 QB 342).

In addition to the offence at s. 5(1) being an arrestable offence, there also appears to be a general power of arrest available to any person in respect of anyone found committing the offence (s. 5(3)).

A power of search with regard to these offences is contained in the Sexual Offences Act 1956, s. 42 which states:

> *Where it is made to appear by information on oath before a justice of the peace that there is reasonable cause to suspect that any house or part of a house is used by a woman for purposes of prostitution, and that a man residing in or frequenting the house is living wholly or in part on her earnings, the justice may issue a warrant authorising a constable to enter and search the house and to arrest the man.*

10.6.4 Woman Exercising Control over Prostitute

**Offence — Woman Exercising Control over Prostitute —
Sexual Offences Act 1956, s. 31**
Triable either way. Seven years' imprisonment on indictment; six months' imprisonment summarily.
(*Arrestable offence*)

The Sexual Offences Act 1956, s. 31 states:

> *It is an offence for a woman for purposes of gain to exercise control, direction or influence over a prostitute's movements in a way which shows she is aiding, abetting or compelling her prostitution.*

Keynote

There is no need to show that the prostitute(s) in question are 'common prostitutes'. As with the above provisions, 'control, direction or influence' can cover a wide range of activities in a descending order of seriousness. Running a telephone service that provides 'call girls' to clients can amount to this offence (*Attorney-General's Reference (No. 2 of 1995)* [1996] 3 All ER 860).

The provisions of the Criminal Evidence (Amendment) Act 1997 do not apply to this offence (**see Evidence and Procedure, chapter 16**).

10.6.5   Brothels

Offence — Keeping a Brothel — Sexual Offences Act 1956, ss. 33–36
Triable summarily. Six months' imprisonment and/or a fine.
(No specific power of arrest)

The Sexual Offences Act 1956, ss. 33–36 state:

33.   It is an offence for a person to keep a brothel, or to manage, or act or assist in the management of, a brothel.

34.   It is an offence for the lessor or landlord of any premises or his agent to let the whole or part of the premises with the knowledge that it is to be used, in whole or in part, as a brothel, or, where the whole or part of the premises is used as a brothel, to be wilfully a party to that use continuing.

35.—(1)   It is an offence for the tenant or occupier, or person in charge, of any premises knowingly to permit the whole or part of the premises to be used as a brothel.
. . .

36.   It is an offence for the tenant or occupier of any premises knowingly to permit the whole or part of the premises to be used for the purposes of habitual prostitution.

Keynote

Premises resorted to for the purposes of homosexual 'lewdness' can also be brothels (Sexual Offences Act 1967, s. 6).

Keeping premises exclusively for one's own use as a prostitute does not amount to keeping a brothel under s. 33 (*Stevens* v *Christy* (1987) 85 Cr App R 249). However, for the offence under s. 36, the use of the relevant premises by one prostitute is enough. Again, the *prostitute* does not commit this offence, but the tenant or other occupier who knowingly permits the premises (or part of them) to be used for habitual prostitution does.

The provisions of the Criminal Evidence (Amendment) Act 1997 do not apply to these offences (**see Evidence and Procedure, chapter 16**).

Offence — Keeping Disorderly House — Common Law
Triable on indictment. Unlimited sentence.
(Arrestable offence)

It is an offence at common law to keep a disorderly house.

Keynote

A brothel is a place to which people resort for the purposes of unlawful sexual intercourse with more than one prostitute. However, it is not necessary that full sexual intercourse takes place or is even offered. A massage parlour where other acts of lewdness or indecency for sexual gratification are offered may be a brothel.

Again there may be practical difficulties in proving the required level of knowledge by a defendant, particularly in the case of landlords. Under s. 36, the offence is complete if the relevant premises are used by a single prostitute for the purposes of his/her habitual prostitution.

To prove the Dickensian-sounding offence of keeping a disorderly house you must show that the house is 'open' (i.e. to customers); that it is unregulated by the restraints of morality; and that it is run in a way that violates law and good order (*R v Tan* [1983] QB 1053).

There must be 'knowledge' on the part of the defendant that a house is being so used (*Moores* v *DPP* [1992] QB 125).

The offence also requires some persistence and will not cover a single instance, e.g. of an indecent performance (*Moores* above).

The licensing of sex shops and sex cinemas is provided for by sch. 3 to the Local Government (Miscellaneous Provisions) Act 1982.

10.6.6 Soliciting

Offence — Soliciting by Common Prostitutes — Street Offences Act 1959, s. 1
Triable summarily. Fine.
(Preserved power of arrest)

The Street Offences Act 1959, s. 1 states:

> *(1)   It shall be an offence for a common prostitute to loiter or solicit in a street or public place for the purpose of prostitution.*
> *(2)   . . .*
> *(3)   A constable may arrest without warrant anyone he finds in a street or public place and suspects, with reasonable cause, to be committing an offence under this section.*
> *(4)   For the purposes of this section 'street' includes any bridge, road, lane, footway, subway, square, court, alley or passage, whether a thoroughfare or not, which is for the time being open to the public; and the doorways and entrances of premises abutting on a street (as hereinbefore defined), and any ground adjoining and open to a street, shall be treated as forming part of the street.*

Offence — Soliciting by Men 'Kerb-crawling' —
Sexual Offences Act 1985, ss. 1, 2 and 4
Triable summarily. Fine.
(No specific power of arrest)

The Sexual Offences Act 1985, ss. 1, 2 and 4 states:

> *1.—(1)   A man commits an offence if he solicits a woman (or different women) for the purpose of prostitution—*
> *(a)   from a motor vehicle while it is in a street or public place; or*
> *(b)   in a street or public place while in the immediate vicinity of a motor vehicle that he has just got out of or off,*
> *persistently or . . . in such manner or in such circumstances as to be likely to cause annoyance to the woman (or any of the women) solicited, or nuisance to other persons in the neighbourhood.*

> *2.—(1)   A man commits an offence if in a street or public place he persistently solicits a woman (or different women) for the purpose of prostitution.*

> *4.—(1)   References in this Act to a man soliciting a woman for the purpose of prostitution are references to his soliciting her for the purpose of obtaining her services as a prostitute.*

Keynote

Before a prosecution is brought under s. 1, it is usual for the prostitute to have been cautioned for that offence at least twice in the last 12 months. This procedure is different from that of cautioning of offenders generally; it only relates to offences of soliciting under s. 1 and the details of the person concerned are recorded in a register kept for that purpose at a police station. The reasoning behind this procedure appears to be to give the person in question an opportunity to 'reform'. It also addresses the cyclical effect of arrest–fine–re-offend to earn money to pay fines.

Note that, with the introduction of the 'final warning scheme' under the Crime and Disorder Act 1998 (as to which, **see Evidence and Procedure, chapter** 7) a 'prostitute's caution' can no longer be given to females under 18. For further discussion in relation to young prostitutes, **see chapter 11**.

Clearly having your name recorded in a register of 'common prostitutes' is not without some stigma. Entries in the register may be used in order to show that the woman is in fact a 'common prostitute'. Any woman who wishes to dispute the interpretation of her actions as 'soliciting' can apply to a court within 14 days of a caution being given for that caution to be expunged.

A common prostitute need not actually be in the street or public place when committing the above offence. She could be in the windows of a house or on a balcony provided her solicitations can reach a person who is in a street or public place.

The power of arrest under the Street Offences Act 1959 is preserved by s. 26 and sch. 2 of the Police and Criminal Evidence Act 1984.

The Criminal Justice and Police Act 2001 makes provision for the offence under s. 1 of the Sexual Offences Act 1985 above to become an 'arrestable offence'. At the time of writing, this part of the 2001 Act had not been brought into force.

In the case of a prosecution for kerb-crawling you must show that there was a *likelihood* of nuisance or annoyance being caused. You do not have to show that it actually *was* caused by the defendant's conduct. Whether or not such nuisance was likely to be caused to people within the neighbourhood is a question of fact, to be determined by having regard to the type of neighbourhood involved (*Paul* v *DPP* (1989) 90 Cr App R 173).

In order to prove the 'persistent' element, you will need to show that the defendant's behaviour took place on more than one occasion. This might involve recording two or more approaches by him towards the same person or separate approaches made towards more than one person.

'Street' for the purposes of kerb-crawling is the same as the definition given in the Street Offences Act 1959, s. 1(4) above. Neither statute defines 'public place'. Generally the guidance developed by the courts under other statutes (e.g. the Road Traffic Act 1988; **see Road Traffic, chapter** 1) may be used in determining whether or not a particular place meets the criteria.

If a person persistently follows another person in a way which causes the victim anxiety, the offence of harassment may apply, **see General Police Duties, chapter 3**.

Offence — Placing an Advertisement — Criminal Justice and Police Act 2001, s. 46
Triable Summarily. Six months' imprisonment and/or fine.
(*Arrestable offence*)

The Criminal Justice and Police Act 2001, s. 46 states:

> *(1)   A person commits an offence if—*
>   *(a)   he places on, or in the immediate vicinity of a public telephone, an advertisement relating to prostitution, and*
>   *(b)   he does so with the intention that the advertisement should come to the attention of any other person or persons*

Keynote

Advertising the services of a prostitute by leaving stickers or cards in telephone kiosks has been held not to amount to 'soliciting' — *Weisz* v *Monahan* [1962] 1 WLR 262. Although the publisher of the stickers could be charged with living on immoral earnings (as to which **see para. 10.6.3**), this has not been particularly helpful in relation to the people who are found placing the advert themselves. The above offence now addresses this conduct specifically and makes it an 'arrestable offence' under s. 24(2) of the Police and Criminal Evidence Act 1984 (**see General Police Duties, chapter 2**).

In proving this offence you must show that, in placing the advertisement, the defendant intended that it should come to the attention of someone else. This does not seem to be a particularly onerous requirement and will be helped by evidence of the degree of care that was taken in placing the card, sticker etc., together with its actual position. The advertisement must be for the services of a prostitute — male or female — or for premises at which such services are offered (s. 46(2)). Whether or not an advertisement 'relates to prostitution' is a question of fact. Where a reasonable person would consider that the particular advertisement was 'related to prostitution' there is a presumption that it meets the requirements of this section (s. 46(3)). This presumption is however rebuttable (as to which **see Evidence and Procedure, chapter 11**)

'Public telephone' here means any telephone which is

- located in a public place *and*
- made available for use by the public or a section of the public

and includes any kiosk, booth, acoustic hood, shelter or other structure housing or attached to the telephone — (s. 46(5)).

Given this wide definition, the offence will cover the placing of advertisements on or within the immediate vicinity of, not just the telephone itself, but also the kiosk, booth etc. Therefore, although the magistrate(s) will decide whether an act fell within the immediate vicinity as a question of fact, the offence is capable of being committed by placing advertisements on pavements or shop windows immediately adjacent to a public telephone kiosk.

Section 46(5) gives a very specific definition of 'public place' for the purposes of this offence, namely:

- any place to which the public have or are permitted to have access, (on payment or otherwise), *other than*
- a place to which children under 16 years of age are not permitted to have access (by law or otherwise), or
- premises used wholly or mainly as residential premises

This means that public areas where children under 16 are not allowed, either because they are prevented by law (e.g. licensing laws) or for some other reason (e.g. where a landowner is holding a public event and has barred children from attending), will not be caught by this legislation. This offence comes into force on 1 September 2001.

Although limited to public telephones and their coverings (as defined above), this offence can be extended by regulations to cover other public structures. At the time of writing no such regulations had been made.

Offence — Importuning by Men — Sexual Offences Act 1956, s. 32
Triable either way. Two years' imprisonment on indictment; six months' imprisonment and/or a fine summarily.
(Statutory power of arrest under certain circumstances)

The Sexual Offences Act 1956, s. 32 states:

It is an offence for a man persistently to solicit or importune in a public place for immoral purposes.

Keynote

The requirements for proving 'persistence' are the same as those for kerb-crawling above. The purpose for which the defendant is importuning (or urging others) must be 'immoral' but they need not be criminal. What is immoral will be a question of fact for the jury/magistrate(s).

Section 41 of the Act states that any person may arrest without warrant a person found committing an offence under s. 32 but that a constable may only do so in accordance with s. 25 of the Police and Criminal Evidence Act 1984 (as to which, **see General Police Duties, chapter 2**).

10.7   Incest

Offence — Incest — Sexual Offences Act 1956, ss. 10 and 11
Triable on indictment. Male with girl under 13 (life imprisonment).
(Serious arrestable offence)
Otherwise (seven years' imprisonment).
(Arrestable offence)

The Sexual Offences Act 1956, ss. 10 and 11 state:

10.—(1)   It is an offence for a man to have sexual intercourse with a woman whom he knows to be his grand-daughter, daughter, sister or mother.
(2)   In the foregoing subsection 'sister' includes half-sister, and for the purposes of that subsection any expression importing a relationship between two people shall be taken to apply notwithstanding that the relationship is not traced through lawful wedlock.

SEXUAL OFFENCES

11.—(1) It is an offence for a woman of the age of sixteen or over to permit a man whom she knows to be her grandfather, father, brother or son to have sexual intercourse with her by her consent.
(2) In the foregoing subsection 'brother' includes half-brother, and for the purposes of that subsection any expression importing a relationship between two people shall be taken to apply notwithstanding that the relationship is not traced through lawful wedlock.

Offence — Inciting Girl under Sixteen to have Incestuous Sexual Intercourse — Criminal Law Act 1977, s. 54
Triable either way. Two years' imprisonment on indictment; six months' imprisonment and/or a fine summarily.
(No specific power of arrest)

The Criminal Law Act 1977, s. 54 states:

(1) It is an offence for a man to incite to have sexual intercourse with him a girl under the age of sixteen whom he knows to be his grand-daughter, daughter or sister.
(2) In the preceding subsection 'man' includes boy, 'sister' includes half-sister, and for the purposes of that subsection any expression importing a relationship between two people shall be taken to apply notwithstanding that the relationship is not traced through lawful wedlock.

Keynote

For the above offences under the Sexual Offences Act 1956 the consent of the Director of Public Prosecutions is required before prosecution.

As incest is outlawed as much in the interests of genetics as ethics, it can only be committed by sexual intercourse. That is also the reason why the offence is restricted to granddaughters, daughters, sisters and mothers. The offence of incest can only be committed if the intercourse is with a person who the woman knows to be her grandfather, father, brother or son. This again makes the presumption that, while a *grandfather* is generally still capable of fathering more children, a *grandson* is unlikely to reach sexual maturity while his grandmother is still of child-bearing age. Although there have been some well-publicised examples of grandmothers bearing children, it was envisaged as very unlikely by the legislators.

The requirement as to 'knowledge' of the particular familial relationship means that you must prove that element of the *mens rea* in order to convict someone of incest.

Sections 1 and 2 of the Criminal Evidence (Amendment) Act 1997 extending the power to take non-intimate samples without consent apply to this offence and also to conspiracies, attempts or incitements in the circumstances set out in that Act (**see Evidence and Procedure, chapter 16**).

10.8   Buggery

Offence — Buggery — Sexual Offences Act 1956, s. 12
Triable on indictment. When committed with person under 16 or an animal (life imprisonment).
(Serious arrestable offence if person under 16)
Where the defendant is 21 or over and the other person is under 18 (five years' imprisonment).
(Arrestable offence)
Otherwise (two years' imprisonment).

The Sexual Offences Act 1956, s. 12 states:

131

(1)   It is [an offence] for a person to commit buggery with another person otherwise than in circumstances described in subsection (1A) or (1AA) below or with an animal.

(1A)   The circumstances first referred to in subsection (1) are that the act of buggery takes place in private and both parties have attained the age of sixteen.

(1AA)   The other circumstances so referred to are that the person is under the age of sixteen and the other party has attained that age.

(1B)   An act of buggery by one man with another shall not be treated as taking place in private if it takes place—

(a)   when more than two persons take part or are present; or

(b)   in a lavatory to which the public have or are permitted to have access, whether on payment or otherwise.

(1C)   In any proceedings against a person for buggery with another person it shall be for the prosecutor to prove that the act of buggery took place otherwise than in private or that one of the parties to it had not attained the age of sixteen.

Keynote

Buggery amounts to anal intercourse with a male, female or animal. It also includes anal *or vaginal* intercourse by a male or female with an animal (e.g. a sheep (see *R* v *Cozins* (1834) 6 C & P 351)).

To prove buggery you must show evidence of penetration to some degree.

The differences in age limits for lawful consensual sexual activity have been successfully challenged as a violation by the state of an individual's right to private life (Article 8 of the European Convention on Human Rights) and freedom from discrimination (Article 14 of the Convention) on several occasions. The European Commission of Human Rights has held that such age differences *did* amount to a violation of those rights (*Sutherland* v *United Kingdom* [1998] EHRLR 117). As a result, the government has introduced the Sexual Offences (Amendment) Act 2000. The legislation, some of the most controversial in recent criminal law, created considerable disagreement between the House of Commons and the House of Lords. Nevertheless, the 2000 Act received Royal Assent, reducing the minimum age at which a person, whether male or female, may lawfully consent to buggery from 18 years to 16 years (in England and Wales) as of 8 January 2001, thereby equalising the age of consent for sexual activity whether it be heterosexual or homosexual.

Despite the controversial nature of this legislation, it still fails address some of the issues raised, both by the courts (see *ADT* v *United Kingdom* [2000] Crim LR 1009) and the Home Office (see *Setting the Boundaries*, July 2000) — principally the issue of privacy. Although the 1956 Act has been amended in relation to the respective *ages* of those involved in buggery and 'gross indecency'(**see para. 10.9**), there are still restrictions on how many people might be involved at any one time in order for the relevant behaviour between men to be regarded as taking place *in private* — restrictions which do not apply to other types of heterosexual activity. In light of the judgment in *ADT* (above), it will be difficult to defend the fact that acts of buggery/gross indecency involving the participation or even the presence of more than two people are still outlawed. Arguably the imposition of the privacy requirement (see below) still amounts to an unjustifiable interference with an individual's right to respect for private life (under Article 8; **see General Police Duties, chapter 2**). Nevertheless, the effect of the new legislation is that consensual buggery between males aged 16 or over, when carried out in private, is not an offence (see the Sexual Offences Act 1967, s. 1). Although s. 12 sets out the — fairly common — occasions when such an act will be deemed not to be in private, other occasions will be a question of fact for the jury/magistrate(s) to decide in the light of all the circumstances. It is worth noting that age is only one of the matters that potentially prevent this type of sexual activity from being an offence; privacy and consent are also key elements.

Where one of the parties to an offence of buggery is under 16 years of age, that person does not commit the offence themselves. This provision reflects the view that, in cases where older men are sexually exploiting minors, it is more appropriate to regard the minors as 'victims' of the adult offender rather than criminalising the behaviour of both. If both parties are under 16, however, that element of exploitation is less likely to be present and both commit the offence.

Anyone suffering from a severe mental handicap is unable to give consent to buggery and buggery without consent amounts to rape (see above).

Other 'homosexual' acts which are carried out in private (i.e. not more than two people present or not in public lavatory) are made lawful provided they are consensual and the parties have reached the age of 16 (Sexual Offences Act 1967, s. 1). 'Homosexual' act is defined at s. 1(7) as being buggery or gross indecency *between men*. For gross indecency, **see para. 10.9**.

A mistaken belief as to the age of the other person, however reasonable, is no defence.

In any proceedings involving an offence of buggery, the burden of proving the elements of privacy, consent and age falls on the prosecution.

The consent of the Director of Public Prosecutions is required before bringing a prosecution for this offence.

Offence — Assault with Intent to Commit Buggery — Sexual Offences Act 1956, s. 16
Triable on indictment. Ten years' imprisonment.
(*Arrestable offence*)

The Sexual Offences Act 1956, s. 16 states:

It is an offence for a person to assault another person with intent to commit buggery.

Keynote

This is a crime of *specific intent* (**see chapter 1**). As buggery without consent is rape (**see para. 10.4**), there may be an offence of attempted rape in such circumstances, provided the defendant's actions go beyond mere preparation to commit the substantive offence. (For criminal attempts generally, **see chapter 3**.)

Offence — Procuring Another to Commit Buggery — Sexual Offences Act 1967, s. 4
Triable on indictment. Two years' imprisonment.
(*No specific power of arrest*)

The Sexual Offences Act 1967, s. 4 states:

(1)   A man who procures another man to commit with a third man an act of buggery which by reason of section 1 of this Act is not an offence shall be liable [for an offence].

Keynote

Under s. 4(1) the procuration of a man to commit buggery with a third man will amount to an offence even though the intended act of buggery itself is not an offence. This is in contrast with the situation where gross indecency is involved (see below).

10.9 Gross Indecency

Offence — Gross Indecency — Sexual Offences Act 1956, s. 13
Triable either way. If defendant is 21 or over and other person is under 16
(five years' imprisonment).
(Arrestable offence)
Otherwise (two years' imprisonment) on indictment; six months' imprisonment
and/or fine summarily.

The Sexual Offences Act 1956, s. 13 states:

It is an offence for a man to commit an act of gross indecency with another man, otherwise than in the circumstances described below, whether in public or private, or to be a party to the commission by a man of an act of gross indecency with another man, or to procure the commission by a man of an act of gross indecency with another man.

The circumstances referred to above are that the man is under the age of sixteen and the other man has attained that age.

Keynote

There is no need to prove actual physical contact in making out this offence.

It is not an offence for men aged 16 or more to engage in acts of gross indecency in private (Sexual Offences Act 1967, s. 1). This age limit was reduced from 18 years by the Sexual Offences (Amendment) Act 2000 (**see para. 10.8**).

As with the offence of buggery (above) the person who is under 16 years of age does not commit the offence themselves (**see para. 10.8**).

In bringing charges under the above section the burden of proving that the act was not in 'private', was not consensual or that a party was under 16 years of age will still rest with the prosecution (Sexual Offences Act 1967, s. 1(6)). 'In private' has the same meaning as the expression under s. 12(1A) and (1B) of the 1956 Act (i.e. no more than two people present and not in a public lavatory). For the potential incompatability of this requirement with the European Convention on Human Rights, **see para. 10.8**.

Whether an act is grossly indecent is a question of fact for the jury/magistrate(s) to determine in each case. If a person carries out an indecent assault (**see para. 10.10**) which amounts to gross indecency, the offence is classed as a 'serious arrestable offence', **see General Police Duties, chapter 2**.

The consent of the Director of Public Prosecutions is required before bringing a prosecution for this offence.

(For further offences against children, including the new offence of 'abuse of a position of trust', **see chapter 11**.)

The Sexual Offences Act 1967, s. 4(3) states:

> *It shall not be an offence under section 13 of the [Sexual Offences Act 1956] for a man to procure the commission by another man of an act of gross indecency with the first-mentioned man which by reason of section 1 of this Act is not an offence under the said section 13.*

Keynote

This means it is not an offence for one man to procure another man to commit an act of gross indecency under the circumstances outlined above (i.e. both are 16 years or more and acting in private). This age was reduced from 18 years to 16 years by the Sexual Offences (Amendment) Act 2000.

10.10   Indecent Assault

Offence — Indecent Assault — Sexual Offences Act 1956, ss. 14 and 15
Triable either way. Ten years' imprisonment on indictment; six months' imprisonment and/or fine summarily.
(Serious arrestable offence where act involves gross indecency; otherwise arrestable offence)

The Sexual Offences Act 1956, ss. 14 and 15 state:

> *14.—(1)   It is an offence, . . . for a person to make an indecent assault on a woman.*
> *(2)   A girl under the age of sixteen cannot in law give any consent which would prevent an act being an assault for the purposes of this section.*
>
> *15.—(1)   It is an offence for a person to make an indecent assault on a man.*
> *(2)   A boy under the age of sixteen cannot in law give any consent which would prevent an act being an assault for the purposes of this section.*

Keynote

Indecent assault is simply an assault committed in circumstances of indecency. For there to be an indecent assault there must be an *assault* (**see chapter 8**). In the well-known case of *Fairclough* v *Whipp* [1951] 2 All ER 834 the defendant invited a child to touch his penis. The court held that there was no assault (however, see the Indecency with Children Act 1960 (**chapter 11**)). However, in keeping with the elements required for an assault, it is not essential that there be an actual *battery*. There need not be any indecent *touching* of the victim — or even a threat of indecent touching (*R* v *Sargeant* (1997) 161 JP 127).

What must be shown is that the defendant committed an assault — as discussed at **chapter 8** — under circumstances of indecency.

The assault or the accompanying circumstances must be capable of being regarded as indecent, that is, they must contravene ordinary standards of decency. Words may make an assault 'indecent' but the test remains an objective one and the secret thoughts or perverted intentions of a defendant cannot make an otherwise innocuous act 'indecent' (like a sales assistant gaining gratification from removing a customer's shoe in a shoe shop). However, if the act is inherently indecent (like spanking someone's buttocks), you do not need to show that a victim actually appreciated the 'indecent' nature of the assault (*R* v *Court* [1989] AC 28). This was reiterated by the Court of Appeal in a recent case where the defendant induced three female victims to take part in a survey of breast cancer. Believing the defendant to be medically qualified, the victims allowed him to examine their breasts. The Court held that there had been no true consent to the touching of the women's breasts. As the touching was overtly indecent, the only issue was that of consent and consequently the defendant's appeal was dismissed (*R* v *Tabassum* [2000] Crim LR 686). These features have caused some practical difficulties in cases involving sado-masochism (see *R* v *Brown* [1994] 1 AC 212). The legal and moral arguments which have raged over the extent to which the law should regulate the sexual conduct of consenting adults have occupied the courts for some considerable time but the general principles are discussed in **chapter 8**.

Where a child is involved — as in some sensationalised cases of schoolchildren 'eloping' with adults — there may be an indecent assault even though the victim 'consents'.

In *Crown Prosecution Service* v *K*, *The Times*, 7 November 2000, the Court of Appeal held that a genuine belief by a defendant that a girl was over 16 years of age did not provide a defence to a charge of indecent assault on a girl under that age under s. 14(1) of the Sexual Offences Act 1956. This decision means that the issue of age in relation to the s. 14 offence is one of strict liability. This is a curious situation, given that defendants *can* claim an honest belief as to the age of a child as a defence in relation to the offence under s. 1(1) of the Indecency with Children Act 1960 (as to which, **see para. 11.4.6**). Arguments in the case of *K* that this statutory effect was incompatible with his rights under Article 6 of the European Convention on Human Rights were not upheld.

10.11   Administering Drugs for Unlawful Sexual Intercourse

Offence — Administering Drugs for Unlawful Sexual Intercourse with a Woman — Sexual Offences Act 1956, s. 4
Triable on indictment. Two years' imprisonment.
(No specific power of arrest)

The Sexual Offences Act 1956, s. 4 states:

(1)   It is an offence for a person to apply or administer to, or cause to be taken by, a woman any drug, matter or thing with intent to stupefy or overpower her so as thereby to enable any man to have unlawful sexual intercourse with her.

Keynote

This is a crime of *specific intent* (**see chapter 1**), which is particularly relevant if the defendant claims to have been intoxicated in some way at the time. There is nothing to exclude alcohol from the provisions of this offence. If sexual intercourse takes place while the woman is so overpowered or stupefied there will almost certainly be a further *prima facie* offence of rape (**see para. 10.4**). The use of the so-called 'date-rape' drugs has increased significantly over recent years. For details of the substances currently being sold/used for such purposes, the advice of the National Criminal Intelligence Service should be sought.

For the offence of poisoning, **see chapter 9**.

For the meaning of 'unlawful sexual intercourse', **see para. 10.6.1**.

10.12   Indecent Exposure

Although it is often trivialised, the behaviour of those who indecently expose themselves in public is both distressing and often symptomatic of a psychological disorder which can manifest itself in other, far more destructive ways.

Offence — Outraging Public Decency — Common Law
Triable on indictment. Unlimited powers of sentence.
(Arrestable offence)

It is an offence at common law to commit an act of a lewd, obscene or disgusting nature and outrage public decency.

Keynote

This offence is committed by the deliberate commission of an act that is, *per se*, lewd, obscene or disgusting (*R v Rowley* [1991] 4 All ER 649). If an act is not lewd, obscene etc. then the motives or intentions of the defendant cannot make it so. Therefore, where the defendant's acts involved leaving messages that were not in themselves obscene in public toilets, his motives (to induce young boys to engage in gross indecency with him) did not bring his actions under this offence (*Rowley* above). In *Rowley* the court cited a speech by Lord Simon in *Knuller (Publishing, Printing and Promotions) Ltd v DPP* [1973] AC 435. Lord Simon had said that 'outraging public decency' goes considerably beyond offending the sensibilities of, or even shocking, reasonable people and that the recognised minimum standards of decency were likely to vary from time to time.

The offence can be committed by exposing the penis or engaging in simulated sexual acts (*R v Mayling* [1963] 3 QB 717) but it may also be committed in other ways and is not restricted to offences committed by men.

The act must be committed where it might be seen by the public generally and it must be shown that more than one person could have seen the act take place (*R v Walker* [1996] 1 Cr App R 111). For this purpose the general public *will include police officers* trying to detect offences (see the Town Police Clauses Act 1847 below).

It is not necessary to prove that someone was *in fact* annoyed or insulted (*R v May* (1989) 91 Cr App R 157).

This common law offence is punishable with imprisonment 'at large', i.e. there is no limit on the term of imprisonment that a court may pass. For this reason it is an offence for which a person aged 21 years or over (who has not been previously convicted) can be sentenced to five years' imprisonment or more — making it an 'arrestable offence' (**see General Police Duties, chapter 2**).

Offence — Indecent Exposure — Vagrancy Act 1824, s. 4
Triable summarily. Three months' imprisonment and/or a fine.
(Statutory power of arrest)

The Vagrancy Act 1824, s. 4 states:

> *It is an offence . . . [for any] person wilfully, openly, lewdly and obscenely to expose his person, . . . with intent to insult any female . . .*

Keynote

Here it must be proved that the defendant exposed his penis; the fact that it was erect may go towards proving that his conduct was both 'wilful' and intended to insult (in this case a female). There must be proof that the person exposed his penis for this offence; no other part of the body will suffice (*Evans* v *Ewels* [1972] 2 All ER 22). There is no requirement that this offence be committed in public (*Ford* v *Falcone* [1971] 2 All ER 1138).

Although it had been thought that the general power of arrest provided by s. 6 was limited to people *other* than police officers, the Court of Appeal has made it clear that the power does apply to police officers and that it has been unaffected by the Police and Criminal Evidence Act 1984, ss. 24 and 26 (*Gapper* v *Chief Constable of Avon and Somerset* [1998] 4 All ER 248). The power under s. 6 allows 'any person whatsoever' to apprehend and take before a justice or deliver to a constable, any person found committing an offence against the Act.

Offence — Indecent Exposure — Town Police Clauses Act 1847, s. 28
Triable summarily. Three months' imprisonment and/or a fine.
(No specific power of arrest)

The Town Police Clauses Act 1847, s. 28 states:

> *Every person who in any street, to the obstruction, annoyance, or danger of the residents or passengers . . . wilfully and indecently exposes his person . . . [commits an offence].*

Keynote

The Town Police Clauses Act 1847 does not apply in the Metropolitan Police District.

The basic elements are the same as under the Vagrancy Act 1824 except that there is no need to prove an intent to insult a female and it cannot be committed in private. 'Passengers' includes foot-passengers (pedestrians) but it *will not include police officers* who are in a public lavatory *for the purposes of detecting offences* (*Cheeseman* v *DPP* [1991] 2 WLR 1105).

CHAPTER ELEVEN

OFFENCES AGAINST CHILDREN AND OTHER VULNERABLE PEOPLE

11.1 Introduction

Although many of the offences in this chapter could also be grouped under their respective headings elsewhere, they have been put into a separate chapter to reflect the significance of the victims — children and other vulnerable groups such as those suffering from a mental disability. Although this chapter sets out the substantive offences, the manner and level of proof required in bringing such cases to trial is dealt with in **Evidence and Procedure**.

11.2 Child Abduction

There are two offences of abducting children, one which applies to people 'connected with the child' and the second by others.

11.2.1 Person Connected with Child

**Offence — Child Abduction — Person Connected with Child —
Child Abduction Act 1984, s. 1**
Triable either way. Seven years' imprisonment on indictment; six months' imprisonment and/or a fine summarily.
(**Arrestable offence**)

The Child Abduction Act 1984, s. 1 states:

(1) Subject to subsections (5) and (8) below, a person connected with a child under the age of 16 commits an offence if he takes or sends the child out of the United Kingdom without the appropriate consent.

OFFENCES AGAINST CHILDREN AND OTHER VULNERABLE PEOPLE

'Connected with a Child'

The Child Abduction Act 1984, s. 1 states:

> (2)   A person is connected with the child for the purposes of this section if—
>   (a)   he is a parent of a child; or
>   (b)   in the case of a child whose parents were not married to each other at the time of his birth, there are reasonable grounds for believing that he is the father of the child; or
>   (c)   he is a guardian of the child; or
>   (d)   he is a person in whose favour a residence order is in force with respect to the child; or
>   (e)   he has custody of the child.

'Appropriate Consent'

The Child Abduction Act 1984, s. 1 states:

> (3)   In this section 'the appropriate consent' in relation to a child, means—
>   (a)   the consent of each of the following—
>   (i)   the child's mother;
>   (ii)   the child's father, if he has parental responsibility for him;
>   (iii)   any guardian of the child;
>   (iv)   any person in whose favour a residence order is in force with respect to the child;
>   (v)   any person who has custody of the child; or
>   (b)   the leave of the court granted under or by virtue of any provision of Part II of the Children Act 1989; or
>   (c)   if any person has custody of the child, the leave of the court which awarded custody to him.

Keynote

This offence can only be committed by those people listed in s. 1(2). To be guilty they must take or send the child out of the United Kingdom. The taking or sending must be shown to have been done without the consent of *each* of those persons listed in s. 1(3)(a) above.

Defence

The Child Abduction Act 1984, s. 1 states:

> (4)   A person does not commit an offence under this section by taking or sending a child out of the United Kingdom without obtaining the appropriate consent if—
>   (a)   he is a person in whose favour there is a residence order in force with respect to the child, and
>   (b)   he takes or sends him out of the United Kingdom for a period of less than one month.
> (4A)   Subsection (4) above does not apply if the person taking or sending the child out of the United Kingdom does so in breach of an order under Part II of the Children Act 1989.
> (5)   A person does not commit an offence under this section by doing anything without the consent of another person whose consent is required under the foregoing provisions if—
>   (a)   he does it in the belief that the other person—
>   (i)   has consented; or
>   (ii)   would consent if he was aware of all the relevant circumstances; or
>   (b)   he has taken all reasonable steps to communicate with the other person but has been unable to communicate with him; or
>   (c)   the other person has unreasonably refused to consent.

140

Keynote

Note the specific defence (at s. 1(5)) — if the defendant believes that the appropriate person has consented or would have consented had they known of the circumstances.

A further provision (s. 1(5A)) states that s. 1(5)(c) will not apply if the person who refused to consent is a person:

- in whose favour there is a residence order in force with respect to the child; or

- who has custody of the child; or

- is, by taking or sending the child out of the United Kingdom, acting in breach of a court order in the United Kingdom.

The consent of the Director of Public Prosecutions is needed before a charge of child abduction is brought under this section (s. 4(2)).

11.2.2 Person Not Connected with Child

Offence — Child Abduction — Person Not Connected with Child — Child Abduction Act 1984, s. 2

Triable either way. Seven years' imprisonment on indictment; six months' imprisonment and/or a fine summarily.
(*Arrestable offence*)

The Child Abduction Act 1984, s. 2 states:

(1) Subject to subsection (3) below, a person other than one mentioned in subsection (2) below, commits an offence if, without lawful authority or reasonable excuse, he takes or detains a child under the age of 16—
(a) so as to remove him from the lawful control of any person having lawful control of the child: or
(b) so as to keep him out of the lawful control of any person entitled to lawful control of the child.
(2) The persons are—
(a) where the father and mother of the child in question were married to each other at the time of his birth, the child's father and mother;
(b) where the father and mother of the child in question were not married to each other at the time of his birth, the child's mother; and
(c) any other person mentioned in section 1(2)(c) to (e) above.

Keynote

This offence requires the taking or detaining of a child under 16 years. This will include keeping a child in the place where he/she is found and inducing the child to remain with the defendant or another person. You must show that the defendant acted without lawful authority or reasonable excuse. Unlike kidnapping, the consent of the victim is irrelevant. Proving the absence of reasonable excuse could be difficult. Clearly a defendant could argue, particularly in the case of a very young child, that he/she was acting in the child's best interests, a claim which might be difficult to refute.

Sections 1 and 2 of the Criminal Evidence (Amendment) Act 1997 extending the power to take non-intimate samples without consent apply to this offence and also to conspiracies, attempts or incitements in the circumstances set out in that Act (**see Evidence and Procedure, chapter 16**).

Defence

The Child Abduction Act 1984, s. 2 states:

> (3) . . . it shall be a defence for [the defendant] to prove—
>   (a) where the father and mother of the child in question were not married to each other at the time of his birth—
>   (i) that he is the child's father; or
>   (ii) that, at the time of the alleged offence, he believed, on reasonable grounds, that he was the child's father; or
>   (b) that, at the time of the alleged offence, he believed that the child had attained the age of 16.

Keynote

Section 2(3)(b) provides a defence if the accused can show that he/she believed the child to be 16 or over. Given the appearance, dress and behaviour of children in their early teens, this defence may not be too difficult to establish in many cases. This should be contrasted with some sexual offences involving children (see below).

11.3 Child Cruelty

Offence — Child Cruelty — Children and Young Persons Act 1933, s. 1
Triable either way. Ten years' imprisonment on indictment, six months' imprisonment and/or a fine summarily.
(Arrestable offence)

The Children and Young Persons Act 1933, s. 1 states:

> (1) If any person who has attained the age of 16 years and has responsibility for any child or young person under that age, wilfully assaults, ill-treats, neglects, abandons, or exposes him, or causes or procures him to be assaulted, ill-treated, neglected, abandoned, or exposed, in a manner likely to cause him unnecessary suffering or injury to health (including injury to or loss of sight, or hearing, or limb or organ of the body, and any mental derangement), that person shall be guilty of [an offence] . . .

Keynote

This offence applies to any person of 16 years or more who is responsible for someone under 16 years. In determining the age of either the defendant or the victim the courts will have regard to the provisions of s. 99 of the 1933 Act which allows a presumption of age to be made by the court in the absence of proof to the contrary.

A person who has parental responsibility for a child or any other legal liability to maintain him/her will be presumed to have 'responsibility' for that child even if the person does not have care of him/her (s. 17(1)(a)). Carers such as baby-sitters may be deemed to have 'responsibility' for a child in their care (s. 17(1)(b)).

This offence can be committed either by acts or omission and there is no need to show any resulting harm to the victim.

Sections 1 and 2 of the Criminal Evidence (Amendment) Act 1997 also apply to this offence (and to conspiracies, attempts or incitements in the circumstances set out in that Act) (**see Evidence and Procedure, chapter 16**).

The Children and Young Persons Act 1933, s. 1 states:

> *(2)   For the purposes of this section—*
>
> *(a)   a parent or other person legally liable to maintain a child or young person or the legal guardian of a child or young person shall be deemed to have neglected him in a manner likely to cause injury to his health if he has failed to provide adequate food, clothing, medical aid or lodging for him, or if, having been unable otherwise to provide such food, clothing, medical aid or lodging, he has failed to take steps to procure it to be provided under the enactment applicable in that behalf . . .*

Keynote

Failing to get adequate medical treatment or to get help from the relevant agencies in securing food and clothing may amount to an offence under this section.

It is unclear whether 'wilful' in this context includes objective recklessness (**see chapter 1**), or whether the defendant must have given some thought to the relevant risk of injury or harm to the child. This element is particularly important where parents or those responsible for a child are of low intelligence and unable to appreciate the possible consequences of their actions or, more often, their *inaction*. In cases of doubt, the advice of the Crown Prosecution Service should be sought.

11.4   Sexual Offences Against Children

11.4.1   Intercourse with Girl under 13

Offence — Unlawful Sexual Intercourse with Girl under 13 —
Sexual Offences Act 1956, s. 5
Triable on indictment. Life imprisonment.
(***Serious arrestable offence***)

The Sexual Offences Act 1956, s. 5 states:

> *It is [an offence] for a man to have unlawful sexual intercourse with a girl under the age of 13.*

11.4.2   Intercourse with Girl under 16

Offence — Sexual Intercourse with Girl under 16 —
Sexual Offences Act 1956, s. 6
Triable either way. Two years' imprisonment on indictment; six months' imprisonment and/or a fine summarily.
(***No specific power of arrest***)

The Sexual Offences Act 1956, s. 6 states:

> *(1)   It is an offence, subject to the exceptions mentioned in this section, for a man to have unlawful sexual intercourse with a girl under the age of 16.*
>
> *(2)   Where a marriage is invalid under section two of the Marriage Act 1949 or section one of the Age of Marriage Act 1929 (the wife being a girl under the age of 16), the invalidity does not make the husband guilty of an offence under this section because he has sexual intercourse with her, if he believes her to be his wife and has reasonable cause for the belief.*
>
> *(3)   A man is not guilty of an offence under this section because he has unlawful sexual intercourse with a girl under the age of 16, if he is under the age of 24 and has not previously been charged with a like offence, and he believes her to be of the age of 16 or over and has reasonable cause for the belief. In this subsection, 'a like offence' means an offence under this section or an attempt to commit one . . .*

143

Keynote

This offence is generally referred to as 'USI' (unlawful sexual intercourse). An offence of having unlawful sexual intercourse with a girl under 16 must be prosecuted within 12 months of the act complained of. Both offences under ss. 5 and 6 are ones of strict liability as to age at the time of intercourse. That element can be proved by documentation or the evidence of a parent. (For the meaning of 'unlawful sexual intercourse', **see chapter 10**.) Note the defence under s. 6(3) above only applies to a person under the age of 24 who has unlawful sexual intercourse with a girl who is at least 13 but under 16.

See also **chapter 10** for the offence of inciting a girl under 16 to have incestuous sexual intercourse.

The Sexual Offences (Amendment) Act 2000 introduces a new offence for a person of 18 years or more abusing a position of trust towards a person under 18 years of age (**see para. 11.4.9**).

11.4.3   **Permitting Girls to Use Premises**

Offence — Permitting Girls to Use Premises — Sexual Offences Act 1956, s. 25
Triable on indictment. Life imprisonment.
(*Arrestable offence*)

The Sexual Offences Act 1956, s. 25 states:

It is [an offence] for a person who is the owner or occupier of any premises, or who has, or acts or assists in, the management or control of any premises, to induce or knowingly suffer a girl under the age of thirteen to resort to or be on those premises for the purpose of having unlawful sexual intercourse with men or with a particular man.

Offence — Permitting Girls to Use Premises — Sexual Offences Act 1956, s. 26
Triable either way. Two years' imprisonment on indictment; six months' imprisonment and/or a fine summarily.
(*No specific power of arrest*)

The Sexual Offences Act 1956, s. 26 states:

It is an offence for a person who is the owner or occupier of any premises, or who has, or acts or assists in, the management or control of any premises, to induce or knowingly suffer a girl . . . under the age of sixteen, to resort to or be on those premises for the purpose of having unlawful sexual intercourse with men or with a particular man.

Keynote

For the meaning of 'unlawful sexual intercourse', **see chapter 10**.

In order to prove the above offences under ss. 25 and 26 you must show that the defendant knew that the girls were on the premises for the purpose of having unlawful sexual intercourse.

It is also a summary offence to allow a child aged four years of more but under 16 to reside in or to frequent a brothel (Children and Young Persons Act 1933, s. 3).

144

11.4.4   Causing or Encouraging Prostitution with or Intercourse or Indecent Assault on Girl under 16

Offence — Causing or Encouraging of, Intercourse with, or Indecent Assault on, Girl under 16 — Sexual Offences Act 1956, s. 28
Triable on indictment. Two years' imprisonment.
(*No specific power of arrest*)

The Sexual Offences Act 1956, s. 28 states:

(1)   It is an offence for a person to cause or encourage the prostitution of, or the commission of unlawful sexual intercourse with, or of an indecent assault on, a girl under the age of 16 for whom he is responsible.

(2)   Where a girl has become a prostitute, or has had unlawful sexual intercourse, or has been indecently assaulted, a person shall be deemed for the purposes of this section to have caused or encouraged it, if he knowingly allowed her to consort with, or to enter or continue in the employment of, any prostitute or person of known immoral character.

(3)   The persons who are to be treated for the purposes of this section as responsible for a girl are (subject to subsection (4) of this section)—

(a)   her parents;

(b)   any person who is not a parent of hers but who has parental responsibility for her; and

(c)   any person who has care of her.

(4)   An individual falling within subsection 3(a) or (b) of this section is not to be treated as responsible for a girl if—

(a)   a residence order under the Children Act 1989 is in force with respect to her and he is not named in the order as the person with whom she is to live; or

(b)   a care order under that Act is in force with respect to her.

(5)   If, on a charge of an offence against a girl under this section, the girl appears to the court to have been under the age of 16 at the time of the offence charged, she shall be presumed for the purposes of this section to have been so, unless the contrary is proved.

Keynote

This offence is not limited to prostitution, but also includes the condoning of an indecent assault. It applies to people who 'are responsible' for girls under 16 which will include parents, guardians and anyone into whose charge a child has been given. Giving a girl under 16 alcohol in the knowledge that it will allow someone else to commit an indecent assault on them amounts to this offence (*R* v *Drury* (1974) 60 Cr App R 195). It would also amount to aiding and abetting an indecent assault (**see chapters 2 and 10**).

Home Office/Department of Health guidance (Home Office Circular 20/2000: Children Involved in Prostitution) points out that males and females under 18 years of age who are involved in prostitution are primarily victims of abuse. As such they ought to be diverted from the abusive activity rather than prosecuted. In exceptional circumstances, the guidance suggests, a prosecution might be appropriate and, where the offence is admitted, the 'final warning scheme' may be used (**see Evidence and Procedure, chapter 7**).

If a person responsible for a girl under 16 is present and is effectively controlling the situation (i.e. they could intervene to prevent the indecent assault), failing to act may amount to this offence (*R* v *Ralphs* (1913) 9 Cr App R 86). For the meaning of 'unlawful sexual intercourse', **see chapter 10**.

11.4.5   Taking out of Possession

Offence — Taking Unmarried Girl under 18 out of Possession of Parent/Guardian for Unlawful Sexual Intercourse — Sexual Offences Act 1956, s. 19
Triable on indictment. Two years' imprisonment.
(No specific power of arrest)

The Sexual Offences Act 1956, s. 19 states:

(1)   It is an offence, subject to the exception mentioned in this section, for a person to take an unmarried girl under the age of 18 out of the possession of her parent or guardian against his will, if she is so taken with the intention that she shall have unlawful sexual intercourse with men or with a particular man.

(2)   A person is not guilty of an offence under this section because he takes such a girl out of the possession of her parent or guardian as mentioned above, if he believes her to be of the age of 18 or over and has reasonable cause for the belief.

(3)   In this section 'guardian' means any person having parental responsibility for or care of the girl.

Offence — Taking Unmarried Girl under 16 out of Possession of Parent/Guardian — Sexual Offences Act 1956, s. 20
Triable on indictment. Two years' imprisonment.
(No specific power of arrest)

The Sexual Offences Act 1956, s. 20 states:

(1)   It is an offence for a person acting without lawful authority or excuse to take an unmarried girl under the age of 16 out of the possession of her parent or guardian against his will.

(2)   In the foregoing subsection 'guardian' means any person having parental responsibility for or care of the girl.

Keynote

It must be shown that the victim in these cases was still 'in the possession' of her parent/guardian. This is an archaic expression but generally requires that the girl is not living a life independent of her parent/guardian. It must also be shown that there was an element of 'taking', i.e. persuading or helping the girl to leave home or to stay away. The offences can only be committed in respect of a girl but can be committed by a man or a woman. Although there is no specific statutory power of arrest attached to these offences, the arrestable offences of false imprisonment and kidnapping may apply in some cases (**see chapter 9**).

For the offence under s. 19 it is not necessary to show that unlawful sexual intercourse actually took place but it must be the intention of the person/people taking the victim that she was to have unlawful sexual intercourse at some point with men or a particular man. Taking a girl in order that she marry a man will not fall under this section (but it may come under s. 17; **see para. 10.6.2**).

For a similar offence where the victim is suffering from a mental impairment, **see para. 11.5.2**.

The defence available under s. 19(2) requires both a belief by the defendant that the victim was 18 or over *and* reasonable cause for that belief. The burden of proof in this case will lie upon the defendant (s. 47).

Although appearing in the Sexual Offences Act 1956, the offence under s. 20 says nothing about any sexual motive and provides no specific defence. The person must, however, be shown to have acted without lawful authority (e.g. under the Children Act 1989; **see para. 11.4.11**) or excuse (e.g. in order to protect the child's life in an emergency).

11.4.6   Indecency with Children

Offence — Indecency with Children — Indecency with Children Act 1960, s. 1
Triable either way. Ten years' imprisonment on indictment; six months' imprisonment and/or a fine summarily.
(*Arrestable offence*)

The Indecency with Children Act 1960, s. 1 states:

> *(1)   Any person who commits an act of gross indecency with or towards a child under the age of 16, or who incites a child under that age to such an act with him or another, shall [commit an offence]*
> . . .
> *(2)   . . .*
> *(3)   References in the Children and Young Persons Act 1933, to the offences mentioned in the first schedule to that Act shall include offences under this section.*

Keynote

This offence was enacted to deal with occasions where no contact is actually made with the child or where the defendant is passive. It can be committed by masturbating in the presence of children (provided the defendant knows that the children are aware of what is going on (*R* v *Francis* (1988) 88 Cr App R 127) and also by inviting children to touch one's genitals (*R* v *Speck* [1977] 2 All ER 859).

There will be occasions where the distinction between this offence and the more general one of indecent assault is difficult to make (see *R* v *Sargeant* (1997) 161 JP 127 and **chapter 10**).

Following the House of Lords' decision in *B (A Minor)* v *DPP* [2000] 2 WLR 452), an honest belief that the child concerned is 16 will now amount to a defence to a charge under s. 1(1). This decision reverses earlier decisions of the Divisional Court.

Leaving notes in a public lavatory trying to encourage young boys to get in touch with the defendant was held not to amount to an attempt at committing the above offence, even though the defendant's ultimate motive in meeting the boys was to commit acts of gross indecency with them (*R* v *Rowley* [1991] 4 All ER 649).

Sections 1 and 2 of the Criminal Evidence (Amendment) Act 1997 also apply to this offence (and to conspiracies, attempts or incitements in the circumstances set out in that Act) **(see Evidence and Procedure, chapter 16)**.

Where a person is charged with this offence, the Youth Justice and Criminal Evidence Act 1999 imposes certain restrictions on the introduction of evidence or the asking of questions relating to the victim's sexual behaviour **(see Evidence and Procedure, chapter 6)**.

11.4.7 Indecent Photographs

Offence — Indecent Photographs — Protection of Children Act 1978, s. 1
Triable either way. Ten years' imprisonment on indictment; six months' imprisonment and/or a fine summarily.
(*Serious arrestable offence*)

The Protection of Children Act 1978, s. 1 states:

> (1)   It is an offence for a person—
> (a)   to take, or permit to be taken or to make, any indecent photograph or pseudo-photograph of a child . . .; or
> (b)   to distribute or show such indecent photographs or pseudo-photographs; or
> (c)   to have in his possession such indecent photographs or pseudo-photographs, with a view to their being distributed or shown by himself or others; or
> (d)   to publish or cause to be published any advertisement likely to be understood as conveying that the advertiser distributes or shows such indecent photographs or pseudo-photographs, or intends to do so.
> (2)   For purposes of this Act, a person is to be regarded as distributing an indecent photograph or pseudo-photograph if he parts with possession of it to, or exposes or offers it for acquisition by, another person.
> (3)   . . .
> (4)   Where a person is charged with an offence under subsection (1)(b) or (c), it shall be a defence for him to prove—
> (a)   that he had a legitimate reason for distributing or showing the photographs or pseudo-photographs or (as the case may be) having them in his possession; or
> (b)   that he had not himself seen the photographs or pseudo-photographs and did not know, nor had any cause to suspect, them to be indecent.
> (5)   References in the Children and Young Persons Act 1933 (except in sections 15 and 99) to the offences mentioned in Schedule 1 to that Act shall include an offence under subsection (1)(a) above.

Offence — Indecent Photographs — Criminal Justice Act 1988, s. 160
Triable either way. Five years' imprisonment on indictment; six months' imprisonment and/or a fine.
(*Arrestable offence*)

The Criminal Justice Act 1988, s. 160 states:

> (1)   It is an offence for a person to have any indecent photograph or pseudo-photograph of a child in his possession.
> (2)   Where a person is charged with an offence under subsection (1) above, it shall be a defence for him to prove—
> (a)   that he had a legitimate reason for having the photograph or pseudo-photograph in his possession; or
> (b)   that he had not himself seen the photograph or pseudo-photograph and did not know, nor had any cause to suspect, it to be indecent; or
> (c)   that the photograph or pseudo-photograph was sent to him without any prior request made by him or on his behalf and that he did not keep it for an unreasonable time.

Keynote

Once the defendant realises, *or should realise*, that material is indecent, any distribution, showing or retention of the material with a view to its being distributed will probably result in an offence under the 1978 Act if the person depicted turns out to be a child (*R v Land* [1999] QB 65). This is because s. 160(4) provides no defence of mistake as to a child's age.

The Criminal Justice Act 1988 makes it an offence simply to possess an indecent photograph of a child.

A person will be a 'child' for the purposes of both Acts above if it appears from the evidence as a whole that he/she was, at the material time, under the age of 16 (Protection of Children Act 1978, s. 2(3) and Criminal Justice Act 1988, s. 160(4)).

However, if the impression conveyed by a pseudo-photograph is that the person shown is a child or where the predominant impression is that the person is a child, that pseudo-photograph will be treated for these purposes as a photograph of a child, notwithstanding that some of the physical characteristics shown are those of an adult (s. 7(8) of the 1978 Act).

'Pseudo-photographs' include computer images and the above offences will cover the situation where part of the photograph is made up of an adult form. These recent amendments to the legislation are designed to tackle the proliferation of child pornography on the Internet and other computer programs. Downloading images from the Internet will amount to 'making' a photograph for the purposes of s. 1(1)(a) of the 1978 Act (*R* v *Bowden* [2000] 2 WLR 1083). However, if the computer automatically stores the images in its temporary memory while the user browses images on the Internet, he/she cannot be said to have 'made' those images for the purposes of s. 1(1)(a) of the 1978 Act above (*Atkins* v *DPP* [2000] 2 All ER 425). Nevertheless, evidence indicating an interest in paedophile material generally can be relevant to show that it was more likely than not that a file containing an indecent image of a child *had* been created deliberately. Such evidence has been held by the Court of Appeal to be relevant for this purpose, along with evidence showing how a computer had been used to access paedophile news groups, chatlines and websites (*R* v *Mould*, *The Times*, 21 October 2000). A further decision on the making of a 'pseudo-photograph' has held that an image consisting of two parts of two different photographs taped together (the naked body of a woman taped to the head of a child) would not suffice (*Goodland* v *DPP*, *The Times*, 8 March 2000). In that case the Divisional Court accepted that such an image, *if photocopied*, could fall within the meaning of a 'pseudo-photograph' — a fine distinction, the practical effect of which seems difficult to defend. The Court of Appeal has confirmed that the offence under s. 1(1)(a) is justified by the requirement to protect children from being exploited and does not contravene Article 8 or Article 10 of the European Convention on Human Rights (*R* v *Smethurst*, *The Times*, 13 April 2001).

A legitimate purpose for possessing such material might be where someone has the material as an exhibits officer or as a training aid for police officers or social workers.

The consent of the Director of Public Prosecutions is needed before prosecuting an offence under the Protection of Children Act 1978.

Distributing will include lending or offering to another.

Note that although the offences include video recordings, possession of exposed but undeveloped film (i.e. film in the form in which it is taken out of a camera) does not appear to be covered. The offence at s. 1(1)(b) and (c) of the 1978 Act can only be proven if the defendant showed/distributed the photograph etc. or intended to show or distribute the photograph etc. *to someone else*. This is clear from the decisions in *R* v *Fellows* [1997] 1 Cr App R 244 and *R* v *T*, *The Times*, 12 February 1998. If no such intention can be proved, or if the defendant only had the photographs etc. for his/her own use, the appropriate charge would be under the 1988 Act.

Sections 1 and 2 of the Criminal Evidence (Amendment) Act 1997 apply to an offence under s. 1 of the Protection of Children Act 1978 (and to conspiracies, attempts or incitements in the circumstances set out in the 1997 Act) (see **Evidence and Procedure, chapter 16**).

See also s. 49 of the Customs and Excise Management Act 1979 in respect of the importation of indecent material.

11.4.8 Harmful Publications

Offence — Harmful Publications — Children and Young Persons (Harmful Publications) Act 1955, s. 2
Triable summarily. Four months' imprisonment and/or a fine.
(**No specific power of arrest**)

The Children and Young Persons (Harmful Publications) Act 1955, s. 2 states:

(1) A person who prints, publishes, sells or lets on hire a work to which this Act applies, or has any such work in his possession for the purpose of selling it or letting it on hire, shall be guilty of an offence . . .

Keynote

A prosecution for this somewhat archaic offence can only be brought with the consent of the Attorney-General (or Solicitor-General). The sort of 'works' to which the Act applies are set out in s. 1 and include books, magazines or other like works of a kind likely to fall into the hands of children or young persons which consist wholly or mainly of stories told in pictures which portray:

- the commission of crimes; or
- acts of violence or cruelty; or
- incidents of a repulsive or horrible nature;

in such a way that the work as a whole would tend to corrupt a child or young person.

Power of Search

A search warrant may be issued under s. 3 of the 1955 Act.

Defence

The Children and Young Persons (Harmful Publications) Act 1955, s. 2 states:

(1) . . . in any proceedings taken under this subsection against a person in respect of selling or letting on hire a work or of having it in his possession for the purpose of selling it or letting it on hire, it shall be a defence for him to prove that he had not examined the contents of the work and had no reasonable cause to suspect that it was one to which this Act applies.

11.4.9   Abuse of Position of Trust

Offence — Abuse of Position of Trust — Sexual Offences Act 2000, s. 3

Triable either way. Five years' imprisonment on indictment six months' imprisonment and/or fine summarily.
(*Arrestable offence*)

The Sexual Offences Act 2000, s. 3 states:

(1)   *Subject to subsections (2) and (3) below, it shall be an offence for a person aged 18 or over—*
   (a)   *to have sexual intercourse (whether vaginal or anal) with a person under that age; or*
   (b)   *to engage in any other sexual activity with or directed towards such a person,*
if (in either case) he is in a position of trust in relation to that person.
(2)   *Where a person ('A') is charged with an offence under this section of having sexual intercourse with, or engaging in any other sexual activity with or directed towards, another person ('B'), it shall be a defence for A to prove that, at the time of the intercourse or activity—*
   (a)   *he did not know, and could not reasonably have been expected to know, that B was under 18;*
   (b)   *he did not know, and could not reasonably have been expected to know, that B was a person in relation to whom he was in a position of trust; or*
   (c)   *he was lawfully married to B.*

Keynote

This new offence was created to address the increasingly common situation where those placed in a position of trust over young people have exploited that position, and the opportunities it provides, for sexual gratification.

The 2000 Act excludes sexual activity that took place between two people who were in both a position of trust and a sexual relationship before the Act came into force (January 2001) (s. 3(3)).

A key element to this offence is showing the existence of a position of trust. On most occasions this will arise as a result of the defendant's work within a particular institution or organisation. A starting point is to establish that the defendant is *regularly involved in caring for, training, supervising or being in sole charge of people under 18* within one of the relevant settings (see s. 4(7)). You will then need to establish that the victim was within one of those settings. The relevant settings are:

- Detention in an institution by virtue of a court order or under an enactment. This would include some situations where the younger person is detained under the criminal justice system or under immigration or mental health legislation (s. 4(2)).

- Accommodation in local authority or voluntary homes. This would include some situations where the younger person is accommodated in a foster home, receiving residential care or in local authority accommodation (s. 4(3)).

- Accommodation and care within a hospital, residential care home, community home or nursing home. This would include some situations where the younger person is being treated for physical, mental or learning disabilities and will include private hospitals as well as NHS accommodation (s. 4(4)).

- Full-time education in an educational institution. This only covers situations where the younger person is registered or enrolled as a pupil in that or a related establishment (s. 4(5) and (8)).

A position of trust may also exist under conditions specified by statutory instrument made by the Home Secretary (s. 4(1)).

In summary, you must show that the victim fell within the relevant settings of **CARE**:

C — court order or other lawful detention
A — accommodation within a local authority or voluntary home
R — residential home, hospital or community home
E — education on a full-time basis

or any circumstances prescribed by statutory instrument.

For the full and precise extent of these settings, the interpretation provisions in s. 4 should be consulted.

Having established that a position of trust exists, it is necessary to prove the relevant sexual intercourse or activity. Sexual intercourse includes any degree of penetration either of the anus or the vagina. The test as to whether any other activity that took place is 'sexual activity' is an objective one. Sexual activity means any activity which *a reasonable person would regard as sexual in all the circumstances* (s. 3(5)). This will not include any activity which a reasonable person would only regard as sexual if they knew of the intentions, motives or feelings of the parties. This is similar to the test for indecent assault (as to which, **see chapter 10**). For example, a routine physical examination of a person under 18 by a registered medical practitioner within a care home would generally not be regarded as 'sexual' for this purpose. Even if the doctor or the patient harboured any hidden sexual motive at the time of the examination, that hidden motive would not bring the activity within the definition of 'sexual activity' here.

The wording of s. 3(1)(b) shows that it is not necessary to prove any touching or physical contact between the parties and that sexual activity *towards* the younger person can be enough.

In raising the statutory defence, the defendant must prove that, at the time of the alleged offence, he/she he did not in fact know, *nor could reasonably have been expected to know*:

- that the younger person was under 18; or

- that a position of trust existed between them.

It will also be a defence if the person can prove that he/she was lawfully married to the other person.

11.4.10 Sex Offenders Act 1997

Part II of the Sex Offenders Act 1997 provides for certain sexual offences committed outside the United Kingdom to be treated as if they had been committed in England, Wales or Northern Ireland. These provisions are clearly aimed at protecting children abroad (see also the Sexual Offences (Conspiracy and Incitement) Act 1996).

For these provisions to apply, the offence must have been committed outside the UK by a person who is a British citizen (see the British Nationality Act 1981) or who is resident in the UK (s. 7(2)).

The relevant offences are listed in sch. 2 of the Sex Offenders Act 1997. The following offences under the Sexual Offences Act 1956 are covered by sch. 2:

- intercourse with girl under 13 (s. 5)
- intercourse with girl between 13 and 16 (s. 6).

The following offences under the Sexual Offences Act 1956 are covered by sch. 2, provided the victim is under 16:

- rape (s. 1)
- buggery (s. 12)
- indecent assault (ss. 14 and 15)
- assault with intent to commit buggery (s. 16).

Other offences covered by sch. 2 are:

- indecent conduct towards a child (Indecency with Children Act 1960, s. 1);
- indecent photographs of children (Protection of Children Act 1978).

Schedule 2 goes on to include other offences under the law relating to Northern Ireland.

It also includes attempting, conspiracy, incitement and aiding and abetting the offences set out.

11.4.11 Protection of Children

Although many of the general provisions restricting the behaviour of sex offenders have been targeted at paedophiles (**see chapter 10**), there are several significant areas of legislation which are aimed specifically at the protection of children, in both a sexual context and in other areas where their well-being is jeopardised.

Criminal Justice and Court Services Act 2000

The Criminal Justice and Court Services Act 2000 introduced a number of measures aimed at preventing unsuitable people from working with children. What follows is a summary of some of the relevant provisions of the Act; for further detail see Home Office Circular 45/2000.

Part II of the 2000 Act introduces the concept of disqualification orders. These orders are aimed at disqualifying people who present a threat to children from working in certain jobs and positions. A key feature of disqualification orders is the fact that a court *must* impose them when defendants are convicted of certain offences unless, having regard to all the circumstances, the court is satisfied that it is unlikely that the defendant will commit any further offences against *any* child (ss. 28 and 29). Broadly, the requirement to pass a disqualification order arises when:

- the defendant, being 18 or over, is convicted of an 'offence against a child'. 'Offences against a child' are set out in sch. 4 to the Act (**see appendix 3**) and generally include most offences involving sexual activity, the use of violence and some drug-related offences (the list specifically includes the military or service law equivalent of these offences).

- A senior court passes a 'qualifying sentence' on the defendant for that offence. A qualifying sentence is generally a sentence of 12 months' imprisonment or more, a hospital or guardianship order (s. 30). 'Senior court' here means the Crown Court and the Court of Appeal. Again, these concepts are specifically extended to cover sentences imposed under service law by courts-martial and the Courts-Martial Appeal Court.

For most purposes under this part of the Act, 'child' means a person under 18.

Once an order is imposed, the person becomes a 'disqualified person' for the purposes of the Act. A person can also become 'disqualified' if he/she appears on a statutory list of unsuitable or unfit people (see below).

Offences — Applying for position while Disqualified — Criminal Justice and Court Services Act 2000, s. 35

Triable either way. Five years' imprisonment on indictment; six months' and/or fine summarily.
(*Arrestable offence*)

Section 35 states:

> *(1)   An individual who is disqualified from working with children is guilty of an offence if he knowingly applies for, offers to do, accepts or does any work in a regulated position.*
> *(2)   An individual is guilty of an offence if he knowingly—*
> *(a)   offers work in a regulated position to, or procures work in a regulated position for, an individual who is disqualified from working with children, or*
> *(b)   fails to remove such an individual from such work.*
> *(3)   It is a defence for an individual charged with an offence under subsection (1) to prove that he did not know, and could not reasonably be expected to know, that he was disqualified from working with children.*

Keynote

There are two offences associated with being a disqualified person. The first offence arises where a disqualified person knowingly applies for, offers to do, accepts or does any work in a regulated position (s. 35(1)). Given the specific defence available (see below), it would seem that the requirement of 'knowingly' here relates to the act of applying, offering or accepting work in a regulated position. The offence would therefore not be made out if the application, offer, etc. were made without the disqualified person's knowledge or agreement. Regulated positions are generally those where the person's normal duties include working with children, whether in the public, private or voluntary sectors and also in certain senior management roles such as social services and children's charities.

The statutory defence to s. 35(1) applies if the defendant can show that he/she neither knew, nor could reasonably have been expected to know that he/she was disqualified (a difficult scenario to envisage let alone prove).

The second offence arises where a person offers or procures work in a regulated position for a person who is disqualified from working with children or fails to remove such an individual from that work (s. 35(2)). This offence is clearly aimed at employers, though it would clearly extend beyond those circumstances and it does not have the statutory defence available. This seems slightly odd given that, of the two, a prospective employer is far less likely to know of a person's disqualification than the person disqualified.

Reviews and Appeals

The Criminal Justice and Court Services Act 2000 makes provision for a person to appeal against the imposition of a disqualification order and also to have such orders reviewed after a minimum period. More significantly for the police, s. 34 makes provision for a chief officer of police (or director of social services) to apply to the High Court to restore a disqualification order if it can be shown that:

- the person who was once subject to the order has acted (either before the order ceased or after) in such a way

- as to give reasonable cause to believe that an order is necessary

- to protect children in general or any children in particular

- from serious harm from that person.

If these conditions are made out, the High Court *must* reinstate the disqualification order.

In addition to the provisions under the Criminal Justice and Court Services Act 2000, there are several pieces of legislation that exist for the protection of children generally. Two key statutes relating to the protection of children are:

- the Protection of Children Act 1999
- the Children Act 1989.

Protection of Children Act 1999

The Protection of Children Act 1999 was passed to provide greater safeguards for children and to increase the restrictions on those who would seek to gain access to children in order to exploit them. One of the main pillars of the 1999 Act is the creation of a comprehensive and accessible information network. Such a network will:

- provide a consolidated list of people who are deemed to represent a particular risk to children, and

- make that list more accessible to employers and other agencies whose responsibilities include the protection of children.

The 1999 Act brings together two existing lists currently maintained by the Department of Health (the 'Consultancy List') and the Department for Education and Employment ('List 99') for the purposes of identifying those people who are unsuitable to work with children. It also makes provision for relevant organisations to apply to the Criminal Record Bureau for criminal record certificates and criminal conviction certificates utilising the relevant provisions of the Police Act 1997.

The Consultancy List maintained by the Secretary of State for the Department of Health providing access to employers' records on people considered to be unsuitable for work with children has been held not to infringe the human rights of those included on it — (R v *Worcester County Council and Secretary of State for the Department of Health, ex parte W* (2000) LTL 12 September).

OFFENCES AGAINST CHILDREN AND OTHER VULNERABLE PEOPLE

The 1999 Act also creates a number of statutory duties upon child care organisations and those involved in the employment of people in child care positions, as well as establishing a tribunal to hear appeals from individuals whose names appear on the relevant list.

Children Act 1989

The Children Act 1989 represents the most comprehensive piece of legislation affecting children ever enacted in England and Wales. Throughout the Act, which makes provision for the care and treatment of children in virtually every aspect of their development, there is a common theme of the child's rights.

Among those rights are the right to protection from harm and the Act imposes many duties on local authorities. It also provides powers for the protection of children and, in particular, for situations where emergency protection is needed.

Police Protection

Section 46 of the Children Act 1989 states:

> *(1)   Where a constable has reasonable cause to believe that a child would otherwise be likely to suffer significant harm, he may—*
> *(a)   remove the child to suitable accommodation and keep him there; or*
> *(b)   take such steps as are reasonable to ensure the the child's removal from any hospital, or other place, in which he is then being accommodated is prevented.*
> *(2)   For the purposes of this Act, a child with respect to whom a constable has exercised his powers under this section is referred to as having been taken into police protection.*
> *(3)   As soon as is reasonably practicable after taking a child into police protection, the constable concerned shall—*
> *(a)   inform the local authority within whose area the child was found of the steps that have been, and are proposed to be, taken with respect to the child under this section and the reasons for taking them;*
> *(b)   give details to the authority within whose area the child is ordinarily resident ('the appropriate authority') of the place at which the child is being accommodated;*
> *(c)   inform the child (if he appears capable of understanding)—*
> *(i)   of the steps that have been taken with respect to him under this section and of the reasons for taking them; and*
> *(ii)   of the further steps that may be taken with respect to him under this section;*
> *(d)   take such steps as are reasonably practicable to discover the wishes and feelings of the child;*
> *(e)   secure that the case is inquired into by an officer designated for the purposes of this section by the chief officer of the police area concerned; and*
> *(f)   where the child was taken into police protection by being removed to accommodation which is not provided—*
> *(i)   by or on behalf of a local authority; or*
> *(ii)   as a refuge, in compliance with the requirements of section 51,*
> *secure that he is moved to accommodation which is so provided.*
> *(4)   As soon as is reasonably practicable after taking a child into police protection, the constable concerned shall take such steps as are reasonably practicable to inform—*
> *(a)   the child's parents;*
> *(b)   every person who is not a parent of his but who has parental responsibility for him; and*
> *(c)   any other person with whom the child was living immediately before being taken into police protection,*
> *of the steps that he has taken under this section with respect to the child, the reasons for taking them and the further steps that may be taken with respect to him under this section.*
> *(5)   On completing any inquiry under subsection (3)(e), the officer conducting it shall release the child from police protection unless he considers that there is still reasonable cause for believing that the child would be likely to suffer significant harm if released.*

(6) No child may be kept in police protection for more than 72 hours.

(7) While a child is being kept in police protection, the designated officer may apply on behalf of the appropriate authority for an emergency protection order to be made under section 44 with respect to the child.

(8) An application may be made under subsection (7) whether or not the authority know of it or agree to its being made.

(9) While a child is being kept in police protection—

(a) neither the constable concerned nor the designated officer shall have parental responsibility for him; but

(b) the designated officer shall do what is reasonable in all the circumstances of the case for the purpose of safeguarding or promoting the child's welfare (having regard in particular to the length of the period during which the child will be so protected).

(10) Where a child has been taken into police protection, the designated officer shall allow—

(a) the child's parents;

(b) any person who is not a parent of the child but who has parental responsibility for him;

(c) any person with whom the child was living immediately before he was taken into police protection;

(d) any person in whose favour a contact order is in force with respect to the child;

(e) any person who is allowed to have contact with the child by virtue of an order under section 34; and

(f) any person acting on behalf of any of those persons,

to have such contact (if any) with the child as, in the opinion of the designated officer, is both reasonable and in the child's best interests.

(11) Where a child who has been taken into police protection is in accommodation provided by, or on behalf of, the appropriate authority, subsection (10) shall have effect as if it referred to the authority rather than to the designated officer.

Keynote

For most purposes of the 1989 Act, someone who is under 18 years old is a 'child' (s. 105).

'Harm' means ill treatment or the impairment of health and development; 'development' includes physical, intellectual, emotional, social or behavioural and 'health' means physical or mental health (s. 31(9)). 'Ill treatment' includes sexual abuse and forms of ill treatment that are not physical (s. 31(9)).

When determining whether harm to a child's health or development is 'significant', the child's development will be compared with that which could reasonably be expected of a similar child (s. 31(10)).

The power under s. 46 is split into two parts:

• a power to remove a child to suitable accommodation and keep him/her there, and

• a power to take reasonable steps to prevent the child's removal from a hospital or other place.

Every local authority must receive and provide accommodation for children in police protection where a request is made under s. 46(3)(f) above (s. 21).

The requirement under s. 46(3)(c) to give the child information, reflects the 1989 Act's theme that children should have some influence over their own destiny.

Section 46(3)(e) is a reference to the appropriate 'designated officer' for that police station. However, the responsibility for ensuring that the case is inquired into by that officer, together with the other responsibilities under s. 46(3) and the responsibility for taking steps to inform people under s. 46(4) rests with the police officer exercising the power under s. 46.

The responsibilities imposed by s. 46(5), (9)(b) and (10) rest with the designated officer.

Under s. 46(7), the designated officer may apply for an 'emergency protection order' under s. 44. Such an order allows the court to order the removal of the child to certain types of accommodation and to prevent the child's removal from any other place (including a hospital) where he/she was being accommodated immediately before the making of the order (s. 44(4)). An emergency protection order gives the applicant 'parental responsibility' for the child while it is in force. It also allows the court to make certain directions in relation to contact with the child and a medical or psychiatric assessment of them. Section 44A allows the court to make an order excluding certain people from a dwellinghouse where the child lives and to attach a power of arrest accordingly.

The longest a child can spend in police protection is 72 hours (s. 46(6)).

Under s. 47(1)(b), when a local authority is informed that a child is in police protection, they have a duty to make 'such enquiries as they consider necessary to enable them to decide whether they should take any action to safeguard' the child.

A court may issue a warrant for a constable to assist a relevant person to enter premises in order to enforce an emergency protection order.

Offence — Acting in Contravention of Protection Order or Power Exercised under s. 46 — Children Act 1989, s. 49
Triable summarily. Six months' imprisonment.
(No specific power of arrest)

The Children Act 1989, s. 49 states:

> *(1)   A person shall be guilty of an offence if, knowingly and without lawful authority or reasonable excuse, he—*
> *(a)   takes a child to whom this section applies away from the responsible person;*
> *(b)   keeps such a child away from the responsible person; or*
> *(c)   induces, assists or incites such a child to run away or stay away from the responsible person.*
> *(2)   This section applies in relation to a child who is—*
> *(a)   in care;*
> *(b)   the subject of an emergency protection order; or*
> *(c)   in police protection,*
> *and in this section 'the responsible person' means any person who for the time being has care of him by virtue of the care order, the emergency protection order, or section 46, as the case may be.*

Keynote

Although there is no specific power of arrest, the general arrest condition under s. 25(3)(e) of the Police and Criminal Evidence Act 1984 is likely to apply (**see General Police Duties, chapter 2**).

It is arguable that, in the case of a child who is under 16, the person would also commit an offence under the Child Abduction Act 1984 (**see para. 11.2**).

There is also a power of entry under s. 17(1)(e) of the 1984 Act for 'saving life and limb' (see **General Police Duties, chapter 2**).

Where a child is taken in contravention of s. 49 above, the court may issue a 'recovery order' under s. 50. Such an order, which is also available where a child is missing or has run away, requires certain people to produce the child to an authorised person (which includes a constable (s. 50(7)(b)) or to give certain information about the child's whereabouts to a constable or officer of the court (s. 50(3)). It can also authorise a constable to enter any premises and search for the child.

Under s. 102 of the 1989 Act a court may issue a warrant to enter premises in connection with certain provisions of the Act which regulate children's homes, foster homes, child-minding premises and nursing homes for children. Section 102 allows for constables to assist any person in the exercise of their powers under those provisions. It also makes allowances for a constable to be accompanied by a medical practitioner, nurse or health visitor (s. 102(3)).

11.4.12 Disclosure of Child's Whereabouts

Where a child is reported missing problems can arise once he/she is discovered to be safe and well but one of the parents wants the police to disclose the whereabouts of the child. This situation arose in *S v S (Chief Constable of West Yorkshire Police Intervening)* [1999] 1 All ER 281 and the Court of Appeal provided some clarification of the issues. In that case the mother left home with her three-year-old child after a marriage breakdown. The father reported the child's absence to the police who found the child and her mother in a refuge. At the request of the mother, the police advised the father that both she and the child were safe but refused to disclose their whereabouts. The father applied *ex parte* (i.e. without telling the police) to the County Court which then made an order under s. 33 of the Family Law Act 1986, requiring the police to disclose the information. The chief constable was granted leave to intervene and, following another order from the court to disclose the child's whereabouts, the chief constable appealed. Butler-Sloss LJ (one of the key figures behind the drafting of the Children Act 1989), gave the finding of the Court of Appeal. The Court held that it was only in exceptional circumstances that the police should be asked to divulge the whereabouts of a child under a s. 33 order. Their primary role in such cases should continue to be finding missing children and ensuring their safety.

However, Butler-Sloss LJ went on to say that, in such cases:

- The police are *not* in a position to give 'categoric assurances' of confidentiality to those who provide information as to the whereabouts of a child. The most they could say is that, other than by removing the child, it would be *most unlikely* that they would have to disclose the information concerning the child's whereabouts.

- An order under s. 33 provides for the information to be disclosed to the court, not to the other party or his/her solicitor.

- An order under s. 33 should not normally be made in respect of the police without their being present (*ex parte*).

11.4.13 Other Protective Legislation

A number of statutes provide protection for children from certain activities and substances. In addition to those relating to vehicles (as to which, **see Road Traffic**), these include:

- Giving intoxicating liquor to a child under 5 (Children and Young Persons Act 1933, s. 5).

- Confiscation of alcohol from a person under 18 (Confiscation of Alcohol (Young Persons) Act 1997 (**see General Police Duties, chapter 10**)).

- Offence of being drunk in charge of a child under 7 (Licensing Act 1902, s. 2(1)).

- Selling tobacco or cigarette papers to person under 16 (Children and Young Persons Act 1933, s. 7(1)).

- Exposing child under 12 to risk of burning (Children and Young Persons Act 1933, s. 11).

- Requirement for retailers and vending machine owners to display warning signs regarding cigarettes (Children and Young Persons (Protection from Tobacco) Act 1991).

- Requirement to provide safety attendants in buildings where entertainment is provided for children (Children and Young Persons Act 1933, s. 12).

- Restrictions on the employment of children (Children and Young Persons Act 1933, Part II).

- Restrictions on dangerous performances involving children (Children and Young Persons Act 1963, s. 37).

- Restrictions on children under 14 riding horses on roads without helmets (Protective Headgear for Young Riders Act 1990).

11.5   People Suffering from Mental Impairment

11.5.1   Sexual Offences against the Mentally Impaired

The Sexual Offences Act 1956 creates certain offences for the protection of people who might be unable to understand the nature of, or to consent to, sexual intimacy. Somewhat politically incorrectly, the Act terms such people as 'defectives', defining them at s. 45 as:

> . . . *[persons] suffering from a state of arrested or incomplete development of mind which includes severe impairment of intelligence and social functioning.*

In addition, there is a specific offence of a man under certain circumstances having sexual intercourse with a psychiatric patient (see below).

Offence — Sexual Intercourse with Mental Defective — Sexual Offences Act 1956, s. 7
Triable on indictment. Two years' imprisonment.
(No specific power of arrest)

The Sexual Offences Act 1956, s. 7 states:

(1) It is an offence, subject to the exception mentioned in this section, for a man to have unlawful sexual intercourse with a woman who is a defective.

The defence is stated at s. 7 as:

(2) A man is not guilty of an offence under this section because he has unlawful sexual intercourse with a woman if he does not know and has no reason to suspect her to be a defective.

Offence — Procurement — Sexual Offences Act 1956, s. 9
Triable on indictment. Two years' imprisonment.
(No specific power of arrest)

The Sexual Offences Act 1956, s. 9 states:

(1) It is an offence, subject to the exception mentioned in this section, for a person to procure a woman who is a defective to have unlawful sexual intercourse in any part of the world.

The defence is stated at s. 9 as:

(2) A person is not guilty of an offence under this section because he procures a defective to have unlawful sexual intercourse, if he does not know and has no reason to suspect her to be a defective.

Offence — Owner/Occupier allowing Woman Mental 'Defective' to Use Premises — Sexual Offences Act 1956, s. 27
Triable on indictment. Two years' imprisonment.
(No specific power of arrest)

The Sexual Offences Act 1956, s. 27 states:

(1) It is an offence, subject to the exception mentioned in this section, for a person who is the owner or occupier of any premises, or who has, or acts or assists in, the management or control of any premises, to induce or knowingly suffer a woman who is a defective to resort to or be on those premises for the purpose of having unlawful sexual intercourse with men or with a particular man.

The defence is stated at s. 27 as:

(2) A person is not guilty of an offence under this section because he induces or knowingly suffers a defective to resort to or be on any premises for the purpose mentioned, if he does not know and has no reason to suspect her to be a defective.

Keynote

The legal burden (**see Evidence and Procedure, chapter 11**) in proving the specific defences shown above falls upon the defence (s. 49 of the 1956 Act).

All the above offences apply to female victims, with the offence under s. 7(1) only being capable of commission by a man. Where the alleged victim is male, the offences of rape or indecent assault may apply (**see chapter 10**).

161

OFFENCES AGAINST CHILDREN AND OTHER VULNERABLE PEOPLE

Offence — Sexual Intercourse with Patients — Mental Health Act 1959, s. 128
Triable on indictment. Two years' imprisonment.
(*No specific power of arrest*)

The Mental Health Act 1959, s. 128 states:

(1)   Without prejudice to section seven of the Sexual Offences Act 1956, it shall be an offence, subject to the exception mentioned in this section,—
(a)   for a man who is an officer on the staff of or is otherwise employed in, or is one of the managers of, a hospital or mental nursing home to have unlawful sexual intercourse with a woman who is for the time being receiving treatment for mental disorder in that hospital or home, or to have such intercourse on the premises of which the hospital or home forms part with a woman who is for the time being receiving such treatment there as an out-patient;
(b)   for a man to have unlawful sexual intercourse with a woman who is a mentally disordered patient and who is subject to his guardianship under the Mental Health Act 1983 or is otherwise in his custody or care under the Mental Health Act 1983 or in pursuance of arrangements under Part III of the National Assistance Act 1948 or the National Health Service Act 1977, or as a resident in a residential care home within the meaning of Part I of the Registered Homes Act 1984.

The defence is stated at s. 128 as:

(2)   It shall not be an offence under this section for a man to have sexual intercourse with a woman if he does not know and has no reason to suspect her to be a mentally disordered patient.

The Sexual Offences Act 1967, s. 1 states:

(3)   A man who is suffering from severe mental handicap cannot in law give any consent which, by virtue of subsection (1) of this section, would prevent a homosexual act from being an offence, but a person shall not be convicted, on account of the incapacity of such a man to consent, of an offence consisting of such an act if he proves that he did not know and had no reason to suspect that man to be suffering from severe mental handicap.
(3A)   In subsection (3) of this section 'severe mental handicap' means a state of arrested or incomplete development of mind which includes severe impairment of intelligence and social functioning.
(4)   Section 128 of the Mental Health Act 1959 (prohibition on men on the staff of a hospital, or otherwise having responsibility for mental patients, having sexual intercourse with women patients) shall have effect as if any reference therein to having unlawful sexual intercourse with a woman included a reference to committing buggery or an act of gross indecency with another man.

Keynote

This offence requires the consent of the Director of Public Prosecutions before any prosecution can be brought. It can only be committed by a man who is in some way employed in the hospital or home where the patient is receiving treatment. Given that requirement, it is unlikely that the specific defence in s. 128(2) of the 1959 Act would apply in many cases.

Sections 1 and 2 of the Criminal Evidence (Amendment) Act 1997 also apply to this offence (and to conspiracies, attempts or incitements in the circumstances set out in that Act) (**see Evidence and Procedure, chapter 16**).

Where a person is charged with this offence, the Youth Justice and Criminal Evidence Act 1999 imposes certain restrictions on the introduction of evidence or the asking of questions relating to the victim's sexual behaviour (**see Evidence and Procedure, chapter 6**).

11.5.2   **Abduction**

**Offence — Abduction of Woman Mental Defective from Parent/Guardian —
Sexual Offences Act 1956, s. 21**
Triable on indictment. Two years' imprisonment.
(**No specific power of arrest**)

The Sexual Offences Act 1956, s. 21 states:

> *(1)   It is an offence, subject to the exception mentioned in this section, for a person to take a woman
> who is a defective out of the possession of her parent or guardian against his will, if she is so taken
> with the intention that she shall have unlawful sexual intercourse with men or with a particular man.*

The defence is stated at s. 21 as:

> *(2)   A person is not guilty of an offence under this section because he takes such a woman out of
> the possession of her parent or guardian as mentioned above, if he does not know and has no reason
> to suspect her to be a defective.*

Keynote

Although no specific power of arrest is provided, the additional arrestable offence of
kidnapping should be considered (**see chapter 9**).

The elements in relation to this offence are the same as those for abduction under
s. 19 (**see chapter 10**).

11.5.3   **Protection of People Suffering from Mental Disorders**

The Mental Health Act 1983 provides for the care and treatment of people suffering
from mental disorders and supplies powers for enforcing some of its provisions.

If those powers are executed in good faith, the 1983 Act also provides some protection
against criminal and civil liability for the police officers and care workers who use them
(see s. 139).

The 1983 Act is supported by a Code of Practice that sets out guidance for the police
and other agencies when dealing with people suffering from mental disorders.

Mentally Disordered People Found in Public Places

Section s. 136 of the Mental Health Act 1983 creates a power for police officers to
remove such a person under certain conditions.

Section 136 states:

> *(1)   If a constable finds in a place to which the public have access a person who appears to him
> to be suffering from mental disorder and to be in immediate need of care or control, the constable may,
> if he thinks it necessary to do so in the interests of that person or for the protection of other persons,
> remove that person to a place of safety within the meaning of section 135 above.*
> *(2)   A person removed to a place of safety under this section may be detained there for a period
> not exceeding 72 hours for the purpose of enabling him to be examined by a registered medical
> practitioner and to be interviewed by an approved social worker and of making any necessary
> arrangements for his treatment or care.*

Keynote

Given the number of people who are suffering from some form of mental disorder and who are receiving 'care in the community', this a significant power which is provided for the protection of the person themselves and of others.

The power places a lot of responsibility and latitude on the officer who must decide whether:

- the person is suffering from mental disorder (see below)

- the person is in immediate need of care or control, and

- it is necessary in the person's interest or for someone else's protection that he/she be removed to a place of safety

before the power is applicable. This power appears to be consistent with Article 5 of the European Convention on Human Rights which sets out the limited circumstances where the detention or arrest of an individual will be permitted (**see General Police Duties, chapter 2**).

The definition of 'mental disorder' under s. 1(2) is very wide and means:

- mental illness

- arrested or incomplete development of mind

- psychopathic disorder (a persistent disorder or disability resulting in abnormally aggressive or seriously irresponsible conduct)

- any other disorder or disability of mind.

Under s. 135(6), a 'place of safety' is:

- residential accommodation provided by social services

- a hospital

- a police station

- a mental nursing home, or

- any other suitable place where the occupier is willing to receive the patient temporarily.

Anyone being taken to a place of safety or detained at such a place will be treated as being in legal custody (s. 137(1)). (This expression is only relevant in relation to escaping and assisting in an escape; it is very different from 'in police detention' used under s. 118 of the Police and Criminal Evidence Act 1984. A mentally disordered person removed from a public place is *not* in police detention even if taken to a police station.)

OFFENCES AGAINST CHILDREN AND OTHER VULNERABLE PEOPLE

Although the power to remove a person to a place of safety under s. 136(1) is classed among the powers of arrest preserved by s. 26 and sch. 2 to the Police and Criminal Evidence Act 1984 (**see General Police Duties, chapter 2**), it is not strictly speaking a power of arrest.

It is an offence to assist someone removed under s. 136 to escape (see s. 128).

Warrant to Search for Patients

Where there is reasonable cause to suspect that a person believed to be suffering from a mental disorder has been, or is being ill-treated or neglected or is unable to care for himself/herself and is living alone, a warrant may be issued by a magistrate (s. 135).

The warrant allows a constable to enter any premises specified and to remove the person to a place of safety. In doing so, the officer must be accompanied by a social worker and a doctor (s. 135(4)).

A warrant may also be issued in respect of a patient ordered to be detained by a court.

Power to Retake Escaped Patients

Section 138 provides a power to retake people who have been in legal custody under the 1983 Act.

A person removed to a place of safety under s. 136 or a person removed under a warrant, who subsequently escapes while being taken to or detained in a place of safety, cannot be retaken after 72 hours have elapsed. That time period starts either when the person escapes or when his/her liability to be detained began, whichever expires first (s. 138(3)). This means that, if the person escapes *before* reaching the place of safety, the 72 hours begins then; if the person escapes *from* the place of safety, the 72 hours begins at the time he/she arrived there.

There is also a power for a court to issue a warrant for the arrest of a convicted mental patient who is unlawfully at large (Criminal Justice Act 1977, s. 72(3)).

Ambit of the Mental Health Act 1983

The ambit of the Mental Health Act 1983 was recently reviewed in *St George's NHS Trust* v *S, The Times*, 8 May 1998, by the Court of Appeal. There it was held that:

- The 1983 Act should not be invoked to overrule the decision of a patient concerning medical treatment simply because that decision appears to be irrational.

- A person detained under the 1983 Act should not be forced to receive medical treatment which is not connected with his/her mental condition unless his/her capacity to give consent is seriously diminished.

CHAPTER TWELVE

THEFT AND RELATED OFFENCES

12.1   Introduction

Theft, and the offences associated with it, cover some of the most commonly encountered offences in English — and Welsh — criminal law.

Given the volume of such crimes, together with the social consequences to victims and the communities in which they live, this area of criminal law has a significant impact on the work of all police officers and support staff.

In an attempt to address the high volume crime arising out of vehicle thefts, the government has introduced new legislation in the form of the Vehicle (Crime) Act 2001. The Act received Royal Assent on 110 April 2001, and introduces some of the recommendations of the Vehicle Crime Reduction Team made up of ACPO, the Home Office, the Association of British Insurers, Driver and Vehicle Licensing Agency, and a number of other motor industry groups.

The 2001 Act creates powers to regulate motor salvage businesses in the UK, gives police the right of entry to registered premises without a warrant and makes requirements in relation to suppliers of vehicle number plates (**see Road Traffic, chapter 12**).

At the time of writing, the Vehicles (Crime) Act 2001 was not in force.

12.2   Theft

Offence — Theft — Theft Act 1968, s. 1
Triable either way. Seven years' imprisonment on indictment; six months' imprisonment and/or a fine summarily.
(Arrestable offence)

The Theft Act 1968, s. 1 states:

(1)   A person is guilty of theft if he dishonestly appropriates property belonging to another with the intention of permanently depriving the other of it; and 'thief' and 'steal' shall be construed accordingly.

Keynote

It is important to understand each element of this offence. The Theft Act 1968 provides some detailed guidance as to parts of the above definition, while our common law has clarified some of the others.

In order for an offence of theft to exist, each element of the definition must be proved and those elements are considered in detail below.

This is a 'trigger' offence under s. 63B of the Police and Criminal Evidence Act 1984 which can activate police powers to require a sample from a person in police detention to ascertain the presence of a specified Class A drug in some force areas (**see Evidence and Procedure, chapter 15**).

12.2.1 Dishonestly

If a person cannot be shown to have acted 'dishonestly', he/she is not guilty of theft. The decision as to whether or not a defendant was in fact dishonest is one for the jury or magistrate(s). Although there are countless examples of when a person would be acting dishonestly, the 1968 Act sets out a number of specific circumstances where the relevant person will *not* be treated as dishonest.

The Theft Act 1968, s. 2 states:

> *(1)   A person's appropriation of property belonging to another is not to be regarded as dishonest—*
> *(a)   if he appropriates the property in the belief that he has in law the right to deprive the other of it, on behalf of himself or of a third person; or*
> *(b)   if he appropriates the property in the belief that he would have the other's consent if the other knew of the appropriation and the circumstances of it; or*
> *(c)   (except where the property came to him as trustee or personal representative) if he appropriates the property in the belief that the person to whom the property belongs cannot be discovered by taking reasonable steps.*
> *(2)   A person's appropriation of property belonging to another may be dishonest notwithstanding that he is willing to pay for the property.*

Keynote

In all three instances it is the person's *belief* that is important.

- Under s. 2(1)(a) if a person in dispute with a bookmaker believes he/she has a legal contractual right to take something of a value equal to his/her unpaid winnings from the bookmaker's stand, that person will not be regarded as dishonest — even though gambling debts are not legally enforceable. His/her belief need not even be reasonable, only honestly held, and could be based on a 'mistake' (contrast the general defence of mistake, **see chapter 4**.

- Under s. 2(1)(b) the person appropriating the property must believe both elements, i.e. that the other person would have consented had he/she known of the appropriation *and the circumstances of it*. If a member of a police station tea club is desperate for a cigarette and takes cash from the tea club kitty which colleagues occasionally use for such 'emergencies', the taker might well argue that s. 2(1)(b) applies. If, however, the money is taken to boost the Christmas kitty of another shift, the second condition may defeat them! Although the person need not have given his/her consent to the appropriation, the presence of such consent may be very relevant in establishing the honest existence of the defendant's belief. It is suggested that this element of theft, namely the element of *dishonesty* is where the issue of consent properly belongs and not in the element of 'appropriation' as discussed below.

- Under s. 2(1)(c), the belief has to be in relation to the likelihood of discovering the 'owner' by taking reasonable steps. Both the nature and value of the property, together with the attendant circumstances, will be relevant. The chances of finding the owner of a valuable, monogrammed engagement ring found after a theatre performance would be considerably greater than those of discovering the owner of a can of beer found outside Twickenham stadium following a Six Nations match between Wales and England. Again, it is the defendant's *belief* at the time of the appropriation that is important here, not that the defendant went on to *take* reasonable steps to discover the person to whom the property belongs.

Under s. 2(2), if a person appropriates another's property, leaving money or details of where he/she can be contacted to make restitution will not *of itself* negate dishonesty (see *Boggeln* v *Williams* [1978] 1 WLR 873). The wording of s. 2(2) gives latitude to a court where the defendant was willing to pay for the property. The subsection says that such an appropriation *may* be dishonest, not that it *will always* be dishonest.

12.2.2   Dishonesty: The Ruling in *Ghosh*

Section 2 will not cater for every circumstance and indeed ss. 2 to 6 only affect the interpretation of the basic elements of theft as set out in s. 1 unless the Act says otherwise (s. 1(3)). Since the case of *R* v *Ghosh* [1982] QB 1053 there has been a requirement for juries to be given some form of direction where the issue of dishonesty is raised. As well as clarifying that the defendant's dishonesty is a matter for a jury to decide, the Court of Appeal in *Ghosh* also identified two aspects which the jury should consider when so deciding. If s. 2 is not applicable or helpful then a jury must decide:

- whether, according to the ordinary standards of reasonable and honest people, what was done was 'dishonest'; and, if it was

- whether 'the defendant himself must have realised that what was done was dishonest' *by those standards*.

This test against the standards of reasonable and honest people means that a defendant who has a purely *subjective* belief that he/she is doing what is morally right (e.g. an anti-vivisectionist taking animals from a laboratory) can still be 'dishonest'. The ruling applies to other offences under the Theft Act 1968 and the original case arose from charges of deception (as to which, **see chapter 13**). The *Ghosh* test is probably the source of the questions so loved by some interviewing officers: 'But what would an *honest* person have done?' or 'What would have been the *honest* thing to do?'

12.2.3   Appropriates

The Theft Act 1968, s. 3 states:

> *(1)   Any assumption by a person of the rights of an owner amounts to an appropriation, and this includes, where he has come by the property (innocently or not) without stealing it, any later assumption of a right to it by keeping or dealing with it as owner.*

Keynote

It is important to note that there can be an 'appropriation' without any criminal liability and appropriation itself does not amount to an offence; it describes one of the circumstances that must exist before a charge of theft can be made out. An appropriation requires no mental state on the part of the appropriator. It is an objective act.

Where an appropriation takes place and is accompanied by the required dishonesty and intention to deprive permanently, there will be a theft.

When and where the particular act amounting to an appropriation took place is therefore of critical importance when bringing a charge of theft; it is also vital when establishing other offences such as robbery (**see para. 12.3**), aggravated burglary (**see para. 12.5**) and handling stolen goods (**see para. 12.11**).

R v *Gomez*

The decision of the House of Lords in *R* v *Gomez* [1993] AC 442 is significant in the development of the meaning of 'appropriation'. Gomez worked in a shop in London. He was approached by a friend who asked him to accept two building society cheques in exchange for some expensive electrical goods from the shop. Knowing the cheques to be stolen, Gomez took them to his store manager asking him to authorise the supply of goods. Gomez assured the manager that the cheques had been confirmed and that they were 'as good as cash'. With this reassurance the manager authorised the supply of the goods. Gomez paid the cheques into the store's account and the large quantity of electrical goods was dispatched to Gomez's friend. Some time later, the cheques were returned with a 'not to pay' order on them as they had been reported stolen.

Gomez was arrested for theft of the electrical goods, together with his friend, and sent for trial. There, counsel for Gomez submitted that there was no case to answer in respect of the theft because the store manager had authorised their supply and therefore there had been no 'appropriation' under s. 3(1) of the Theft Act 1968. The submission was rejected by the trial judge but was upheld on appeal on the grounds that, when Gomez's friend took possession of the electrical goods, he was entitled to do so under the terms of the contract of sale entered into by the store manager. The Court went on to say that, although the contract of sale my have been 'voidable' (that is, the other parties to it could have it set aside because they had been duped into it), nevertheless the goods were transferred to Gomez's friend with the express authority of the 'owner' (the store manager).

On the appeal by the Director of Public Prosecutions to the House of Lords, Lord Keith followed an earlier case (*Lawrence* v *Metropolitan Police Commissioner* [1972] AC 626). His Lordship disagreed with the argument that an act expressly or impliedly authorised by the owner can never amount to an 'appropriation' and pointed out that the decision in *Lawrence* was a direct contradiction of that proposition. The House of Lords upheld the men's convictions for theft and accepted that there are occasions where property can be 'appropriated' for the purposes of the Theft Act 1968, *even though the owner has given his/her consent or authority*.

A number of issues come from this decision:

- *Taking or depriving*. First, it is not necessary that the property be 'taken' in order for there to be an appropriation (contrast this with the offence under s. 12 of taking a conveyance, **see para. 12.7**), neither need the owner be 'deprived' of the property. Similarly, there is no need for the defendant to 'gain' anything by an appropriation which can also be caused by damaging or destroying property (*R* v *Graham* [1997] 1 Cr App R 395). (For offences involving criminal damage, **see chapter 14.**)

- *Consent.* Secondly, it is irrelevant to the issue of appropriation whether or not the owner consented to that appropriation (again, contrast the offence under s. 12, **see para. 12.7**). This is well illustrated in *Lawrence*, the decision followed by the House of Lords in *Gomez*. In *Lawrence* a tourist gave his wallet full of unfamiliar English currency to a taxi driver for the latter to remove the correct fare. The driver in fact helped himself to ('appropriated') far more than the amount owed. It has held that the fact that the wallet and its contents were handed over freely (with consent) by the owner did not prevent the taxi driver's actions from amounting to an 'appropriation' of it. The Court of Appeal appears — at least on one occasion — to have interpreted *Gomez* as deciding that consent *obtained by fraud* is irrelevant to the issue of appropriation (see *R* v *Mazo* [1997] 2 Cr App R 518). However, there is no such restriction placed on the decision in *Gomez* and it seems safe to assume that *no* consent given by the owner of property can prevent it being 'appropriated' for the purposes of the Theft Act 1968. This creates a considerable overlap with offences of deception (**see chapter 13**).

- *Interfering with goods.* Our higher courts were greatly concerned for a number of years by the swapping of price labels on goods displayed for sale in shops and whether or not such behaviour amounted to an appropriation. A third point that is now clear from the decision in *Gomez* is that simply swapping the price labels on items displayed for sale in a shop *would* amount to an 'appropriation'. This is because to do so, irrespective of any further intention, involves an assumption of one of the owner's rights in relation to the property. If that appropriation were accompanied by the required circumstances of dishonesty and intention to deprive, then there would be a *prima facie* case of theft.

- *More than one appropriation.* A fourth point apparent from *Gomez* is that there may be an appropriation of the same property on more than one occasion. However, once property has been *stolen* (as opposed to merely appropriated), that same property cannot be stolen again by the same thief (*R* v *Atakpu* [1994] QB 69). Appropriation can also be a continuing act, that is, it can include the whole episode of entering and ransacking a house and the subsequent removal of property (*R* v *Hale* (1978) 68 Cr App R 415). Therefore identifying the exact point at which property was appropriated with the requisite intention and accompanying dishonesty can cause practical difficulties, particularly in cases involving cheques and credit transactions. The advice of the Crown Prosecution Service should be sought in such cases.

Summary

The House of Lords was recently asked to rule on whether a person could 'appropriate' property belonging to another where the other person made her an absolute gift of property, retaining no proprietary interest in the property or any right to resume or recover it (*R* v *Hinks* [2000] 3 WLR 1590). In that case the defendant had befriended a middle aged man of limited intelligence who had given her some £60,000 over a period of time. The defendant was charged with five counts of theft and, after conviction, eventually appealed to the House of Lords. Their Lordships held that:

- in a prosecution for theft it was unnecessary to prove that the taking was without the owner's consent (as in *Lawrence* above);

- it was immaterial whether the act of appropriation was done with the owner's consent or authority (as in *Gomez*); and

- *Gomez* therefore gave effect to s. 3(1) by treating 'appropriation' as a neutral word covering 'any assumption by a person of the rights of an owner'.

Although consistent with earlier cases, this approach creates a few problems. If acceptance of the gift were treated as an 'appropriation', the defendant would seem to have had a belief that she had a right to deprive the donor of the property (**see para. 12.2.1**) and therefore she was not 'dishonest'. Further, under s. 5 of the 1968 Act (**see para. 12.2.5**) the prosecution has to prove that, at the time of the alleged appropriation, the relevant property belonged to another. In *Hinks* the defendant had been validly given the property, therefore it is difficult to see how the money still belonged to the donor at the time of appropriation.

These and other concerns were raised by Lord Hobhouse who pointed out that ss. 1 to 6 should be read as a whole and that attempts to 'compartmentalise' each element only lead to contradictions. However, he was in a minority and the case decision stands, compartments and all.

If a person, having come by property — innocently or not — without stealing it, later assumes any rights to it by keeping it or treating it as his/her own, then he/she 'appropriates' that property (s. 3(1)).

An exception to these circumstances is provided by s. 3 which states:

> (2)   Where property or a right or interest in property is or purports to be transferred for value to a person acting in good faith, no later assumption by him of rights which he believed himself to be acquiring shall, by reason of any defect in the transferor's title, amount to theft of the property.

Keynote

If a person buys a car in good faith and gives value for it (i.e. a reasonable price) but then discovers it has been stolen, his/her refusal to return it to the vendor will not, without more, *attract liability for theft*. Without s. 3(2) the retention of the vehicle would be caught by s. 3(1). This narrow exemption does not mean however that the innocent purchaser gets good title to the car (see *National Employers' Mutual Insurance Association* v *Jones* [1990] AC 24).

12.2.4   Property

The Theft Act 1968, s. 4 states:

> (1)   'Property' includes money and all other property, real or personal, including things in action and other intangible property.
> (2)   A person cannot steal land, or things forming part of land and severed from it by him or by his directions, except in the following cases, that is to say—
> (a)   when he is a trustee or personal representative, or is authorised by power of attorney, or as liquidator of a company, or otherwise, to sell or dispose of land belonging to another, and he

appropriates the land or anything forming part of it by dealing with it in breach of the confidence reposed in him; or

    (b)   when he is not in possession of the land and appropriates anything forming part of the land by severing it or causing it to be severed, or after it has been severed; or

    (c)   when, being in possession of the land under a tenancy, he appropriates the whole or part of any fixture or structure let to be used with the land.

For purposes of this subsection 'land' does not include incorporeal hereditaments; 'tenancy' means a tenancy for years or any less period and includes an agreement for such a tenancy, but a person who after the end of a tenancy remains in possession as statutory tenant or otherwise is to be treated as having possession under the tenancy, and 'let' shall be construed accordingly.

    (3)   A person who picks mushrooms growing wild on any land, or who picks flowers, fruit or foliage from a plant growing wild on any land, does not (although not in possession of the land) steal what he picks unless he does it for reward or for sale or other commercial purpose.

For purposes of this subsection 'mushroom' includes any fungus, and 'plant' includes any shrub or tree.

    (4)   Wild creatures, tamed or untamed, shall be regarded as property; but a person cannot steal a wild creature not tamed nor ordinarily kept in captivity, or the carcase of any such creature, unless either it has been reduced into possession by or on behalf of another person and possession of it has not since been lost or abandoned, or another person is in course of reducing it into possession.

Keynote

Under s. 4(1) 'things in action' would include patents and trademarks and other things which can only be enforced by legal action as opposed to physical possession. Other intangible property would include software programs and perhaps credits accumulated on 'smart cards'. Confidential information — such as the contents of an examination paper (!) — is not intangible property *per se* (see *Oxford* v *Moss* (1978) 68 Cr App R 183). However, the document itself would be property. It has been accepted by the Court of Appeal that contractual rights obtained by buying a ticket for the London Underground may amount to a 'thing in action' (see *R* v *Marshall* [1998] 2 Cr App R 282), though this view is extremely contentious.

Cheques will be property as they are pieces of paper (albeit of very little intrinsic value). The contents of a bank or building society account, however, are also a 'thing in action' that can be stolen *provided the account is in credit or within the limits of an agreed overdraft facility* (*R* v *Kohn* (1979) 69 Cr App R 395). Therefore reducing the credit balance in one account, and transferring a like sum into your own account amounts to an 'appropriation' within the meaning of s. 1. This principle (set out in *Kohn*) was reaffirmed in *R* v *Williams (Roy)*, *The Times*, 25 October 2000 by the Court of Appeal. (For an alternative offence where someone else is deceived into transferring a credit balance to another account, see chapter 13).

Under s. 4(2) you cannot generally steal land even though it is 'property' for the purposes of criminal damage (**see chapter 14**). It also seems that the restrictions relating to land as 'property' under s. 4(2) above do not apply to offences of obtaining property by deception (see *Blackstone's Criminal Practice*, 2001, section B5.27. For the offence of obtaining property by deception, **see chapter 13**. If you are a trustee or personal representative or someone in a position of trust to dispose of land belonging to another you can be guilty of stealing it.

If you are in possession of land under a tenancy then things forming part of that land to be used with it are 'property'. Such fittings and fixtures (including fireplaces, fitted kitchens etc.) would be particularly relevant to agricultural tenants or those occupying council property.

Section 4(3) obliquely includes mushrooms, flowers, fruit and foliage in the ambit of 'property' unless they are growing wild on any land. If they are so growing, then the person picking them must be shown to have done so for reward, sale or other commercial purpose in order to be guilty of theft. It is arguable that, if the person does not have such a *purpose at the time of the picking*, any later intention to sell the fruit etc. may not bring it within the provisions of s. 4(3).

Section 4(4) appears slightly confusing in that the subsection acknowledges that all wild creatures are 'property' but goes on to qualify the occasions when they will be capable of supporting a charge of theft. Once a person has reduced it into possession (say, by trapping, capturing or shooting it), a wild animal can be 'stolen', as it can during the process of so reducing it into possession. If the animal is lost or abandoned after it has been reduced into possession or killed then it cannot be 'stolen'.

These provisos appear to relate more to the concept of 'belonging to another' (see below) than 'property'.

Pets and animals that are tamed or ordinarily kept in captivity are always property for the purposes of theft.

What is not Property?

Human bodies are not property (*Doodeward* v *Spence* (1907) 6 CLR 406) although a driver has been convicted of stealing a specimen of his own urine (*R* v *Welsh* [1974] RTR 478). This principle was upheld by the Court of Appeal in *R* v *Kelly* [1999] QB 621, after the conviction of two people involved in the theft of body parts from the Royal College of Surgeons. The court upheld the convictions for theft on the grounds that the process of *alteration* (amputation, dissection and preservation) which the body parts had undergone did make them 'property' for the purposes of the 1968 Act. The common law rule was that there is no property in a corpse and any change to that rule would have to be made by Parliament.

Electricity is the subject of a specific offence (**see para. 12.10**).

12.2.5   Belonging to Another

The Theft Act 1968, s. 5 states:

> *(1)   Property shall be regarded as belonging to any person having possession or control of it, or having in it any proprietary right or interest (not being an equitable interest arising only from an agreement to transfer or grant an interest).*
> *(2)   Where property is subject to a trust, the persons to whom it belongs shall be regarded as including any person having a right to enforce the trust, and an intention to defeat the trust shall be regarded accordingly as an intention to deprive of the property any person having that right.*

Keynote

Property can be 'stolen' from any person who has possession or control or a right or interest in that property. In one case where the defendant sneaked into a garage to recover his own recently-repaired car, he was convicted of stealing the car which at the time 'belonged to' the garage proprietor who had possession and control of it (*R* v *Turner (No. 2)* [1971] 1 WLR 901). In determining whether or not a person had 'possession' of property for the purposes of s. 5(1), the period of possession can be finite (i.e. for a given number of hours, days etc.) or infinite (*R* v *Kelly* [1998] 3 All ER 741).

It is not necessary to show who does own the property — only that it 'belongs to' someone other than the defendant. (For rights of the Crown under the Treasure Act 1996 and other statutes, see *Blackstone's Criminal Practice*, 2001, section B4.18.)

When a cheque is written, that will create a 'thing in action'. That thing in action belongs only to the payee. Therefore a payee of a cheque cannot 'steal' the thing in action which it creates (*R* v *Davies* (1988) 88 Cr App R 347). The piece of paper on which a cheque is printed will also be property — however low in value (**see para. 12.2.4**).

In proving theft, you must show that the property belonged to another *at the time of the appropriation*. This requirement has caused some difficulty where a defendant's decision not to pay for goods has been made *after* property passed to him/her. In such cases (e.g. people refusing to pay for meals after they have eaten or deciding to drive off having filled their car with petrol), the proper charge has been one of deception or making off without payment (**see chapter 13**). But it should be remembered that the appropriation can be an extended and continuing act (*R* v *Atakpu* [1994] QB 69). The House of Lords' ruling in *Gomez* raises some questions over such cases, **see para. 12.2.3**). As the consent of the owner is irrelevant to the issue of 'appropriation', the key element in such cases is whether the property 'belonged to another' at the time of the act of appropriation. If ownership of the property had passed to the defendant *before* he/she appropriated it (e.g. by virtue of the Sale of Goods Act 1979; see *Edwards* v *Ddin* [1976] 1 WLR 942) then this element of theft would not be made out and an alternative charge should be considered.

12.2.6 Obligations Regarding Another's Property

The Theft Act 1968, s. 5 states:

> (3)   *Where a person receives property from or on account of another, and is under an obligation to the other to retain and deal with that property or its proceeds in a particular way, the property or proceeds shall be regarded (as against him) as belonging to the other.*

Keynote

'Obligation' means a legal obligation, not simply a moral one (*R* v *Hall* [1973] QB 126). Whether or not such an obligation exists is a matter of law for a trial judge to decide (*R* v *Dubar* [1994] 1 WLR 1484).

Instances under s. 5(3) most commonly involve receiving money from others to retain and use in a certain way (e.g. travel agents taking deposits; solicitors holding funds for mortgagees; or pension fund managers collecting contributions (*R* v *Clowes (No. 2)* [1994] 2 All ER 316)). The Court of Appeal has held that one effect of s. 5(3), is that property can be regarded as belonging to another even where it does not 'belong' to them on a strict interpretation of civil law (*R* v *Klineberg* [1999] 1 Cr App R 427). In that case the defendants collected money from customers in their timeshare business. Although the customers were told that their deposits would be placed with an independent trustee, the defendants paid the sums into their company account, thereby breaching the 'obligation' under s. 5(3) to deal with the money in a particular way. Section 5(3) would also include, say, the owners of shopping malls where coins thrown into a fountain are to be donated to charity; if the owners did not deal with those coins in the way intended, the provisions of s. 5(3) may well apply.

12.2.7   Obligation to Restore Another's Property

The Theft Act 1968, s. 5 states:

> *(4)   Where a person gets property by another's mistake, and is under an obligation to make restoration (in whole or in part) of the property or its proceeds or of the value thereof, then to the extent of that obligation the property or proceeds shall be regarded (as against him) as belonging to the person entitled to restoration, and an intention not to make restoration shall be regarded accordingly as an intention to deprive that person of the property or proceeds.*

Keynote

Before s. 5(4) was enacted, an employee who was mistakenly credited with extra money in his/her bank account could not be prosecuted for larceny (the predecessor of theft) (*Moynes* v *Cooper* [1956] 1 QB 439). In such circumstances under s. 5(4) the employee will be liable for stealing the extra money if he/she keeps it (see *Attorney-General's Reference (No. 1 of 1983)* [1985] QB 182 where a police officer's account was credited with money representing overtime which she had not actually worked).

Section 5(4) only applies where someone *other than the defendant* has made a mistake. It is clear that such a mistake can be a mistake as to a material fact; whether or not a mistake as to *law* would be covered is unclear.

Again, the obligation to make restoration is a *legal* one and, as with s. 5(3), an unenforceable or moral obligation will not be covered by s. 5(4). (See *R* v *Gilks* [1972] 1 WLR 1341 where a betting shop mistakenly paid out winnings against the wrong horse. As gambling debts are not legally enforceable the defendant was not under 'an obligation' to restore the money and therefore s. 5(4) did not apply.)

For offences invoving money transfers, **see chapter 13**.

12.2.8   Intention of Permanently Depriving

If you cannot prove an intention permanently to deprive you cannot prove theft (see *R* v *Warner* (1970) 55 Cr App R 93).

If there is such an intention at the time of the appropriation, giving the property back later will not alter the fact and the charge will be made out (*R* v *McHugh* (1993) 97 Cr App R 335).

In certain circumstances s. 6 may help in determining the presence or absence of such an intention.

The Theft Act 1968, s. 6 states:

> *(1)   A person appropriating property belonging to another without meaning the other permanently to lose the thing itself is nevertheless to be regarded as having the intention of permanently depriving the other of it if his intention is to treat the thing as his own to dispose of regardless of the other's rights; and a borrowing or lending of it may amount to so treating it if, but only if, the borrowing or lending is for a period and in circumstances making it equivalent to an outright taking or disposal.*

Keynote

The key feature of s. 6(1) is the intention to treat 'the thing' as one's own to dispose of regardless of the other's rights. An example of such a case would be where property is 'held to ransom' (*R* v *Coffey* [1987] Crim LR 498). The borrowing or lending of another's property is specifically caught within s. 6(1). If a person takes property from his/her employer (e.g. carpet tiles) and uses it in a way which makes restoration unlikely or impossible (e.g. by laying them in his/her living room), then s. 6(1) will apply (see *R* v *Velumyl* [1989] Crim LR 299).

Similarly, if a person borrowed a season ticket causing the owner to miss a match, s. 6(1) would help prove the required intention because the circumstances of the borrowing make it equivalent to an outright taking.

The Theft Act 1968, s. 6 states:

> (2)   Without prejudice to the generality of subsection (1) above, where a person, having possession or control (lawfully or not) of property belonging to another, parts with the property under a condition as to its return which he may not be able to perform, this (if done for purposes of his own and without the other's authority) amounts to treating the property as his own to dispose of regardless of the other's rights.

Keynote

Section 6(2) deals with occasions such as pawning another's property. If there is a likelihood that the defendant will be unable to meet the conditions under which he/she parted with another person's property, s. 6(2) would help in proving an intention permanently to deprive.

12.3   Robbery

Offence — Robbery — Theft Act 1968, s. 8
Triable on indictment. Life imprisonment.
(**Arrestable offence**)

The Theft Act 1968, s. 8 states:

> (1)   A person is guilty of robbery if he steals, and immediately before or at the time of doing so, and in order to do so, he uses force on any person or puts or seeks to put any person in fear of being then and there subjected to force.

Keynote

For there to be a robbery, there must be a theft and, consequently, dishonesty (*R* v *Robinson* [1977] Crim LR 173. The defendant must either:

- Use *force* on any person. If the force used is applied, not to the person directly but to his/her property (such as pulling a shopping basket or handbag from his/her hand), this may still be robbery as the force has still been applied, albeit indirectly (*Corcoran* v *Anderton* (1980) 71 Cr App R 104).

  Or

- Put, or seek to put, *any* person in fear of being then and there subjected to force. It is not enough to threaten to use force on some future occasion, or to use force at some place other than at the scene, nor is it enough to show simply that the victim was frightened; you must show that the defendant put or sought to put the victim in fear of being then and there subjected to force (see *R* v *Khan* (2001) LTL 9 April).

As the force must be used *in order to steal*, it would seem to follow that an accidental application of force during a theft would not be enough to prove robbery.

The force used or threatened must be on or towards *any* person, not necessarily the person from whom the theft is committed. Although the wording does not make it clear, it appears that any person means any person *other than the defendant*. Pretending to use force on an accomplice in order to compel a third person to part with his/her property would probably not come within the parameters of the offence as the defendant would not in reality be 'using' force on the accomplice nor seeking to put him/her in fear of being then and there subjected to such force.

Whether force has been used or a person so put in fear will be a question of fact for a jury (*R* v *Dawson* (1976) 64 Cr App R 170). If force or the fear of force is proved, it must also be shown that it was used at the time or *immediately* before the theft, and *in order to carry out the theft*. If the defendant used force in order to escape having stolen property from another, then this element would not be satisfied. It is important to remember, however, that appropriation (**see para. 12.2.3**) can be regarded as a continuing act. If you can show that when a defendant used force on another, he/she was still in the throes of appropriating property, this element will be satisfied.

Robbery is a 'trigger' offence under s. 63B of the Police and Criminal Evidence Act 1984 which can activate police powers to require a sample from a person in police detention in some police areas to ascertain the presence of a specified Class A drug (**see Evidence and Procedure, chapter 15**).

12.4 Burglary

12.4.1 Section 9(1)(a)

Offence — Burglary — Theft Act 1968, s. 9
Triable on indictment if 'ulterior offence' is so triable, or if committed in dwelling and violence used; otherwise triable either way. Fourteen years' imprisonment (if building/part of building is dwelling, otherwise ten years' imprisonment on indictment; six months' imprisonment and/or a fine summarily.
(*Arrestable offence*)

The Theft Act 1968, s. 9 states:

(1)   A person is guilty of burglary if—
   (a)   he enters any building or part of a building as a trespasser and with intent to commit any such offence as is mentioned in subsection (2) below; or . . .
   (2)   The offences referred to in subsection (1)(a) above are offences of stealing anything in the building or part of a building in question, of inflicting on any person therein any grievous bodily harm or raping any person therein, and of doing unlawful damage to the building or anything therein.

Keynote

There are two types of burglary. The first one is concerned with the defendant's *intentions when entering the building or part of a building*. Entry into a building or part of a building must be 'effective and substantial' (*R* v *Collins* [1973] QB 100).

178

The defendant does not need to get his/her whole body into the building; provided that the entry is deliberate (i.e. not accidental), an entry by part of the body will be sufficient. A defendant may use an object as an extension of themselves to 'enter' and ultimately the question of whether they entered or not will be one of fact for a jury or magistrate(s).

The defendant's entry must be trespassory, that is, without any express or implied permission. Often permission is given conditionally, as with a householder inviting a television engineer to inspect his/her television, or a shopkeeper inviting shoppers to browse through goods on display. In such cases, entry becomes trespassory if someone goes beyond that condition, for instance by taking a TV set (*R* v *Jones* [1976] 1 WLR 672) or going behind the counter in a shop (*R* v *Walkington* [1979] 1 WLR 1169). In order to prove that an entry was trespassory it must be shown that the defendant knew that he/she did not have permission, or was at least reckless as to that fact.

Burglary under s. 9(1)(a) is a crime of *ulterior intent*, that is, in addition to the deliberate entry as a trespasser, the defendant must be shown to have had one of the ulterior intentions listed at s. 9(2). These intentions must coincide with the trespassory entry, that is, they must have been formed in the mind of the defendant by the time he/she enters the building/part of a building. This requirement is a further example of the principle that *mens rea* and *actus reus* must coincide (**see chapter 2**). This requirement for the relevant ulterior intention should be contrasted with burglary under s. 9(1)(b) (**see para. 12.4.2**) which only requires that the trespasser goes on to do certain things inside the building/part of a building. This distinction is particularly important in relation to defences (**see chapter 4**).

Sections 1 and 2 of the Criminal Evidence (Amendment) Act 1997 extending the power to take non-intimate samples without consent apply to all offences of burglary including aggravated burglary (**see para. 12.5**) and also to conspiracies, attempts or incitements in the circumstances set out in that Act (**see Evidence and Procedure, chapter 16**).

This is a 'trigger' offence under s. 63B of the Police and Criminal Evidence Act 1984 which can activate police powers to require a sample from a person in police detention to ascertain the presence of a specified Class A drug in some police areas (**see Evidence and Procedure, chapter 15**).

Building

The Theft Act 1968 s. 9 states:

> *(4)   References in subsections (1) and (2) above to a building, . . . and . . . to a building which is a dwelling, shall apply also to an inhabited vehicle or vessel, and shall apply to any such vehicle or vessel at times when the person having a habitation in it is not there as well as at times when he is.*

Keynote

The effect of s. 9(4) is to include house boats or vehicles used as dwellings. There is a general requirement for 'buildings' to have some degree of permanence (*Norfolk Constabulary* v *Seekings* [1986] Crim LR 167). An unfinished house can be a building for the purposes of burglary (*R* v *Manning* (1871) LR 1 CCR 338), as can an industrial freezer (*B* v *Leathley* [1979] Crim LR 314).

Intentions at the Time of Entry

The intentions must be as follows:

- Stealing — this means an intention to commit theft under s. 1 (**see para. 12.2**). It will not include abstracting electricity because abstracting under s. 13 is not stealing (*Low* v *Blease* [1975] Crim LR 513) (**see para. 12.10**), neither will it include taking a conveyance (**see para. 12.7**). The property which the defendant intends to steal must be in a building or part of a building.

- Inflicting grievous bodily harm — this will present practical difficulties if no grievous bodily harm is ultimately inflicted or if the defendant did not carry a weapon. If grievous bodily harm is inflicted (**see chapter 8**), then the second offence under s. 9(1)(b) below would apply. In proving an intention to commit grievous bodily harm under s. 9(1)(a), it is not necessary to prove that an assault was actually committed (*Metropolitan Police Commissioner* v *Wilson* [1984] AC 242).

- Raping any person — the intended victim may be male or female. Again proof of such an intention will be difficult (**see chapter 10**). Where a person is charged with this offence, the Youth Justice and Criminal Evidence Act 1999 imposes certain restrictions on the introduction of evidence or the asking of questions at trial relating to the victim's sexual behaviour (**see Evidence and Procedure, chapter 6**).

- Causing unlawful damage — this includes damage, not only to the building but to anything in it (**see chapter 14**).

Conditional Intent

Provided the required intention can be proved, it is immaterial whether or not there is anything 'worth stealing' within the building (*R* v *Walkington* [1979] 1 WLR 1169). Presumably the same will be true if the person whom the defendant intends to rape or to cause serious harm is not in the building or part of the building at the time (see also criminal attempts, **chapter 3**).

12.4.2   **Section 9(1)(b)**

Offence — Burglary — Theft Act 1968, s. 9
(see para. 12.4.1)

The Theft Act 1968, s. 9 states:

> *(1)   A person is guilty of burglary if—*
> . . .
> *(b)   having entered any building or part of a building as a trespasser he steals or attempts to steal anything in the building or that part of it or inflicts or attempts to inflict on any person therein any grievous bodily harm.*

Keynote

The second type of burglary involves a defendant's behaviour *after* entering a building or part of a building.

The defendant must have entered the building or part of a building as a trespasser; it is not enough that he/she subsequently became a trespasser by exceeding a condition of entry (e.g. hiding in the public area of a shop during open hours until the shop closes). However, where a person has entered a particular building (such as a shop or a pub) lawfully and without trespassing, if he/she later moves to *another part* of the building as a trespasser, this element of the offence will be made out.

Example

D enters a public house near closing time with a friend who buys him a drink from the bar. D's entry onto that part of the premises has been authorised by the implied licence extended to members of the adult public by the publican and therefore D is not a trespasser. D then goes into the lavatories to use them as such. At this point he has entered another part of a building but again his entry is made under the implied licence to customers wishing to use the lavatories. While inside the lavatory area, D decides to hide until closing time in order to avoid buying his friend a drink. He hides inside one of the cubicles. At this point, although D's intention in hiding may be considered a little mean-spirited, he has none of the required intentions for the purposes of s. 9(1)(a) (**see para. 12.4.1**).

Once the publican has shut the pub for the night, D leaves the lavatory and walks into the bar area. Now D has entered *a part of a building as a trespasser* because the licence extended to members of the public by the publican certainly does not cover wandering around in the bar after it has been closed. Having no particular intention at this point, however, D has still not committed an offence of burglary.

On seeing the gaming machines in the public bar, D decides to break into them and steal the money inside. At this point, although he has *two* of the required intentions for s. 9(1)(a) (an intention to steal and an intention to cause unlawful damage), those intentions were formed *after* his entry. Therefore, D has not committed burglary under s. 9(1)(a). Because he has not stolen/attempted to steal or inflicted/attempted to inflict grievous bodily harm on any person therein, D has not committed burglary under s. 9(1)(b) either.

D then breaks open a gaming machine. At this point he commits burglary under s. 9(1)(b). This is because, having entered a part of a building (the public bar area) as a trespasser (because the pub is closed and D knows that to be the case), he *attempts to steal*. If he simply damaged the machine without an intention of stealing the contents, D would not commit this offence because causing unlawful damage is only relevant to the offence under *s. 9(1)(a)*.

It has been argued that, if a defendant's intentions at the time of entering a building or part of a building are dishonest then he/she would automatically become a trespasser because any conditional or implied permission from the occupier to enter would not include someone with dishonest intentions. Such an argument would mean that all shoplifters could be charged with burglary (an argument which is unlikely to endear you to your Crime Manager!). Whether or not this argument has any merit, one thing is clear in relation to trespassers in cases of burglary. There is a doctrine at common law that an unlawful act by a person lawfully on premises has a retrospective effect, rendering the person's presence trespassory *ab initio* ('from the outset'). This means that, even if a person has entered the land lawfully, any later wrongdoing would make his/her whole entry and presence on the premises trespassory. Clearly this would have a significant effect on the number of offences that could be classified as burglaries and would support the argument above. Thankfully, the common law doctrine has been held not to apply to burglary (see *R v Collins* [1973] QB 100).

Unlike s. 9(1)(a), there are only two further elements to the offence under s. 9(1)(b) — the subsequent theft/attempted theft of anything in the building or part of it, and the subsequent inflicting/attempted inflicting of grievous bodily harm to any person therein.

This is also a 'trigger' offence under s. 63B of the Police and Criminal Evidence Act 1984 which can activate police powers to require a sample from a person in police detention to ascertain the presence of a specified Class A drug in some police areas (**see Evidence and Procedure, chapter 15**).

12.5   Aggravated Burglary

Offence — Aggravated Burglary — Theft Act 1968, s. 10
Triable on indictment. Life imprisonment.
(*Arrestable offence*)

The Theft Act 1968, s. 10 states:

>   *(1)   A person is guilty of aggravated burglary if he commits any burglary and at the time has with him any firearm or imitation firearm, any weapon of offence or any explosive.*

Keynote

The 'time' at which the defendant must have the weapon etc. with him/her is critical and will depend on the type of burglary with which he/she is charged. If the defendant is charged with an offence under s. 9(1)(a), he/she must be shown to have had the weapon *at the time of entry*. Therefore if several people are charged with the offence of aggravated burglary, it must be shown that one of the defendants who actually entered the building had the weapon with them (*R v Klass* [1998] 1 Cr App R 453). If the charge is brought under s. 9(1)(b), he/she must be shown to have had the weapon *at the time of stealing or inflicting grievous bodily harm*.

Example

A person (X) enters a house as a trespasser intending to steal the contents. While inside, X is disturbed by the occupier. X grabs a kitchen knife from the kitchen and threatens the occupier.

If charged with burglary under s. 9(1)(a), X does not, on these facts alone, commit the offence of aggravated burglary because he did not have the weapon (kitchen knife) *at the time* of the burglary. If, however, X grabs the knife from the kitchen and stabs the occupier, *inflicting grievous bodily harm*, he commits the offence of burglary under s. 9(1)(b) *and at the time* has with him a weapon of offence. (See *R v O'Leary* (1986) 82 Cr App R 341.) Therefore X would be guilty of aggravated burglary. Similarly, if X followed the occupier into another part of the house intending to stab him, he would commit aggravated burglary.

'Has with him' will require a degree of immediate control (*R v Pawlicki* [1992] 1 WLR 827) and will normally be the same as 'carrying' (*Klass* above).

In cases where a defendant has been found entering a building with a weapon, it will not be necessary to prove any intention to use that weapon during the burglary (*R v Stones* [1989] 1 WLR 156).

For other offences involving weapons, **see General Police Duties, chapter 6**.

The aggravated form of burglary is also a 'trigger' offence under s. 63B of the Police and Criminal Evidence Act 1984 which can activate police powers to require a sample from a person in police detention to ascertain the presence of a specified Class A drug in some police forces (**see Evidence and Procedure, chapter 15**).

12.5.1 Firearm/Weapon of Offence/Explosive

The Theft Act 1968, s. 10 states:

> *(1) . . . and for this purpose—*
> *(a) 'firearm' includes an airgun or pistol, and 'imitation firearm' means anything which has the appearance of being a firearm, whether capable of being discharged or not, and*
> *(b) 'weapon of offence' means any article made or adapted for use for causing injury to or incapacitating a person, or intended by the person having it with him for such use; and*
> *(c) 'explosive' means any article manufactured for the purpose of producing a practical effect by explosion, or intended by the person having it with him for that purpose.*

Keynote

The 'person' whom the article is intended to injure or incapacitate under s. 9(1)(b) above need not be a person in the building/part of a building. If a burglar has a weapon that he/she intends to use to injure or incapacitate someone unconnected with the building/part of a building, he/she may be tempted to use that weapon during the course of the burglary; the very consequence behind the creation of this offence (see *Stones* above).

It would appear that the defendant must at least know they have an article with them *and* that the article is in fact a weapon of offence (see *Blackstone's Criminal Practice*, 2001, section B4.80).

Note the additional element of articles made, adapted or intended for 'incapacitating' a person. This is broader than the other legislation defining weapons and would include rope, binding tape, chloroform, handcuffs and CS spray.

12.6 Removal of Articles from Places Open to the Public

Offence — Removal of Articles — Theft Act 1968, s. 11
Triable either way. Five years' imprisonment on indictment; six months' imprisonment and/or a fine summarily.
(*Arrestable offence*)

The Theft Act 1968, s. 11 states:

> *(1) Subject to subsections (2) and (3) below, where the public have access to a building in order to view the building or part of it, or a collection or part of a collection housed in it, any person who without lawful authority removes from the building or its grounds the whole or part of any article*

displayed or kept for display to the public in the building or that part of it or in its grounds shall be guilty of an offence.

For this purpose, 'collection' includes a collection got together for a temporary purpose, but references in this section to a collection do not apply to a collection made or exhibited for the purpose of effecting sales or other commercial dealings.

Keynote

This is a specific offence designed for circumstances where there is no intention of permanently depriving the owner of property. If a person borrows a painting or a sculpture to enjoy in his/her own home for a while, intending to put it back later, he/she may commit this offence. The important features are:

- the access to the public must be for the purpose of viewing the building or part of the building or the collection or part of the collection

- the article(s) removed must be in the building or grounds for the purpose of public display but not for sale, and

- the article(s) must be removed therefrom.

If paintings are swapped around or hidden somewhere else in a gallery, this offence would not be made out. Neither would it be made out if the removed article was not part of a displayed 'collection', such as cleaning materials in a gallery caretaker's cupboard (although with some of our contemporary artists this distinction may be difficult to make). Articles placed in a church for religious worship are not necessarily 'kept for display' but may have a functional role in which case the offence would not apply (*R* v *Barr* [1978] Crim LR 244).

12.6.1 Public Access

The Theft Act 1968, s. 11 states:

(2) It is immaterial for purposes of subsection (1) above, that the public's access to a building is limited to a particular period or particular occasion; but where anything removed from a building or its grounds is there otherwise than as forming part of, or being on loan for exhibition with, a collection intended for permanent exhibition to the public, the person removing it does not thereby commit an offence under this section unless he removes it on a day when the public have access to the building as mentioned in subsection (1) above.

Keynote

If the building is usually open for the public to view a collection or exhibition, it is possible to commit this offence even on days when it is actually closed.

12.6.2 Lawful Authority

The Theft Act 1968, s. 11 states:

(3) A person does not commit an offence under this section if he believes that he has lawful authority for the removal of the thing in question or that he would have it if the person entitled to give it knew of the removal and the circumstances of it.

Keynote

There does not appear to be any requirement that the defendant's belief be a reasonable one, simply that he/she had that belief at the time of the removal of the articles. Where the defendant alleges that he/she had such a belief, the onus will be on the prosecution to prove that no such belief existed (see *R* v *MacPherson* [1973] RTR 157, a case involving a similar provision under s. 12(6)).

12.7   Taking a Conveyance without Consent

Offence — Taking a Conveyance without the Owner's Consent — Theft Act 1968, s. 12
Triable summarily. Six months' imprisonment and/or a fine.
(*Arrestable offence*)

The Theft Act 1968, s. 12 states:

> *(1) Subject to subsections (5) and (6) below, a person shall be guilty of an offence if, without having the consent of the owner or other lawful authority, he takes any conveyance for his own or another's use or, knowing that any conveyance has been taken without such authority, drives it or allows himself to be carried in or on it.*

Keynote

As with other offences requiring the absence of consent, any 'consent' given must be true consent if the defendant is to avoid liability. The identity of the person taking the conveyance may be of particular importance to the owner (i.e. he/she would not lend his/her car to just anybody). If that can be shown to be the case, consent would be negated by the taker pretending to be someone to whom the owner would not ordinarily lend the vehicle. However, if it cannot be shown that the person's identity was of importance to the owner (e.g. where the owner is a car hire company), simply pretending to be someone else and producing a driving licence in another's name would not, of itself, be enough to negate any 'consent' (see *Whittaker* v *Campbell* [1984] QB 318).

Where the consent is obtained by a misrepresentation as to the purpose or destination of the journey, that misrepresentation has been held not to negate the consent (see *R* v *Peart* [1970] 2 QB 672). This seems difficult to reconcile with the defence at s. 12(6) (see below).

Going beyond the express or implied permission of the owner may also negate consent (*R* v *Phipps* (1970) 54 Cr App R 300). This is often encountered where employees deviate substantially from an agreed route in their employer's vehicle or take the vehicle for a purpose entirely different from that permitted.

Lawful authority may come from many different sources. A police officer removing a vehicle which is obstructing traffic after an accident or an agent of a finance company re-possessing a vehicle would be examples of such authority. In addition, s. 12(6) provides:

> *A person does not commit an offence under this section by anything done in the belief that he has lawful authority to do it or that he would have the owner's consent if the owner knew of his doing it and the circumstances of it.*

THEFT AND RELATED OFFENCES

There are similarities here with the element of dishonesty under the Theft Act 1968, s. 2(1)(b) (**see para. 12.2.1**). In order to attract the exemption under this subsection the person taking the conveyance must show:

- a belief that he/she had lawful authority at the time of the taking, or

- a belief that he/she would have the owner's consent had the owner known *of the taking and the circumstances of it.*

Example

If a police officer at a Police Training Centre usually allows her colleague to use her motor cycle to go to a local gym on Tuesdays and Thursdays, the colleague might be able to claim that s. 12(6) applies if he took the motor cycle for that purpose one Tuesday without prior permission. However, if he were to take her Nissan Micra to use in a time trials competition one Sunday afternoon without her consent, subsection (6) is unlikely to apply.

This offence, together with its aggravated form below, is a 'trigger' offence under s. 63B of the Police and Criminal Evidence Act 1984 which can activate police powers to require a sample from a person in police detention to ascertain the presence of a specified Class A drug in some force areas (**see Evidence and Procedure, chapter 15**).

12.7.1 Conveyance

The Theft Act 1968, s. 12(7) states:

> *(a) 'conveyance' means any conveyance constructed or adapted for the carriage of a person or persons whether by land, water, or air, except that it does not include a conveyance constructed or adapted for use only under the control of a person not carried in or on it, and 'drive' shall be construed accordingly . . .*

Keynote

It can be seen that this definition includes cars, motor cycles, boats or aircraft. It would also extend to pedal cycles but for the provisions of s. 12(5) which creates a parallel offence for such conveyances (**see para. 12.9**). The definition does not extend to hand carts or to animals used as conveyances, such as horses.

12.7.2 Taking for Own or Another's Use

To prove this offence you must show that the vehicle or conveyance was moved. It does not matter by how little the vehicle is moved but simply starting the engine is not enough (*R* v *Bogacki* [1973] QB 832) nor is hiding in a car or doing anything else in it while it is stationary. It is also worth noting that, as the offence is triable summarily only, there can be no 'attempt' (Criminal Attempts Act 1981, s. 1(1) and (4)). This is the case even though the 'offence' of attempting to take a conveyance still appears in sch. 2, part II of the Road Traffic Offenders Act 1988 (**see Road Traffic**).

The vehicle/conveyance must be 'taken', even if it is put onto another vehicle to do so (*R* v *Pearce* [1973] Crim LR 321, where a rubber dinghy was put on the roof rack of a car and taken away). The taking must be for the taker's or someone else's ultimate use as a conveyance. Pushing someone's car around the corner as a practical joke satisfies the first part ('taking') but not the second 'for one's own or another's use as a conveyance' (*R v Stokes* [1983] RTR 59). This is because, although the defendant may have 'taken' the conveyance, he/she did not do so for someone ultimately to use it as such. If the practical joker pushed the car round the corner in order for a friend to then start it out of earshot and drive it to a further location the offence *would* be committed at the time of pushing the car.

Where a person got into a Land Rover that was blocking his path and released the handbrake, allowing the vehicle to coast for several hundred metres, it was held that his actions satisfied both elements (*R v Bow* (1976) 64 Cr App R 54). This is because getting into (or onto) a conveyance and moving it is necessarily amounts to *taking it for use as a conveyance*, therefore the motives of a defendant in so doing are irrelevant. These decisions fit with the older notions of an offence of 'stealing a ride' rather than the vehicle itself.

Once a conveyance has been 'taken' it cannot be 'taken' again by the same person before it has been recovered (*R v Spriggs* [1994] RTR 1). This accords with the position in relation to the repeated theft of the same property by the same thief (**see para. 12.2.3**). However, where the original taker abandons the conveyance, it may be 'taken' by a further defendant and the original taker may be responsible for further offences arising out of its use before it is recovered (**see para. 12.8**).

The person taking a vehicle or conveyance must do so intentionally, i.e. not simply by moving it accidentally (*Blayney v Knight* (1974) 60 Cr App R 269).

12.7.3 Allowing Self to be Carried

If you cannot prove who took a vehicle/conveyance, you may be able to show that a defendant allowed himself/herself to be carried in or on it. You must also show that the defendant *knew* that the conveyance had been taken without the required consent or authority. It must also be shown that there was some movement of the vehicle while the defendant was in it (*R v Diggin* (1980) 72 Cr App R 204).

If, as often happens, all the occupants of a car so taken deny having been the driver, they can all be charged under this element of the offence provided there is sufficient evidence of *mens rea*.

12.8 Aggravated Vehicle-taking

Given the frequency of offences under s. 12, together with the anti-social and dangerous consequences, the offence of aggravated vehicle-taking was introduced.

Offence — Aggravated Vehicle Taking — Theft Act 1968, s. 12A
Triable either way. If the accident under s. 12A(2)(b) caused death (five years' imprisonment), otherwise two years' imprisonment and/or a fine on indictment; six months' imprisonment and/or a fine summarily.
(Arrestable offence)

The Theft Act 1968, s. 12A states:

(1) Subject to subsection (3) below, a person is guilty of aggravated taking of a vehicle if—

(a) he commits an offence under section 12(1) above (in this section referred to as a 'basic offence') in relation to a mechanically propelled vehicle; and

(b) it is proved that, at any time after the vehicle was unlawfully taken (whether by him or another) and before it was recovered, the vehicle was driven, or injury or damage was caused, in one or more of the circumstances set out in paragraphs (a) to (d) of subsection (2) below.

(2) The circumstances referred to in subsection (1)(b) above are—

(a) that the vehicle was driven dangerously on a road or other public place;

(b) that, owing to the driving of the vehicle, an accident occurred by which injury was caused to any person;

(c) that, owing to the driving of the vehicle, an accident occurred by which damage was caused to any property, other than the vehicle;

(d) that damage was caused to the vehicle.

Keynote

There must first of all be an offence under s. 12(1) — including an offence of 'being carried' — and the conveyance involved must be a 'mechanically propelled vehicle' (**see Road Traffic, chapter 1**).

You need only prove that *one* of the consequential factors occurred before the vehicle was recovered (*Dawes* v *Director of Public Prosecutions* [1995] 1 Cr App R 65).

If the person taking the car disposes of it in a way that amounts to an intention permanently to deprive the owner of it, he/she may commit an offence of theft.

'Dangerous driving' will require the same proof as the substantive offence (**see Road Traffic, chapter 2**). There is no need to show any lack of care in the driving of the vehicle to prove s. 12A(2)(b), (c) or (d) (see *R* v *Marsh* [1997] 1 Cr App R 67). A vehicle will be 'recovered' once it has been restored to its owner or other lawful possession or custody (s. 12A(8)). This would include occasions where a vehicle has come into the possession of the police.

Sections 1 and 2 of the Criminal Evidence (Amendment) Act 1997 also apply to an offence under s. 12A where the vehicle is involved in an accident which causes the death of any person (and to conspiracies or incitements in the circumstances set out in that Act) (**see Evidence and Procedure, chapter 16**).

Defence

The Theft Act 1968, s. 12A(3) states:

A person is not guilty of an offence under this section if he proves that, as regards any such proven driving, injury or damage as is referred to in subsection (1)(b) above, either—

(a) the driving, accident or damage referred to in subsection (2) above occurred before he committed the basic offence; or

(b) he was neither in nor on nor in the immediate vicinity of the vehicle when that driving, accident or damage occurred.

Keynote

Once the prosecution has proved the occurrence of one of the aggravating factors above, it is for the defendant to prove one of the specific defences set out under s. 12A(3). Such proof will have to meet the lower standard of 'balance of probabilities' rather than the standard imposed upon the prosecution, namely 'beyond a reasonable doubt' (**see Evidence and Procedure, chapter 11**).

'Immediate vicinity' is not defined but will be a question of fact for the jury/magistrate(s) to determine in each case.

12.9 Pedal Cycles

It is a separate summary offence (punishable with a fine) for a person, without having the consent of the owner or other lawful authority, to take a pedal cycle for his/her own or another's use, or to ride a pedal cycle knowing it to have been taken without such authority (Theft Act 1968, s. 12(5)). The defence under s. 12(6) (**see para. 12.7**) also applies to pedal cycles.

For other offences involving pedal cycles, **see Road Traffic, chapter 15**.

12.10 Abstracting Electricity

Offence — Abstracting Electricity — Theft Act 1968, s. 13
Triable either way. Five years' imprisonment on indictment;
six months' imprisonment and/or a fine summarily.
(*Arrestable offence*)

The Theft Act 1968, s. 13 states:

A person who dishonestly uses without due authority, or dishonestly causes to be wasted or diverted, any electricity shall [be guilty of an offence].

Keynote

As electricity is not 'property' (**see para. 12.2.4**), a specific offence was created to deal with its dishonest use or waste. For this reason electricity cannot be 'stolen' and therefore its dishonest use or wastage cannot form an element of burglary (**see para. 12.4**). Diverting a domestic electrical supply so as to bypass the meter or using another's telephone without authority (*Low* v *Blease* [1975] Crim LR 513) would be examples of this offence, as would unauthorised surfing on the Internet by an employee at work, provided in each case that dishonesty was present.

For the summary offence of fraudulently using a telephone system, see the Telecommunications Act 1984, s. 42.

12.11 Handling Stolen Goods

Offence — Handling Stolen Goods — Theft Act 1968, s. 22
Triable either way. Fourteen years' imprisonment on indictment; six months' imprisonment and/or a fine summarily.
(*Arrestable offence*)

The Theft Act 1968, s. 22 states:

(1) A person handles stolen goods if (otherwise than in the course of the stealing) knowing or believing them to be stolen goods he dishonestly receives the goods, or dishonestly undertakes or assists in their retention, removal, disposal or realisation by or for the benefit of another person, or if he arranges to do so.

Keynote

Handling can only be committed *otherwise than in the course of stealing*. Given the extent of theft and the fact that it can be a continuing act (**see para. 12.2**), it is critical to identify at what point the theft of the relevant property ended. It is also useful, in cases of doubt, to include alternative charges.

You must show that the defendant *knew* or *believed* the goods to be stolen. Mere suspicion, however strong, will not be enough (*R* v *Griffiths* (1974) 60 Cr App R 14). Deliberate 'blindness' to the true identity of the goods would suffice but the distinction is a fine one in practice. It can be very difficult to prove knowledge or belief on the part of, say, a second-hand dealer who 'asks no questions'. Because there are practical difficulties in proving the required *mens rea*, s. 27(3) of the 1968 Act makes special provision to allow evidence of the defendant's previous convictions, or previous recent involvement with stolen goods, to be admitted (**see Evidence and Procedure**).

Dishonestly retaining goods may amount to theft (**see para. 12.2**), in which case that is the relevant charge.

'Goods' will include money and every other description of property except land, and includes things severed from the land by stealing (s. 34(2)(b) of the Act).

12.11.1 Stolen Goods

The Theft Act 1968, s. 24 states:

(1)   The provisions of this Act relating to goods which have been stolen shall apply whether the stealing occurred in England or Wales or elsewhere, and whether it occurred before or after the commencement of this Act, provided that the stealing (if not an offence under this Act) amounted to an offence where and at the time when the goods were stolen; and references to stolen goods shall be construed accordingly.

(2)   For purposes of those provisions references to stolen goods shall include, in addition to the goods originally stolen and parts of them (whether in their original state or not),—

(a)   any other goods which directly or indirectly represent or have at any time represented the stolen goods in the hands of the thief as being the proceeds of any disposal or realisation of the whole or part of the goods stolen or of goods representing the stolen goods; and

(b)   any other goods which directly or indirectly represent or have at any time represented the stolen goods in the hands of a handler of the stolen goods or any part of them as being the proceeds of any disposal or realisation of the whole or part of the stolen goods handled by him or of goods so representing them.

(3)   But no goods shall be regarded as having continued to be stolen goods after they have been restored to the person from whom they were stolen or to other lawful possession or custody, or after that person and any other person claiming through him have otherwise ceased as regards those goods to have any right to restitution in respect of the theft.

(4)   For purposes of the provisions of this Act relating to goods which have been stolen (including subsections (1) to (3) above) goods obtained in England or Wales or elsewhere either by blackmail or in the circumstances described in section 15(1) of this Act shall be regarded as stolen; and 'steal', 'theft' and 'thief' shall be construed accordingly.

. . .

(7)   Subsection (8) below applies for purposes of provisions of this Act relating to stolen goods (including subsection (4) above).

(8)   References to stolen goods include money which is dishonestly withdrawn from an account to which a wrongful credit has been made, but only to the extent that the money derives from the credit.

Keynote

If goods are not stolen there is no handling. Whether they are so stolen is a question of fact for a jury or magistrate(s). There is no need to prove that the thief, blackmailer, deceiver etc. has been convicted of the primary offence before prosecuting the alleged handler, neither is it always necessary to *identify* who that person was.

Goods obtained by deception and blackmail are included in the definition of 'stolen goods' under s. 24(4). Clearly goods gained through robbery or burglary will, by definition, be 'stolen' as theft is an intrinsic element of both offences.

'Wrongful credits' are included within the meaning of stolen goods under certain circumstances and are dealt with later in this chapter (**see para. 12.17**).

Section 24 Explained

Under s. 24(1) a person can still be convicted of handling if the goods were stolen outside England and Wales but only if the goods were taken under circumstances which amounted to an offence in the other country.

Under s. 24(2), goods will be classed as stolen only if they are the property which was originally stolen or if they have at some time represented the *proceeds* of that property in the hands of the thief or a 'handler'.

Therefore if a video cassette recorder (VCR) is stolen, sold to an unsuspecting party who then part exchanges it for a new one at a high street retailer, the first VCR will be 'stolen' goods, the new one will not. If the person buying the original VCR *knew* or *believed* that it was stolen, the new VCR would be treated as stolen goods.

Tracing the proceeds of theft, deception, blackmail etc. can be complex; proving them to be stolen even more so. There is an overlap between this legislation — which deals with goods that have been stolen — and other legislation such as the Criminal Justice Act 1988 which relates to criminally-obtained property generally or the Drug Trafficking Act 1994. For further guidance see *Blackstone's Criminal Practice*, 2001, section B22.

Under s. 24(3), once goods have been restored to lawful possession they cease to be stolen. This situation formerly caused practical problems when police officers recovered stolen property but waited for it to be collected by a handler (see *Houghton* v *Smith* [1975] AC 476). Since the Criminal Attempts Act 1981 and the common-law rulings on 'impossibility' (**see chapter 3**), this has been less problematic. In such cases you may consider:

- Theft — collecting the property will be an 'appropriation'.

- Handling — an *arrangement* to come and collect stolen goods will probably have been made while they were still 'stolen'.

- Criminal attempt — the person collecting the goods has gone beyond merely preparing to handle them.

Section 24(4) widens the occasions on which goods will be deemed to be stolen goods beyond strictly theft-based offences such as burglary and robbery.

12.11.2 Proof that Goods were Stolen

The Theft Act 1968, s. 27 states:

> *(4)   In any proceedings for the theft of anything in the course of transmission (whether by post or otherwise), or for handling stolen goods from such a theft, a statutory declaration made by any person that he dispatched or received or failed to receive any goods or postal packet, or that any goods or postal packet when dispatched or received by him were in a particular state or condition, shall be admissible as evidence of the facts stated in the declaration, subject to the following conditions:—*
>
> > *(a)   a statutory declaration shall only be admissible where and to the extent to which oral evidence to the like effect would have been admissible in the proceedings: and*
> >
> > *(b)   a statutory declaration shall only be admissible if at least seven days before the hearing or trial a copy of it has been given to the person charged, and he has not, at least three days before the hearing or trial or within such further time as the court may in special circumstances allow, given the prosecutor written notice requiring the attendance at the hearing or trial of the person making the declaration.*
>
> *(5)   This section is to be construed in accordance with section 24 of this Act; and in subsection (3)(b) above the reference to handling stolen goods shall include any corresponding offence committed before the commencement of this Act.*

12.11.3 Handling

Despite some views to the contrary, there is only one offence of handling stolen goods (albeit made up of many facets). Therefore to charge a defendant without specifying a particular form of handling is not bad for duplicity (*R* v *Nicklin* [1977] 1 WLR 403). However, the offence can be divided for practical purposes into two parts:

- *receiving/arranging to receive* stolen goods, in which case the defendant acts for his/her own benefit, and

- *assisting/acting for the benefit of another* person, in which case that assistance to another or benefit of another must be proved.

12.11.4 Receiving

Often used as shorthand for handling stolen goods generally, this is a specific part of the overall offence. Receiving does not require the physical reception of goods and can extend to exercising control over them. Things in action — such as bank credits from a stolen cheque — can be 'received'.

'Arranging to receive' would cover circumstances which do not go far enough to constitute an attempt — that is, actions which *are* merely preparatory to the receiving of stolen goods may satisfy the elements under s. 22 even though they would not meet the criteria under the Criminal Attempts Act 1981 (**see chapter 3**).

If the goods have yet to be stolen, then s. 22 would not apply and the offence of conspiracy (**see chapter 3**) should be considered (see *R* v *Park* (1987) 87 Cr App R 164).

12.11.5 Assisting/Acting for Another's Benefit

Assisting or acting for the benefit of another can be committed by misleading police officers during a search (see *R* v *Kanwar* [1982] 1 WLR 845).

Disposing of the stolen goods or assisting in their disposal or realisation usually involves physically moving them or converting them into a different form (see *R* v *Forsyth* [1997] 2 Cr App R 299).

If the only person 'benefiting' from the defendant's actions is the defendant himself/herself, this element of the offence will not be made out (*R* v *Bloxham* [1983] 1 AC 109).

Similarly, if the only 'other' person to benefit is a co-accused on the same charge, the offence will not be made out (*R* v *Gingell, The Times*, 21 May 1999).

12.12 Power to Search for Stolen Goods

The Theft Act 1968, s. 26 states:

> *(1) If it is made to appear by information on oath before a justice of the peace that there is reasonable cause to believe that any person has in his custody or possession or on his premises any stolen goods, the justice may grant a warrant to search for and seize the same; but no warrant to search for stolen goods shall be addressed to a person other than a constable except under the authority of an enactment expressly so providing.*
> *(2) . . .*
> *(3) Where under this section a person is authorised to search premises for stolen goods, he may enter and search the premises accordingly, and may seize any goods he believes to be stolen goods.*
> *(4) . . .*
> *(5) This section is to be construed in accordance with section 24 of this Act; and in subsection (2) above the references to handling stolen goods shall include any corresponding offence committed before the commencement of this Act.*

Keynote

Section 26 provides a general power to search for and seize stolen goods, whether identified in the search warrant or not and magistrates are entitled to act on material provided by the police that gives rise to a reasonable belief that stolen goods will be found (*R* v *Chief Constable of Kent, ex parte R Cruikshank Ltd* (2001) ILR 2 April).

For the provisions governing the application for, and the execution of warrants, **see General Police Duties, chapter 2** and **Evidence and Procedure, chapter 4**.

12.13 Advertising Rewards

Offence — Advertising a Reward — Theft Act 1968, s. 23
Triable summarily. Fine.
(**No specific power of arrest**)

The Theft Act 1968, s. 23 states:

> *Where any public advertisement of a reward for the return of any goods which have been stolen or lost uses any words to the effect that no questions will be asked, or that the person producing the goods will be safe from apprehension or inquiry, or that any money paid for the purchase of the goods or advanced by way of loan on them will be repaid, the person advertising the reward and any person who prints or publishes the advertisement shall [commit an offence].*

Keynote

This offence applies to both the person advertising such a reward and the person/ company who prints or publishes that advertisement. This second aspect of the offence attracts 'strict liability', in that there is no need to demonstrate any particular *mens rea* on the part of the printer/publisher (*Denham v Scott* (1983) 77 Cr App R 210). The important features are the fact that no questions will be asked or that the person will be given some form of 'immunity' from arrest or investigation. There is no mention of any promise of immunity from prosecution or civil claim.

12.14 Going Equipped

Offence — Going Equipped for Stealing etc. — Theft Act 1968, s. 25
Triable either way. Three years' imprisonment on indictment;
six months' imprisonment and/or a fine summarily.
(*Arrestable offence*)

The Theft Act 1968, s. 25 states:

(1)   *A person shall be guilty of an offence if, when not at his place of abode, he has with him any article for use in the course of or in connection with any burglary, theft or cheat.*

Keynote

The power of search under s. 1 of the Police and Criminal Evidence Act 1984 applies to this offence (**see General Police Duties, chapter 2**).

A person's place of abode means where he/she resides; it does not include his/her place of business (unless, presumably, they are one and the same place) (*R v Bundy* [1977] 2 All ER 382). If a person lives in a vehicle then that vehicle will be regarded only as their 'place of abode' if it is parked at the place where the person 'abides' or intends to 'abide' (*Bundy*). Therefore it would seem that, if a person is found in his/her vehicle away from such a site and at the time has with them articles as described under s. 25, they would commit this offence.

'Has with him' is a narrower requirement than 'possession' and, as with aggravated burglary (**see para. 12.5**) generally means that the article must be readily accessible (**see General Police Duties, chapters 5 and 6**).

You do not need to prove that the person having the article with them intended to use it themselves and it will be enough to show that the person intended it to be used *by someone* for one of the purposes in s. 25(1) (*R v Ellames* [1974] 3 All ER 130). Simply being a passenger in a car where such an article is found is not enough to prove the offence (*R v Lester* (1955) 39 Cr App R 157). The articles must be for some future use; it is not enough to show that the defendant had articles that *had been used* in the course of, or in connection with, one of the proscribed offences.

If the articles are found at the defendant's place of abode then an alternative offence under the Criminal Damage Act 1971 (**see chapter 14**) may be appropriate.

If you can prove that the article was made, adapted or intended (**see General Police Duties, chapter 6**) for burglary, theft or cheat, that fact will be evidence that the person had it with him/her for that purpose (s. 25(3)) — a provision that probably seems more helpful than it really is, given that, in many cases, it is simply stating the obvious.

Article can mean almost any object but does not include *animate* objects, e.g. a trained monkey (see *Daly* v *Cannon* [1954] 1 All ER 315).

Theft for these purposes will include the offence of taking a conveyance (as to which, **see para. 12.7**) and 'cheat' means an offence under s. 15 (as to which, **see chapter 13**) (s. 25(5)).

In addition to it being an arrestable offence (**see General Police Duties, chapter 2**) there is a power for any person — other than a constable — to arrest without warrant anyone who is, or who with reasonable cause is suspected to be committing this offence (s. 25(4)). For guidance on the applicability of such powers of arrest to police officers, see Home Office circular 88/85.

This is a 'trigger' offence under s. 63B of the Police and Criminal Evidence Act 1984 which can activate police powers to require a sample from a person in police detention to ascertain the presence of a specified Class A drug in some force areas (**see Evidence and Procedure, chapter 15**).

12.15   Making Off Without Payment

Offence — Making Off Without Payment — Theft Act 1978, s. 3
Triable either way. Two years' imprisonment on indictment; six months' imprisonment and/or a fine summarily.
(Statutory power of arrest)

The Theft Act 1978, s. 3 states:

(1)   Subject to subsection (3) below, a person who, knowing that payment on the spot for any goods supplied or service done is required or expected from him, dishonestly makes off without having paid as required or expected and with intent to avoid payment of the amount due shall be guilty of an offence.
(2)   For purposes of this section 'payment on the spot' includes payment at the time of collecting goods on which work has been done or in respect of which service has been provided.
(3)   Subsection (1) above shall not apply where the supply of the goods or the doing of the service is contrary to law, or where the service done is such that payment is not legally enforceable.
(4)   Any person may arrest without warrant anyone who is, or whom he, with reasonable cause, suspects to be, committing or attempting to commit an offence under this section.

Keynote

This offence is traditionally included alongside deception offences (**see chapter 13**). This is slightly misleading as making off without payment differs from the other offences above in that there is *no requirement for any deception*. Practically, however, making off is an easier offence to prove and can be used where a deception cannot be supported by the evidence available. This offence is most frequently committed by motorists who drive off without paying for petrol, diners who run off after a meal and 'punters' who jump out of taxi cabs (see *DPP* v *Ray* [1974] AC 370; *Edwards* v *Ddin* [1976] 1 WLR 942; *R* v *Brooks* (1982) 76 Cr App R 66). Some problems can arise in cases of alleged theft where the ownership in the property has passed to the defendant before the act of appropriation (**see para. 12.2.5**); this offence offers a solution to some such cases.

Unlike the offence of 'obtaining services by deception' under the Theft Act 1978, s. 1 (**see chapter 13**), this offence excludes occasions where the supply of goods or services is contrary to law or is not legally enforceable (s. 3(3)). Making off without payment after the provision of an unlawful service, or one for which payment is not legally enforceable (e.g. betting), would not then be caught by s. 3 though it might be an offence under s. 1. If there is some doubt as to whether the defendant has actually 'made off' from the spot then he/she can be charged with attempting the offence.

You must also prove an intention to *avoid* payment; simply delaying payment due or making someone wait for payment is not enough. In *R v Vincent* [2001] 1 WLR 1172, the Court of Appeal has recently acknowledged a 'loophole' in s. 3. Circumstances in which this loophole might operate can be illustrated as follows:

* A person checks into an hotel and runs up a substantial bill.

* The person deceives the proprietor into agreeing that the bill will be settled at some later date (as opposed to on departure).

* Having gained that agreement, the person checks out of the hotel and never makes any payment.

The Court pointed out that, in such a situation, there was no longer an expectation of payment at the time when the person checked out of the hotel. This expectation had been removed by the agreement; the fact that the agreement had been obtained dishonestly did not reinstate the expectation of payment on departure. The Court identified that the offence under s. 3 is a simple and straightforward one which applies to a limited set of circumstances only (and which, fortunately for the defendant, were not covered by the above facts). The limited scope of this offence would suggest that alternative charges of theft and/or deception should be considered. If there has been an operating deception, an offence under s. 2(1)(b) may be appropriate (**see chapter 13**). If the person driving or running away from the garage, restaurant, taxi cab etc. does so because he/she feels aggrieved at the service received or is in dispute with the supplier, then the question of dishonesty should be considered against the standards of ordinary, honest people (per *R v Ghosh* [1982] QB 1053 (**see para. 12.2.2**)).

For the application of 'any person' powers of arrest, **see General Police Duties, chapter 2**.

12.16 Blackmail

Offence — Blackmail — Theft Act 1968, s. 21
Triable on indictment. Fourteen years' imprisonment.
(***Arrestable offence***)

The Theft Act 1968, s. 21 states:

(1) A person is guilty of blackmail if, with a view to gain for himself or another or with intent to cause loss to another, he makes any unwarranted demand with menaces; and for this purpose a demand with menaces is unwarranted unless the person making it does so in the belief—
(a) that he has reasonable grounds for making the demand; and
(b) that the use of the menaces is a proper means of reinforcing the demand.

(2) The nature of the act or omission demanded is immaterial, and it is also immaterial whether the menaces relate to action to be taken by the person making the demand.

Keynote

You must show that a defendant acted either with a view to gain for himself/herself or another or with intent to cause loss to another. There is no requirement for dishonesty, deception or theft and the offence is aimed at the making of the demands rather than the consequences of them. Although gaining may cause loss to another, the two elements are distinct.

Section 34 of the 1968 Act states:

(2) For the purposes of this Act—
(a) 'gain' and 'loss' are to be construed as extending only to gain or loss in money or other property, but as extending to any such gain or loss whether temporary or permanent; and—
(i) 'gain' includes by keeping what one has, as well as a gain by getting what one has not; and
(ii) 'loss' includes a loss by not getting what one might get, as well as a loss by parting with what one has . . .

Keynote

Therefore keeping what you already have can amount to a 'gain'. Similarly, not getting something that you might expect to get can be a 'loss'.

Example

Consider an example used later in relation to 'obtaining a pecuniary advantage' (**see chapter 13**). A person makes unwarranted demands with menaces with a view to getting a sports fixture cancelled and thereby to avoid losing money that he/she has bet on the outcome of that fixture. Here it could be argued that the intention of keeping what the defendant already had (the money at risk on the bet) amounts to 'gain' as defined under s. 34(2). Similarly, the intention of preventing others getting what they might have got (their winnings or the club's earnings) could amount to a 'loss'.

12.16.1 Criminal Conduct

The offence of blackmail is complete when the demand with menaces is made. It does not matter whether the demands bring about the desired consequences or not. If a demand is made by letter, the act of making it is complete when the letter is posted. The letter does not have to be received (*Treacy* v *DPP* [1971] AC 537).

Menaces will include threats which must be significant *to the victim*. If a threat bears a particular significance for a victim (such as being locked in the boot of a car to someone who is claustrophobic) that will be enough, provided the defendant was aware of that fact. If a victim is particularly timid and the defendant knows it, that timidity may be taken into account when assessing whether or not the defendant's conduct was 'menacing' (*R* v *Garwood* [1987] 1 WLR 319).

For offences involving malicious and threatening communications, **see General Police Duties, chapter 3**.

12.16.2   Unwarranted?

If a defendant raises the issue that his/her demand was reasonable and proper, you will have to prove that he/she did not believe:

• that he/she had reasonable grounds for making the demand, and

• that the use of the particular menaces employed was not a proper means of reinforcing it.

The defendant's *belief* will be a subjective one and therefore could be entirely unreasonable. However, if the threatened action would itself be unlawful (such as a threat to rape the victim) then it is unlikely that the courts would accept any claim by a defendant that he/she believed such a demand to be 'proper' (see *R* v *Harvey* (1980) 72 Cr App R 139).

12.17   Retaining a Wrongful Credit

Offence — Dishonestly Retaining a Wrongful Credit — Theft Act 1968, s. 24A
Triable either way. Ten years' imprisonment on indictment; six months' imprisonment and/or a fine summarily.
(*Arrestable offence*)

The Theft Act 1968, s. 24A states:

(1)   A person is guilty of an offence if—
(a)   a wrongful credit has been made to an account kept by him or in respect of which he has any right or interest;
(b)   he knows or believes that the credit is wrongful; and
(c)   he dishonestly fails to take such steps as are reasonable in the circumstances to secure that the credit is cancelled.
(2)   References to a credit are to a credit of an amount of money.
(3)   A credit to an account is wrongful if it is the credit side of a money transfer obtained contrary to section 15A of this Act.
(4)   A credit to an account is also wrongful to the extent that it derives from—
(a)   theft;
(b)   an offence under section 15A of this Act;
(c)   blackmail; or
(d)   stolen goods.
(5)   In determining whether a credit to an account is wrongful, it is immaterial (in particular) whether the account is overdrawn before or after the credit is made.
(6)   . . .
(7)   Subsection (8) below applies for purposes of provisions of this Act relating to stolen goods (including subsection (4) above).
(8)   References to stolen goods include money which is dishonestly withdrawn from an account to which a wrongful credit has been made, but only to the extent that the money derives from the credit.
(9)   In this section 'account' and 'money' shall be construed in accordance with section 15B of this Act.

Keynote

This offence was prompted by the decision in *R* v *Preddy* [1996] AC 815. The Law Commission were anxious to ensure that the transferee of funds obtained dishonestly could be charged with 'handling' those funds. As there were considerable problems created by applying the existing legislation under s. 22 (**see para. 12.11**), these further offences were introduced.

The wrongful credit to an account can occur in two ways: it may come from the circumstances outlined under s. 15A (**see chapter 13**); or it may come from one of the dishonest sources set out in s. 24A(4) above.

Again, the type of 'account' involved is the same as for the offence under s. 15A(1) (**see chapter 13**). Therefore these offences will generally be restricted to transactions involving the crediting of accounts held with financial institutions.

There is a requirement for dishonesty (as to which, **see para. 12.2.2**). However, there is no requirement for any *deception*.

The effects of s. 24A(8) are that *money* derived from credit received under ss. 15A and 24A of the Theft Act 1968 may amount to stolen goods. The provisions governing the status of the credit itself (i.e. not as cash but as a 'thing in action') are more complicated. If the proceeds of a theft by A are paid into his/her bank account they are stolen goods because they represent the stolen goods in the hands of the thief (s. 24(4)).

If they are then transferred into B's bank account, they cease to be stolen goods. This is because the 'thing in action' (the credit balance) created by the transfer in B's name is a different 'thing in action' from the one originally created by A (see *R* v *Preddy* [1996] AC 815). As such, the credit balance in B's name has never represented the proceeds of the theft *in the hands of the thief*. If B withdraws money from the credited account, that money then, by virtue of s. 24A(8), becomes stolen goods once more.

To quote from *Blackstone's Criminal Practice*, 2001, section B4.147:

> It may seem strange that the proceeds of A's original theft can be classed as stolen goods when paid into A's own bank account, cease to be so classified when effectively 'transferred' to B's account, and yet revert to being stolen goods when dishonestly withdrawn as cash by B; but such is now the law.

This offence is also unusual in that the *actus reus* not only *can be* satisfied by an 'omission', but necessarily *involves* an omission or a failure to act (**see chapter 2**).

For the relationship between s. 15A and s. 24A, **see chapter 13**.

CHAPTER THIRTEEN

DECEPTION AND FRAUD

13.1 Introduction

Deception offences are closely related to theft and other offences involving dishonesty. The most important element in such offences is the presence of the operating act of 'deception'.

The Theft Act 1968, s. 15 states:

> *(4)* '*. . . deception' means any deception (whether deliberate or reckless) by words or conduct as to fact or as to law, including a deception as to the present intentions of the person using the deception or any other person.*

As deception offences require dishonesty — a largely subjective concept — then the 'recklessness' referred to above should be *subjective* (**see chapter 1**), that is, the defendant must have given some thought to his/her conduct (see *R* v *Goldman* [1997] Crim LR 894). The special provisions of s. 2 of the Theft Act 1968 in relation to dishonesty (**see chapter 12**) do not directly apply to deception offences but the *Ghosh* directions as to what might be considered dishonest do apply. Dishonesty and deception are two distinct elements and the presence of a defendant's intention to deceive is not necessarily proof that he/she was dishonest (see *R* v *Clarke* [1996] Crim LR 824).

The general essence of a 'deception' is behaviour that induces someone to believe that something is, or might be, true. For that reason, offences involving falsification of documents are also included in this chapter.

Without more, deception itself is not an offence; there must be other intentions or consequences springing from the deception, together with the element of dishonesty referred to above.

13.1.1 Words or Conduct

The courts have accepted that some omissions can be a deception (e.g. deliberately omitting to fill out forms (*R* v *Shama* [1990] 1 WLR 661)). It is difficult therefore to see how the inclusion of 'words or conduct' adds anything other than a checklist against which to assess a defendant's behaviour when proving the elements of deception. In some circumstances silence and failure to act can amount to 'conduct' for the purposes of supporting a criminal deception (*R v Rai* [2000] 1 Cr App R 233). In *Rai* the defendant remained silent when council workers came to his home in order to install a downstairs bathroom for his elderly mother who had lived there. Although his mother had died between the placing of the order and subsequent installation, the defendant failed to tell the workers of this material change in circumstances and allowed them to go ahead with their work. The Court of Appeal held that this behaviour was enough to support a charge of obtaining a service by deception (as to which, see below). In the offences which follow, the particular consequences (such as the parting with property or the provision of a service) must be brought about by the deception.

There are particular difficulties in relation to credit cards and charge cards where the person being 'deceived' is not entirely convinced by the deception or is aware that the deceiver is simply exceeding his/her authorised credit limit. For a discussion of these cases, see *Blackstone's Criminal Practice*, 2001, section B5.9.

If the 'target' of the deception is not actually deceived by the words or conduct then there will only have been an attempted deception. Although there is no clear authority on the issue, it would appear that this requirement means that a machine cannot be deceived and any offences committed by fooling a machine or computer would not amount to deception. Because of this restriction and the increase in the number of commercial transactions carried out solely by interaction with a machine (e.g. purchases of goods and services over the telephone by keying in details of debit cards), there has been some pressure for a change in the law. Despite this pressure, the Law Commission has declined to recommend the creation of a new offence of 'fraud' which would do away with the need for an operating deception. For the time being, therefore, if a person orders goods or services simply by dialing up an automated database and keying in false details of a 'Switch' card over the telephone, he/she does not commit any offence involving deception (though there would clearly be other offences).

For the situation in relation to forgery of documents etc. designed to 'fool' machines, **see para. 13.7.2**.

If the deceit is practised *after* the desired consequences (e.g. the obtaining of property or services), there will be no operating deception (see *R v Collis-Smith* [1971] Crim LR 716), but there may still be other offences (such as making off without payment, **see chapter 12**).

13.2 Obtaining Property

Offence — Obtaining Property by Deception — Theft Act 1968, s. 15
Triable either way. Ten years' imprisonment on indictment; six months' imprisonment and/or a fine summarily.
(Arrestable offence)

The Theft Act 1968, s. 15 states:

(1) A person who by any deception dishonestly obtains property belonging to another, with the intention of permanently depriving the other of it, shall on conviction on indictment be liable . . .

(2) For purposes of this section a person is to be treated as obtaining property if he obtains ownership, possession or control of it, and 'obtain' includes obtaining for another or enabling another to obtain or to retain.

(3) Section 6 above shall apply for purposes of this section, with the necessary adaptation of the reference to appropriating, as it applies for purposes of section 1.

Keynote

'Property' for these purposes is generally the same as for the offence of theft (**see chapter 12**). However, the restrictions in relation to 'property' contained in s. 4(2)–(4) of the 1968 Act do not appear to apply to this offence. Therefore it would seem that you can 'obtain' land by deception. Where the property obtained is a bank credit or the offence involves the issuing of a cheque, the situation is complicated by the decision in *R* v *Preddy* [1996] AC 815. Although there may be an offence under s. 15A (**see para. 13.6.1**), which was introduced as a result of *Preddy*, the advice of the Crown Prosecution Service should be sought.

'Obtaining' as defined under s. 15(2) is very broad and also includes enabling another to *retain* property. A defendant practising a deception to enable *himself/herself* to retain property would not fall into this definition.

As mentioned above, you must prove a connection between the deception practised and the obtaining of the property.

Example

A man (X) goes to the goods collection point in an electrical superstore. Falsely claiming that he has ordered and paid for a computer game for his son's birthday, X says he would like to collect the game but has lost the receipt. The sales assistant believes him and gives him the computer game. The following week X gives the game to his delighted son.

In these circumstances you must prove that:

- X used a *deception* — by both his *words* and *conduct* he *deliberately* misrepresented *facts* about himself and the pre-paid order for goods

- X acted *dishonestly* — implicit in his behaviour

- X *obtained property* — he gained control of (including actual possession) the computer game

- the goods *belonged to another* — the electrical store

- X *intended to deprive* the other of the goods *permanently* — he gave the game to his son (note that s. 6 of the Theft Act 1968 applies to this offence (**see chapter 12**)).

If the sales assistant had not been fooled by the deception but had felt sorry for X's son and gave him the game anyway, this offence would not be made out. There would, however, have been an attempted deception (**see chapter 3**). Since the House of Lords' decision in *R* v *Gomez* [1993] AC 442 (**see chapter 12**), there may also be an offence of theft. In fact, following that ruling, many offences under s. 15 will also be chargeable as offences of theft without the need to prove the operating deception.

If, instead of deceiving the assistant into giving him the game, X had deceived him into giving his son a free session on a coin-operated video game in the store, no *property* would have been obtained. A *service* would have been obtained and the proper charge would be one of obtaining a service by deception under the Theft Act 1978, s. 1 (**see para. 13.4**).

This is a 'trigger' offence under s. 63B of the Police and Criminal Evidence Act 1984 which can activate police powers in some police areas to ascertain the presence of a specified Class A drug (**see Evidence and Procedure, chapter 15**).

13.3 Obtaining a Pecuniary Advantage

Offence — Obtaining a Pecuniary Advantage by Deception — Theft Act 1968, s. 16

Triable either way. Five years' imprisonment on indictment; six months' imprisonment and/or a fine summarily.

(*Arrestable offence*)

The Theft Act 1968, s. 16 states:

> *(1)   A person who by any deception dishonestly obtains for himself or another any pecuniary advantage shall on conviction on indictment be liable . . .*
> *(2)   The cases in which a pecuniary advantage within the meaning of this section is to be regarded as obtained for a person are cases where—*
> *(a)   [repealed]*
> *(b)   he is allowed to borrow by way of overdraft, or to take out any policy of insurance or annuity contract, or obtains an improvement of the terms on which he is allowed to do so; or*
> *(c)   he is given the opportunity to earn remuneration or greater remuneration in an office or employment, or to win money by betting.*

Keynote

The elements of deception and dishonesty are the same as those for s. 15 above. This offence is really about deceiving people in order to bring about certain types of opportunity. Helpfully, the House of Lords have decided that a defendant need not be shown to have actually profited by his/her actions, only that his/her deception brought about the consequences listed at s. 16(2)(b) or (c) (*DPP* v *Turner* [1974] AC 537).

13.3.1 Pecuniary Advantage: Overdraft Facility

Once the overdraft facility is created the offence under s. 16(2)(b) is complete. There is no need for anyone to use that facility or to overdraw (*R* v *Watkins* [1976] 1 All ER 578). If the facility was used, there would be an overlap with s. 15 above, as property (money) would have been obtained.

Other credit facilities — such as loans or credit agreements — will not suffice for this section (however, **see para. 13.4**).

13.3.2 Pecuniary Advantage: Insurance

If a 21-year-old disqualified driver deceived an insurer into issuing him an insurance policy in the belief that he was 50 years' old with a clean licence, this offence would be appropriate.

13.3.3 Pecuniary Advantage: Opportunity to Earn etc.

Again, it is the securing of the *opportunity* which matters here. If someone who is self-employed seeks to deceive prospective clients by claiming to have professional qualifications, this offence may apply (*R* v *Callender* [1992] 3 WLR 501).

Under the second part of the offence at s. 16(2)(c), the requirement is for the opportunity *to win money* by betting. This does not appear to be the same as to *avoid losing money* by betting, an important distinction when considering offences involving the disruption of sporting events where money has already been staked on the outcome.

13.4   Obtaining Services

Offence — Obtaining Services by Deception — Theft Act 1978, s. 1
Triable either way. Five years' imprisonment on indictment; six months' imprisonment and/or a fine summarily.
(*Arrestable offence*)

The Theft Act 1978, s. 1 states:

(1)   A person who by any deception dishonestly obtains services from another shall be guilty of an offence.

(2)   It is an obtaining of services where the other is induced to confer a benefit by doing some act, or causing or permitting some act to be done, on the understanding that the benefit has been or will be paid for.

Keynote

Deception and dishonesty are the same as for those offences under the 1968 Act. The main difference between this and the offence of obtaining property is that here *the person providing the service* must be induced to do so by the deception, that is, he/she must be the 'target' of the deception. Although there is no mention of obtaining a service for *another*, the Court of Appeal has accepted that such behaviour could amount to an offence under s. 1 (*R* v *Nathan* [1997] Crim LR 835). As with the offence of obtaining property, the deception could be aimed at a third party. Again, there may be some overlap with other deception offences. A service provided by a hotel may include property such as a meal. Conversely, the delivery of goods will include an element of service. To illustrate the possible extent of overlap between deception offences consider the following example.

Example

A person replies to a job advertisement for a child minder. Falsely claiming to have a recognised qualification in child care, he is offered a job which includes remuneration, accommodation, meals and the use of the family car.

By applying for the job and availing himself of the attendant benefits, the person apparently commits many of the offences considered in this chapter.

13.4.1   Service

There is nothing in the section which requires the service to be a lawful or contractual one.

There were considerable problems involved with prosecuting offences under s. 1 where the service obtained was the granting of a loan. The courts had decided that loan agreements, even those procured by deception, were not covered by s. 1 of the 1978 Act and s. 16 of the 1968 Act only extends to overdraft facilities.

However, Parliament has amended s. 1 of the 1978 Act (Theft (Amendment) Act 1996, s. 4(1)) by inserting s. 1(3) which states:

(3)   Without prejudice to the generality of subsection (2) above, it is an obtaining of services where the other is induced to make a loan, or to cause or permit a loan to be made, on the understanding that any payment (whether by way of interest or otherwise) will be or has been made in respect of the loan.

Keynote

This new subsection puts the quite common situation of obtaining a loan by deception squarely within the offence of obtaining services.

13.5 Evading Liability

Offence — Evading Liability by Deception — Theft Act 1978, s. 2
Triable either way. Five years' imprisonment on indictment; six months' imprisonment and/or a fine summarily.
(*Arrestable offence*)

The Theft Act 1978, s. 2 states:

(1) Subject to subsection (2) below, where a person by any deception—
(a) dishonestly secures the remission of the whole or part of any existing liability to make a payment, whether his own liability or another's; or
(b) with intent to make permanent default in whole or in part on any existing liability to make a payment, or with intent to let another do so, dishonestly induces the creditor or any person claiming payment on behalf of the creditor to wait for payment (whether or not the due date for payment is deferred) or to forgo payment; or
(c) dishonestly obtains any exemption from or abatement of liability to make a payment; he shall be guilty of an offence.
(2) For purposes of this section 'liability' means legally enforceable liability; and subsection (1) shall not apply in relation to a liability that has not been accepted or established to pay compensation for a wrongful act or omission.
(3) For purposes of subsection (1)(b) a person induced to take in payment a cheque or other security for money by way of conditional satisfaction of a pre-existing liability is to be treated not as being paid but as being induced to wait for payment.
(4) For purposes of subsection (1)(c) 'obtains' includes obtaining for another or enabling another to obtain.

Keynote

Deception and dishonesty have the same meaning as in the other offences above.

This section creates three distinct offences. One feature which all three offences share is the requirement for a *legal liability*. In the case of s. 2(1)(a) and (b) that liability must already be in existence whereas the wording of s. 2(1)(c) makes provision for both existing and newly-created liabilities.

If the liability is not legally enforceable (such as a betting agreement or an agreement to provide an immoral service) none of the three offences will apply.

Section 2(2) excludes any liability to pay compensation in relation to a wrongful act or omission where that liability has not been accepted or established.

13.5.1 Elements of the Offences

To prove the offence under s. 2(1)(a) you must show that a defendant secured a release from all or part of an existing liability to make a payment. If a person orders and accepts delivery of goods and then dishonestly convinces the supplier that they have been paid for, he/she would commit this offence. Note that because the deception in such a case is not committed at the time of the goods being obtained, s. 15 of the 1968 Act (obtaining property by deception) is not applicable. Section 2(1)(a) makes provision for the situation where the liability is *another* person's liability, not just the defendant's.

Under s. 2(1)(b) there is a requirement to prove an intent to make permanent default, that is, not just to put creditors off or to delay payment to them. Perhaps the best examples of such offences are those involving 'dud' cheques which, by virtue of s. 2(3), will amount to an inducement to wait for payment. Section 2(1)(b) makes provision for the situation where the defendant's intentions are to let *another person* make permanent default on *any* existing liability.

An 'abatement' is a reduction in a liability to make a payment. Such an abatement under s. 2(1)(c) might be obtained when someone falsely claims to be a student in order to get into a cinema at a discounted rate. In such circumstances, the person's deception as to his/her status (i.e. as a paid-up member of the Students' Union) may also be an offence under s. 1 (see *R* v *Adams* [1993] Crim LR 525).

Section 2(1)(c) makes no provision in respect of obtaining an exemption from, or abatement of a liability *for another* to make a payment. It may therefore be argued that, given the specific inclusion of such provisions in s. 2(1)(a) and (b), this was an intentional omission by the legislators. However, the approach of the Court of Appeal in *Nathan* (**see para. 13.4**) may also be adopted in such circumstances.

13.5.2   Overlap

As with the other deception offences, there will be occasions when offences under s. 2 of the 1978 Act will overlap. Consider the following example:

Example

X orders a lawnmower from a mail order catalogue, never intending to pay for it. When it is delivered to X's house some weeks later, the delivery driver asks for both payment in full for the mower and also for the delivery charges. X, who ordered the goods, falsely states that he has already paid a 50 per cent deposit and is only liable for the remainder. He also falsely states that when he placed the order he was told delivery would be free. The delivery driver and the mail order company accept the 50 per cent payment (made with a worthless cheque) and the 'purchaser', X, then sells the lawnmower at a car boot sale.

In these circumstances X may commit:

- Theft — by dishonestly appropriating the mower intending to deprive the supplier of it permanently.

- Obtaining property by deception — by dishonestly deceiving the mail order company from the outset into giving him control of the mower, intending permanently to deprive them of it.

- Obtaining a service by deception — because X never intended to pay for the mower or the delivery service he has induced the mail order company to confer that benefit on the understanding that it had been/will be paid for.

- Evading liability by deception — X has, by his deceptions dishonestly secured a release from his existing liability to pay for the mower and its delivery.

- Dishonestly inducing the company and its agent to wait for payment, intending to make permanent default.

- Dishonestly obtaining an abatement of his liability to pay for the mower and an exemption from paying for its delivery.

Clearly there are some charges which more readily lend themselves to these circumstances, but the example serves to show the potential overlap in even relatively straightforward theft and deception offences. In cases of doubt, the advice of the Crown Prosecution Service should be sought.

13.6   Offences Relating to Bank Accounts

There are two recent offences which have been created to deal specifically with circumstances where defendants cause bank or building society accounts to be credited or debited, or where they dishonestly retain funds which have been wrongly credited to their account. The first offence was discussed in **chapter 12** (**see para. 12.17**). The second one is set out below, followed by an explanation of how the offences relate to each other in practice.

13.6.1   Obtaining Money Transfer

Offence — Obtaining Money Transfer by Deception — Theft Act 1968, s. 15A
Triable either way. Ten years' imprisonment on indictment; six months' imprisonment and/or a fine summarily.
(**Arrestable offence**)

The Theft Act 1968, s. 15A states:

> *(1)   A person is guilty of an offence if by any deception he dishonestly obtains a money transfer for himself or another.*
> *(2)   A money transfer occurs when—*
> *(a)   a debit is made to one account,*
> *(b)   a credit is made to another, and*
> *(c)   the credit results from the debit or the debit results from the credit.*
> *(3)   References to a credit and to a debit are to a credit of an amount of money and to a debit of an amount of money.*
> *(4)   It is immaterial (in particular)—*
> *(a)   whether the amount credited is the same as the amount debited;*
> *(b)   whether the money transfer is effected on presentment of a cheque or by another method;*
> *(c)   whether any delay occurs in the process by which the money transfer is effected;*
> *(d)   whether any intermediate credits or debits are made in the course of the money transfer;*
> *(e)   whether either of the accounts is overdrawn before or after the money transfer is effected.*

Keynote

This offence was introduced by the Theft (Amendment) Act 1996, s. 1 to close a gap in the law relating to deception. In a case involving a complicated mortgage fraud (*R v Preddy* [1996] AC 815) the House of Lords had accepted that there had been no *property belonging to another* to support a charge of obtaining property by deception under s. 15 (**see para. 13.2**), neither had there been an obtaining of a 'service' (**see para. 13.4**). As a result of the Theft (Amendment) Act 1996, s. 4, the provision of a loan *is* now a 'service' for these purposes.

The above offence now caters for such occasions. As this is new law there has been no opportunity for the courts to interpret its application. The Law Commission, however, felt that the wording in s. 15A(2) was wide enough to cover occasions where the amount credited from one account is different from the amount debited or vice-versa. It should also cover circumstances where there is a delay in the debit or credit on either account or where the debit/credit is made in error and later corrected.

'Dishonestly' and 'deception' will have the same meaning as in the other offences in this chapter. Remember that if a person dishonestly presents a cheque from another person's account and that cheque is honoured, there has been an old fashioned appropriation (**see para. 12.2.3**) of the contents (which can be 'property'; **see para. 12.2.4**). Therefore there would be a theft and the principle in *Preddy* would not apply (*R* v *Williams (Roy)*, *The Times*, 25 October 2000).

An 'account' means an account kept with a bank or a person carrying on a business which falls within s. 15B which states:

> *A business falls within this subsection if—*
> *(a)   in the course of the business money received by way of deposit is lent to others; or*
> *(b)   any other activity of the business is financed, wholly or to any material extent, out of the capital of or the interest on money received by way of deposit;*
> *and 'deposit' here has the same meaning as in section 35 of the Banking Act 1987 (fraudulent inducement to make a deposit).*

Keynote

An 'account' for the purpose of an offence under s. 15A(1) must be an account kept with a bank or a person carrying on a business that falls within s. 15B. As such, the offence will generally be restricted to transactions involving the crediting and debiting of accounts held with financial institutions.

13.6.2   Relationship Between s. 15A and s. 24A

The offence(s) could be committed in the following ways:

- Where a defendant dishonestly obtains a transfer of funds, by a deception, from the bank account of a friend into his/her own bank account. In such a case there would be two overlapping offences; the offence of obtaining a money transfer by deception (s. 15A, above) and the further offence (s. 24A) of *retaining* the credit once it had been obtained in that way (**see chapter 12**).

- Where a defendant is authorised to operate his/her employer's account and steals funds from it, transferring them to his/her own account. The defendant would commit both theft (**see chapter 12**), and also the offence of dishonestly retaining a wrongful credit (s. 24A).

- Where a defendant uses any form of dishonest deception to get a person to transfer funds from his/her own account into that of a third person. The defendant would commit the offence of dishonestly obtaining a money transfer (s. 15A) and the third party, if they dishonestly failed to take reasonable steps to secure its cancellation, would commit the offence under s. 24A.

- Where a defendant dishonestly obtains a money transfer by deception and then, sometime later, draws the cash out of his/her account. The defendant commits an offence under s. 15A, an offence under s. 24A and theft (**see chapter 12**). The cash will be 'stolen goods' for the purposes of s. 22 (**see chapter 12**) and anyone who receives it under the conditions specified in s. 22 will be guilty of 'handling'.

13.7   Falsification of Documents and Other Instruments

In addition to the offence of deception, there are a series of closely-related offences which deal with falsification of documents or other 'instruments'. As with some deception offences, there will be circumstances which appear to support charges under several different enactments such as false accounting, using a false instrument or obtaining property by deception.

13.7.1   False Accounting

Offence — False Accounting — Theft Act 1968, s. 17
Triable either way. Seven years' imprisonment on indictment; six months' imprisonment and/or a fine summarily.
(***Arrestable offence***)

The Theft Act 1968, s. 17 states:

(1)   Where a person dishonestly, with a view to gain for himself or another or with intent to cause loss to another,—
(a)   destroys, defaces, conceals or falsifies any account or any record or document made or required for any accounting purpose; or
(b)   in furnishing information for any purpose produces or makes use of any account, or any such record or document as aforesaid, which to his knowledge is or may be misleading, false or deceptive in a material particular;
he shall [commit an offence].
(2)   For purposes of this section a person who makes or concurs in making in an account or other document an entry which is or may be misleading, false or deceptive in a material particular, or who omits or concurs in omitting a material particular from an account or other document, is to be treated as falsifying the account or document.

Keynote

This section creates two offences: destroying, defacing etc. accounts and documents; and using false or misleading accounts or documents in furnishing information.

An offence under s. 17 can be committed by omission as well as by an act. Failing to make an entry in an accounts book, altering a till receipt or supplying an auditor with records that are incomplete may, if accompanied by the other ingredients, amount to an offence.

Unlike theft there is no requirement to prove an intention permanently to deprive but there is a need to show dishonesty (as to both points, **see chapter 12**). The requirement as to gain and loss is the same as for blackmail (**see chapter 12**).

The misleading, false or deceptive nature of the information furnished under s. 17(1)(b) must be 'material' to the defendant's overall purpose, i.e. the ultimate gaining or causing of loss. Such an interpretation means that the defendant's furnishing of information need not relate directly to an accounting process and could be satisfied by lying about the status of a potential finance customer (see *R* v *Mallet* [1978] 1 WLR 820).

Where the documents falsified are not intrinsically 'accounting' forms, such as insurance claim forms filled out by policyholders, you must show that those forms are treated for accounting purposes by the victim (*R* v *Sundhers* [1998] Crim LR 497).

There is also a further offence (triable and punishable as the above offences), of company officers making false statements with intent to deceive members or creditors (Theft Act 1968, s. 19).

13.7.2 Forgery

The traditional image of forgery conjures up images of skilled printers with inky fingers using sophisticated plates to create high quality bank notes. In reality the offences classed as forgery include virtually every kind of document *except* bank notes. Coins and currency are the subject of a separate group of offences classed as counterfeiting and are dealt with later in this chapter.

Many of the offences dealt with below are divided into two categories:

* Offences where there is an *intention* by the defendant to pass the document, note or coin off as being genuine. These, more serious offences, attract higher penalties and are *arrestable offences* (as to which, **see General Police Duties, chapter 2**).

* Offences where there is no requirement to prove any *ulterior* intent.

False Instruments

Offence — Making a False Instrument with Intent — Forgery and Counterfeiting Act 1981, s. 1
Triable either way. Ten years' imprisonment on indictment; six months' imprisonment and/or a fine summarily.
(Arrestable offence)

The Forgery and Counterfeiting Act 1981, s. 1 states:

> *A person is guilty of forgery if he makes a false instrument, with the intention that he or another shall use it to induce somebody to accept it as genuine, and by reason of so accepting it to do or not to do some act to his own or any other person's prejudice.*

Offence — Using a False Instrument with Intent — Forgery and Counterfeiting Act 1981, s. 3
Triable either way. Ten years' imprisonment on indictment; six months' imprisonment and/or a fine summarily.
(Arrestable offence)

The Forgery and Counterfeiting Act 1981, s. 3 states:

It is an offence for a person to use an instrument which is, and which he knows or believes to be, false, with the intention of inducing somebody to accept it as genuine, and by reason of so accepting it to do or not to do some act to his own or any other person's prejudice.

Offence — Copying a False Instrument with Intent — Forgery and Counterfeiting Act 1981, s. 2
Triable either way. Ten years' imprisonment on indictment; six months' imprisonment and/or a fine summarily.
(Arrestable offence)

The Forgery and Counterfeiting Act 1981, s. 2 states:

It is an offence for a person to make a copy of an instrument which is, and which he knows or believes to be, a false instrument, with the intention that he or another shall use it to induce somebody to accept it as a copy of a genuine instrument, and by reason of so accepting it to do or not to do some act to his own or any other person's prejudice.

Offence — Using a Copy of a False Instrument with Intent — Forgery and Counterfeiting Act 1981, s. 4
Triable either way. Ten years' imprisonment on indictment; six months' imprisonment and/or a fine summarily.
(Arrestable offence)

The Forgery and Counterfeiting Act 1981, s. 4 states:

It is an offence for a person to use a copy of an instrument which is, and which he knows or believes to be, a false instrument, with the intention of inducing somebody to accept it as a copy of a genuine instrument, and by reason of so accepting it to do or not to do some act to his own or any other person's prejudice.

Keynote

The essence of these offences is that they concern documents or instruments which purport to be something which they are not; that is, they 'tell a lie about themselves'.

In the defining terms used by s. 9 of the 1981 Act they are:

(1) An instrument is false for the purposes of this Part of this Act—
(a) if it purports to have been made in the form in which it is made by a person who did not in fact make it in that form; or
(b) if it purports to have been made in the form in which it is made on the authority of a person who did not in fact authorise its making in that form; or
(c) if it purports to have been made in the terms in which it is made by a person who did not in fact make it in those terms; or
(d) if it purports to have been made in the terms in which it is made on the authority of a person who did not in fact authorise its making in those terms; or
(e) if it purports to have been altered in any respect by a person who did not in fact alter it in that respect; or
(f) if it purports to have been altered in any respect on the authority of a person who did not in fact authorise the alteration in that respect; or
(g) if it purports to have been made or altered on a date on which, or at a place at which, or otherwise in circumstances in which, it was not in fact made or altered; or
(h) if it purports to have been made or altered by an existing person but he did not in fact exist.

212

Keynote

The list of ways in which instruments can be false might be remembered by the following mnemonic. An instrument may be false if:

F it falsely claims to have been made in a **F**orm or in terms by, or on the authority of, another

A it falsely claims to have been **A**ltered by, or on the authority of, another

L it **L**ies about the date, place or any other circumstances in which it claims to have been made or altered

S it falsely claims to have been made or altered by **S**omeone who did not in fact

E **E**xist.

This list is exhaustive; if an instrument cannot be brought under one of these heads it will not be regarded as 'false'. However, you do not have to specify which of the heads an action comes under in a charge or indictment.

Section 9 goes on to say that:

> *A person is to be treated for the purposes of this Part of this Act as making a false instrument if he alters an instrument so as to make it false in any respect (whether or not it is false in some other respect apart from that alteration).*

An 'instrument' is defined in s. 8 of the 1981 Act which states:

> *(1)   Subject to subsection (2) below, in this Part of this Act 'instrument' means—*
> *(a)   any document, whether of a formal or informal character;*
> *(b)   any stamp issued or sold by the Post Office;*
> *(c)   any Inland Revenue stamp; and*
> *(d)   any disc, tape, sound track or other device on or in which information is recorded or stored by mechanical, electronic or other means.*
> *(2)   A currency note within the meaning of Part II of this Act is not an instrument for the purposes of this Part of this Act.*
> *(3)   A mark denoting payment of postage which the Post Office authorise to be used instead of an adhesive stamp is to be treated for the purposes of this Part of this Act as if it were a stamp issued by the Post Office.*
> *(4)   In this Part of this Act 'Inland Revenue stamp' means a stamp as defined in section 27 of the Stamp Duties Management Act 1891.*

Keynote

The reference at s. 8(1)(d) above does not extend to electronic impulses keyed into a computer and therefore simply 'hacking' into a computer cannot amount to forgery (*R v Gold* [1988] AC 1063). For the offences under the Computer Misuse Act 1990, **see General Police Duties, chapter 11**).

Note that 'document' is not defined. As discussed above, this definition does not include currency notes which are the subject of a specific offence (see counterfeiting below).

Specific Instruments

In addition to the above offences which apply to any instrument, there are several specific offences which apply to specific types of 'formal' instrument.

Offence — Having Custody or Control of Specific Instruments and Materials with Intent — Forgery and Counterfeiting Act 1981, s. 5(1) and (3)

Triable either way. Ten years' imprisonment on indictment; six months' imprisonment and/or a fine summarily.
(Arrestable offence)

The Forgery and Counterfeiting Act 1981, s. 5 states:

(1)   It is an offence for a person to have in his custody or under his control an instrument to which this section applies which is, and which he knows or believes to be, false, with the intention that he or another shall use it to induce somebody to accept it as genuine, and by reason of so accepting it to do or not to do some act to his own or any other person's prejudice.
(2)   . . .
(3)   It is an offence for a person to make or to have in his custody or under his control a machine or implement, or paper or any other material, which to his knowledge is or has been specially designed or adapted for the making of an instrument to which this section applies, with the intention that he or another shall make an instrument to which this section applies which is false and that he or another shall use the instrument to induce somebody to accept it as genuine, and by reason of so accepting it to do or not to do some act to his own or any other person's prejudice.

Offence — Having Custody or Control of Specific Instruments and Materials — Forgery and Counterfeiting Act 1981, s. 5(2) and (4)

Triable either way. Two years' imprisonment on indictment; six months' imprisonment and/or a fine summarily.
(No specific power of arrest)

The Forgery and Counterfeiting Act 1981, s. 5 states:

(2)   It is an offence for a person to have in his custody or under his control, without lawful authority or excuse, an instrument to which this section applies which is, and which he knows or believes to be, false.
(3)   . . .
(4)   It is an offence for a person to make or to have in his custody or under his control any such machine, implement, paper or material, without lawful authority or excuse.

The instruments to which the above offences under s. 5 apply are:

(5)   . . .
  (a)   money orders;
  (b)   postal orders;
  (c)   United Kingdom postage stamps;
  (d)   Inland Revenue stamps;
  (e)   share certificates;
  (f)   passports and documents which can be used instead of passports;
  (g)   cheques;
  (h)   travellers' cheques;
  (j)   cheque cards;
  (k)   credit cards;
  (l)   certified copies relating to an entry in a register of births, adoptions, marriages or deaths and issued by the Registrar General, the Registrar General for Northern Ireland, a registration officer or a person lawfully authorised to register marriages; and
  (m)   certificates relating to entries in such registers.
(6)   In subsection (5)(e) above 'share certificate' means an instrument entitling or evidencing the title of a person to a share or interest—
  (a)   in any public stock, annuity, fund or debt of any government or state, including a state which forms part of another state; or
  (b)   in any stock, fund or debt of a body (whether corporate or unincorporated) established in the United Kingdom or elsewhere.

Prejudice and Induce

The *ulterior intent* (**see chapter 1**) of *inducing* somebody to accept an instrument with the result that he/she does something to his/her own *prejudice* must be read in the light of s. 10 of the 1981 Act which states:

> (1) Subject to subsections (2) and (4) below, for the purposes of this Part of this Act an act or omission intended to be induced is to a person's prejudice if, and only if, it is one which, if it occurs—
>
> (a) will result—
>
> (i) in his temporary or permanent loss of property; or
>
> (ii) in his being deprived of an opportunity to earn remuneration or greater remuneration; or
>
> (iii) in his being deprived of an opportunity to gain a financial advantage otherwise than by way of remuneration; or
>
> (b) will result in somebody being given an opportunity—
>
> (i) to earn remuneration or greater remuneration from him; or
>
> (ii) to gain a financial advantage from him otherwise than by way of remuneration; or
>
> (c) will be the result of his having accepted a false instrument as genuine, or a copy of a false instrument as a copy of a genuine one, in connection with his performance of any duty.
>
> (2) An act which a person has an enforceable duty to do and an omission to do an act which a person is not entitled to do shall be disregarded for the purposes of this Part of this Act.
>
> (3) In this Part of this Act references to inducing somebody to accept a false instrument as genuine, or a copy of a false instrument as a copy of a genuine one, include references to inducing a machine to respond to the instrument or copy as if it were a genuine instrument or, as the case may be, a copy of a genuine one.

Keynote

This section extends the meaning of inducing someone to accept something as genuine to *machines*. This extension, which deals with occasions where machines are 'fooled' by a false instrument is in direct contrast to the situation where an operating *deception* is concerned (**see para. 13.1**). Therefore, it would seem that you can be guilty of making, possessing etc. a false instrument intending that it will be used to induce a machine to accept it as genuine, but you could not be guilty, on the same facts, of an offence requiring a 'deception'. The extension is limited to offences under Part I of the 1981 Act and therefore does not apply to offences contained elsewhere such as counterfeiting (as to which, see below).

Police Powers

A warrant to search for and seize false instruments and materials may be issued under s. 7 of the 1981 Act.

13.7.3 Acknowledging Bail

Offence — Acknowledging Bail in the Name of Another — Forgery Act 1861, s. 34
Triable on indictment. Seven years' imprisonment.
(*Arrestable offence*)

The Forgery Act 1861, s. 34 states:

> Whosoever, without lawful authority or excuse (the proof whereof shall lie on the party accused), shall in the name of any other person acknowledge any recognisance or bail, . . .or judgment or any deed or other instrument, before any court, judge, or other person lawfully authorized in that behalf, shall be guilty of [an offence].

Keynote

Provided the bail or recognisance is valid, this offence would appear to apply equally to bail granted by a court or the police.

13.7.4 Counterfeiting

The offences of counterfeiting apply to currency notes and coins. These terms are defined within the Forgery and Counterfeiting Act 1981, s. 27, which states:

> (1) In this Part of this Act—
> 'currency note' means—
>> (a) any note which—
>>> (i) has been lawfully issued in England and Wales, Scotland, Northern Ireland, any of the Channel Islands, the Isle of Man or the Republic of Ireland; and
>>> (ii) is or has been customarily used as money in the country where it was issued; and
>>> (iii) is payable on demand; or
>> (b) any note which—
>>> (i) has been lawfully issued in some country other than those mentioned in paragraph (a)(i) above; and
>>> (ii) is customarily used as money in that country; and
> 'protected coin' means any coin which—
>> (a) is customarily used as money in any country: or
>> (b) is specified in an order made by the Treasury for the purposes of this Part of this Act.

Section 28 defines counterfeit as:

> (1) For the purposes of this Part of this Act a thing is a counterfeit of a currency note or of a protected coin—
>> (a) if it is not a currency note or a protected coin but resembles a currency note or protected coin (whether on one side only or on both) to such an extent that it is reasonably capable of passing for a currency note or protected coin of that description; or
>> (b) if it is a currency note or protected coin which has been so altered that it is reasonably capable of passing for a currency note or protected coin of some other description.
> (2) For the purposes of this Part of this Act—
>> (a) a thing consisting of one side only of a currency note, with or without the addition of other material, is a counterfeit of such a note;
>> (b) a thing consisting—
>>> (i) of parts of two or more currency notes; or
>>> (ii) of parts of a currency note, or of parts of two or more currency notes, with the addition of other material,
> is capable of being a counterfeit of a currency note.
> (3) References in this Part of this Act to passing or tendering a counterfeit of a currency note or a protected coin are not to be construed as confined to passing or tendering it as legal tender.

Keynote

Currency notes and protected coins can therefore originate from another country (see, however, the offences under ss. 18 and 19 below).

Given the imminent arrival of the Euro, it might be anticipated that this area of criminal law becomes more prominent in day-to-day police work.

Counterfeit currency or coins can be either:

- things which are not in fact currency notes or coins but which resemble them sufficiently enough to be passed as such

- things which *are* in fact currency notes or coins but which have been altered to resemble different ones.

The National Criminal Intelligence Service (NCIS) is responsible for collating intelligence on counterfeit currency and they can provide expert evidence and advice in investigations. The government has made provision for the counterfeiting of Euro notes prior to circulation in January 2002. For details see Home Office Circular 10/2000.

Offence — Making Counterfeit Note or Coin with Intent — Forgery and Counterfeiting Act 1981, s. 14(1)
Triable either way. Ten years' imprisonment on indictment; six months' imprisonment and/or a fine summarily.
(*Arrestable offence*)

The Forgery and Counterfeiting Act 1981, s. 14 states:

(1)   It is an offence for a person to make a counterfeit of a currency note or of a protected coin, intending that he or another shall pass or tender it as genuine.

Keynote

Although there is a requirement to prove an ulterior intent, there is no need to show that the defendant intended to induce someone to do something to his/her own prejudice.

Offence — Having Custody or Control of Counterfeit Note or Coin with Intent — Forgery and Counterfeiting Act 1981, s. 16(1)
Triable either way. Ten years' imprisonment on indictment; six months' imprisonment and/or a fine summarily.
(*Arrestable offence*)

The Forgery and Counterfeiting Act 1981, s. 16 states:

(1)   It is an offence for a person to have in his custody or under his control any thing which is, and which he knows or believes to be, a counterfeit of a currency note or of a protected coin, intending either to pass or tender it as genuine or to deliver it to another with the intention that he or another shall pass or tender it as genuine.

Offence — Passing Counterfeit Notes or Coins with Intent — Forgery and Counterfeiting Act 1981, s. 15(1)(a) and (b)
Triable either way. Ten years' imprisonment and/or a fine on indictment; six months' imprisonment and/or a fine summarily.
(*Arrestable offence*)

The Forgery and Counterfeiting Act 1981, s. 15 states:

(1)   It is an offence for a person—
(a)   to pass or tender as genuine any thing which is, and which he knows or believes to be, a counterfeit of a currency note or of a protected coin; or
(b)   to deliver to another any thing which is, and which he knows or believes to be, such a counterfeit, intending that the person to whom it is delivered or another shall pass or tender it as genuine.

Offence — Having Custody or Control of Materials for Counterfeiting with Intent — Forgery and Counterfeiting Act 1981, s. 17(1)
Triable either way. Ten years' imprisonment and/or a fine on indictment; six months' imprisonment and/or a fine summarily.
(*Arrestable offence*)

The Forgery and Counterfeiting Act 1981, s. 17 states:

DECEPTION AND FRAUD

(1) It is an offence for a person to make, or to have in his custody or under his control, any thing which he intends to use, or to permit any other person to use, for the purpose of making a counterfeit of a currency note or of a protected coin with the intention that it be passed or tendered as genuine.

Offence — Making Counterfeit Note or Coin — Forgery and Counterfeiting Act 1981, s. 14(2)
Triable either way. Two years' imprisonment on indictment; six months' imprisonment and/or a fine summarily.
(No specific power of arrest)

The Forgery and Counterfeiting Act 1981, s. 14 states:

(2) It is an offence for a person to make a counterfeit of a currency note or of a protected coin without lawful authority or excuse.

Offence — Having Custody or Control of Counterfeit Note or Coin — Forgery and Counterfeiting Act 1981, s. 16(2)
Triable either way. Two years' imprisonment and/or a fine on indictment; six months' imprisonment and/or a fine summarily.
(No specific power of arrest)

The Forgery and Counterfeiting Act 1981, s. 16 states:

(2) It is an offence for a person to have in his custody or under his control, without lawful authority or excuse, any thing which is, and which he knows or believes to be, a counterfeit of a currency note or of a protected coin.
(3) It is immaterial for the purposes of subsections (1) and (2) above that a coin or note is not in a fit state to be passed or tendered or that the making or counterfeiting of a coin or note has not been finished or perfected.

Offence — Delivering Counterfeit Notes or Coins — Forgery and Counterfeiting Act 1981, s. 15(2)
Triable either way. Two years' imprisonment and/or a fine on indictment; six months' imprisonment and/or a fine summarily.
(No specific power of arrest)

The Forgery and Counterfeiting Act 1981, s. 15 states:

(2) It is an offence for a person to deliver to another, without lawful authority or excuse, any thing which is, and which he knows or believes to be, a counterfeit of a currency note or of a protected coin.

Offence — Having Custody or Control of Materials for Counterfeiting — Forgery and Counterfeiting Act 1981, s. 17(2) and (3)
Triable either way. Two years' imprisonment and/or a fine on indictment; six months' imprisonment and/or a fine summarily.
(No specific power of arrest)

The Forgery and Counterfeiting Act 1981, s. 17 states:

(2) It is an offence for a person without lawful authority or excuse—
(a) to make; or
(b) to have in his custody or under his control,
any thing which, to his knowledge, is or has been specially designed or adapted for the making of a counterfeit of a currency note.

(3) Subject to subsection (4) below, it is an offence for a person to make, or to have in his custody or under his control, any implement which, to his knowledge, is capable of imparting to any thing, a resemblance—
 (a) to the whole or part of either side of a protected coin; or
 (b) to the whole or part of the reverse of the image on either side of a protected coin.

Defence

Section 17(4) of the 1981 Act states:

(4) It shall be defence for a person charged with an offence under subsection (3) above to show—
 (a) that he made the implement or, as the case may be, had it in his custody or under his control, with the written consent of the Treasury; or
 (b) that he had lawful authority otherwise than by virtue of paragraph (a) above, or a lawful excuse, for making it or having it in his custody or under his control.

Keynote

This defence only applies to s. 17(3) above. In all other cases the legal burden (**see Evidence and Procedure, chapter 11**) to disprove lawful authority lies with the prosecution.

Police Powers

A warrant to search for and seize counterfeit currency and materials may be issued under s. 24 of the 1981 Act.

British Currency and Coins

Offence — Reproducing British Currency Note —
Forgery and Counterfeiting Act 1981, s. 18
Triable either way. Fine.
(**No specific power of arrest**)

The Forgery and Counterfeiting Act 1981, s. 18 states:

(1) It is an offence for any person, unless the relevant authority has previously consented in writing, to reproduce on any substance whatsoever, and whether or not on the correct scale, any British currency note or any part of a British currency note.
(2) In this section—
 'British currency note' means any note which—
 (a) has been lawfully issued in England and Wales, Scotland or Northern Ireland; and
 (b) is or has been customarily used as money in the country where it was issued; and
 (c) is payable on demand; and
'the relevant authority', in relation to a British currency note of any particular description, means the authority empowered by law to issue notes of that description.

Offence — Making Imitation British Coins —
Forgery and Counterfeiting Act 1981, s. 19
Triable either way. Fine.
(**No specific power of arrest**)

The Forgery and Counterfeiting Act 1981, s. 19 states:

(1) It is an offence for a person—

 (a) to make an imitation British coin in connection with a scheme intended to promote the sale of any product or the making of contracts for the supply of any service; or

 (b) to sell or distribute imitation British coins in connection with any such scheme, or to have imitation British coins in his custody or under his control with a view to such sale or distribution, unless the Treasury have previously consented in writing to the sale or distribution of such imitation British coins in connection with that scheme.

 (2) In this section—

 'British coin' means any coin which is legal tender in any part of the United Kingdom; and

 'imitation British coin' means any thing which resembles a British coin in shape, size and the substance of which it is made.

Keynote

These offences require no *ulterior* intent that anyone be fooled into thinking that the notes or coins are genuine. They are offences of *basic* intent (**see chapter 1**), and are designed to prevent any duplication under the proscribed circumstances. If any fraudulent use was made or intended then one of the earlier offences discussed above would be committed.

CHAPTER FOURTEEN

CRIMINAL DAMAGE

14.1 Introduction

Damage to property has many consequences. As well as the immediate financial impact upon the owner, criminal damage affects:

- The environment.

- Community safety — it is well-documented that graffiti and visible damage to buildings can create a widespread fear of crime and sense of lawlessness. This is particularly true where the nature of the damage and/or the selection of the victim is intended to intimidate and is one of the reasons behind the creation of a 'racially aggravated' form of criminal damage.

- The economy — in many cases of criminal damage the 'hidden' victims are often insurance companies, businesses and local communities.

All of these areas should be considered when dealing with offences of criminal damage, particularly when submitting compensation schedules with a proposed prosecution file.

The most important recent development in this area is the introduction of racially aggravated criminal damage under the Crime and Disorder Act 1998.

A further important development in the area of damage to property can be found in Protocol 1, Article 1 of the European Convention on Human Rights which gives individuals a right to peaceful enjoyment of their property and possessions. For the effects of the Convention and the Human Rights Act 1998 generally, **see General Police Duties**.

14.1.1 Types of Offence

There are extensive civil remedies available for people whose property is damaged by others. In cases involving a course of conduct or behaviour that causes widespread public nuisance, other offences and remedies may apply (**see General Police Duties, chapter 3**). The law regulating *criminal* damage, however, is largely contained within one statute, the Criminal Damage Act 1971. This Act deals with occasions where a person:

- actually damages or destroys the property of another (simple damage)

- damages or destroys his/her own property or that of another where there are 'aggravating' factors or circumstances (aggravated damage)

- threatens to damage or destroy property

- has articles to be used for damaging or destroying property

- commits an offence which is 'racially aggravated'.

14.2   Simple Damage

Offence — Simple Damage — Criminal Damage Act 1971, s. 1(1)
Triable either way. Ten years' imprisonment on indictment; six months' imprisonment and/or a fine summarily.
(***Arrestable offence***)

Offence — Racially Aggravated — Crime and Disorder Act 1998, s. 30(1)
Triable either way. Fourteen years' imprisonment and/or a fine on indictment; six months' imprisonment and/or a fine summarily.
(***Arrestable offence***)

The Criminal Damage Act 1971, s. 1 states:

(1)   A person who without lawful excuse destroys or damages any property belonging to another intending to destroy or damage any such property or being reckless as to whether any such property would be destroyed or damaged shall be guilty of an offence.

Keynote

Although triable either way, if the cost of the property destroyed or the damage done is less than £5,000, the offence is to be tried summarily (Magistrates' Courts Act 1980, s. 22). If the damage in such a case was caused by fire (arson) (**see para. 14.4**) then this rule will not apply.

The fact that the substantive offence is, by virtue of the value of the damage caused, triable only summarily does not make simple damage a 'summary offence' for all other purposes. If it did, you could only be found guilty of *attempting* to commit criminal damage if the value of the intended damage was more than £5,000 (because the Criminal Attempts Act 1981 does not extend to summary offences (**see chapter 3**). Therefore, where a defendant tried to damage a bus shelter in a way that would have cost far less than £5,000 to repair, his argument that he had only attempted what was in fact a 'summary offence' was dismissed by the Divisional Court (*R* v *Bristol Magistrates, ex parte E* [1998] 3 All ER 798).

The racially aggravated form of this offence (see below) is triable either way irrespective of the cost of the damage.

For the special evidential provisions in relation to criminal damage offences (under s. 9), **see Evidence and Procedure**.

Racially Aggravated Damage

The racially aggravated circumstances set out at s. 28(1)(a) of the Crime and Disorder Act 1998 (**see General Police Duties, chapter 3**) deal with situations where the defendant demonstrates hostility:

- at the time of
- or immediately before or after

committing the offence, towards the *victim* and that hostility is *based on the victim's membership or presumed membership of a racial group*. To clarify such situations in relation to racially aggravated damage, s. 30(3) provides that the person to whom the property belongs or is treated as belonging, will be treated as the 'victim'.

This provision is helpful where the aggravated offence is one under s. 28(1)(a) — the 'demonstration' type of aggravation — and the property is privately owned.

Where the property is owned by a corporate body (e.g. a bus shelter or tube station) however, there will clearly be problems in proving that the defendant's hostility was based on the *victim's* membership/presumed membership of a racial group. Even though property for these purposes may be treated as belonging to more than one person (**see para. 14.2.5**) this means that, where the damage is caused by racist graffiti in publicly-owned places or in property owned by large corporations, the most suitable charge will probably be under s. 28(1)(b) of the Act — by far the harder to prove.

The provisions of s. 30 of the Crime and Disorder Act 1998 only apply to the offence of 'simple' damage under s. 1(1) of the 1971 Act; they do not apply to any of the other offences in this chapter.

14.2.1 Lawful excuse

Section 5 of the Criminal Damage Act 1971 provides for two occasions where a defendant may have a 'lawful excuse'. These can be remembered as 'permission' (s. 5(2)(a)) and 'protection' (s. 5(2)(b)). Both involve the belief of the defendant. The wording of s. 5 indicates that these particular defences are not the only ones available to a charge of criminal damage and other general defences (**see chapter 4**) may apply.

Permission

A person shall be treated as having lawful excuse under s. 5(2):

(a) if at the time of the act or acts alleged to constitute the offence he believed that the person or persons whom he believed to be entitled to consent to the destruction of or damage to the property in question had so consented, or would have so consented to it if he or they had known of the destruction or damage and its circumstances . . .

Keynote

An example of 'lawful excuse' under s. 5(2)(a) would be if you, as a police officer, were asked by a motorist to help them get into their partner's car after locking the keys inside. If, during that attempt you damaged the rubber window surround, s. 5(2)(a) would provide you with a statutory defence to any later charge of criminal damage by the owner. The key elements here would be:

• the consent of someone whom you believed to be entitled to consent to that damage, and

• the circumstances under which it was caused.

If the driver was not available and your reason for opening the door was to get a better look at some personal documents for intelligence purposes, it is unlikely that the driver or the owner would have consented, either to the damage or the circumstances in which it was caused. Therefore you could not use this particular defence.

Protection

A person shall be treated as having lawful excuse under s. 5(2):

> (b)   if he destroyed or damaged or threatened to destroy or damage the property in question or, in the case of a charge of an offence under section 3 above, intended to use or cause or permit the use of something to destroy or damage it, in order to protect property belonging to himself or another or a right or interest in property which was or which he believed to be vested in himself or another, and at the time of the act or acts alleged to constitute the offence he believed—
> (i)   that the property, right or interest was in immediate need of protection; and
> (ii)   that the means of protection adopted or proposed to be adopted were or would be reasonable having regard to all the circumstances.

Keynote

Situations where such a defence can be used involve causing damage to property in order to protect other property. This defence also applies to the offence of having articles for causing damage (**see para. 14.6**). Key features of this defence are the immediacy of the need to protect the property and the reasonableness of the means of protection adopted. In a case involving 'peace campaigners' it was held that the threat presented by a possible nuclear attack in the future did not excuse the carrying of a hacksaw for cutting through the perimeter fence of an airbase (*R* v *Hill* (1988) 89 Cr App R 74).

The 1971 Act goes on to say that it is immaterial whether a 'belief' above was justified as long as it was honestly held (s. 5(3)). This is a largely subjective test as to what was going through a defendant's mind at the time — or perhaps what was *not* going through his/her mind! In *Jaggard* v *Dickinson* [1981] QB 527 the defendant had broken a window to get into a house. Being drunk at the time, she had got the wrong house but the court accepted that her belief (that it was the right house and that the owner would have consented) had been honestly held, and that it did not matter whether that belief was brought about by intoxication, stupidity, forgetfulness or inattention. (For further discussion of drunkenness as a defence generally, **see chapter 4**.) That is not to say, however, that *any* honestly held belief will suffice. An example of someone claiming — though unsuccessfully — a defence under both s. 5(2)(a) and (b) can be seen in *Blake* v *DPP* [1993] Crim LR 586. There the defendant was a vicar who wished to protest against Great Britain's involvement in the Gulf War. In order to mark his disapproval, the defendant wrote a quotation from the Bible in ink on a pillar in front of the Houses of Parliament. He claimed:

- that he was carrying out God's instructions and therefore had a lawful excuse based on his belief that God was the person entitled to consent to such damage and that He had in fact consented or would have done so (s. 5(2)(a)); and

- that he had damaged the property as a reasonable means of protecting other property located in the Gulf from being damaged by warfare (s. 5(2)(b)).

Perhaps unsurprisingly the Divisional Court did not accept either proposition holding that, in the first case a belief in The Almighty's consent was not a 'lawful excuse' and, in the second, that the defendant's conduct was too remote from any immediate need to protect property in the Gulf States. The test in relation to the defendant's belief appears then to be largely subjective (i.e. what was/was not going on in his/her head at the time) but with an objective element in that the judge/magistrate(s) must decide whether, on the facts as believed by the defendant, his/her acts were capable of protecting property.

A similar approach has been tried more recently in a case where the defendant was arrested after making 22 cuts in a perimeter fence of a base where nuclear warheads were produced. The defendant claimed that the activity at the base was unlawful in international law and therefore acts to prevent that activity amounted to a lawful excuse under the 1971 Act. The Divisional Court did not accept this argument, nor the argument that the defendant's acts were merely an expression of her opinion under Article 10 of the European Convention on Human Rights (as to which, **see General Police Duties, chapter 2**) (*Hutchinson* v *Newbury Magistrates' Court, The Independent,* 9 October 2000).

The Act also states, at s. 5(4), that a right or interest in property includes any right or privilege in or over land, whether created by grant, licence or otherwise.

Section 5(5) allows for other general defences (**see chapter 4**) at criminal law to apply in addition to those listed under s. 5.

It is not an offence to damage your own property unless there are aggravating circumstances (**see para. 14.3**). Even if the intention in doing so is to carry out some further offence — such as a fraudulent insurance claim — this fact still does not make it an offence under s. 1(1) of the Criminal Damage Act 1971 (*R* v *Denton* [1981] 1 WLR 1446). (It may, however, give rise to other offences of dishonesty (**see chapter 12**).)

14.2.2 *Mens Rea*

An offence of criminal damage under s. 1(1) can be proved by showing that the defendant was 'reckless' (**see chapter 1**). As with most criminal offences requiring recklessness as to consequences, the recklessness here is *objective* which will mean proving that:

- the defendant does an act which *in fact* creates an obvious risk that property will be destroyed or damaged, and

- when doing the act, the defendant either has not given any thought to the possibility of there being such a risk or has recognised that there was some risk involved and has nevertheless gone on to do it

(per Lord Diplock in *Metropolitan Police Commissioner* v *Caldwell* [1982] AC 341).

The risk of damage at the time of the defendant's conduct need only be apparent to a *reasonable* person. It is not necessary to show that the risk would have been obvious to the defendant had he/she stopped to think about what he/she was doing; neither need it be shown that the risk would have been obvious to a person of the same age or state of mind as the defendant (*R* v *Coles* [1995] 1 Cr App R 157).

Example

A group of youths in a shopping precinct walk up to a grocery display and begin juggling with some apples. They drop several apples, some of which smash on the pavement while others are soiled and bruised.

By juggling with the fruit the youths have created an obvious risk that the apples (property) will be damaged. As the risk to the property would have been obvious to any reasonable bystander watching their antics the youths are 'reckless' for the purposes of the Criminal Damage Act 1971, *whether or not they had given any thought to the risk themselves.*

14.2.3 Destroy or Damage

Although a key feature of the 1971 Act, the terms 'destroy' or 'damage' are not defined. The courts have taken a wide view when interpreting these terms. 'Destroying' property would suggest that it has been rendered useless but there is no need to prove that 'damage' to property is in any way permanent or irreparable. In the example above, the apples which were smashed were clearly 'destroyed'; those which were soiled, even though they could be washed, would probably be unfit for sale and therefore 'damaged' for the purposes of s. 1(1).

Whether an article has been damaged will be a question of fact for each court to determine on the evidence before it. Situations where courts have accepted that property has been damaged include the defacing of a pavement by an artist using only water-soluble paint (*Hardman* v *Chief Constable of Avon and Somerset* [1986] Crim LR 330) and the erasure of electronically-stored data on a circuit card (*Cox* v *Riley* (1986) 83 Cr App R 54 — see now the Computer Misuse Act 1990, **General Police Duties, chapter 11**). It has also been held by the Divisional Court that graffiti smeared in mud can amount to damage, even though it is easily washed off (*Roe* v *Kingerlee* [1986] Crim LR 735).

14.2.4 Property

Property is defined in the 1971 Act by s. 10 which states:

   (1)   In this Act 'property' means property of a tangible nature, whether real or personal, including money and—

(a)   including wild creatures which have been tamed or are ordinarily kept in captivity and any other wild creatures or their carcasses if, but only if, they have been reduced into possession . . . or are in the course of being reduced into possession; but
(b)   not including mushrooms growing wild on any land or flowers, fruit or foliage of a plant growing wild on any land.
. . .

Keynote

This definition has similarities with the definition of 'property' for the purposes of theft (**see chapter 12**) but 'real' property (i.e. land and things attached to it) can be damaged even though it cannot be stolen. Trampling flower beds, digging up cricket pitches, chopping down trees in a private garden and even pulling up genetically-modified crops may all amount to criminal damage if accompanied by the required circumstances.

It is important to remember when dealing with disputes involving pets or farm animals that they are property for the purposes of this Act. Cases of horses being mutilated would, in addition to the offence of 'cruelty' itself (**see General Police Duties, chapter 8**), amount to criminal damage. There may also be occasions — such as domestic or neighbour disputes — involving harm or cruelty to such animals where it will be more appropriate and effective to consider offences under the 1971 Act, together with the powers which they attract under the Police and Criminal Evidence Act 1984 for arrestable offences (**see General Police Duties, chapter 2**).

14.2.5   Belonging to Another

Section 10(2) states:

(2)   Property shall be treated for the purposes of this Act as belonging to any person—
(a)   having the custody or control of it;
(b)   having in it any proprietary right or interest (not being an equitable interest arising only from an agreement to transfer or grant an interest); or
(c)   having a charge on it.

Keynote

This extended meaning of 'belonging to another' is similar to that used in the Theft Act 1968 (**see chapter 12**). One result is that if a person damages his/her own property, he/she may still commit the offence of simple criminal damage if that property also 'belongs to' someone else.

14.3   Aggravated Damage

Offence — Aggravated Damage — Criminal Damage Act 1971, s. 1(2)
Triable on indictment. Life imprisonment.
(*Arrestable offence*)

The Criminal Damage Act 1971, s. 1 states:

(2)   A person who without lawful excuse destroys or damages any property, whether belonging to himself or another—

227

CRIMINAL DAMAGE

(a)   intending to destroy or damage any property or being reckless as to whether any property would be destroyed or damaged; and
(b)   intending by the destruction or damage to endanger the life of another or being reckless as to whether the life of another would be thereby endangered;
shall be guilty of an offence.

Keynote

The aggravating factor in this offence, and the reason why it attracts such a heavy maximum sentence, is the ulterior intention of endangering life or recklessness as to whether life is endangered. As such, evidence of self-induced intoxication may provide a defence to a charge under this section (**see chapter 4**). This form of 'aggravation' should not be confused with the 'racially aggravated' form of criminal damage.

The reference to 'without lawful excuse' does not refer to the statutory excuses under s. 5 (**see para. 14.2.1**) which are not applicable here, but to general excuses such as self-defence or the prevention of crime (**see chapter 4**).

In order to prove a defendant's recklessness you will need to apply the objective test used in *Caldwell* (**see para. 14.2.2**), that is, would the risk have been obvious to a reasonable person watching the defendant's behaviour?

You must also show that the defendant either intended or was reckless as to each of the following consequences:

* the damage being caused, and
* the *resultant* danger to life.

It does not matter that the *actual* damage caused by the defendant turned out to be minor. What matters is the *potential* for damage and danger created by the defendant's conduct.

Where a defendant set fire to furniture in a house which was unoccupied at the time, the court nevertheless found him guilty of this offence. The court's reasoning for doing so turned on the fact that, had a reasonable bystander been present, he/she would have seen the possible risk that the fire might cause to the lives of others in the area, even though with hindsight it was shown that there had been no likelihood of the fire spreading to neighbouring properties (*R* v *Sangha* [1988] 1 WLR 519). In this case there was clearly recklessness as to the damage caused *and* recklessness as to the danger to life *presented by the damage*. In contrast, where a defendant fired a weapon through a window pane he was clearly reckless as to the damage his actions would cause. However, the court felt that, even though two people were standing behind the window and that they were obviously put in some danger, it was the *missile* which endangered their lives and not the result of the damage. Therefore the court held that the defendant was not guilty of this particular offence (*R* v *Steer* [1988] AC 111). This distinction seems to be a fine one, particularly if you are the person behind the window.

If someone were to smash the windscreen of a moving car or to cause a large display window to collapse into a busy street, this would probably be enough to support a charge under s. 1(2) (see *R* v *Webster* [1995] 2 All ER 168).

14.4   Arson

Offence — Arson — Criminal Damage Act 1971, s. 1(3)
Triable either way. Life imprisonment on indictment; where life is not endangered six months' imprisonment and/or a fine summarily.
(*Arrestable offence*)

The Criminal Damage Act 1971, s. 1 states:

> *(3)   An offence committed under this section by destroying or damaging property by fire shall be charged as arson.*

Keynote

In any of the above cases of criminal damage, if the destruction or damage is caused by fire, the offence will be charged as 'arson'. Given the potential for extensive damage and danger to life that fire-raising has, the restrictions on the mode of trial for simple damage under s. 1(1) (**see para. 14.2**) do not apply to cases of arson.

As arson is a 'violent offence' for the purposes of the Powers of Criminal Courts (Sentencing) Act 2000, those convicted of it are covered by the statutory provisions relating to sexual and violent offenders (**see chapter 10**).

Aggravated damage caused by arson is triable only on indictment and carries a maximum penalty of life imprisonment.

Sections 1 and 2 of the Criminal Evidence (Amendment) Act 1997 extending the power to take non-intimate samples without consent apply to this offence and also to conspiracies, attempts or incitements in the circumstances set out in that Act (**see Evidence and Procedure, chapter 16**).

14.5   Threats to Destroy or Damage Property

Offence — Threats to Destroy or Damage Property —
Criminal Damage Act 1971, s. 2
Triable either way. Ten years' imprisonment on indictment; six months' imprisonment and/or a fine summarily.
(*Arrestable offence*)

The Criminal Damage Act 1971, s. 2 states:

> *A person who without lawful excuse makes to another a threat, intending that that other would fear it would be carried out,—*
> *(a)   to destroy or damage any property belonging to that other or a third person; or*
> *(b)   to destroy or damage his own property in a way which he knows is likely to endanger the life of that other or a third person;*
> *shall be guilty of an offence.*

Keynote

This is an offence of *intention*, that is, the key element is the defendant's intention that the person receiving the threat fears it would be carried out.

The s. 2 offence, which originates from the need to tackle protection racketeers, is very straightforward: there is no need to show that the other person actually feared or even believed that the threat would be carried out. There is no need to show that the defendant intended to carry it out; nor does it matter whether the threat was even capable of being carried out.

Example

If a person, enraged by a neighbour's inconsiderate parking, shouts over the garden wall, '*When you've gone to bed I'm going to T-cut that heap with paint stripper!*', the offence will be complete, provided you can show that the person making the threat intended the neighbour to fear it would be carried out.

For other offences involving threats, harassment or nuisance, **see General Police Duties, chapter 3.**

14.6 Having Articles with Intent to Destroy or Damage Property

Offence — Having Articles with Intent to Destroy or Damage Property — Criminal Damage Act 1971, s. 3
*Triable either way. Ten years' imprisonment on indictment;
six months' imprisonment and/or a fine summarily.*
(*Arrestable offence*)

The Criminal Damage Act 1971, s. 3 states:

> *A person who has anything in his custody or under his control intending without lawful excuse to use it or cause or permit another to use it—*
> *(a)   to destroy or damage any property belonging to some other person; or*
> *(b)   to destroy or damage his own or the user's property in a way which he knows is likely to endanger the life of some other person;*
> *shall be guilty of an offence.*

Keynote

Often referred to as 'possessing articles' for causing damage, this offence is, in reality, far wider than that. Although it also originates from the need to control organised crime, this offence covers *anything* which a defendant has '*in his custody or under his control*', a deliberately broader term than 'possession'. (Compare this with the narrower expression — 'has with him' — used in the law preventing the carrying of weapons, **see General Police Duties, chapter 6** and the Theft Act 1968, **chapter 12.**)

As a result, this offence applies to graffiti 'artists' carrying aerosols, advertisers with adhesives for sticking illicit posters and neighbours with paint stripper. The key element, once again, is an *intention*. This time the required intention is that the 'thing' be used to cause criminal damage to another's property or to the defendant's own property in a way which he/she knows is likely to endanger the life of another. Such articles are not 'prohibited' articles for the purposes of the power of stop and search under s. 1 of the Police and Criminal Evidence Act 1984 (**see General Police Duties, chapter 2**).

If the person's intention is to use the articles for contaminating goods or making it appear that goods have been contaminated, a separate offence exists under the Public Order Act 1986, s. 38(3) (**see para. 14.7**).

A conditional intent — that is, an intent to use something to cause criminal damage if the need arises — will be enough (*R* v *Buckingham* (1976) 63 Cr App R 159).

Just as it is not an offence to damage your own property in a way which endangers no-one else, neither is it an offence to have something which you intend to use to cause damage under those circumstances.

Example

If the owner of a 10 metre high conifer decides to trim the top with a chainsaw and a ladder, putting himself — but no-one else — at considerable risk, he commits no offence, either by causing the damage or by having the chainsaw. If he intends to fell the tree in a way which a reasonable bystander would say presents a danger to his neighbours or passers by, then he may commit offences on both counts.

Police Powers

In addition to the police powers which this offence attracts (by virtue of its being an arrestable offence; **see General Police Duties, chapter 2**), there is a statutory power to apply to a magistrate for a search warrant under s. 6.

14.7 Contamination or Interference with Goods

**Offence — Contamination or Interference with Goods —
Public Order Act 1986, s. 38(1)**
*Triable either way. Ten years' imprisonment and/or a fine on indictment;
six months' imprisonment and/or a fine summarily.*
(Arrestable offence)

The Public Order Act 1986, s. 38 states:

(1) It is an offence for a person, with the intention—
(a) of causing public alarm or anxiety, or
(b) of causing injury to members of the public consuming or using the goods, or
(c) of causing economic loss to any person by reason of the goods being shunned by members of the public, or
(d) of causing economic loss to any person by reason of steps taken to avoid any such alarm or anxiety, injury or loss,
to contaminate or interfere with goods, or make it appear that goods have been contaminated or interfered with, or to place goods which have been contaminated or interfered with, or which appear to have been contaminated or interfered with in a place where goods of that description are consumed, used, sold or otherwise supplied.
(2) It is also an offence for a person, with any such intention as is mentioned in paragraph (a), (c) or (d) of subsection (1), to threaten that he or another will do, or to claim that he or another has done, any of the acts mentioned in that subsection.
(3) It is an offence for a person to be in possession of any of the following articles with a view to the commission of an offence under subsection (1)—
(a) materials to be used for contaminating or interfering with goods or making it appear that goods have been contaminated or interfered with, or

    (b)   goods which have been contaminated or interfered with, or which appear to have been contaminated or interfered with.

    (4) . . .

    (5)   In this section 'goods' includes substances whether natural or manufactured and whether or not incorporated in or mixed with other goods.

    (6)   The reference in subsection (2) to a person claiming that certain acts have been committed does not include a person who in good faith reports or warns that such acts have been, or appear to have been, committed.

Keynote

Section 38 creates two offences. The first involves the contamination of, interference with or placing of goods with the intentions set out at s. 38(1)(a)–(d). This is a crime of 'specific' intent (**see chapter 1**) and the particular intention of the defendant must be proved.

Section 38(2) involves the making of threats to do, *or* the claiming *to have done* any of the acts in s. 38(1), with any of the intentions set out at s. 38(1)(a), (c) or (d). It is difficult to see how a threat or claim made with the intention of causing injury to the public (s. 38(1)(b)) would not also amount to an intention to cause them alarm or anxiety.

Section 38(6) allows for people to communicate warnings in good faith where such acts appear to have been committed.

Where threats to contaminate goods are made there may also be grounds for charging blackmail (**see chapter 12**). This type of 'product' sabotage is increasing, evidenced by the increasingly elaborate sealing devices used by manufacturers. Perhaps the most notorious example of this offence — and the overlap with blackmail — is the case of *R v Witchelo* (1992) 13 Cr App R (S) 371 where the defendant, a police officer, was sentenced to 13 years' imprisonment after obtaining £32,000 from food producers to whom he had sent threatening letters.

Additionally, where the defendant's behaviour is designed to influence the government, to intimidate the public or where it creates a serious risk to health and safety, the offences may fall within the definition of 'terrorism' under the Terrorism Act 2000. For a full discussion of this area, **see General Police Duties, chapter 4**.

CHAPTER FIFTEEN

OFFENCES AGAINST THE ADMINISTRATION OF JUSTICE AND PUBLIC INTEREST

15.1 Introduction

This chapter deals with the various offences which can be seen as an interference with the machinery of justice. Some such offences, such as perjury and tendering false statements in evidence, affect the administration of justice directly while others like corruption have an indirect effect on the public interest.

15.2 Perjury

Offence — Perjury in Judicial Proceeding — Perjury Act 1911, s. 1
Triable on indictment. Seven years' imprisonment.
(**Arrestable offence**)

The Perjury Act 1911, s. 1 states:

(1)   If any person lawfully sworn as a witness or as an interpreter in a judicial proceeding wilfully makes a statement material in that proceeding, which he knows to be false or does not believe to be true, he shall be guilty of perjury . . .
(2)   The expression 'judicial proceeding' includes a proceeding before any court, tribunal, or person having by law power to hear, receive, and examine evidence on oath.
(3)   Where a statement made for the purposes of a judicial proceeding is not made before the tribunal itself, but is made on oath before a person authorised by law to administer an oath to the person who makes the statement, and to record or authenticate the statement, it shall, for the purposes of this section, be treated as having been made in a judicial proceeding.

Keynote

To commit this offence a defendant must have been *lawfully sworn* (see the Evidence Act 1851, s. 16). The statement made in 'judicial proceeding' can be one given orally before the court or tribunal, or it can be given in the form of an affidavit (sworn statement). If a witness tenders a false statement (MG 11) used under the Criminal Justice Act 1967, s. 89 he/she commits a separate, lesser offence (**see para. 15.3**).

'Wilful' in this case means deliberate as opposed to accidental.

A 'statement material in that proceeding' means that the content of the evidence tendered in that case must have some importance to it and not just be of passing relevance. Whether something is material to a case is a question of law for a judge to decide. Whether a motorist had taken a drink between the time of his/her having a road traffic accident and being breathalysed would be such a material issue, and to get a witness to provide false evidence about that matter would be a 'statement material in that proceeding' (*R* v *Lewins* (1979) 1 Cr App R (S) 246).

To prove perjury you must also show that the defendant *knew* the statement to be false or *did not believe it to be true*. Technically, many defendants who are convicted after entering a 'not guilty' plea commit perjury but it would hardly be practical to investigate and prosecute each occasion where that happens!

Evidence of an opinion provided by a witness who does not genuinely hold such an opinion may also be perjury.

Perjury may be proved by using a court transcript or the evidence of others who were present at the proceeding in question (see Perjury Act 1911, s. 14).

Corroboration is required in cases of perjury (see Perjury Act 1911, s. 13 and **Evidence and Procedure, chapter 11**). The requirement for corroboration is solely in relation to the *falsity* of the defendant's statement. There is no requirement under s. 13 for corroboration of the fact that the defendant *actually made* the alleged statement, nor that he/she knew or believed it to be untrue. However, as that corroboration can be documentary and may even come from the defendant's earlier conduct (*R* v *Threlfall* (1914) 10 Cr App R 112) this requirement does not appear to present much of a hurdle to the prosecution.

Evidence given by live TV link under the provisions of the Criminal Justice Act 1988, s. 32 is also subject to the offence of perjury.

15.2.1 Aiding and Abetting

Offence — Aiding and Abetting Perjury — Perjury Act 1911, s. 7
If principal offence is contrary to s. 1 triable on indictment. Seven years' imprisonment.
(*Arrestable offence*)
Otherwise either way. Two years' imprisonment on indictment;
six months' imprisonment and/or a fine summarily.
(*No specific power of arrest*)

The Perjury Act 1911, s. 7 states:

> *(1)   Every person who aids, abets, counsels, procures, or suborns another person to commit an offence against this Act shall be liable to be proceeded against, indicted, tried and punished as if he were a principal offender.*
> *(2)   Every person who incites . . . another person to commit an offence against this Act shall be guilty of [an offence].*

Keynote

'Subornation' is the same as procuring. This specific section does not appear to add anything to the general offences of aiding and abetting principal offenders (**see chapter 2**).

15.3   Offences Similar to Perjury

Offence — False Testimony of Unsworn Child Witness — Children and Young Persons Act 1933, s. 38(2)
Triable summarily. Punishment as per text of subsection.
(No specific power of arrest)

The Children and Young Persons Act 1933, s. 38 states:

> (2)   If any child whose evidence is received unsworn . . . wilfully gives false evidence in such circumstances that he would, if the evidence had been given on oath, have been guilty of perjury, he shall be liable on summary conviction to be dealt with as if he had been summarily convicted of an indictable offence punishable in the case of an adult with imprisonment.

Offence — False Statements in Criminal Proceedings — Criminal Justice Act 1967, s. 89
Triable either way. Two years' imprisonment and/or a fine on indictment;
six months' imprisonment and/or a fine summarily.
(No specific power of arrest)

The Criminal Justice Act 1967, s. 89 states:

> (1)   If any person in a written statement tendered in evidence in criminal proceedings by virtue of section . . . 9 of this Act, or in proceedings before a court-martial . . . wilfully makes a statement material in those proceedings which he knows to be false or does not believe to be true, he shall be liable . . .
> (2)   The Perjury Act 1911 shall have effect as if this section were contained in that Act.

Offence — False Statements in Criminal Proceedings — Magistrates' Courts Act 1980, s. 106
Triable either way. Two years' imprisonment and/or a fine on indictment;
six months' imprisonment and/or a fine summarily.
(No specific power of arrest)

The Magistrates' Courts Act 1980, s. 106 states:

> (1)   If any person in a written statement tendered in evidence in criminal proceedings by virtue of section 102 above wilfully makes a statement material in those proceedings which he knows to be false or does not believe to be true, he shall be liable . . .
> (2)   The Perjury Act 1911 shall have effect as if this section were contained in that Act.

Offence — False Statements on Oath — Perjury Act 1911, s. 2
Triable either way. Seven years' imprisonment and/or a fine on indictment;
six months' imprisonment and/or a fine summarily.
(Arrestable offence)

The Perjury Act 1911, s. 2 states:

If any person—
(1)   being required or authorised by law to make any statement on oath for any purpose, and being lawfully sworn (otherwise than in a judicial proceeding) wilfully makes a statement which is material for that purpose and which he knows to be false or does not believe to be true; . . .
he shall be [guilty of an offence].

Keynote

The first two offences cover witnesses who tender false statements, either in criminal proceedings themselves (Criminal Justice Act 1967) or in place of depositions at a committal hearing (Magistrates' Courts Act 1980). The third offence covers the making of false statements under an oath which is not sworn in connection with a judicial proceeding.

The offence under s. 38 of the Children and Young Persons Act 1933 will be replaced by s. 57 of the Youth Justice and Criminal Evidence Act 1999, when it comes into force.

The Perjury Act 1911 makes further provision for the making of false statements in relation to mariage licences (s. 3) and the making of false statements in relation to the registration of births and deaths (s. 4). Both sections carry seven years' imprisonment on indictment and are therefore *arrestable offences*.

The 1911 Act also creates offences of making false declarations and of suppressing documents. For a full discussion of these offences, see *Blackstone's Criminal Practice*, 2001, section B14.

15.4   Perverting the Course of Justice

Offence — Perverting the Course of Justice — Common Law
Triable on indictment. Life imprisonment and/or a fine.
(*Arrestable offence*)

It is an offence at common law to do an act tending and intended to pervert the course of public justice.

Keynote

Although traditionally referred to — and charged — as 'attempting' to pervert the course of justice, it is recognised that behaviour which is *aimed* at perverting the course of public justice does just that and the substantive offence should be charged (see *R v Williams* (1991) 92 Cr App R 158).

Perverting the course of justice requires positive acts by the defendant, not merely standing by and allowing an injustice to take place. The offence will include cases where evidence is deliberately destroyed, concealed or falsified as well as cases where witnesses and jurors are intimidated (**see para. 15.5**).

Admitting to a crime to enable the true offender to avoid prosecution would fall under this offence (*R v Devito* [1975] Crim LR 175), as would abusing your authority as a police officer to excuse someone of a criminal charge (*R v Coxhead* [1986] RTR 411). Other examples include:

- making a false allegation of an offence (*R* v *Goodwin* (1989) 11 Cr App R (S) 194 (rape))

- giving another person's personal details when being reported for an offence (*R* v *Hurst* (1990) 12 Cr App R (S) 373)

- destroying and concealing evidence of a crime (*R* v *Kiffin* [1994] Crim LR 449).

It is important that the requisite intention is proved in every case as that intention cannot be implied, even from admitted facts (*R* v *Lalani* [1999] 1 Cr App R 481).

15.5 Intimidating Witnesses and Jurors

There are several statutory measures designed to protect witnesses, jurors and others involved in the judicial process. These can be separated into measures aimed at protecting those involved in *criminal* trials and/or investigations and offences aimed at protecting those involved in other proceedings.

The first measure can be found in the Criminal Justice and Public Order Act 1994.

Offence — Intimidating Witnesses and Jurors— Criminal Justice and Public Order Act 1994, s. 51
Triable either way. Five years' imprisonment and/or a fine on indictment; six months' imprisonment and/or a fine summarily.
(*Arrestable offence*)

The Criminal Justice and Public Order Act 1994, s. 51 states:

(1)   A person commits an offence if—
  (a)   he does an act which intimidates, and is intended to intimidate, another person ('the victim'),
  (b)   he does the act knowing or believing that the victim is assisting in the investigation of an offence or is a witness or potential witness or a juror or potential juror in proceedings for an offence, and
  (c)   he does it intending thereby to cause the investigation or the course of justice to be obstructed, perverted or interfered with.
(2)   A person commits an offence if—
  (a)   he does an act which harms, and is intended to harm, another person or, intending to cause another person to fear harm, he threatens to do an act which would harm that other person,
  (b)   he does or threatens to do the act knowing or believing that the person harmed or threatened to be harmed ('the victim'), or some other person, has assisted in an investigation into an offence or has given evidence or particular evidence in proceedings for an offence, or has acted as a juror or concurred in a particular verdict in proceedings for an offence, and
  (c)   he does or threatens to do it because of that knowledge or belief.
(3)   For the purposes of subsections (1) and (2) it is immaterial that the act is or would be done, or that the threat is made—
  (a)   otherwise than in the presence of the victim, or
  (b)   to a person other than the victim.
(4)   The harm that may be done or threatened may be financial as well as physical (whether to the person or a person's property) and similarly as respects an intimidatory act which consists of threats.
(5)   The intention required by subsection (1)(c) and the motive required by subsection (2)(c) above need not be the only or the predominating intention or motive with which the act is done or, in the case of subsection (2), threatened.

237

Keynote

As discussed above, this section is aimed at protecting people involved in the investigation or trial of criminal offences.

These offences are designed to exist alongside the common-law offence of perverting the course of justice (**see para. 15.4**) and there will be circumstances which may fall under the both statutory and the common-law offences. Such behaviour may also be punishable as a contempt of court, see *Blackstone's Criminal Practice*, 2001, section B14.59 and **para. 15.9** below.

The wording of s. 51(1) to (3) was altered by sch. 4 to the Youth Justice and Criminal Evidence Act 1999, to reflect the courts' interpretations of the elements of the offence. This part of sch. 4 came into force on 14 April 2000.

This is an offence of 'specific intent' (**see chapter** 1) or perhaps even multiple intent as it must be shown that the act was done with the intentions set out in s. 51(1)(a) and (c). It must also be shown that the defendant knew or believed the other person to be assisting in the investigation of an offence or that he/she was going to testify/appear on the injury in proceedings for an offence.

For 'knowing or believing' in this context the prosecution must present evidence that an investigation was in fact being carried out at the time of the alleged offence *R* v *Singh* [2000] 1 Cr App R 31.

Section 51(2) provides a similar offence for acts done or threatened in the knowledge or belief that the person, *or another person*, has so assisted or taken part in proceedings. Doing acts to third parties in order to intimidate or harm the relevant person is also covered by this offence (s. 51(3)). Making threats by telephone will amount to 'doing an act to another' (*DPP* v *Mills* [1997] QB 300).

Section 51(8) creates a statutory presumption under certain circumstances that the defendant had the required motive at the time of his/her actions or threats.

Making a *threat* via a third person knowing it will be passed on and that the ultimate recipient would be intimidated by it amounts to an offence under s. 51(1) (*Attorney-General's Reference (No. 1 of 1999)* (1999) 149 NLJ 975).

The intention to obstruct, pervert or interfere with the course of justice need not be the only or even the main intention (s. 51(5)).

Intimidation of Witnesses in Other Proceedings

In addition to the measures aimed at protecting those involved in the investigation and trial of criminal offences, there are further statutory measures designed to protect witnesses and others who are (or may become) involved in other proceedings. Guidance on the practical application of these measures can be found in Home Office Circular 12/2001.

**Offence — Intimidation of Witnesses —
Criminal Justice and Police Act 2001, s. 39**
*Triable either way. Five years' imprisonment on indictment; six months' imprisonment
and/or fine summarily.*
(Arrestable offence)

The Criminal Justice and Police Act 2001, s. 39 states:

(1) A person commits an offence if—

   (a) he does an act which intimidates, and is intended to intimidate, another person ('the victim');

   (b) he does the act—

     (i) knowing or believing that the victim is or may be a witness in any relevant proceedings; and

     (ii) intending, by his act, to cause the course of justice to be obstructed, perverted or interfered with;

and

   (c) the act is done after the commencement of those proceedings.

Keynote

This offence has some similarities to the Criminal Justice and Public Order Act 1994 offence in the earlier paragraph. References to doing an act include threats — against a person and/or their property — and the making of any other statement (s. 39(6)). The key difference is that this offence is concerned with protecting people who are in some way connected with 'relevant proceedings' which are *'any proceedings in or before the Court of Appeal, the High Court, the Crown Court or any county or magistrates' court which are not proceedings for an offence'* (s. 41(1)). This means that the offence will be relevant if the proceedings involved are civil proceedings in the higher courts or the county court or if they are non-offence proceedings in the Crown Court or magistrates' court. Examples of the latter would be a hearing to deal with a breach of a community order or an application for an anti-social behaviour order (as to which **see General Police Duties, chapter 3**). You must show that the relevant proceedings had already commenced by the time of the offence.

As with the Criminal Justice and Public Order Act offence, this requires proof of 'multiple' intent in that, as well as showing the intimidatory act, it must also be shown that the elements set out at s. 39(1)(a)–(c) are present. However, if you can prove that the defendant:

   (a) did any act that intimidated, and was intended to intimidate, another person, and

   (b) that he/she did that act knowing or believing that that other person was or might be a 'witness' in any relevant proceedings that had already commenced,

there will be a presumption that the defendant did the act with the intention of causing the course of justice to be obstructed, perverted or interfered with (s. 39(3)) This presumption is, however, rebuttable (as to which **see Evidence and Procedure, chapter 11**). 'Witness' here is a very wide expression and extends to anyone who provides, or is able to provide, any information, document or other thing which might be used in evidence in those proceedings (see s. 39(5)).

In proving the offence it is immaterial whether the act:

- is done in the presence of the victim;
- is done to the victim him/herself or to another person

or whether or not the intention to obstruct, pervert or interfere with the course of justice is the main intention of the person doing it (s. 39(2)).

This offence is intended to exist alongside the common law offence of perverting the course of justice (as to which **see para. 15.4**) and will come into force on 1 August 2001.

Offence — Harming Witnesses — Criminal Justice and Police Act 2001, s. 40

Triable either way. Five years' imprisonment on indictment; six months' imprisonment and/or fine summarily.

(Arrestable offence)

The Criminal Justice and Police Act 2001, s. 40 states:

(1)   A person commits an offence if in circumstances falling within subsection (2)—

(a)   he does an act which harms, and is intended to harm, another person; or

(b)   intending to cause another person to fear harm, he threatens to do an act which would harm that other person.

(2)   The circumstances fall within this subsection if—

(a)   the person doing or threatening to do the act does so knowing or believing that some person (whether or not the person harmed or threatened or the person against whom harm is threatened) has been a witness in relevant proceedings; and

(b)   he does or threatens to do that act because of that knowledge or belief.

Keynote

A distinction between this and the s. 39 offence is that the offence above refers to someone who *has been* (or is believed to have been) a witness in relevant proceedings. Again, 'witness' is very wide and extends to anyone who has provided any information, document etc. which was (or might have been) used in evidence in those proceedings (see s. 40(7)). For 'relevant proceedings' see the s. 39 offence. This offence is aimed is the general protection of people who have been involved in relevant proceedings. Therefore there is no requirement here for any intention to pervert or interfere with the course of justice. The harm caused or threatened does not have to directed towards the witness themselves; the key element is the motivation of the defendant. In relation to that motivation, the Act creates a presumption as follows — If you can prove that, between the start of the proceedings and one year after they are concluded, the defendant:

(a)   did an act which harmed, and was intended to harm, another person, or

(b)   threatened to do an act which would harm another person intending to cause that person to fear harm

with the knowledge or belief required by s. 40(2)(a) above, he/she will be presumed to have acted because of that knowledge or belief (s. 40(3)). Again, this is rebuttable (**see Evidence and Procedure, chapter 11**). It is immaterial whether the act or threat is made (or would be carried out) in the presence of the person who is or would be harmed, or of the person threatened or whether the motive mentioned in s. 40(2)(b) is the main motive. The harm done or threatened can be physical or financial and can be made to a person or property (s. 40(4)), This offence will come into force on 1 August 2001.

15.6   Assisting Offenders

Offence — Assisting Offenders — Criminal Law Act 1967, s. 4

Triable on indictment; either way if original offence is either way. Where sentence for original offence is fixed by law (ten years' imprisonment and/or a fine on indictment; six months' imprisonment and/or a fine summarily). Where sentence for original offence is fourteen years (seven years' imprisonment and/or a fine on indictment; six months' imprisonment and/or a fine summarily). Where sentence for original offence is ten years (five years' imprisonment and/or a fine on indictment; six months' imprisonment and/or a fine summarily).

(*Arrestable offence*)

Otherwise (three years' imprisonment and/or a fine on indictment; six months' imprisonment and/or a fine summarily).

(*No specific power of arrest*)

The Criminal Law Act 1967, s. 4 states:

(1) Where a person has committed an arrestable offence, any other person who, knowing or believing him to be guilty of the offence or of some other arrestable offence, does without lawful authority or reasonable excuse any act with intent to impede his apprehension or prosecution shall be guilty of an offence.

(1A) In this section and section 5 . . . 'arrestable offence' has the meaning assigned to it by section 24 of the Police and Criminal Evidence Act 1984.

Keynote

This offence must involve some positive act by the defendant; simply doing or saying nothing will not suffice.

Although there is no duty on people to assist the police in their investigations generally (though, **see chapter 8**), this offence and the one below create a negative duty not to interfere with investigations after an offence has taken place.

For there to be an offence under s. 4 or 5 (**para. 15.7**) there must first have been an arrestable offence committed by someone. (For arrestable offences generally, **see General Police Duties, chapter 2**.) That arrestable offence must, in the case of the above offence, have been committed by the 'assisted' person.

The defendant can commit the offence before the person he/she has assisted is convicted of committing the relevant arrestable offence.

It must be shown that the defendant knew or believed the person to be guilty of that, *or some other* arrestable offence. Therefore, if the defendant believed that the 'assisted' person had committed a robbery when in fact he/she had committed a theft, that mistaken part of the defendant's belief will not prevent a conviction for this offence.

By analogy with the requirements for handling stolen goods (**see chapter 12**) mere *suspicion*, however strong, that the 'assisted' person had committed an arrestable offence will not be enough.

This offence requires the consent of the Director of Public Prosecutions before a prosecution is brought (s. 4(4)).

A procedural problem arises where the 'arrestable offence' assisted is taking a conveyance under s. 12 of the Theft Act 1968 (**see chapter 12**). As that offence is triable only summarily, it would seem that *assisting* the offence would have to be tried on indictment.

This offence cannot be 'attempted' (Criminal Attempts Act 1981, s. 1(4)).

Sections 1 and 2 of the Criminal Evidence (Amendment) Act 1997 extending the powers to take non-intimate samples without consent apply to this offence if the arrestable offence assisted is murder and also to conspiracies and incitements in the circumstance set out in that Act (**see Evidence and Procedure, chapter 16**).

15.7 Concealing Arrestable Offences

Offence — Concealing Arrestable Offences — Criminal Law Act 1967, s. 5
Triable on indictment; either way if original offence is triable either way. Two years' imprisonment on indictment; six months' imprisonment and/or a fine summarily.
(No specific power of arrest)

The Criminal Law Act 1967, s. 5 states:

(1) Where a person has committed an arrestable offence, any other person who, knowing or believing that the offence or some other arrestable offence has been committed, and that he has

information which might be of material assistance in securing the prosecution or conviction of an offender for it, accepts or agrees to accept for not disclosing that information any consideration other than the making good of loss or injury caused by the offence, or the making of reasonable compensation for that loss or injury, shall be liable . . .

Keynote

This offence also requires the consent of the Director of Public Prosecutions before a prosecution can be brought (s. 5(3)).

It is also excluded from the provisions of the Criminal Attempts Act 1981 (s. 1(4)).

Again, someone must have committed an arrestable offence before this particular offence can be committed.

The main focus of this offence is:

- the acceptance of, or agreement to accept 'consideration' (i.e. anything of value)
- beyond reasonable compensation for loss/injury *caused by the arrestable offence*
- in exchange for not disclosing material information.

'Disclosure' does not appear to be confined to information passed to the police. It would probably extend to other agencies with a duty to investigate offences but is perhaps even wider than that.

This offence requires proof, not only of the defendant's knowledge or belief that an arrestable offence had been committed, but also that he/she has information that might be of material assistance in securing the *prosecution or conviction* of *an offender* for it. Given this very broad wording, the possession of information that might provide useful intelligence in an investigation into arrestable offences may meet the requirements of s. 5, although *proving* that the defendant had the required knowledge or belief presents considerable practical problems.

15.8 Miscellaneous Offences Relating to Offenders

Offence — Escaping — Common Law
Triable on indictment. Unlimited punishment.
(*Arrestable offence*)

It is an offence at common law to escape from legal custody.

Keynote

The 'custody' from which a person escapes must be shown to have been lawful. The offence applies to both police custody (or police detention — see the Police and Criminal Evidence Act 1984, s. 118) or custody following conviction.

People detained under the Mental Health Act 1983, s. 36, are also in lawful custody (**see chapter 11**).

If a defendant uses force to *break out* of a prison or a police station, he/she may commit an offence of prison breach, again at common law and attracting the same punishment and mode of trial as escaping.

Under the Prisoners (Return to Custody) Act 1995, s. 1, a person who has been temporarily released under the Prison Act 1952 commits a summary offence if he/she remains unlawfully at large or fails to respond to an order of recall to prison.

Offence — Assisting Escape — Prison Act 1952, s. 39
Triable on indictment. Ten years' imprisonment.
(Arrestable offence)

The Prison Act 1952, s. 39 states:

Any person who aids any prisoner in escaping or attempting to escape from a prison or who, with intent to facilitate the escape of any prisoner, conveys any thing into a prison or to a prisoner or places any thing anywhere outside a prison with a view to its coming into the possession of a prisoner, shall be guilty of [an offence].

Offence — Harbouring Offenders — Criminal Justice Act 1961, s. 22(2)
Triable either way. Ten years' imprisonment and/or a fine on indictment;
six months' imprisonment and/or a fine summarily.
(Arrestable offence)

The Criminal Justice Act 1961, s. 22 states:

(2) If any person knowingly harbours a person who has escaped from a prison or other institution to which the said section thirty-nine applies, or who, having been sentenced in any part of the United Kingdom or in any of the Channel Islands or the Isle of Man to imprisonment or detention, is otherwise unlawfully at large, or gives to any such person any assistance with intent to prevent, hinder or interfere with his being taken into custody, he shall be liable . . .

Keynote

The offences under s. 39 of the 1952 Act and s. 22 of the 1961 Act do not apply to a prisoner who escapes while in transit to or from prison (*R v Moss* (1985) 82 Cr App R 116).

There is a particular offence, punishable by two years' imprisonment, of inducing or assisting a patient detained in a mental hospital to escape or to absent themselves without leave (Mental Health Act 1983, s. 128). (For powers in relation to mentally-disordered people generally, **see chapter 11.**)

It also appears that there is a common law offence of forcibly rescuing another from lawful custody (see *Blackstone's Criminal Practice*, 2001, section B14.57).

Offence — Wasting Police Time — Criminal Law Act 1967, s. 5(2)
Triable summarily. Six months' imprisonment and/or a fine.
(No specific power of arrest)

The Criminal Law Act 1967, s. 5 states:

(2) Where a person causes any wasteful employment of the police by knowingly making to any person a false report tending to show that an offence has been committed, or to give rise to apprehension for the safety of any persons or property, or tending to show that he has information material to any police inquiry, he shall be liable . . .

Keynote

It is widely thought that there is a minimum number of hours which must be wasted before a prosecution can be brought for this offence. There is no reliable authority on this point but the consent of the Director of Public Prosecutions is needed before a prosecution can be brought under s. 5(2). Consideration should also be given to the offence of perverting the course of justice (**see para. 15.4**).

15.9   Contempt of Court

Acts which amount to contempt of court can be divided into criminal and civil contempt. Criminal contempt is defined at common law as 'behaviour involving interference with the due administration of justice' (*Attorney-General* v *Newspaper Publishing plc* [1988] Ch 333 and see *Blackstone's Criminal Practice*, 2001, section B14.59).

Contempt can be committed in many different ways including misbehaviour in court, publication of matters prejudicial to a trial and taking photographs inside a court building. For a full explanation of the subject together with the extensive powers of courts to deal with contempt, see *Blackstone's Criminal Practice*, 2001, section B14.59 *et seq.*

15.10   Corruption

Corruption offences, like conspiracies (**see chapter 3**), can be divided into common law and statutory offences.

Offence — Corruption — Common Law
Triable on indictment. Unlimited punishment.
(***Arrestable offence***)

'[A person] accepting an office of trust concerning the public is answerable criminally to [the Crown] for misbehaviour in his office' (*R* v *Bembridge* (1783) 3 Doug 327 and see *Blackstone's Criminal Practice*, 2001, section B15.1).

Keynote

As well as a public official accepting a bribe (which would amount to 'misbehaviour'), it is also a similar offence at common law to *bribe* such an office-holder.

In addition to these offences, there are two overlapping statutory offences of corruption (see below).

Offence — Corruption — Public Bodies Corrupt Practices Act 1889, s. 1
Triable either way. Seven years' imprisonment and/or a fine on indictment;
six months' imprisonment and/or a fine summarily.
(***Arrestable offence***)

The Public Bodies Corrupt Practices Act 1889, s. 1 states:

(1)   Every person who shall by himself or by or in conjunction with any other person, corruptly solicit or receive, or agree to receive, for himself, or for any other person, any gift, loan, fee, reward, or advantage whatever as an inducement to, or reward for, or otherwise on account of any member, officer, or servant of a public body as in this Act defined, doing or forbearing to do anything in respect of any matter or transaction whatsoever, actual or proposed, in which the said public body is concerned, shall be guilty of [an offence].

(2)   Every person who shall by himself or by or in conjunction with any other person corruptly give, promise, or offer any gift, loan, fee, reward, or advantage whatsoever to any person, whether for the benefit of that person or of another person, as an inducement to or reward for or otherwise on account of any member, officer, or servant of any public body as in this Act defined, doing or forbearing to do anything in respect of any matter or transaction whatsoever, actual or proposed, in which such public body as aforesaid is concerned, shall be guilty of [an offence].

Keynote

The consent of the Attorney-General (or Solicitor-General) is required before bringing a prosecution for this offence.

The meaning of the word 'corruptly' is circular in that it has been usefully held to be 'doing an act which the law forbids as tending to corrupt'! (See *R* v *Wellburn* (1979) 69 Cr App R 254.) The offence of corruption under s. 1(1) is concerned with the 'instigation of a corrupt bargain'. This was reaffirmed recently by the Court of Appeal in *R* v *Harrington* (2000) LTL 29 September. That case involved the defendant asking for money from someone who was being investigated for 'fixing' a horse race. The defendant claimed that he could make the case 'go away' but said that he would need money in order to bribe the police officer conducting the investigation. The defendant never met the officer in question, nor did he ever communicate with him. The person whom the defendant asked for the money was acting as an informant and there was never any intention that the police officer investigating the case was going to be 'bribed' into dropping it. The Court held that it was not necessary to prove an intention by the defendant that the corrupt transaction would actually involve a public official or an employee of a public body in order to establish the state of mind required by the offence. Consequently, the defendant's conviction was upheld. (For some general issues arising out of covert police operations, **see para. 3.6.**)

Giving improper gifts, payments or favours to officers or servants of a public body would usually amount to corruption.

As with the common law, both the giving and the receiving of the gift can amount to this offence. It will not be a defence for either the giver or the recipient to show that the latter was not in fact influenced by it (*R* v *Parker* (1985) 82 Cr App R 69). There are circumstances where there will be a rebuttable presumption (**see Evidence and Procedure, chapter 11**) that any gift etc. was given or received corruptly (see below).

Offence — Corruption of Agents — Prevention of Corruption Act 1906, s. 1
Triable either way. Seven years' imprisonment and/or a fine on indictment;
six months' imprisonment and/or a fine summarily.
(*Arrestable offence*)

The Prevention of Corruption Act 1906, s. 1 states:

(1)   If any agent corruptly accepts or obtains, or agrees to accept or attempts to obtain, from any person, for himself or for any other person, any gift or consideration as an inducement or reward for doing or forbearing to do, or having after the passing of this Act done or forborne to do, any act in relation to his principal's affairs or business, or for showing or forbearing to show favour or disfavour to any person in relation to his principal's affairs or business; or

If any person corruptly gives or agrees to give or offers any gift or consideration to any agent as an inducement or reward for doing or forbearing to do, or for having after the passing of this Act done or forborne to do, any act in relation to his principal's affairs or business, or for showing or forbearing to show favour or disfavour to any person in relation to his principal's affairs or business; or

If any person knowingly gives to any agent, or if any agent knowingly uses with intent to deceive his principal, any receipt, account, or other document in respect of which the principal is interested, and which contains any statement which is false or erroneous or defective in any material particular, and which to his knowledge is intended to mislead the principal;

he shall be guilty of [an offence] . . .

(2) For the purposes of this Act the expression 'consideration' includes valuable consideration of any kind; the expression 'agent' includes any person employed by or acting for another; and the expression 'principal' includes an employer.

(3) A person serving under the Crown or under any corporation or any . . . borough, county, or district council, or any board of guardians, is an agent within the meaning of this Act.

Keynote

The consent of the Attorney-General or the Solicitor-General is required before a prosecution can be brought under s. 1. There is an overlap between this offence and the offence under s. 1 of the 1889 Act. However, 'agent' does not include persons such as local counsellors who would fall under the Public Bodies Corrupt Practices Act 1889. Examples of the corruption of agents range from the securing of Ministry of Defence contracts in return for personal payments of £2 million (*R v Foxley* (1995) 16 Cr App R (S) 879) to the attempted bribery of police officers with free meals in a restaurant (*R v Oxdemir* (1985) 7 Cr App R (S) 382).

15.11 Illegal Entry to the United Kingdom

One of the most controversial and pressing policing issues at the start of the 21st century has arisen from the enormous increase in illegal entry to the United Kingdom. The law regulating immigration is substantial, extending far beyond the scope of this Manual. That legislation has itself been reinforced by a raft of additional measures contained in the Immigration and Asylum Act 1999 designed to address the issues arising from asylum seekers and also from those criminals who specialise in smuggling illegal entrants into the country. Specialist advice is available from the Home Office in all these areas. However, there are several key offences — and accompanying powers — that are immediately relevant to police officers who may find themselves dealing with incidents involving people suspected of having entered the UK unlawfully or of having assisted others to do so.

15.11.1 Illegal Entry

Offence — Illegal Entry — Immigration Act 1971, s. 24
Triable summarily. Six months' imprisonment and/or fine.
(*Specific power of arrest*)

The Immigration Act 1971, s. 24 states:

(1) A person who is not a British citizen shall be guilty of an offence . . .
in any of the following cases—
(a) if contrary to this Act he knowingly enters the United Kingdom in breach of a deportation order or without leave;
(aa) . . .
(b) if, having only a limited leave to enter or remain in the United Kingdom, he knowingly either—

> (i)   remains beyond the time limited by the leave; or
> (ii)   fails to observe a condition of the leave;
> (c)   if, having lawfully entered the United Kingdom by virtue of section 8(1) above, he remains without leave beyond the time allowed by section 8(1);
> (d)   if, without reasonable excuse, he fails to comply with any requirement imposed on him under Schedule 2 to this Act to report to a medical officer of health or the chief administrative medical officer of a Health and Social Services Board, or to attend, or submit to a test or examination, as required by such an officer;
> (e)   if, without reasonable excuse, he fails to observe any restriction imposed on him under Schedule 2 or 3 to this Act as to residence, as to his employment or occupation or as to reporting to the police or to an immigration officer;
> (f)   if he disembarks in the United Kingdom from a ship or aircraft after being placed on board under Schedule 2 or 3 to this Act with a view to his removal from the United Kingdom;
> (g)   if he embarks in contravention of a restriction imposed by or under an Order in Council under section 3(7) of this Act.

Offence — Use of Deception — Immigration Act 1971, s. 24A
Triable either way. Two years' imprisonment on indictment; six months' imprisonment and/or fine summarily.
(Specific power of arrest)

The Immigration Act 1971, s. 24A states:

> A person who is not a British citizen is guilty of an offence if, by means which include deception by him—
> (a)   he obtains or seeks to obtain leave to enter or remain in the United Kingdom; or
> (b)   he secures or seeks to secure the avoidance, postponement or revocation of enforcement action against him.

Keynote

The first offence above (s. 24) is concerned generally with non-British citizens who enter the UK illegally or who 'overstay' having been granted only limited leave to be here; it also addresses occasions where such people disregard some other lawful requirements placed upon them. The reference in s. 24(1)(c) to 'section 8(1)' refers to the special provisions made for seamen, aircrew, etc. landing lawfully in the UK.

The second offence (s. 24A) is relatively new and is broadly aimed at the more calculated actions by non-British citizens to get (or try to get) leave to enter or stay in the UK, or to evade deportation. 'Deception' here would appear to have its ordinary meaning and is not defined within the 1971 Act (for specific deception offence, **see chapter 13**). It is worth noting that the relevant criminal conduct (*actus reus*: **see chapter 2**) by the defendant here can be *any means which include deception by him/her*. Therefore, although the entire course of conduct by the defendant need not amount to a deception, it will be necessary to show that the defendant himself/herself carried out some act of deception (e.g. giving false details, providing misleading information, etc.). It will not be enough for this offence to show that someone else practised a deception in order to bring about the consequences at s. 24A(a) and (b) for another person (but see below for further offence of assisting and harbouring).

The power of arrest for both offences is set out below. Note that it does not extend to the offence under s. 24(1)(d).

Power of Arrest

The Immigration Act 1971, s. 28A states:

> *(1)   A constable or immigration officer may arrest without warrant a person—*
> *(a)   who has committed or attempted to commit an offence under section 24 or 24A; or*
> *(b)   whom he has reasonable grounds for suspecting has committed or attempted to commit such an offence.*
> *(2)   But subsection (1) does not apply in relation to an offence under section 24(1)(d).*

Keynote

Whether there are 'reasonable grounds for suspecting' that a person has committed or attempted to commit the offence(s) is a question of fact to be decided in the light of all the circumstances. Generally the arresting officer will have to show that the grounds on which he/she acted would have been enough to give rise to that suspicion in a 'reasonable person' (see *Nakkuda Ali* v *Jayaratne* [1951] AC 66). 'Suspicion' requires a lower degree of certainty than *belief* and has been described as '. . . a state of conjecture or surmise when proof is lacking' (*Shaaben Bin Hussein* v *Chong Fook Kam* [1970] AC 492 (per Lord Devlin)).

That suspicion can be based on any evidence, even if the evidence itself would be inadmissible at trial (e.g. because it is hearsay — **see Evidence and Procedure**). Therefore it can arise from information given to the officer by a colleague, an informant or even anonymously (see *O'Hara* v *Chief Constable of the Royal Ulster Constabulary* [1997] AC 286). For a further discussion of these and related issues involving powers of arrest, **see General Police Duties, chapter 2**).

As discussed above, the power of arrest does not apply where the only offence committed or suspected is that under s. 24(1)(d).

15.11.2   Assisting and Harbouring

Offence — Assisting and Harbouring — Immigration Act 1971, s. 25
Triable either way. Ten years' imprisonment on indictment; six months and/or fine summarily.
(*Arrestable offence*)

The Immigration Act 1971, s. 25 states:

> *(1)   Any person knowingly concerned in making or carrying out arrangements for securing or facilitating*
> *(a)   the entry into the United Kingdom of anyone whom he knows or has reasonable cause for believing to be an illegal entrant;*
> *(b)   the entry into the United Kingdom of anyone whom he knows or has reasonable cause for believing to be an asylum claimant; or*
> *(c)   the obtaining by anyone of leave to remain in the United Kingdom by means which he knows or has reasonable cause for believing to include deception,*
> *shall be guilty of an offence.*

Keynote

This offence requires that the defendant acted 'knowingly' and this will be a key element in securing any conviction.

An actual entry into the UK is not a necessary ingredient of the offence under either s. 25(1)(a) or (b) and it will be enough to show that the person assisted by the defendant was an 'illegal entrant' or 'asylum claimant' (*R* v *Eyck* [2000] 1 WLR 1389).

Whereas the earlier offences under s. 24 and 24A have a specific power of arrest, this offence is an arrestable offence under the Police and Criminal Evidence Act 1984, s. 24 by virtue of its penalty (**see General Police Duties**).

Where a person has been arrested for an offence under s. 25(1)(a) or (b) above, a police officer may detain any vehicle or certain smaller ships and aircraft where he/she has reasonable grounds for *believing* (as opposed to 'suspecting'; **see para 15.11.1**) that:

- the vehicle, ship or aircraft has been used or was intended to be used in carrying out the arrangements in respect of the offence, and

- the person arrested is the owner, driver or, in the case of a ship or aircraft, the captain (see ss. 25A and 25(6)).

There is a further, summary offence under s. 25(2) of knowingly harbouring anyone whom the defendant knows or has reasonable cause for believing to be either an illegal immigrant or a person who has committed an offence under s. 24(1)(b) or (c) above. This offence has no specific power of arrest without warrant but there is provision for magistrates to issue a warrant to enter premises, search for and arrest a suspect of this offence (s. 28B). Warrants under s. 28B may also been sworn out in respect of people suspected of offences under s. 24(1)(a)–(f) or s. 24A (as to which, **see para. 15.11.1**).

APPENDIX ONE

MISUSE OF DRUGS ACT 1971, SCHEDULE 2

CONTROLLED DRUGS
PART I   CLASS A DRUGS

1.   The following substances and products, namely:—
    (a)   Acetorphine.
Alfentanil.
Allylprodine.
Alphacetylmethadol.
Alphameprodine.
Alphamethadol.
Alphaprodine.
Anileridine.
Benzethidine.
Benzylmorphine (3-benzylmorphine).
Betacetylmethadol.
Betameprodine.
Betamethadol.
Betaprodine.
Bezitramide.
Bufotenine.
Cannabinol, except where contained in cannabis or cannabis resin.
Cannabinol derivatives.
Carfentanil.
Clonitazene.
Coca leaf.
Cocaine.
Desomorphine.
Dextromoramide.
Diamorphine.
Diampromide.
Diethylthiambutene.
Difenoxin (1-(3-cyano-3, 3-diphenylpropyl)-4-phenylpiperidine-4-carboxylic acid).
Dihydrocodeinone O-carboxymethyloxime.

Dihydromorphine.
Dimenoxadole.
Dimepheptanol.
Dimethylthiambutene.
Dioxaphetyl butyrate.
Diphenoxylate.
Dipipanone.
Drotebanol (3,4-dimethoxy-17-methylmorphinan-6 β, 14-diol).
Ecgonine, and any derivative of ecgonine which is convertible to ecgonine or to cocaine.
Ethylmethylthiambutene.
Eticyclidine.
Etonitazene.
Etorphine.
Etoxeridine.
Etryptamine.
Fentanyl.
Furethidine.
Hydrocodone.
Hydromorphinol.
Hydromorphone.
Hydroxypethidine.
Isomethadone.
Ketobemidone.
Levomethorphan.
Levomoramide.
Levophenacylmorphan.
Levorphanol.
Lofentanil.
Lysergamide.

Lysergide and other *N*-alkyl derivatives
  of lysergamide.
Mescaline.
Metazocine.
Methadone.
Methadyl acetate.
Methyldesorphine.
Methyldihydromorphine
  (6-methyldihydromorphine).
Metopon.
Morpheridine.
Morphine.
Morphine methoromide, morphine
  N-oxide and other pentavalent nitrogen
  morphine derivatives.
Myrophine.
Nicomorphine (3,6-dinicotinoyl-
  morphine).
Noracymethadol.
Norlevorphanol.
Normethadone.
Normorphine.
Norpipanone.
Opium, whether raw, prepared or
  medicinal.
Oxycodone.
Oxymorphone.
Pethidine.
Phenadoxone.
Phenampromide.
Phenazocine.
Phencyclidine.
Phenomorphan.
Phenoperidine.
Piminodine.

Piritramide.
Poppy-straw and concentrate
  of poppy-straw.
Proheptazine.
Properidine (1-methyl-4-phenyl-
  piperidine-4-carboxylic acid
  isopropyl ester).
Psilocin.
Racemethorphan.
Racemoramide.
Racemorphan.
Rolicyclidine.
Sufentanil.
Tenocylidine.
Thebacon.
Thebaine.
Tilidate.
Trimeperidine.
4-Bromo-2,5-dimethoxy-α-
  methylphenethylamine.
4-Cyano-2-dimethylamino-4,
  4-diphenylbutane.
4-Cyano-1-methyl-4-phenyl-piperidine.
N,N-Diethyltryptamine.
N,N-Dimethyltryptamine.
2,5-Dimethoxy-α,
  4-dimethylphenethylamine.
N-Hydroxy-tenamphetamine
1-Methyl-4-phenylpiperidine-
  4-carboxylic acid.
2-Methyl-3-morpholino-1,
  1-diphenylpropanecarboxylic acid.
4-Methyl-aminorex
4-Phenylpiperidine-4-carboxylic acid
  ethyl ester.

(b)   any compound (not being a compound for the time being specified in subparagraph (a) above) structurally derived from tryptamine or from a ring-hydroxy tryptamine by substitution at the nitrogen atom of the sidechain with one or more alkyl substituents but no other substituent;

(c)   any compound (not being methoxyphenamine or a compound for the time being specified in subparagraph (a) above) structurally derived from phenethylamine, an *N*-alkylphenethylamine, α-methyl-phenethylamine, an *N*-alkyl-α-methylphenethylamine, α-ethylphenethylamine, or an *N*-alkyl-α-ethyl-phenethylamine by substitution in the ring to any extent with alkyl, alkoxy, alkylenedioxy or halide substituents, whether or not further substituted in the ring by one or more other univalent substituents.

(d)   any compound (not being a compound for the time being specified in subparagraph (a) above) structurally derived from fentanyl by modification in any of the following ways, that is to say,

(i)   by replacement of the phenyl portion of the phenethyl group by any heteromonocycle whether or not further substituted in the heterocycle;

(ii)   by substitution in the phenethyl group with alkyl, alkenyl, alkoxy, hydoxy, halogeno, haloalkyl, amino or nitro groups;

(iii)   by substitution in the piperidine ring with alkyl or alkenyl groups;

(iv)   by substitution in the aniline ring with alkyl, alkoxy, alkylenedioxy, halogeno or haloalkyl groups;

(v)   by substitution at the 4-position of the piperidine ring with any alkoxycarbonyl or alkoxyalkyl or acyloxy group;

(vi)   by replacement of the *N*-propionyl group by another acyl group;

(e)   any compound (not being a compound for the time being specified in subparagraph (a) above) structurally derived from pethidine by modification in any of the following ways, that is to say,

(i)   by replacement of the 1-methyl group by an acyl, alkyl whether or not unsaturated, benzyl or phenethyl group, whether or not further substituted;

(ii)   by substitution in the piperidine ring with alkyl or alkenyl groups or with a propano bridge, whether or not further substituted;

(iii)   by substitution in the 4-phenyl ring with alkyl, alkoxy, aryloxy, halogeno or haloalkyl groups;

(iv)   by replacement of the 4-ethoxycarbonyl by any other alkoxycarbonyl or any alkoxyalkyl or acyloxy group;

(v)   by formation of an *N*-oxide or of a quaternary base.

2.   Any stereoisomeric form of a substance for the time being specified in paragraph 1 above not being dextromethorphan or dextrorphan.

3.   Any ester or ether of a substance for the time being specified in paragraph 1 or 2 above not being a substance for the time being specified in part II of this schedule.

4.   Any salt of a substance for the time being specified in any of paragraphs 1 to 3 above.

5.   Any preparation or other product containing a substance or product for the time being specified in any of paragraphs 1 to 4 above.

6.   Any preparation designed for administration by injection which includes a substance or product for the time being specified in any of paragraphs 1 to 3 of part II of this schedule.

PART II   CLASS B DRUGS

1.   The following substances and products, namely:—

(a)   Acetyldihydrocodeine.
Amphetamine.
Cannabis and cannabis resin.
Codeine.
Dihydrocodeine.
Ethylmorphine (3-ethylmorphine).
Glutethimide.
Lefetamine.
Mecloqualone.
Methaqualone.
Methcathinone.
Methylamphetamine.
Methylphenidate.
Methylphenobarbitone.
Nicodine.
Nicodicodine
(6-nicotinoyldihydrocodeine).
Norcodeine.
Pentazocine.
Phenmetrazine.
Pholcodine.
Propiram.
Zipeprol.

(b)   Any 5,5 disubstituted barbituric acid.

2.   Any stereoisomeric form of a substance for the time being specified in paragraph 1 of this part of this schedule.

3.   Any salt of a substance for the time being specified in paragraph 1 or 2 of this part of this schedule.

4.   Any preparation or other product containing a substance or product for the time being specified in any of paragraphs 1 to 3 of this part of this schedule, not being a preparation falling within paragraph 6 of part I of this schedule.

PART III   CLASS C DRUGS

1.   The following substances, namely:—

(a)   Alprazolam.
Aminorex.
Benzphetamine.
Bromazepam.
Brotizolam.
Buprenorphine.
Camazepam.
Cathine.
Cathinone.
Chlordiazepoxide.
Chlorphentermine.
Clobazam.
Clonazepam.
Clorazepic acid.
Clotiazepam.
Cloxazolam.
Delorazepam.
Dextropropoxyphene.
Diazepam.
Diethylpropion.
Estazolam.
Ethchlorvynol.
Ethinamate.
Ethyl loflazepate.
Fencamfamin.
Fenethylline.
Fenproporex.
Fludiazepam.
Flunitrazepam.
Flurazepam.
Halazepam.
Haloxazolam.
Ketazolam.
Loprazolam.
Lorazepam.
Lormetazepam.
Mazindol.
Medazepam.
Mefenorex.
Mephentermine.

Meprobamate.
Mesocarb.
Methyprylone.
Midazolam.
Nimetazepam.
Nitrazepam.
Nordazepam.
Oxazepam.Oxazolam.
Pemoline.
Phendimetrazine.

Phentermine.
Pinazepam.
Pipradrol.
Prazepam.
Pyrovalerone.
Temazepam.
Tetrazepam.
Triazolam.
N-Ethylamphetamine.

(b) Atamestane.
Bolandiol.
Bolasterone.
Bolazine.
Boldenone.
Bolenol.
Bolmantalate.
Calusterone.
4-Chloromethandienone.
Clostebol.
Drostanolone.
Enestebol.
Epitiostanol.
Ethyloestrenol.
Fluoxymesterone.
Formebolone.
Furazabol.
Mebolazine.
Mepitiostane.
Mesabolone.
Mestanolone.
Mesterolone.
Methandienone.
Methandriol.

Methenolone.
Methyltestosterone.
Metribolone.
Mibolerone.
Nandrolone.
Norboletone.
Norclostebol.
Norethandrolone.
Ovandrotone.
Oxabolone.
Oxandrolone.
Oxymesterone.
Oxymetholone.
Prasterone.
Propetandrol.
Quinbolone.
Roxibolone.
Silandrone.
Stanolone.
Stanozolol.
Stenbolone.
Testosterone.
Thiomesterone.
Trenbolone.

(c) any compound (not being Trilostane or a compound for the time being specified in sub-paragraph (b) above) structurally derived from 17-hydroxyandrostan-3-one or from 17-hydroxyestran-3-one by modification in any of the following ways, that is to say,

(i) by further substitution at position 17 by a methyl or ethyl group;

(ii) by substitution to any extent at one or more of positions 1, 2, 4, 6, 7, 9, 11 or 16, but at no other position;

(iii) by unsaturation in the carbocyclic ring system to any extent, provided that there are no more than two ethylenic bonds in any one carbocyclic ring;

(iv) by fusion of ring A with a heterocyclic system;

(d) any substance which is an ester or ether (or, where more than one hydroxyl function is available, both an ester and an ether) of a substance specified in sub-paragraph (b) or described in sub-paragraph (c) above;

(e) Chorionic Gonadotrophin (HCG).
Clenbuterol.
Non-human chorionic gonadotrophin.

Somatotropin.
Somatrem.
Somatropin.

2. Any stereoisomeric form of a substance for the time being specified in paragraph 1 of this part of this schedule not being phenylpropanolamine.

3. Any salt of a substance for the time being specified in paragraph 1 or 2 of this part of this schedule.

4. Any preparation or other product containing a substance for the time being specified in any of paragraphs 1 to 3 of this part of this schedule.

PART IV MEANING OF CERTAIN EXPRESSIONS USED IN THIS SCHEDULE

For the purposes of this schedule the following expressions (which are not among those defined in section 37(1) of this Act) have the meanings hereby assigned to them respectively, that is to say—

'cannabinol derivatives' means the following substances, except where contained in cannabis or cannabis resin, namely tetrahydro derivatives of cannabinol and 3-alkyl homologues of cannabinol or of its tetrahydro derivatives;

'coca leaf' means the leaf of any plant of the genus *Erythroxylon* from whose leaves cocaine can be extracted either directly or by chemical transformation;

'concentrate of poppy-straw' means the material produced when poppy-straw has entered into a process for the concentration of its alkaloids;

'medicinal opium' means raw opium which has undergone the process necessary to adapt it for medicinal use in accordance with the requirements of the British Pharmacopoeia, whether it is in the form of powder or is granulated or is in any other form, and whether it is or is not mixed with neutral substances;

'opium poppy' means the plant of the species *Papaver somniferum* L;

'poppy straw' means all parts, except the seeds, of the opium poppy after mowing;

'raw opium' includes powdered or granulated opium but does not include medicinal opium.

APPENDIX TWO

CPS OFFENCES AGAINST THE PERSON CHARGING STANDARD

AGREED BY THE POLICE AND THE CROWN PROSECUTION SERVICE

OFFENCES AGAINST THE PERSON CHARGING STANDARD

INDEX

OFFENCES AGAINST THE PERSON CHARGING STANDARD AGREED BY THE POLICE AND CROWN PROSECUTION SERVICE

1 Charging Standard — Purpose

1.1   The purpose of joint charging standards is to make sure that the most appropriate charge is selected at the earliest opportunity. This will help the police and Crown Prosecutors in preparing the case. Adoption of this joint standard should lead to a reduction in the number of times charges have to be amended which in turn should lead to an increase in efficiency and a reduction in avoidable extra work for the police and the Crown Prosecution Service.

1.2   This joint Charging Standard offers guidance to police officers who have responsibility for charging and to Crown Prosecutors on the most appropriate charge to be preferred in cases relating to offences against the person. The guidance:

- **should not be used** in the determination of any **pre-charge** decision, such as the decision to arrest;
- **does not** override any guidance issued on the use of appropriate alternative forms of disposal **short of charge**, such as cautioning;
- **does not** override the principles set out in the Code for Crown Prosecutors;
- **does not** override the need for consideration to be given in every case as to whether a charge/prosecution is in the public interest;
- **does not** remove the need for each case to be considered on its individual merits or fetter the discretion of the police to charge and the CPS to prosecute the most appropriate offence depending on the particular facts of the case in question.

2 Introduction

2.1   Offences against the person are intended to penalise those who commit assault and acts of violence. The principal offences are contained in the Offences Against the Person Act 1861 ('the Act'). This joint standard gives guidance about the charge which should be preferred if the criteria set out in the Code for Crown Prosecutors are met.

2.2   This standard covers the following offences:

- common assault, contrary to section 39 Criminal Justice Act 1988;
- assault upon a constable in the execution of his duty, contrary to section [89(1)] Police Act [1996];
- assault with intent to resist arrest, contrary to section 38 of the Act;
- assault occasioning actual bodily harm, contrary to section 47 of the Act;
- unlawful wounding/inflicting grievous bodily harm, contrary to section 20 of the Act;
- wounding/causing grievous bodily harm with intent, contrary to section 18 of the Act;
- attempted murder, contrary to section 1(1) Criminal Attempts Act 1981.

3 General Principles: Charging Practice

3.1   You should always have in mind the following general principles when selecting the appropriate charge(s):

(i)   the charge(s) should accurately reflect the extent of the defendant's alleged involvement and responsibility, thereby allowing the Courts the discretion to sentence appropriately;

(ii)   the choice of charges should ensure the clear and simple presentation of the case, particularly where there is more than one defendant;

(iii)   it is wrong to encourage a defendant to plead guilty to a few charges by selecting more charges than are necessary;

(iv)   it is wrong to select a more serious charge which is not supported by the evidence in order to encourage a plea of guilty to a lesser allegation.

4 Common assault, contrary to section 39 Criminal Justice Act 1988

4.1   An offence of common assault is committed when a person either assaults or inflicts a battery upon another person.

4.2   An assault is committed when a person intentionally or recklessly causes another to apprehend the immediate infliction of unlawful force.

4.3   A battery is committed when a person intentionally or recklessly inflicts unlawful force upon another.

4.4   It is a summary only offence which carries a maximum penalty of six months' imprisonment and/or a fine not exceeding the statutory maximum.

4.5   Where there is a battery the defendant should be charged with 'assault by beating': *DPP* v *Little* [1992] 1 All ER 299.

4.6   The only factor which distinguishes common assault from assault occasioning actual bodily harm, contrary to section 47 of the Offences Against the Person Act 1861, is the degree of injury which results.

4.7   Where battery results in injury, a choice of charge is available. The Code for Crown Prosecutors recognises that there will be factors which may properly lead to a decision not to prefer or continue with the gravest possible charge. Thus, although any injury can be classified as actual bodily harm, the appropriate charge will generally be contrary to section 39 where injuries amount to no more than the following:

- grazes;
- scratches;
- abrasions;
- minor bruising;
- swellings;
- reddening of the skin;
- superficial cuts;
- a 'black eye'.

4.8   Always consider the injuries first. In most cases the degree of injury will determine whether the appropriate charge is section 39 or section 47. There will be borderline cases, such as where an undisplaced broken nose has resulted. When the injuries amount to no more than those described at paragraph 4.7 above, any decision to charge an offence contrary to section 47 may be justified in exceptional circumstances, or where the maximum available sentence in the Magistrates' Court would be inadequate.

4.9   As common assault is not an alternative verdict to more serious offences of assault, a jury may only convict of common assault if the count has been preferred in the circumstances set out in section 40 Criminal Justice Act 1988 (see paragraph 11.6 below).

4.10   Where a charge contrary to section 47 has been preferred, the acceptance of a plea of guilty to an added count for common assault will rarely be justified in the absence of a significant change in circumstances that could not have been foreseen at the time of review.

5   Assault on a Constable in the execution of his/her duty, contrary to section [89(1)] Police Act [1996]

5.1   The offence is committed when a person assaults either:

- a constable acting in the execution of his or her duty; or
- a person assisting a constable in the execution of his/her duty.

5.2   It is a summary only offence which carries a maximum penalty of six months' imprisonment and/or a fine not exceeding the statutory maximum.

5.3   If an assault on a constable results in injury of the type described at paragraph 4.7 above, a prosecution under section [89(1)] Police Act [1996] will be appropriate, provided that the officer is acting in the execution of his/her duty.

5.4   Where the evidence that the officer was acting in the execution of his/her duty is insufficient, but proceedings for an assault are nevertheless warranted, the appropriate charge will be under section 39.

5.5   The fact that the victim is a police officer is not, in itself, an exceptional reason for charging an offence contrary to section 47 when the injuries are minor. When the injuries are such that an offence contrary to section 47 would be charged in relation to an assault on a member of the public, section 47 will be the appropriate charge for an assault on a constable.

6   Assault with intent to resist arrest, contrary to section 38 of the Act

6.1   The offence is committed when a person assaults another person with the intent to resist or prevent the lawful apprehension or detainer of himself or another for any offence.

6.2   It is an either way offence which carries a maximum penalty on indictment of two years' imprisonment and/or an unlimited fine. Summarily, the maximum penalty is six months' imprisonment and/or a fine not exceeding the statutory maximum.

6.3   A charge contrary to section 38 may properly be used for assaults on persons other than police officers, for example store detectives, who may be trying to apprehend or detain an offender.

6.4   When a police officer is assaulted, a charge under section [89(1)] will often be more appropriate unless there is clear evidence of an intent to resist apprehension or prevent detainer. Unlike section [89(1)], a charge under section 38 is triable on indictment and may therefore be coupled with other offences to be tried on indictment.

6.5   It is not bad for duplicity to charge 'resist or prevent the lawful apprehension or detainer' etc. in the one count: Rule 7 of the Indictment Rules 1971.

7   Assault occasioning actual bodily harm, contrary to section 47 of the Act

7.1   The offence is committed when a person assaults another, thereby causing actual bodily harm to that other person.

7.2   It is an either way offence which carries a maximum penalty on indictment of five years' imprisonment and/or an unlimited fine. Summarily, the maximum penalty is six months' imprisonment and/or a fine not exceeding the statutory maximum.

7.3   As is made clear in paragraph 4.6 above, the only factor in law which distinguishes a charge under section 39 from a charge under section 47 is the degree of injury. By way of example, the following injuries should normally be prosecuted under section 47:

- loss or breaking of a tooth or teeth;
- temporary loss of sensory functions (which may include loss of consciousness);
- extensive or multiple bruising;
- displaced broken nose;
- minor fractures;
- minor, but not merely superficial, cuts of a sort probably requiring medical treatment (e.g. stitches);
- psychiatric injury which is more than fear, distress or panic. (Such injury will be proved by appropriate expert evidence.)

7.4   Section 47 will also be the appropriate charge in the exceptional circumstances referred to in paragraph 4.8 above.

7.5   A verdict of assault occasioning actual bodily harm may be returned on proof of an assault together with proof of the fact that actual bodily harm was occasioned by the assault. The prosecution are not obliged to prove that the defendant intended to cause some actual bodily harm or was reckless as to whether harm would be caused: *R* v *Savage* [[1992] 1 AC 699].

8   Unlawful wounding/inflicting grievous bodily harm, contrary to section 20 of the Act.

8.1   The offence is committed when a person unlawfully and maliciously, either:

- wounds another person; or
- inflicts grievous bodily harm upon another person.

8.2   It is an either way offence which carries a maximum penalty on indictment of five years' imprisonment and/or an unlimited fine. Summarily, the maximum penalty is six months' imprisonment and/or a fine not exceeding the statutory maximum.

8.3   Wounding means the breaking of the continuity of the whole of the outer skin, or the inner skin within the cheek or lip. It does not include the rupturing of internal blood vessels.

8.4   The definition of wounding may encompass injuries which are relatively minor in nature, for example a small cut or laceration. An assault resulting in such minor injuries should more appropriately be charged contrary to section 47. An offence contrary to section 20 should be reserved for those wounds considered to be serious (thus equating the offence with the infliction of grievous, or serious, bodily harm under the other part of the section).

8.5   Grievous bodily harm means serious bodily harm. Examples of this are:

* injury resulting in permanent disability or permanent loss of sensory function;
* injury which results in more than minor permanent, visible disfigurement;
* broken or displaced limbs or bones, including fractured skull; compound fractures, broken cheek bone, jaw, ribs, etc;
* injuries which cause substantial loss of blood, usually necessitating a transfusion;
* injuries resulting in lengthy treatment or incapacity. (When psychiatric injury is alleged appropriate expert evidence is essential to prove the injury.)

8.6   In accordance with the recommendation in *R* v *McCready* [1978] 1 WLR 1376, if there is any reliable evidence that a sufficiently serious **wound** has been inflicted, then the charge under section 20 should be of unlawful wounding, rather than of inflicting grievous bodily harm. Where both a wound and grievous bodily harm have been inflicted, discretion should be used in choosing which part of section 20 more appropriately reflects the true nature of the offence.

8.7   The prosecution must prove under section 20 that either the defendant intended, or actually foresaw, that the act would cause some harm. It is not necessary to prove that the defendant either intended or foresaw that the unlawful act might cause physical harm of the gravity described in section 20. It is enough that the defendant foresaw that some physical harm to some person, albeit of a minor character, might result: *R* v *Savage* (supra).

9   Wounding/causing grievous bodily harm with intent, contrary to section 18 of the Act

9.1   The offence is committed when a person unlawfully and maliciously, with intent to do some grievous bodily harm, or with intent to resist or prevent the lawful apprehension or detainer of any person, either:

* wounds another person; or
* causes grievous bodily harm to another person.

9.2   It is an indictable only offence which carries a maximum penalty of imprisonment for life.

9.3   For the definition of wounding and grievous bodily harm, see paragraph 8 above.

9.4   The distinction between charges under section 18 and section 20 is one of intent.

9.5   The gravity of the injury resulting is not the determining factor although it may provide some evidence of intent.

9.6   When charging an offence involving grievous bodily harm, consideration should be given to the fact that a section 20 offence requires the **infliction** of harm, whereas a section 18 offence requires the **causing** of harm. This is especially significant when considering alternative verdicts (see paragraph 11 below).

9.7   Factors which may indicate the specific intent include:—

* a repeated or planned attack;
* deliberate selection of a weapon or adaptation of an article to cause injury, such as breaking a glass before an attack;
* making prior threats;
* using an offensive weapon against, or kicking, the victim's head;

9.8   The evidence of intent required is different if the offence alleged is a wounding or the causing of grievous bodily harm with intent to resist or prevent the lawful apprehension or detainer of any person. This part of section 18 is of assistance in more serious assaults upon police officers, where the evidence of an intention to prevent arrest is clear, but the evidence of an intent to cause grievous bodily harm is in doubt.

9.9   It is not bad for duplicity to indict for wounding with intent to cause grievous bodily harm or to resist lawful apprehension in one count, although it is best practice to include the allegations in separate counts. This will enable a jury to consider the different intents and the court to sentence on a clear basis of the jury's finding.

10   Attempted murder, contrary to section 1(1) Criminal Attempts Act 1981

10.1   The offence is committed when a person does an act which is more than merely preparatory to the commission of an offence of murder, and at the time the person has the intention to kill.

10.2   It is an indictable only offence which carries a maximum penalty of imprisonment for life.

10.3   Unlike murder, which requires an intention to kill or cause grievous bodily harm, **attempted murder requires evidence of an intention to kill alone**. This makes it a difficult allegation to sustain and careful consideration must be given to whether the more appropriate charge is under section 18.

10.4   The Courts will pay particular attention to counts of attempted murder and justifiably will be highly critical of any such count unless there is clear evidence of an intention to kill.

10.5   It should be borne in mind that the actions of the defendant must be more than preparatory and although words and threats may provide prima facie evidence of an intention to kill, there may be doubt as to whether they were uttered seriously or were mere bravado.

10.6   Evidence of the following factors may assist in proving the intention to kill:

- calculated planning;
- selection and use of a deadly weapon;
- threats (subject to paragraph 10.5) above;
- severity or duration of attack;
- relevant admissions in interview.

11   Alternative verdicts

11.1   In certain circumstances, it is possible for a jury to find the accused not guilty of the offence charged, but guilty of some other alternative offence. The general provisions are contained in section 6(3), Criminal Law Act 1967, and are supplemented by other provisions which relate to specific offences.

11.2   For offences against the person, the following alternatives may be found by a jury:

causing grievous bodily harm with intent, contrary to section 18 of the Act

- attempting to cause grievous bodily harm with intent;
- inflicting grievous bodily harm, contrary to section 20 of the Act.
- unlawful wounding, contrary to section 20 of the Act.

wounding with intent, contrary to section 18 of the Act

- attempting wounding with intent;
- unlawful wounding, contrary to section 20 of the Act;
- assault occasioning actual bodily harm, contrary to section 47 of the Act.

inflicting grievous bodily harm, contrary to section 20 of the Act

- assault occasioning actual bodily harm, contrary to section 47 of the Act.

unlawful wounding, contrary to section 20 of the Act

- assault occasioning actual bodily harm, contrary to section 47 of the Act.

11.3   It is essential, however, that the charge which most suits the circumstances of the case is always preferred. It will never be appropriate to charge a more serious offence in order to obtain a conviction (whether by plea or verdict) to a lesser offence.

11.4   There is authority to support the proposition that a jury may convict of wounding, contrary to section 20 of the Act, as an alternative to a count of causing grievous bodily harm with intent, contrary to section 18 of the Act: R v *Wilson*, R v *Jenkins & Jenkins* (1983) 77 Cr App R 319 HL, R v *Mandair* [1994] 2 WLR 1376 HL.

11.5   Notwithstanding that authority, prosecutors should nevertheless include a separate count on the indictment alleging wounding, contrary to section 20, where there is a realistic likelihood that the jury will convict the defendant of the lesser offence.

11.6   Common assault is not available as an alternative to any offence contrary to sections 18, 20 or 47 of the Act. A specific count alleging common assault must be included on the indictment pursuant to the provisions of section 40, Criminal Justice Act 1988.

12   Defences to assaults

12.1   Police officers and prosecutors must consider all assaults in the context in which they are allegedly committed. There will be cases in which the surrounding circumstances will be of help in deciding whether to bring criminal proceedings.

12.2   Particular care must be taken in dealing with cases of assault where the allegation is made by a 'victim' who was, at the time, engaged in criminal activity himself. For instance, a burglar who claims to have been assaulted by the occupier of the premises concerned.

12.3   It is lawful for an individual to use reasonable force in the following circumstances:

- in self-defence; or
- to defend another; or
- to defend property; or
- to prevent crime; or
- to lawfully arrest.

12.4   Where the use of force in any of these circumstances is reasonable, the 'assailant' has an absolute defence and charges relating to the assault should not be brought.

12.5   In assessing the reasonableness of the force used, two questions should be asked:

- was the use of force justified in the circumstances? (i.e. was there a need for any force at all?); and
- was the force used excessive in the circumstances?

The courts have indicated that both questions are to be answered on the basis of the facts as the accused *honestly believed* them to be. To that extent it is a *subjective* test. There is, however, an *objective* element to the test, as the court must then go on to ask whether, on the basis of the facts as the accused believed them to be, a reasonable person would regard the force used as reasonable or excessive.

12.6   There can be a fine line, however, between what constitutes reasonable and unreasonable force. When considering whether the force used was reasonable or excessive, it is important to consider the words of Lord Morris in *Palmer* v *R* [1971] AC 814 which emphasise the difficulties often facing someone confronted by an intruder or defending himself against attack:

'If there has been an attack so that defence is reasonably necessary, it will be recognised that a person defending himself cannot weigh to a nicety the exact measure of his defensive action. If the jury thought that in a moment of unexpected anguish a person attacked had only done what he honestly and instinctively thought necessary, that would be the most potent evidence that only reasonable defensive action had been taken . . .'

12.7   Where the police are in doubt about whether a charge should be brought in cases such as these, they should seek the advice of the CPS before charging the defendant.

APPENDIX THREE

CRIMINAL JUSTICE AND COURT SERVICES ACT 2000, SCHEDULE 4

MEANING OF 'OFFENCE AGAINST A CHILD'

1. The offences mentioned in paragraph (a) of subsection (1) of section 26 are—
   (a) an offence under section 1 of the Children and Young Persons Act 1933 (cruelty to children),
   (b) an offence under section 1 of the Infanticide Act 1938 (infanticide),
   (c) an offence under section 5 of the Sexual Offences Act 1956 (intercourse with a girl under 13),
   (d) an offence under section 6 of that Act (intercourse with a girl under 16),
   (e) an offence under section 19 or 20 of that Act (abduction of girl under 18 or 16),
   (f) an offence under section 25 or 26 of that Act (permitting girl under 13, or between 13 and 16, to use premises for intercourse),
   (g) an offence under section 28 of that Act (causing or encouraging prostitution of, intercourse with or indecent assault on, girl under 16),
   (h) an offence under section 1 of the Indecency with Children Act 1960 (indecent conduct towards young child),
   (i) an offence under section 54 of the Criminal Law Act 1977 (inciting girl under sixteen to incest),
   (j) an offence under section 1 of the Protection of Children Act 1978 (indecent photographs of children),
   (k) an offence under section 1 of the Child Abduction Act 1984 (abduction of child by parent),
   (l) an offence under section 160 of the Criminal Justice Act 1988 (possession of indecent photograph of child),
   (m) an offence under section 3 of the Sexual Offences (Amendment) Act 2000 (abuse of trust).

2. The offences mentioned in paragraph (b) of that subsection are—
   (a) murder,
   (b) manslaughter,
   (c) kidnapping,
   (d) false imprisonment,
   (e) an offence under section 18 or 20 of the Offences against the Person Act 1861 (wounding and causing grievous bodily harm),
   (f) an offence under section 47 of that Act (assault occasioning actual bodily harm),
   (g) an offence under section 1 of the Sexual Offences Act 1956 (rape),
   (h) an offence under section 2 or 3 of that Act (procurement of woman by threats or false pretences),
   (i) an offence under section 4 of that Act (administering drugs to obtain or facilitate intercourse),
   (j) an offence under section 14 or 15 of that Act (indecent assault),
   (k) an offence under section 16 of that Act (assault with intent to commit buggery),
   (l) an offence under section 17 of that Act (abduction of woman by force or for the sake of her property),
   (m) an offence under section 24 of that Act (detention of woman in brothel or other premises).

3.   A person falls within this paragraph if—

(a)   he commits an offence under section 16 of the Offences against the Person Act 1861 (threats to kill) by making a threat to kill a child,

(b)   he commits an offence under section 7 of the Sexual Offences Act 1956 (intercourse with defective) by having sexual intercourse with a child,

(c)   he commits an offence under section 9 of that Act (procurement of defective) by procuring a child to have sexual intercourse,

(d)   he commits an offence under section 10 of that Act (incest by a man) by having sexual intercourse with a child,

(e)   she commits an offence under section 11 of that Act (incest by a woman) by allowing a child to have sexual intercourse with her,

(f)   he commits an offence under section 12 of that Act by committing buggery with a child under the age of 16,

(g)   he commits an offence under section 13 of that Act by committing an act of gross indecency with a child,

(h)   he commits an offence under section 21 of that Act (abduction of defective from parent or guardian) by taking a child out of the possession of her parent or guardian,

(i)   he commits an offence under section 22 of that Act (causing prostitution of women) in relation to a child,

(j)   he commits an offence under section 23 of that Act (procuration of girl under 21) by procuring a child to have sexual intercourse with a third person,

(k)   he commits an offence under section 27 of that Act (permitting defective to use premises for intercourse) by inducing or suffering a child to resort to or be on premises for the purpose of having sexual intercourse,

(l)   he commits an offence under section 29 of that Act (causing or encouraging prostitution of defective) by causing or encouraging the prostitution of a child,

(m)   he commits an offence under section 30 of that Act (man living on earnings of prostitution) in a case where the prostitute is a child,

(n)   she commits an offence under section 31 of that Act (woman exercising control over prostitute) in a case where the prostitute is a child,

(o)   he commits an offence under section 128 of the Mental Health Act 1959 (sexual intercourse with patients) by having sexual intercourse with a child,

(p)   he commits an offence under section 4 of the Sexual Offences Act 1967 (procuring others to commit homosexual acts) by—

(i)   procuring a child to commit an act of buggery with any person, or

(ii)   procuring any person to commit an act of buggery with a child,

(q)   he commits an offence under section 5 of that Act (living on earnings of male prostitution) by living wholly or in part on the earnings of prostitution of a child,

(r)   he commits an offence under section 9(1)(a) of the Theft Act 1968 (burglary), by entering a building or part of a building with intent to rape a child,

(s)   he commits an offence under section 4(3) of the Misuse of Drugs Act 1971 by—

(i)   supplying or offering to supply a Class A drug to a child,

(ii)   being concerned in the supplying of such a drug to a child, or

(iii)   being concerned in the making to a child of an offer to supply such a drug,

(t)   he commits an offence of—

(i)   aiding, abetting, counselling, procuring or inciting the commission of an offence against a child, or

(ii)   conspiring or attempting to commit such an offence.

INDEX